Black Market, Cold War

Everyday Life in Berlin, 1946–1949

This book explains how and why Berlin became the symbolic capital of the Cold War. It brings the history of the Cold War down to earth by focusing on the messy accounts of daily struggles to survive rather than seamless narratives of diplomatic exchange. By following Berliners as they made their way from ration offices to the black markets, from allied occupation bureaus to the physical and symbolic battles for the city's streets and squares, Paul Steege anchors his account of this emerging global conflict in the fractured terrain of a city literally shattered by World War II. In this history of everyday life, he claims for Berliners a vital role in making possible Berlin's iconic Cold War status. The world saw an absolutely divided city, but everyday Berliners crossed its many boundaries, and these transgressive practices brought into focus the stark oppositions of the Cold War.

Paul Steege is an associate professor of history at Villanova University and coeditor of the electronic discussion list *H-German*.

Black Market, Cold War

Everyday Life in Berlin, 1946–1949

PAUL STEEGE

Villanova University

CAMBRIDGE UNIVERSITY PRESS
Cambridge, New York, Melbourne, Madrid, Cape Town, Singapore, São Paulo

Cambridge University Press
32 Avenue of the Americas, New York, NY 10013-2473, USA

www.cambridge.org
Information on this title: www.cambridge.org/9780521864961

First published 2007

Printed in the United States of America

A catalog record for this publication is available from the British Library.

Library of Congress Cataloging in Publication Data

Steege, Paul, 1970–
Black market, Cold War : everyday life in Berlin, 1946–1949 / Paul Steege.
   p. cm.
Includes bibliographical references and index.
ISBN-13: 978-0-521-86496-1 (hardback)
ISBN-10: 0-521-86496-8 (hardback)
  1. Berlin (Germany) – History – 1945–1990. 2. Berlin (Germany) – History –
Blockade, 1948–1949. 3. Cold War. 4. Berlin (Germany) – Strategic aspects.
I. Title.
DD881.S738 2007
943'.1550874–dc22   2006019642

ISBN 978-0-521-86496-1 hardback

To my parents

Contents

List of Maps, Tables, and Figures

Maps

Tables

Figures

List of Abbreviations

Abt.:	Section (*Abteilung*)
ACC:	Allied Control Council
ADN:	Universal German News Service (*Allgemeiner Deutscher Nachrichtendienst*)
AdsD:	Archive of Social Democracy (*Archiv der sozialden Demokratie*)
AEG:	General Electric Corporation (*Allgemeine Elektrizitätsgesellschaft*)
AK:	Allied Kommandatura
BA-DDR:	German Federal Archives, GDR Section (*Bundesarchiv, Abteilung DDR*)
BEWAG:	Berlin Electric Company
Bgm.:	Mayor (*Bürgermeister*)
Bl.:	Archival Page (*Blatt*)
BLHA:	Brandenburg Main State Archive (*Brandenburgisches Landeshauptarchiv*)
BPA:	District Party Archive of the Berlin SED (*Bezirksparteiarchiv*)
CDU:	Christian Democratic Union (*Christlich-Demokratische Union*)
CFM:	Council of Foreign Ministers
DBD:	Democratic Farmers' Party of Germany (*Demokratische Bauernpartei Deutschlands*)
DDR:	German Democratic Republic, GDR (*Deutsche Demokratische Republik*)

DWK:	German Economic Commission (*Deutsche Wirtschaftskommission*)
FDGB:	Association of Free German Trade Unions (*Freier Deutscher Gewerkschaftsbund*)
FDJ:	Free German Youth (*Freie deutsche Jugend*)
FRUS:	*Foreign Relations of the United States*
GDR:	German Democratic Republic
GPU:	State Political Directorate (*Gosudarstvennoe Politicheskoe Upravlenie*)
HfGB:	Trade Association for Greater Berlin (*Handelsgesellschaft für Groß-Berlin*)
IHK:	Industry and Trade Office (*Industrie- und Handelskontor*)
Kdo.:	Command (*Kommando*)
KPD:	Communist Party of Germany (*Kommunistische Partei Deutschlands*)
LAB:	Berlin State Archive (*Landesarchiv Berlin*)
LAZ:	(Berlin) State Archive, Contemporary History Collection (*Landesarchiv, Zeitgeschichtliche Sammlung*)
LDP:	Liberal Democratic Party (*Liberal-Demokratische Partei*)
LHAM:	Magdeburg Main State Archive (*Landeshauptarchiv Magdeburg*)
LPB:	State Police Bureau (*Landespolizeibehörde*)
LV:	State Organization (*Landesverband*)
NA:	National Archives (United States)
NDPD:	National-Democratic Party of Germany (*National-Demokratische Partei Deutschlands*)
NKVD:	People's Commissariat of Internal Affairs (*Narodnii Kommissariat. Vnutrennykh Del*)
NL:	Personal papers (*Nachlass*)
NSDAP:	National Socialist (Nazi) Party (*Nationalsozialistische deutsche Arbeiterpartei*)
OB:	(Lord) Mayor (*Oberbürgermeister*)
OMGBS:	Office of Military Government (United States) Berlin Sector
OMGUS:	Office of Military Government (United States)
RBD:	German Railroad Authority (*Reichsbahndirektion*)
Rep.:	Repository (*Repositur*)

RG:	Record Group
RIAS:	Radio in the American Sector
SAG:	Soviet Joint-Stock Company (*Sowjetische Aktiengesellschaft*)
SAPMO:	German Federal Archive, Foundation Archive for the Parties and Mass Organizations of the GDR (*Stiftung Archiv der Parteien und Massenorganisationen der DDR*)
SBZ:	Soviet Zone of Occupation (*Sowjetische Besatzungszone*)
SED:	Sozialistische Einheitspartei Deutschlands (Socialist Unity Party of Germany)
SMA:	Soviet Military Administration (*Sowjetische Militäradministration*)
SPD:	Social Democratic Party of Germany (*Sozialdemokratische Partei Deutschlands*)
Sta. Ort-Nr.:	Location Code
SVAG:	Soviet Military Administration in Germany (*Sovetskaia Voennaia Administratsia v Germanii*)
UGO:	Independent Trade Union Organization/Opposition (*Unabhängige Gewerkschaftsopposition/-organisation*)
VdgB:	Association for Mutual Farmers' Assistance (*Vereinigung der gegenseitigen Bauernhilfe*)
VEB:	People's Factory (*Volkseigene Betrieb*)
VVN:	Association of the Victims of the Nazi Regime (*Vereinigung der Verfolgten des Naziregimes*)
ZK:	Central Committee (*Zentralkomitee*)
ZKK:	Central Control Commission (*Zentrale Kontrollkommission*)

Acknowledgments

This book has survived a long journey, and I am grateful for this opportunity to acknowledge the many acts of generosity that helped it along its way. Its intellectual roots lie in the graduate seminars and workshops of the University of Chicago. The first classroom door I walked through took me into Alf Lüdtke's research seminar on the history of everyday life, a course whose influence on my subsequent work cannot be overestimated. Michael Geyer helped me to frame the big questions, and I hope that he sees his influence in my effort to wrestle with the global implications of everyday life. I am increasingly aware of the subtle ways in which his intellectual encouragement has helped me refine my interests, and I count myself fortunate to have been his student.

My remarkable colleagues in Villanova's history department helped make this a much better book than it might otherwise have been. The opportunity to read their work, engage them in regular conversation, and solicit their comments and criticisms provided the perfect mix of intellectual stimulus and collegiality and reminds me how pleasurable this intellectual work can and should be. Marc Gallicchio, Judy Giesberg, Jeff Johnson, Maghan Keita, Catherine Kerrison, Adele Lindenmeyr, Larry Little, Emmet McLaughlin, Charlene Mires, Rachel O'Toole, and Paul Rosier at various times patiently discussed this evolving project and offered numerous fruitful insights. Particular thanks are due Seth Koven for his generosity on both an intellectual and personal level. His regular encouragement to get to the core issues helped me to clarify my arguments and to reorganize the book in a way that brought those arguments to light.

Late in the project's dissertation stage, Bruce Cumings and Sheila Fitzpatrick raised questions that subsequently influenced its reworking. Thomas Lindenberger, Arnd Bauerkämper, Michael Lemke, Konrad Jarausch, and their colleagues at the Zentrum für Zeithistorische Forschung in Potsdam provided a welcome point of intellectual exchange during my regular trips to Berlin and consistently pointed me in productive directions. I am grateful to Lew Bateman at Cambridge University Press for his interest in this project, for the two anonymous readers whose comments and critiques did much to improve the manuscript, and to Christine Dunn, whose copyediting saved me from myself on many occasions.

The cohort of Central Europeanists during my time at the University of Chicago – Jim Bjork, Melissa Feinberg, Paul Hanebrink, Heikki Lempa, and Andre Wakefield – have been much more than onetime seminar classmates, and their friendship and intellectual engagement are inspiring. Thanks as well to Drew Bergerson, Mo Healy, and Pamela Swett, whose collaboration has helped me grasp more fully the implications of everyday life history. In Philadelphia and elsewhere, a number of colleagues have commented helpfully on portions of this work, especially Belinda Davis, Greg Eghigian, Geoff Eley, Fred Enssle, Martin Geyer, Ron Granieri, David Imhoof, Pieter Judson, Mark Landsman, Andy Lees, Jay Lockenour, and Troy Paddock. Of course, any errors and shortcomings remaining in the book are entirely my own.

My thanks as well to the archivists and staff who helped me find my way to the sources that made this study possible, including those at the Landesarchiv Berlin; the Bundesarchiv in Berlin-Lichterfelde; the National Archives in College Park, Maryland; the Archiv der sozialen Demokratie; the Brandenburgisches Landeshauptarchiv; the Landeshauptarchiv Sachsen-Anhalt; and the Archiv des Polizeipräsidiums, Berlin. At Villanova University, I came to rely on the dependably speedy assistance of the staff at Falvey Library. Donna Blaszkowski in Villanova's office of media technologies and creative design cheerfully accommodated my repeated requests for "small" changes to produce the remarkable maps. Thanks to graduate research assistants Jim Perrin, Catherine Holden, Kirsten Helgesson, Rachel Wineman, and Jeff Ludwig, who helped in many small ways that are hard to discern from the outside. Harold Hurwitz took time to share both his personal experiences in Berlin as well as his scholarly expertise. Martha Mautner generously offered insights into the flavor of life in postwar Berlin that would otherwise have been inaccessible. In Berlin, the Hasselblatt, Kent, and Tui-Lorenzl families deserve particular thanks for so regularly creating a second home for me in the city. Our many years of friendship have enriched me immeasurably. Thanks also to the Bakke, Heyn, and Hoffmann families for sharing their homes when they were away for extended periods. The staff and morning regulars at the Gryphon Café in Wayne, Pennsylvania, created the perfect mix of distraction and intellectual energy without which most of my revisions would never have happened.

I gratefully acknowledge permission to reproduce materials published elsewhere. An earlier version of Chapter 4 appeared in *Central European History* as "Holding on in Berlin: March 1948 and SED Efforts to Control the Soviet Zone." Portions of Chapter 6 appeared as a chapter in *Earth Ways: Framing Geographical Meanings*, published by Lexington Books. Figures 3 and 5–14 appear courtesy of the Landesarchiv Berlin. Figure 4 appears courtesy of the United States National Archives. Research for this project was supported by the Friedrich Ebert Foundation, the Mellon Foundation, the Max-Planck-Institut für Geschichte, Villanova University, and a Bernadotte E. Schmitt Grant from the American Historical Association.

On a much more personal level, my wife Julie has watched this project evolve and patiently endured the occasional obsessions intrinsic to and personal sacrifices demanded by academic life. For her unwavering support and gentle humor, which prevents me from ever taking myself too seriously, I am eternally grateful. She and our two daughters share their boundless enthusiasm for life and are a source of constant joy. Thank you.

In a way, this book's journey began even before I started my graduate studies and reflects an evolving love affair with a city that I first came to know as a teenager – when Berlin was still split by a wall. As an adult, I have had the great fortune to wander through what had been east and west and to revel in the dynamic tensions of this city where a tumultuous past remains close to the surface and a contested future is always just around the corner. And so, supremely aware of the extent to which no work of history can be divorced from the personal story of which its writing is a part, I dedicate this book to my parents, who first took me to Berlin.

A Note on Terminology

The dynamic environment of post–World War II Berlin makes it a particularly fascinating subject, but its fluid political and economic landscape produced a confusing array of terminology, even before two separate administrations came to govern the city. While I have tried to explain these shifting terms in the course of the text, two contexts merit more explicit clarification.

In discussing the main body of German authority in the city, I have retained the German term *Magistrat* throughout the text. Selected by the Berlin city assembly, the councilors who comprised the executive branch of the Berlin government represented something more than a city council, and the term *Magistrat* conveys that most precisely. Additionally, I have translated the term *Oberbürgermeister* as *mayor* and not the more cumbersome *lord mayor*. The three subordinate *Bürgermeister* are thus *deputy mayors*.

Even before the dual currency reforms in 1948, there were several currencies circulating in Berlin: the reichsmark (RM) – the official German currency – rentenmarks – the Weimar-era currency created to help resolve the 1923 hyperinflation crisis – and allied occupation scrip. The 1948 currency reform introduced a new deutsche mark (German mark) in eastern and western flavors. Contemporary documents refer to these currencies in various shorthands, including marks, DM, D-Mark, or even B-Mark (for the west mark in Berlin with a distinct "B" stamp). For the period after 1948, I generally use east mark and west mark to describe the distinct currencies. In order to provide some sense of the fluid and uncertain currency environment facing Berliners at the time, I do, however, retain the diverse currency designations when quoting from contemporary sources.

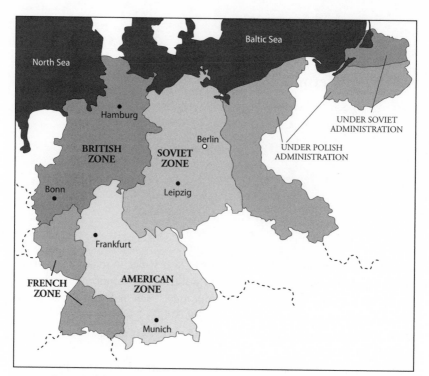

MAP 1. Occupied Germany, 1945–9. *Source:* Villanova University Office of Media Technologies.

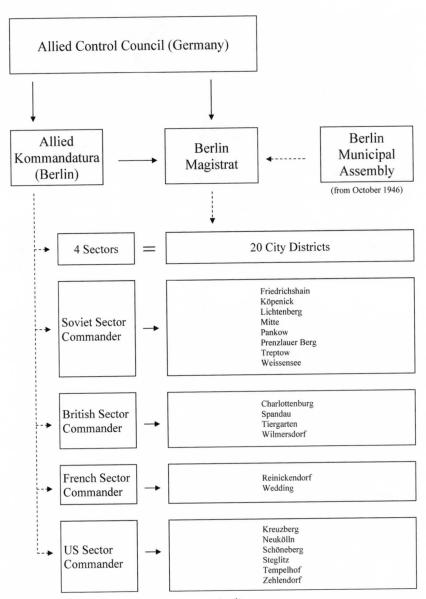

FIGURE I. Lines of authority in postwar Berlin.

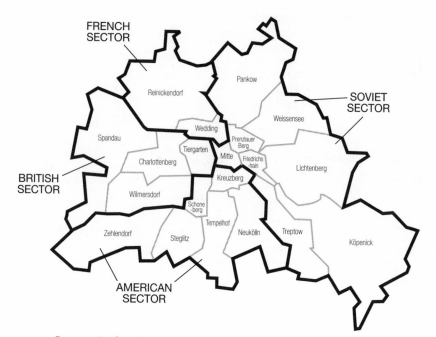

MAP 2. Postwar Berlin: Occupation Sectors and City Districts. *Source:* Villanova University Office of Media Technologies.

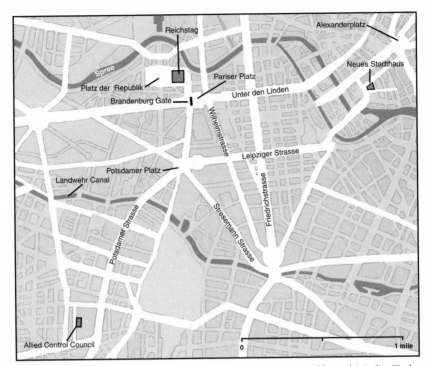

Spree
Reichstag
Alexanderplatz
Neues Stadthaus
Platz der Republik
Pariser Platz
Brandenburg Gate
Unter den Linden
Wilhelmstrasse
Leipziger Strasse
Potsdamer Platz
Friedrichstrasse
Landwehr Canal
Potsdamer Strasse
Stresemann Strasse
Allied Control Council
0   1 mile

MAP 3. Berlin City Center. *Source:* Villanova University Office of Media Technologies.

Introduction

"An Imaginary Wall"

On July 19, 1948, millions of Americans opened up their copy of *Life* magazine to find an article about the blockaded city of Berlin. To help explain the Soviet blockade to its readers, the magazine included a two-page map of the city with the respective occupation sectors and important local landmarks clearly marked (Figure 2). A three-dimensional barrier traced the external boundary of the three western sectors. Its significance was made explicit in the caption: "Blockade of Berlin is shown symbolically in this map, with American, British and French sectors enclosed within *an imaginary wall.*"[1] Thirteen years later, the Berlin Wall would cease to be imaginary, the East German regime rendering *Life*'s explanatory short-hand in concrete with its "antifascist protective barrier" literally cutting off West Berlin from the surrounding countryside. The magazine's illustration bears a striking resemblance to maps of Berlin that graced posters and t-shirts in the 1980s, souvenir Cold War icons in which the Berlin Wall separated sectors filled with the national flags of the respective occupying powers. Although we could perhaps grant the editors at *Life* a kind of eerie foresight about the city's future, the image they used to explain the blockade inaccurately depicted what was happening in and around Berlin that summer. The article described the "Soviet siege of Berlin" as "tight – dangerously tight," overlooking not even "the smallest detail."[2] This version of the blockade is wrong. Throughout 1948 and 1949, Soviet

---

[1] Emmet Hughes, "Berlin under Siege," *Life* (July 19, 1948), 72–3. My emphasis.
[2] Ibid., 26.

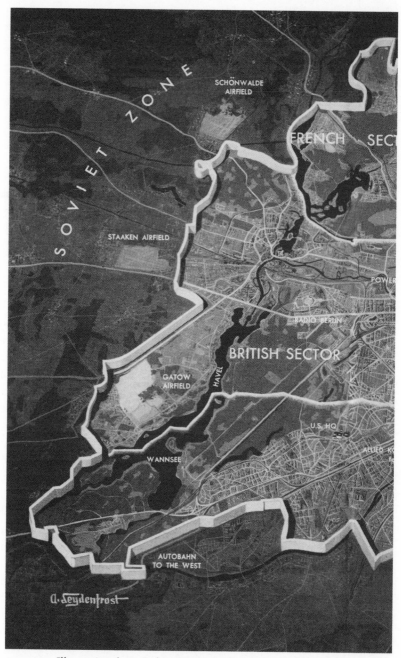

FIGURE 2. Illustration from *Life* magazine, July 19, 1948. The original caption reduces its explanation of a permeable blockade to a "wall" that will not actually exist for another thirteen years: "Blockade of Berlin is shown symbolically in this map, with American, British and French sectors enclosed within an imaginary wall. Concentration of police and power facilities in the Soviet sector

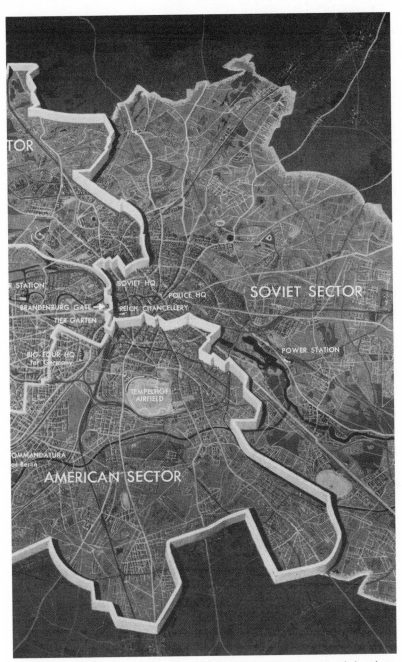

(*center and right*) gives the Russians a tight grip inside the city, and they have closed the Autobahn and railroads (*lower left*) which reach Berlin from west through the Russian zone. American air lift comes in at Tempelhof near downtown area, while British are landing supplies at Gatow and on the Havel (*left*)."

controls never amounted to an airtight barrier around the city's western sectors. While the image of a wall may have heightened the crisis's dramatic power, the Berlin Wall cannot be retroactively constructed in the Berlin of the blockade.

Five decades later, German Chancellor Helmut Kohl and U.S. President Bill Clinton joined thousands of Berliners at Berlin's Tempelhof Airport to celebrate the golden anniversary of the Berlin airlift and the great Western victory it purportedly marked. Standing in front of a representative vintage C-54 as well as a new transport plane dubbed the *Spirit of Berlin*, the speakers testified to the airlift's technical achievement. The heroic drone of its achievements overwhelmed all other aspects of the crisis. Held literally in the shadow of military transport planes, this celebration allowed no room for Berliners other than as passive German victims of Communist aggression or heroic belt-tighteners who refused to knuckle under to Soviet pressure. The gathered crowd heard only one account of Berliners' blockade experiences when a woman described her childhood memories of waiting at the end of the runway to catch chocolate bars dropped by parachute from landing aircraft.[3] In this version of the blockade and airlift, the Berliners – both East and West – who continued to work, trade on the black market, and crowd onto trains into the countryside to barter or steal from farmers' fields vanished, their everyday work of survival reduced to passively waiting for assistance literally to drop from the sky.

But if we turn our gaze back to earth, we see a very different picture: a messy Berlin setting that neither superpower ever truly mastered. By focusing on everyday Berliners as they moved through the city's ruined streets and squares, this book relocates the narrative landmarks that generally demarcate Berlin's emergence as a Cold War flashpoint. It looks to the black market instead of the airlift; the rain-drenched streets of Berlin rather than the Allied Control Council (ACC); and striking Berlin railroaders instead of the Council of Foreign Ministers (CFM). Offering a history from the inside out, this book explores the relationship between

---

[3] See Dan Balz, "Clinton, in Berlin, Joins Kohl to Hail '48 Airlift," *International Herald Tribune* (May 15, 1998). More generally on the anniversary celebrations, see "Beginn der Feiern zum Luftbrückenjubiläum: 12. Mai 1949: Ende der Blockade," *Der Tagesspiegel* (May 12, 1998), 15. For a description of the exploits of the renowned "candy bomber," Gail Halverson, see Ann and John Tusa, *The Berlin Airlift* (New York: Atheneum, 1988), 268–9. There is even an English-language children's book that celebrates the story of the woman who stood in for Berlin at the Tempelhof ceremony: Margot Theis Raven, *Mercedes and the Chocolate Pilot: The True Story of the Berlin Airlift and the Candy that Dropped from the Sky* (Chelsea, MI: Sleeping Bear Press, 2002).

Berliners' day-to-day struggles to survive in the midst of wartime devastation and their part in shaping Berlin as the symbolic capital of the Cold War.[4] While Cold War Berlin may be a familiar location for a well-worn narrative of superpower conflict, this book challenges the assumption that we have always known what that conflict was about and how it worked. The Cold War was not just imposed from above, and this book seeks to negotiate the gaps between the emergence of this crisis "on the ground" in Berlin and its political, symbolic, and historical construction that has resonated far beyond the city.

Telling Berlin Stories, 1946–1949

Rather than trying to fill in those gaps, this study highlights the fragmented nature of Berliners' postwar history. It takes up their stories in 1946 (as opposed to 1945), not out of some contrarian impulse to be different, but because one year after the German surrender, Berliners' day-to-day survival practices were becoming increasingly well-rehearsed, in effect normalizing the "temporary" status of the *postwar*.[5] In October 1946, when the Soviet-supported Socialist Unity Party's (SED) stunning defeat in Berlin's first postwar election occurred, it marked a powerful popular rejection of the Soviet occupier's presumed dominance in the city. But it also made clear that Berliners possessed the ability to assert their power in a potent way – essentially rolling back the Soviets' domination of the city administration. Even at the height of the blockade two years later, Berliners continued to demonstrate their ability and willingness to undermine the exercise of Soviet power in and around the city, not just in their electoral decisions, but even more so in their daily choices about how and where to buy food, run their businesses, and move about the city.

The decision to begin in 1946 serves also to emphasize the Cold War not just as an imposition of international policy but as a product of the tension between high politics and Berliners' material battle to survive. At the very moment of their greatest material desperation, postwar Berliners showed themselves capable of shaping the structures of power within the city, and the election of October 1946 offers the unanticipated moment at which Berliners' dramatic agency bursts to the surface. Three years later,

---

[4] My use of this term evolved out of conversations with Michael Geyer when this project was still in the dissertation stage. David Clay Large also writes about Berlin's symbolic role as the "capital of the Cold War." David Clay Large, *Berlin* (New York: Basic Books, 2000), xviii.

[5] Tony Judt, *Postwar: A History of Europe since 1945* (New York: Penguin, 2005).

when the first open battle of the Cold War seemed to have appropriated the city for a global conflict, the realities of life in a politically divided city undermined the Great Powers' claims to definitive victory or defeat – the Western victors wrestled with the economic and strategic burdens of a West Berlin that they could never abandon; the eastern losers found themselves in charge of a new state that, for all of their rhetorical posturing, the Western powers would never really challenge.

Before the founding of East and West German states in 1949, neither German municipal authorities nor occupation forces successfully met Berliners' basic material needs, a fundamental weakness that remained even as both sides made increasingly assertive claims to a Berlin they defined as an ideological battleground. This slippage played out in unintended consequences that complicated even those outcomes presumed to be most explicitly products of high politics. For the Western powers, the experiences of the blockade and airlift helped transform former enemies into allies and friends but also bound them inextricably to a city that would threaten to ensnare them in an explosion of conflict at least until the building of the Wall in 1961.[6] For the Soviets and the SED, the public relations disaster of defeat concealed the fact that they had achieved what they sought, a Stalinist state in Germany and Western acceptance of a divided Berlin.

While images from Berlin often sum up the triumph and tragedy of the Cold War, a fresh look at Berlin from 1946 to 1949 challenges any reduction of events in Berlin to undiluted highs or lows and unambiguous victories and defeats. Still, these grand "events" continue to define Berlin's Cold War history, and even the most innovative new approaches to Cold War history run the risk of serving primarily to fill in the spaces between the heights of the Cold War's defining events to which these additions serve as subordinate, if at times nonetheless contested, objects.[7] This book endeavors to do something more. By relocating Berlin's Cold War stories, it argues that these moments "betwixt and between" are actually key to unraveling the convoluted workings of a struggle that remains most

<hr/>

[6] Andreas Daum argues that the airlift transformed the city, making "Germany's Berlin" into "America's Berlin." Andreas W. Daum, *Kennedy in Berlin: Politik, Kultur und Emotionen im Kalten Krieg* (Paderborn: Ferdinand Schöningh, 2003), 8 and 39.
[7] While the discussion of filling in historiographical gaps has focused primarily on the possibilities offered by newly available archives, I would argue that a similar sensibility informs the methodological innovations of the "new Cold War history." See the description of the University of North Carolina Press book series of the same name (under the general editorship of John Lewis Gaddis) at http://uncpress.unc.edu/bm-series.html#new (accessed March 16, 2006).

often elaborated in Manichean terms.[8] In the process of unraveling the workings of this first clash of the Cold War, I hope also to clarify some of the reasons that this epic event continues to resonate so powerfully in the world today and to suggest that the Cold War's end has not made a renewed examination of its origins less relevant.

Locating Berlin in the Cold War

The image of an isolated and inaccessible city has dominated accounts of the Berlin Blockade for nearly six decades. According to this confident narrative, the Soviets blockaded Berlin's western sectors for nearly eleven months in 1948 and 1949 in an effort to force the Western Allies to halt their separate currency reform and the formation of a West German state. Supplied by the heroic accomplishments of a Western airlift, West Berliners held out on tight rations until the Soviets backed down, conceding defeat in the first great clash of the Cold War.[9] The agreement negotiated by Phillip Jessup and Jakov Malik to end the blockade in

[8] The idea of "betwixt and between-ness" emerges in Victor Turner's discussion of the liminality that characterizes the experience of initiates during rites of passage among the Ndembu people of south-central Africa. For a general discussion of this liminal condition, see Victor Turner, "Betwixt and Between: The Liminal Period in *Rites de Passage*," in *The Forest of Symbols: Aspects of Ndembu Ritual* (Ithaca and London: Cornell University Press, 1973), 93–110. I discuss more fully the liminal nature of Berlin in the early Cold War in "Finding the there, there: local space, global ritual, and early Cold War Berlin," in *Earth Ways: Framing Geographical Meanings*, Gary Backhaus and John Murungi, eds. (Lanham, MD: Lexington Books, 2004), 155–72.

[9] W. Philips Davison, *The Berlin Blockade: A Study in Cold War Politics* (Princeton: Princeton University Press, 1958), 19–20. Despite its strident Cold War tone, the book located the events of the evolving crisis in Berlin in a framework that most subsequent work has retained without much question. See, e.g, Tusa, *The Berlin Airlift*, 102–5. Michael Haydock, *City under Siege: The Berlin Blockade and Airlift, 1948–1949* (Washington and London: Brassey's, 1999), 123–5. Thomas Parrish, *Berlin in the Balance: The Blockade, the Airlift, the First Major Battle of the Cold War* (Reading, MA: Perseus Books, 1998), 141–2. The former East German historian Gerhard Keiderling is generally more forgiving of Soviet and East German intentions but does not dramatically shift the center of gravity of the events under analysis; see his "*Rosinenbomber über Berlin*": *Währungsreform, Blockade, Luftbrücke, Teilung* (Berlin: Dietz, 1998), 18–28. See also the timeline in Hermann Weber, *DDR Grundriß der Geschichte 1945–1990* (Hannover: Fackelträger Verlag, 1991), 287. The first account to challenge this vision of the blockade was Andreas Hallen and Thomas Lindenberger, "Frontstadt mit Lücken: Ein Versuch über die Halbwahrheiten von Blockade und Luftbrücke," Berliner Geschichtswerkstatt, ed., *Der Wedding – hart an der Grenze: Weiterleben in Berlin nach dem Krieg* (Berlin: Nishen Verlag, 1987). These ideas were developed most fully in William Stivers, "The Incomplete Blockade: Soviet Zone Supply of West Berlin, 1948–49," *Diplomatic History* 21, no. 4. (Fall 1997), 569–602. In a similar vein, see also Volker Koop, *Kein Kampf um Berlin? Deutsche Politik zur Zeit der Berlin-Blockade 1948/1949* (Bonn: Bouvier Verlag, 1998).

May 1949 seemed to draw a neat line under which historians could add up their tidy explanatory sums.[10] It marked the end to a clash – somewhat short of "hot" war – in which Soviet policy thrust (blockade) encountered Western policy parry (airlift), with Berlin simply the arena where the duel took place.

Throughout its postwar history and especially since the building of the Wall in 1961, Berlin served as *the* icon of Cold War conflict, a site for presidential pilgrimages and spy exchanges.[11] Even after the Cold War's end, chunks of the Berlin Wall (or at least multicolored pieces of concrete alleged to come from the Wall) remain one of the most obvious Cold War souvenirs, an artifact of the conflict that presumably defined the city. The West Berlin government's official chronicle of 1946–8 already locates the city's immediate postwar history in the shadow of the growing east-west divide, and most historians of postwar Germany and particularly of postwar Berlin have viewed this period through the lens of the emerging Cold War.[12] From this perspective, events on the ground in Berlin manifested the potent forces driving inevitably toward a total collapse of the postwar occupation regime and the construction of two stable, separate German states that were both "intrinsic products of the Cold War" and "symbols of the broader global conflict."[13] Berlin functioned as the point at which two competing trajectories of power – each to end in a new German state – most directly confronted each other and produced their most explosive conflicts.

---

[10] The Jessup-Malik agreement was reached by representatives of the four occupation powers on May 4, 1949 and called for the lifting eight days later of all restrictions imposed on transportation and communication between Berlin and the western zones since March 1948 as well as between the western zones and the Soviet Zone. On the Jessup-Malik agreement, see Avi Shlaim, *The United States and the Berlin Blockade* (Berkeley and London: University of California Press, 1983) and Phillip C. Jessup, "Park Avenue Diplomacy – Ending the Berlin Blockade," *Political Science Quarterly* 87, no. 3 (September 1972), 377–400.

[11] John F. Kennedy's speech before the Schöneberg town hall in which he pronounced that "ich bin ein Berliner" and Ronald Reagan's call for Mikhail Gorbachev to "tear down this wall" are but two of the most famous. Likewise, the exchange for U-2 pilot Francis Gary Powers on the Glienicke Bridge is simply one among many. For Cold War film and fiction, Berlin has, as well, played a prominent role. Perhaps most famous is John LeCarré's classic cold war tale, *The Spy Who Came in from the Cold* (New York: Coward-McCann, 1964). On the general image of Berlin in the Cold War, see Eric Morris, *Blockade: Berlin and the Cold War* (London: Hamish Hamilton, 1973), 243.

[12] Berlin (West Berlin) Landesarchiv, ed., *Berlin: Behauptung von Freiheit und Selbstverwaltung 1946–1948* (Berlin: Heinz Pitzing Verlag, 1959), 434.

[13] Corey Ross, *The East German Dictatorship: Problems and Perspectives in the Interpretation of the GDR* (London: Arnold, 2002), 2.

The Cold War laid the foundation for two separate postwar histories of East and West Germany: the narrative of western integration and the West German economic miracle contrasted with the ambiguous development of existing socialism in the German Democratic Republic (GDR). These historical trajectories interacted only on the basis of the competition defined and demanded by the Cold War, and the two states' nascent development over the course of these years depended on this clash.[14] British and American officials aggressively facilitated the formation of a separate West German state, and Soviet officials ultimately preferred a subservient partial state to a unified and potentially independent-minded German whole.[15] But trying to establish blame for the division of Germany into two states should not anchor examinations of Germany in the second half of the twentieth century. Instead, a history of postwar Germany must highlight the myriad continuities and ruptures that transcend easy geographical, political, and temporal divides and fit them into a multilayered historical stream that did not end with the start of the Cold War.[16]

In the introduction to the second volume of his history of the Korean War, Bruce Cumings notes that the outbreak of war in 1950 was a "*denouement* mistaken for a beginning."[17] The Berlin Blockade represents a similar confusion of historical trajectory. As soon as historians pronounce it a Cold War battle, they mark it as radically distinct from the German past that immediately preceded it. It becomes a post–World War II contest between East and West in *occupied* Germany and thus hardly a *German* historical event at all. If one follows this line of reasoning, the blockade took place in Berlin only by geographical accident. It was a product of the intersection of Soviet and Western policies and was essentially imposed upon the city from the outside. Berlin assumed

---

[14] William Glenn Gray, *Germany's Cold War: The Global Campaign to Isolate East Germany, 1949–1969* (Chapel Hill and London: University of North Carolina Press, 2003) and Ronald J. Granieri, *The Ambivalent Alliance: Konrad Adenauer, the CDU/CSU, and the West, 1949–1966*, Monographs in German History 9 (New York and Oxford: Berghahn Books, 2003).

[15] For an account that views German division as a product of British and American policy, see Carolyn Woods Eisenberg, *Drawing the Line: The American Decision to Divide Germany, 1944–1949* (Cambridge and New York: Cambridge University Press, 1996).

[16] See Christoph Kleßmann's introduction to *The Divided Past: Rewriting Post-War German History*, Christoph Kleßmann, ed. (Oxford and New York: Berg, 2001), 1–9 and Konrad H. Jarausch and Michael Geyer, *Shattered Past: Reconstructing German Histories* (Princeton: Princeton University Press, 2003), 16–33; also, Catherine Epstein, *The Last Revolutionaries:* (Cambridge, MA: Harvard University Press, 2003).

[17] Bruce Cumings, *The Origins of the Korean War*, vol. 2, *The Roaring of the Cataract 1947–1950* (Princeton: Princeton University Press, 1990), 9. Italics in original.

importance in this evolving clash only as one piece in the larger conflict seen to have emerged in Europe by early 1948. American Military Governor Lucius Clay explained Berlin's significance in an oft-cited message from April 1948:

We have lost Czechoslovakia. Norway is threatened. We retreat from Berlin. When Berlin falls, Western Germany will be next. If we mean ... to hold Europe against Communism, we must not budge. We can take humiliation and pressure short of war in Berlin without losing face. If we withdraw, our position in Europe is threatened. If America does not understand this now, does not know that the issue is cast, then it never will and communism will run rampant. I believe the future of democracy requires us to stay.[18]

Thus, in Clay's polemical declaration, Berlin posed a dilemma that primarily questioned American willingness to recognize the city's overall strategic implications. For Clay's pitch to Washington politicians, this challenge had little to do with the specific struggles in the city. Rather, it lay in the symbolic value of Berlin for a larger strategic concern that had been coming into focus since 1947. In this context, only after the traditional "declarations" of Cold War – the Truman Doctrine and Marshall Plan, the creation of the Cominform, and the gradual consolidation of Soviet power in Eastern Europe – could Berlin matter for the Cold War.[19] Regardless of whether one explains this escalation of international tension as the product of Soviet aggression, American imperialism, or some other causal variation, the blockade was part of a larger teleology of Cold War. In the evolving international calculus for which Berlin functioned as both arena and prize, Berliners' everyday life remained the direct object of the high political predicate.

But neither Germany nor Berlin comprised a vacuum into which the two nascent superpowers were inextricably drawn and within which their inevitable hegemonic clash came to pass.[20] Following the destruction of the Nazi Third Reich, Germany was not an empty space, in either material or political terms. Certainly, the victorious allies – East and West – sought

---

[18] Lucius D. Clay, *Decision in Germany*, reprint (Westport, CT: Greenwood Press, 1970), 361.

[19] "Text of President Truman's Speech on New Foreign Policy," New York Times (March 13, 1947), 2. See Cumings, *The Origins of the Korean War*, 35. See also Charles E. Bohlen, *Witness to History 1929–1969* (New York: W. W. Norton and Company, 1973), 260; and Walter LaFeber, *America, Russia, and the Cold War 1945–1996*, 9th ed. (New York: McGraw-Hill, 2002), esp. chapter 2.

[20] See John Lewis Gaddis, *We Now Know: Rethinking Cold War History* (Oxford: Clarendon Press, 1997), 4. See also Anders Stephanson, "The United States," in *The Origins of the Cold War in Europe*, David Reynolds, ed., 28.

with varying degrees of success to reshape German politics and society. Yet no amount of denazification, decartelization, or democratization (of either the Soviet or Western variety) could erase the residual effects of war, Nazi rule, and the political and economic turmoil that preceded it. At the same time, material crisis and the symbolic density of the German political location shaped and limited the engagement of the Eastern and Western powers with each other.

The historiographical debates on the Cold War have focused primarily on its origins, more specifically on the question: Who was to blame?[21] Here, of course, debate has focused on the two superpowers. Washington and Moscow, and the policies formulated in these cities, emerged as the twin suns around which Cold War scholarship circled.[22] The first efforts to "depolarize" the historiography of the Cold War argued that other state actors – in addition to the two superpowers – played important roles in waging Cold War.[23] Although much of the most recent Cold War history has been dominated by celebratory discoveries from newly accessible East Bloc archives, a range of new scholarship has started to ask a new set of questions of both old and new archival material.[24] An increasing number of social and cultural analyses have further expanded our understanding

[21] For one effort to move beyond this debate on "responsibility," see the introduction to Charles S. Maier, ed., *The Cold War in Europe: Era of a Divided Continent* (New York: Markus Wiener Publishing, Inc., 1991).
[22] The orthodox or traditional view of the Cold War reined supreme in the 1950s and early 1960s. It saw the threat of Soviet expansionism as the primary cause of the Cold War. In the late 1960s, revisionists argued that the Cold War resulted from the Soviets' legitimate responses to American economic imperialism. The postrevisionists challenged this view of American culpability, arguing that parallel misunderstandings and domestic political limitations constrained efforts to counter the tensions of competing state systems in a geo-political arena. For a good summary of the progression of these debates, see Anders Stephanson's chapter on the United States and the Cold War in *The Origins of the Cold War in Europe*, 23–52.
[23] For an explicit discussion of this undertaking, see David Reynolds's introduction to *The Origins of the Cold War in Europe*, esp. pp. 7ff.
[24] Gaddis, *We Now Know*. For a critique of Gaddis and a discussion of recent work on the Cold War that in particular cautions against overvaluing new archival sources, see Melvyn P. Leffler, "The Cold War: What Do 'We Now Know'?," *American Historical Review* 104, no. 2 (April 1999), 519–20. Work drawing on these new sources includes Vojtech Mastny, *The Cold War and Soviet Insecurity: The Stalin Years* (New York and Oxford: Oxford University Press, 1996); Vladislav Zubok and Constantine Pleshakov, *Inside the Kremlin's Cold War: From Stalin to Khruschchev* (Cambridge and London: Harvard University Press, 1996); and Francesca Gori and Silvio Pons, eds., *The Soviet Union and Europe in the Cold War, 1943–53* (New York: St. Martin's Press, 1996). For a critical assessment of post–Cold War "triumphalist" scholarship, see Allen Hunter, ed., *Rethinking the Cold War* (Philadelphia: Temple University Press, 1998).

of the diverse agents engaged in producing the Cold War.[25] International, multiarchival studies have also complicated our sense of coherent Cold War settings, crossing geographic and temporal boundaries as they weave Cold War stories into narratives of decolonization and state formation with altogether different trajectories.[26]

Toward an Everyday Life History of the Cold War

It is easy to recognize the continuity of individual actors (people's lives did not literally start over in 1945), but their memories and practices shaped how they made sense of and engaged their postwar struggles to survive in ways that are perhaps less obvious. Fashioned especially in the midst of economic crisis and the violent clashes on the streets of the Weimar Republic, Berliners' understandings of the intersections between their everyday lives and their symbolic resonance in the city's political stagecraft played a dominant role in contemporary understanding of events in postwar Germany and especially in Berlin. In the contests among Berlin's German politicians as they struggled to re-form a municipal administration and recraft civil society, the language and debates of the 1920s and 1930s continuously reasserted themselves. Even more significantly, this political rhetoric operated in and depended on its ability to resonate in the midst of day-to-day experiences that constituted a dramatically different set of continuities – common experiences of hunger, scarcity, and material crisis such as the 1917 "turnip winter," the hyperinflation of 1923, or the absolute desperation at the height of the Great Depression. These continuities,

---

[25] Reinhold Wagnleitner, *Coca-Colonization and the Cold War: The Cultural Mission of the United States in Austria after the Second World War*, Diana M. Wolf, trans. (Chapel Hill and London: University of North Carolina Press, 1994) and Uta Poiger, *Jazz, Rock, and Rebels: Cold War Politics and American Culture in a Divided Germany* (Berkeley: University of California Press, 2000). Walter Hixson, *Parting the Curtain: Propaganda, Culture, and the Cold War, 1945–1961* (New York: St. Martin's Press, 1997) examines how culture operated beyond the control of policy makers. Similarly, Jessica C. E. Gienow-Hecht, *Transmission Impossible: American Journalism as Cultural Diplomacy in Postwar Germany 1945–1955*, Eisenhower Center Studies on War and Peace (Baton Rouge: Louisiana State University Press, 1999) suggests that Cold War "victories" came *in spite of* American policy makers' misguided efforts to control "undesirable" manifestations of popular culture.

[26] Matthew Connelly, *A Diplomatic Revolution: Algeria's Fight for Independence and the Origins of the Post–Cold War Era* (Oxford and New York: Oxford University Press, 2002) and Mark Bradley, *Imagining Vietnam and America: The Making of Postcolonial Vietnam, 1919–1950* (Chapel Hill and London: University of North Carolina Press, 2000). See also Gray, *Germany's Cold War*.

in turn, provide a vital means to access the workings of the political ruptures that presumably defined life in postwar Berlin while highlighting the role ordinary Berliners played in crafting and defining these seminal events.

While the profound experience of material hardship has hardly vanished from accounts of postwar Berlin, it has served a very different role there from that in West Germany, where it came to be seen as a prelude to the 1948 currency reform and the economic miracle it presumably unleashed.[27] The successful development of a West German democracy rested, it was assumed, on its association with the sustained drive toward economic prosperity and the almost universal experience of plenty. In this version of West German recovery, the postwar experience of material hardship thus constituted a crucial prehistory.[28] Just as the staple before-and-after postcard contrasts images of German tourist sites' postwar destruction with their current splendor, the destruction left by World War II thus becomes merely a necessary beginning for this postwar story and the starting point for *post*war politics.

Postwar Germans' perceptions of supply variations; their constant comparison between individuals, cities, and regions; and the implicit fear that someone else was getting more or better food, clothing, or coal reiterated the inherently political nature of these everyday acts of survival.[29]

---

[27] On the currency reform as a founding myth along the lines of the Boston Tea Party or the transformation of the third estate into the National Assembly, see Lutz Niethammer, "Privat-Wirtschaft: Erinnerungsfragmente einer anderen Umerziehung," in Lutz Niethammer, ed., *"Hinterher merkt man, daß es richtig war, daß es schiefgegangen ist"*: Nachkriegs-Erfahrungen im Ruhrgebiet, vol. 2 of Lebensgeschichte und Sozialkultur im Ruhrgebiet 1930 bis 1960 (Bonn and Berlin: J. H. W. Dietz Nachf., 1983), 83. More generally, on the powerful place of the currency reform in German collective memory, see Christoph Kleßmann and Georg Wagner, eds., *Das gespaltene Land: Leben in Deutschland 1945 bis 1990: Texte und Dokumente* (Munich: C. H. Beck, 1993), ch. 7. For a pathbreaking volume that described a period of crisis that straddled 1945, see *Von Stalinsgrad bis Währungsreform: zur Sozialgeschichte des Umbruchs in Deutschland*, Martin Broszat, Klaus-Dietmar Kenke, and Hans Woller, eds., Quellen und Darstellungen zur Zeitgeschichte 26 (Munich: R. Oldenbourg Verlag, 1988).

[28] Although he critiques the notion of an undifferentiated experience of prosperity in 1950s West Germany, Michael Wildt offers a thoughtful analysis of ways in which the experience of scarcity laid the foundation for the production of a pluralized consumer society. See his *Am Beginn der "Konsumgesellschaf": Mangelerfahrung, Lebeshaltung, Wohlstandshoffnung in Westdeutschland in der fünfziger Jahren*, Forum Zeitgeschichte 3 (Hamburg: Ergebnisse Verlag, 1994), 264–5.

[29] Alf Lüdtke argues against relegating the everyday to the nonpolitical in "Organizational Order or *Eigensinn*? Workers' Privacy and Workers' Politics in Imperial Germany," in *Rites of Power: Symbolism, Ritual, and Politics since the Middle Ages*, Sean Wilentz, ed. (Philadelphia: University of Pennsylvania Press, 1985), 304–5. Michael Wildt, *Der Traum*

The almost universal fear of differentiated supply (and the sense that one's own supply was certainly bad) points to the intersection of competing senses of entitlement, justice, legitimacy, and power that were all bound up with the daily struggle to meet individual supply needs. But the differentiated individual experiences that comprised this battle for survival have disappeared into an iconic account of universal hardship, which helped Germans (East and West) explain and justify the shape of their postwar politics.[30] The myth of a German zero hour (*Stunde null*) – the conviction of the chance to build anew on a slate wiped clean by wartime destruction – served not only to distance the emerging West German democracy from the recent Nazi past but also to separate it from the first, failed German experiment in twentieth-century democracy, the Weimar Republic.[31]

In order to access the productive tension between these continuities and ruptures, this study offers an everyday life history (*Alltagsgeschichte*) of Berlin from 1946 to 1949.[32] This does not mean that it seeks only – or

---

vom Sattwerden: Hunger und Protest Schwarzmarkt und selbsthilfe in Hamburg 1945–1948 (Hamburg: VSA-Verlag, 1986), 9 and Rainer Gries, *Die Rationengesellschaft: Versorgungskampf und Vergleichsmentalität: Leipzig, München und Köln nach dem Kriege* (Münster: Verlag westfälisches Dampfboot, 1991), 13. Alon Confino and Rudy Koshar call for a "history of small steps," which analyzes consumption and the materiality of everyday goods as a way to study history across political regimes. See their "Régimes of Consumer Culture: New Narratives in Twentieth-Century German History," *German History* 19, no. 2 (2001), 154–6.

[30] Elizabeth Heineman emphasizes the particularly gendered component of the experience of Germany's "crisis years" (from the Battle of Stalingrad to the Currency Reform, 1942–8), emphasizing how the integration of memories of victimhood, heroic reconstruction, and moral decline universalized female experiences and claimed them for a new West German *national* identity, while denying their particular applicability to individual women. Elizabeth Heineman, "The Hour of the Woman: Memories of Germany's 'Crisis Years' and West German National Identity," *The American Historical Review* 101, no. 2 (April 1996), 354–95.

[31] Elaborated most famously in F. R. Aleman, *Bonn ist nicht Weimar* (Cologne: Kiepenheuer and Witsch, 1956). On this issue more generally, see Konrad Jarausch, "1945 and the Continuities of German History: Reflections on Memory, Historiography, and Politics," in *Stunde Null: The End and the Beginning Fifty Years Ago*, Occasional Paper no. 20, Geoffrey J. Giles, ed. (Washington, DC: German Historical Institute, 1997), 9–24. More generally on the topic of the German "zero hour" see Harold James, "The Prehistory of the Federal Republic," *Journal of Modern History* 63 (March 1991), 99–115 and Christoph Kleßmann, *Die doppelte Staatsgründung: Deutsche Geschichte 1945–1955*, Studien zur Geschichte und Politik Band 298, 5th ed., (Bonn: Bundeszentrale für politische Bildung, 1991), 37f. Kleßmann prefers the term *Zusammenbruchgesellschaft* to describe the sense of disruption without discounting the continuities of individual actors, institutions, and experiences.

[32] On *Alltagsgeschichte*'s ability to retain awareness of history's continuities and ruptures, see David F. Crew, *Germans on Welfare: From Weimar to Hitler* (Oxford and New York: Oxford University Press, 1998), 6.

merely – to tell stories of daily life. It is concerned not just with the way "ordinary people" lived during the Cold War but with exploring why and particularly *how* everyday life matters for the way the Cold War worked. Everyday life history elaborates not only history "from below" but engages the tension between the everyday lives of "ordinary" persons and the symbolic meanings that they shape, engage, and contest in the spaces through which they move.[33] Thus, this is not only a story of streets and squares but also of administrative offices and police station houses, parliamentary debates and radio broadcasts, the material and conceptual spaces in which these "everyday Berliners" become vital shapers of an international Cold War. It follows a trace that jumps across multiple layers of human action – from the most basic pursuit of the material necessities on which human survival depends to high political debates among international leaders – acknowledging in the process of traversing the gaps between these sites of struggle that all explanations seeking to make sense of such fissure-riven processes will inevitably prove fragmented. By tackling a globalizing description such as the Cold War, the historian of everyday life questions the seamlessness of even the most comprehensive explanation.

Even at the time, political parties, occupation officials, and German administrators tried to assemble some sense of the ways that Berliners understood, participated in, and even contested the policies that were supposedly directing life in the city. Numerous "reports on the popular mood" (*Stimmungsberichte*), filed both with the police and the SED, describe discussions in the public sphere and note signs and posters, current jokes in Berlin cabarets, and even the subjects of children's plays

---

[33] The closest thing to a programmatic statement for the practice of *Alltagsgeschichte* is Alf Lüdtke's introduction to *The History of Everyday Life: Reconstructing Historical Experiences and Ways of Life*, Alf Lüdtke, ed. and William Templer, trans., Princeton Studies in Culture/Power/History (Princeton: Princeton University Press, 1989). See also Thomas Lindenberger, "Everyday History: New Approaches to the History of Post-War Germanies," in *The Divided Past*, 43–67. My thinking on the nature of "everydayness" has also been dramatically influenced by Harry Harootunian, *History's Disquiet: Modernity, Cultural Practice, and the Question of Everyday Life* (New York: Columbia University Press, 2000) and Andrew Stuart Bergerson, *Ordinary Germans in Extraordinary Times: The Nazi Revolution in Hildesheim* (Bloomington and Indianapolis: Indiana University Press, 2004), esp. the appendix. On the political critique inherent in *Alltagsgeschichte*, see Geoff Eley's 1989 review essay, "Labor History, Social History, 'Alltagsgeschichte': Experience, Culture, and the Politics of the Everyday – A New Direction for German Social History?" *The Journal of Modern History* 61, no. 2 (June 1989), 297–343, esp. pp. 300, 313. In a similar vein, Andreas Daum describes part of what he writes as a "microhistory" of John F. Kennedy's 1963 visit to Berlin. See his *Kennedy in Berlin*, 9.

as evidence of the authorities' impotence. Advertisements and newspaper accounts hint provocatively at some of the generally unacknowledged mechanisms with which people coped with supply restrictions. A close reading of these sources makes it possible to recognize regular patterns of language, expression, and explanation, with which they narrated these ambiguous events and helps us gain entry into the places where these everyday actions played out. In July 1948, when a woman set out on behalf of the Prenzlauer Berg District SED to collect opinions from the "working population," she initially encountered problems getting workers in various firms to enter into "discussions." Only after she posed pointed questions did discussions evolve.[34] Thus, even as she offers the reader of her reports access to the voices of workers and customers in a particular bakery and brewery (street addresses included), she also formulates the means to ask questions about the ways that she (re)produced these voices.

This study makes no claim to recover vanished voices of Berlin's past. It does, however, seek to offer a counterpoint to most Cold War histories of the city that remain unwilling even to try to make it onto the streets through which that global conflict's ordinary protagonists moved. Writing in his diary in August 1945, Karl Deutmann described how he and his wife were caught in a police black market raid at the Brandenburg Gate in the city center. The two of them had come from Adlershof on the southeastern edge of Berlin to test their luck in the city. As the authorities moved in, Deutmann and his wife followed the crowd into the ruins of the nearby Blücher Palace (American Embassy). When they discovered that the police already had the building's exits covered, they slipped through a shattered wall, headed through the former propaganda ministry, and finally managed to escape out into the street through another shell hole.[35] Although they managed to elude the police, Deutmann and his wife discovered how the exercise of power in postwar Berlin depended on the ability to master the often obscure passageways within the shattered cityscape. Most of these routes are no longer visible. Already by the 1960s, one visitor

---

[34] "Stimmungsberichte zu der Antwortnote der Sowjetrussischen Regierung an die westlichen Alliierten" (July 17, 1948), Landesarchiv Berlin (hereafter LAB), BPA IV, 4/6/402.

[35] "Aufzeichnungen aus dem Tagebuch von Karl Deutmann aus Adlershof bei Berlin (DHM-Bestand)," entry for August 7, 1945, *Lebendiges virtuelles Museum Online* (http://www.dhm.de/lemo/forum/kollektives_gedaechtnis/010/index.html) (accessed May 5, 2004). The German Historical Museum in Berlin obtained Deutmann's diary from the collection of the former Museum of German History of the GDR but has no further information about him.

returning to the city for the first time since the late 1940s reported that she struggled to find her way – the regrown trees concealed the buildings with which she had grown familiar.[36] But even if we cannot "master" the paths along which ordinary Berliners moved, their fragmentary traces still offer remarkable explanatory possibilities.

[36] Martha Mautner, interview with the author, Washington, DC, July 18, 2003.

I

Postwar Berlin: The Continuities of Scarcity

Wie ihr es immer dreht und wie ihr's immer schiebt
Erst kommt das Fressen, dann kommt die Moral.
Erst muß es möglich sein auch armen Leuten
Vom großen Brotlaib sich ihr Teil zu schneiden.
Denn wovon lebt der Mensch?[1]

The weather in Berlin remained pleasantly mild during the summer of 1946. On only thirty-five days did temperatures surpass 77 degrees.[2] In just a few months Berliners would face a new crisis when one of the coldest winters on record challenged their ability to survive as they huddled in ruined homes and windowless apartments. But now, in the second summer since the end of World War II in Europe, the demands of postwar life had begun to seem remarkably normal. The previous July the four victorious powers had established a central military organ, the Allied Kommandatura (AK), to administer the city's four occupation sectors and preparations were underway to hold Berlin's first postwar elections in October – an effort to provide the city a democratically

---

[1] Bertolt Brecht, *Die Dreigroschenoper* in Siegfried Unseld, ed., *Bertolt Brechts Dreigroschenbuch: Texte, Materialien, Dokumente* (Frankfurt am Main: Suhrkamp Verlag, 1960), 46–7. "However much you twist, whatever lies you tell / Food is the first thing. Morals follow on. / So first make sure that those who now are starving / Get proper helpings when we all start carving / What keeps mankind alive?" *The Threepenny Opera*, Ralph Manheim and John Willet, trans. (New York: Vintage Books, 1977), 55–6. The English translation fails to capture adequately the tension between the animal-like desperation of real hunger and the humanity of moral judgment. The German word *fressen* describes the eating/feeding of animals; for humans, the verb is *essen*.
[2] Hauptamt für Statistik von Groß-Berlin, *Berlin in Zahlen 1947* (Berlin: Berliner Kulturbuch-Verlag, 1949), 47.

elected German administration after twelve years of Nazi rule. Yet even as the three Western powers and the Soviet Union joined together to try the remaining Nazi leadership in Nuremberg and implement the decrees of the ACC that they had established to formulate a coherent regime for postwar Germany, the first cracks began to appear in the allied anti-Hitler coalition. Alternative visions of postwar democracy and the Allies' competing economic interests strained cooperative efforts to rebuild German society and economic and political life. These high political decisions and debates garnered significant and ongoing attention in public discussions and the popular press but played only a subordinate role in Berliners' day-to-day existence. In the former German capital, the material implications of life in a destroyed city mattered more. Faced with real and sustained scarcity, Berliners had to battle to survive, and, for the overwhelming majority of the population, this struggle dominated all aspects of social, cultural, and political life in the city.

A discussion of Cold War politics in Berlin must shift from the rarefied space of international diplomacy and the halls of power to everyday battles to cope with scarcity. In postwar Berlin, these activities comprised the core experiences upon which everything else depended. Throughout the immediate postwar period, Berliners moved through material and symbolic locations shaped by a fundamental tension between the scarcity that dominated their day-to-day lives and the administrative structures that purported to control their material existence. On the surface, that administration seemed to possess incredible power over people's ability to obtain the food and other goods necessary for their survival. Residency checks, ration card allocation, distribution of surplus food and fuel – all these processes lay under the jurisdiction of the various municipal bureaucracies if still subject to occasional intervention of the four occupying powers. In practice, however, the material situation operated quite differently.

For most Berliners, depending on "official" channels remained but one of a wide range of strategies they developed in their ongoing efforts to overcome hunger, the lack of adequate housing, and the general scarcity that dominated the four years after the end of World War II. Very often, these strategies depended on behavior that was technically illegal, at least according to the regulations of the occupation authorities and the emerging civilian administration. But most Berliners' successful reliance on survival strategies that regularly escaped the occupation and German municipal authorities' control ironically facilitated those authorities' ability to assert that control, a process on which Berlin's status as Cold War capital came to depend. In order to delineate the contours of

Cold War Berlin, we must begin by filling in the material spaces in which
this evolving battle for Berlin played out.

Locating Berliners in a Geography of Destruction

Postwar Berlin was a city of debris. Although the first substantial air raids
to target the city struck only in November 1943, Berlin had endured 363
attacks and absorbed 45,517 tons of bombs by the time the war ended.[3]
These air raids and the devastating bombardment of the final Soviet attack
on the city in April 1945 produced some 70 million cubic meters of rubble, 17.5 percent of the wartime total within the boundaries of the 1938
German Reich. The resulting "rubble mountains" scattered across Berlin
eventually formed many of the highest geographic points across the city,
including one where the Americans later placed a principal Cold War
electronic-listening post.[4] Although directors, such as Billy Wilder, came
to make their films in Berlin, this devastation served as much more than
just a backdrop for postwar life. Several years after the war ended, many
streets in Berlin remained restricted to a narrow lane of traffic due to huge
mounds of rubble that continued to spill out into the roadways. The rubble remained a continuous threat to the city's inhabitants: weakened walls
at times gave way, crushing passersby, while munitions buried beneath the
debris projected the explosive violence of the wartime past into the postwar present. Recalling his arrival in the city, American General Lucius
D. Clay, described Berlin as "a city of the dead."[5] Aerial film footage
from the time shows roofless buildings that seem to extend interminably,

---

[3] The first bombs fell on Berlin in August 1940, but it took three years for major air raids to
reach the city. Reinhard Hellwig, ed., *Dokumente deutscher Kriegsschäden: Evakuierte,
Kriegssachgeschädigte, Währungsgeschädigte: die geschichtliche und rechtliche Entwick-
lung*, vol. IV/2, *Berlin –Kriegs- und Nachkriegsschicksal der Reichshauptstadt* (Bonn:
Bundesminister für Vertriebene, Flüchtlinge und Kriegsgeschädigte, 1967), 3–5.
[4] Wolfgang Bohleber, *Mit Marshallplan und Bundeshilfe: Wohnungsbaupolitik in Berlin
1945–1963* (Berlin: Duncker and Humblot, 1990), 29. On the transformations of the
Berlin landscape by the massive process of rubble removal, see Volkmar Fichtner,
*Die anthropogen bedingte Umwandlung des Reliefs durch Trümmeraufschüttungen in
Berlin (West) seit 1945*, Abhandlungen des Geographischen Instituts Anthropogeogra-
phie 21 (Berlin: Selbstverlag des Geographischen Instituts der Freien Universität Berlin,
1977).
[5] Clay, *Decision in Germany*, 21. Wilhelm Schivelbusch suggests that Berlin has never been
associated with destruction by bombs as are Hiroshima or Dresden, in spite of the fact that
Berlin absorbed more bombs and shells than any other city during World War II. Wilhelm
Schivelbusch, *In a Cold Crater: Cultural and Intellectual Life in Berlin, 1945–1948*, Kelly
Barry, trans. (Berkeley: University of California Press, 1998), 1–2.

the shattered walls providing an early assessment ground for the "ruin value" of the Thousand Year Reich.[6]

Wartime destruction cost Greater Berlin 612,000, or 39 percent, of its apartments, and, according to the State Statistical Bureau, the city lost no less than 50 percent of its total prebombardment housing space (*Wohnraum*).[7] In the central portions of the city, the destruction hit especially hard. The central, Mitte district saw 34 percent of its 10,321 buildings totally destroyed and another 17 percent partially destroyed. Building losses amounted to 54.4 percent of prewar totals in the Tiergarten district, 45.5 percent in Friedrichshain, and 39.9 percent in Kreuzberg. Although authorities deemed 11 to 15 percent of buildings in the six central districts repairable, the lack of building materials meant that subsequent years' exposure to the elements pushed many of them into the category of total loss.[8]

Rather than an effective summary of devastation, this description of destruction by percentage only reiterates the fragmented nature of the city and the diverse experience of violence at war's end.[9] The battle for the German capital in the last days of the war completely disrupted the city's food supply, and Berliners frantically held out, making use of whatever resources they could find. Even the Nazi Party acknowledged the growing desperation, issuing guidelines to the population about how to catch frogs and incorporate resources as diverse as tree bark, sawdust, and acorns into increasingly meager diets.[10] In Berlin the chaos of the final days of the war produced a sense of desperation in which questions of food and drink and, for women and girls, fear of rape at the hands of advancing

---

[6] As Albert Speer and Adolf Hitler planned the future capital of the German Reich, they sought to imagine an architecture that would, like the remnants of the classical world, prove equally impressive as ruins. After the Nuremberg War Crimes Tribunal sentenced Speer to twenty years in Berlin's Spandau prison, he obtained a firsthand view of the German capital from the window of the plane returning him to the city. On Albert Speer's "theory of ruin value," see Albert Speer, *Inside the Third Reich*, Richard and Clara Winston, trans. (New York: Collier Books, 1981), 56.

[7] Christian Engeli and Wolfgang Ribbe, "Berlin in der NS-Zeit (1933–1945)," in *Geschichte Berlins*, 2nd ed., vol. 2, *Von der Märzrevolution bis zur Gegenwart*, Wolfgang Ribbe, ed. (Munich: Verlag C. H. Beck, 1988), 1014. See the account of postwar life in a Berlin apartment as described in Ruth Andreas-Friedrich, *Battleground Berlin: Diaries 1945–1948*, Anna Boerresen, trans. (New York: Paragon House Publishers, 1990), 13ff.

[8] Bohleber, *Mit Marshallplan*, 15.

[9] On the basis of these numeric terms, other German cities had lost an even greater *percentage* of their housing stock. In Cologne, for example, only 2 percent of the pre-1939 buildings in the old city center were still standing. Gries, *Rationengesellschaft*, 250.

[10] Gustavo Corni and Horst Gies, *Brot, Butter, Kanonen: Die Ernährungswirtschaft in Deutschland unter der Diktatur Hitlers* (Berlin: Akademie Verlag, 1997), 582.

Soviet soldiers comprised only part of immediate survival concerns. Here, at least, brutal Soviet behavior meshed with Nazi propaganda, crafting a lingering sense of animosity toward the Soviets that would never really disappear. But even in the carnage that marked the war's last act, Berliners experienced the final battle for the city in sporadic fashion when bursts of intense violence interrupted periods of calm that some Berliners used to search out working water pumps or scavenge for food. For the inhabitants of even this one city, the war's ending varied greatly – the fighting hit some districts much harder than others – and these differences quite powerfully shaped these individuals' understandings of their starting places in the postwar world. Their responses to these moments, their willingness or ability to seize initiative, to act when others did not, could dramatically impact their ability to navigate the transition from war to its aftermath.

Crossing a street while shells still whistled overhead to chase down a report of a functioning water tap, slaughtering an ox that happened to wander down the street, or drinking vodka toasts with Russian soldiers on the search for plunder demanded both resources (water buckets, knives, the ability to speak rudimentary Russian) and the willingness to deploy them. While chance certainly played a significant role in the course of events that faced individual Berliners in the last days of April and early May 1945, it also became quite clear that some people proved more adept at taking action and seizing the opportunities that presented themselves in the evolving postwar environment. When she heard a rumor of horse-meat not far from her apartment in the Charlottenburg district of western Berlin, Margret Boveri set out and discovered a crowd gathered around a dead horse, whose body was still warm. Digging in aggressively with her pocket knife, she managed to obtain a large chunk of the lung and a piece of the leg. Arriving home, she still had hours of work, draining off the strangely pink-colored blood, cutting off the hide, and making sausage from the lungs. As she worked, a neighbor reported that the first Russians had arrived on their street, but she stayed in her kitchen, hesitant to track the mess into her front room but also afraid that Soviet soldiers might harbor dangerous suspicions about a woman splattered with blood.[11] For Berliners used to meat appearing neatly on the butcher's counter, this need for almost primal behavior challenged easy notions about their relative civilization.

---

[11] Margret Boveri, *Tage des Überlebens: Berlin 1945* (Munich: Piper Verlag, 1968), 79–80 and 97–9. Andreas-Friedrich, *Battleground Berlin*, 9–10.

Even for people who had opposed the Nazi regime, the implications of this battle for survival proved troubling. Ruth Andreas-Friedrich, a writer who had been part of a circle of anti-Nazi activists, uneasily observed how people poured out of hidden cellars to attempt to get some share of the ox that her friends had decided to slaughter on April 30, 1945. "So that is what the hour of liberation amounts to. Is this the moment we have awaited for twelve years? That we might fight over an ox's liver? And grab what we don't need, take what we never wanted to have? No, that is . . . I don't know what it is. In any case it is something horrifying."[12] Andreas-Friedrich had begun her diary following the Nazi-organized pogrom in November 1938 and maintained it in code throughout the Nazi era. From the outset she hoped to publish her account of resistance and opposition during the Third Reich and defend the moral stature of at least some of those remaining in Germany. An active part of postwar Berlin's intellectual life – she was the licensee and copublisher of the weekly *Sie* – Andreas-Friedrich filled her record of her life in Berlin with meticulous descriptions of her daily life. But her eye for detail also reflected her eye for a future audience, and we should be cautious not to attribute to all Berliners her sense of moral outrage.[13]

In the immediate aftermath of the war, Berliners literally came up from underground, emerging from their basements and air raid shelters, where they had endured the final battle for Berlin. They clambered over and through the contorted passages left in the midst of a battle-scarred cityscape, in search of home, beginning the process of cleaning up in some instances even as the fighting still raged. The schoolgirl Lilli G. recorded her personal encounter with the transition from war to postwar in a few short diary entries:

22.4. [April 22, 1945] Sleeping in the cellar. The Russians have reached Berlin.

25.4. No water! No gas! No light!

26.4. Artillery fire!

27.4. The enemy has reached Kaiserplatz [Wilmersdorf].

28.4. Our building received its 4th artillery hit.

29.4 Our building has approximately 20 hits. Cooking is made very difficult by the ongoing threat to life and limb if you leave the cellar.

---

[12] Andreas-Friedrich, *Battleground Berlin*, 9.

[13] Jörg Drews, afterword to *Battleground Berlin*, 258–9 and Lothar Bluhm, *Das Tagebuch zum Dritten Reich: Zeugnisse der Inneren Emigration von Jochen Klepper bis Ernst Jünger*, Studien zur Literatur der Moderne 20 (Bonn: Bouvier Verlag, 1991), 237–48.

30.4 When the bomb hit, I was at the top of the cellar steps with Frau B. The Russians have arrived. Rapes at night. I not; mother, yes. Some, 5–20 times.

1.5. Russians are going in and out. All the watches are gone. Horses are lying on our beds in the courtyard. The cellars have been broken into.

2.5. The first night of calm. We have come from hell into heaven. We cried when we discovered the blooming lilacs in the courtyard. All radios must be turned in.

6.5. Our building has 21 hits. Cleaned up and packed the whole day. At night, storm. Hid under the bed out of fear that the Russians would come. But the building just rattled from the shelling.

7.5. Swept the street clear. Went to get ration tickets [Nummern] for bread, picked up, cleaned.

8.5. Swept the street. Stood in line for bread. Report that Papa is still alive.

9.5. Ceasefire. There's milk for Margit.

10.5. Picked up.[14]

Within this sparse account, we find only hints of the intensity of violence that she and those around her experienced. The rapes at the hands Soviet soldiers that would become the defining experience for most Berlin women's initial encounters with the occupier from the East are enumerated matter-of-factly, but she hid under the bed, fearing that the "Russians" would come back. Indeed this pervasive fear that women and girls felt in the last days of the war and the immediate aftermath – of going out, of walking alone in a stairwell, of nighttime – becomes a critical context in which to try to make sense of the blurred lines between war and peace.[15] In the midst of this fear, Berliners tried to put things in order, to sweep up the dust and broken glass, to begin to clean up the residue of war in the middle of their kitchens and living rooms.

But even this description suggests a uniformity of experience that is misleading. Residents in outlying districts were much more likely to possess homes with no or only minimal damage (although that also made them targets for occupation seizure). After the fighting stopped, these

[14] Quoted in Susanne zur Nieden, *Alltag im Ausnahmezustand Frauentagebücher im zerstörten Deutschland 1943 bis 1945* (Berlin: Orlanda Frauenverlag, 1993), 91–2. Unless noted to the contrary, all translations are by the author.

[15] Zur Nieden, *Alltag im Ausnahmezustand*, 96. Anonymous, *A Woman in Berlin: Eight Weeks in the Conquered City* (New York: Metropolitan Books, 2005).

different experiences continued to matter a great deal. The extent to which Berliners still had a residence and barterable possessions created unequal starting points for those now forced to cope with the demands of postwar survival. Because some 200,000 apartments had been destroyed only in the last days of the war, this process entailed a massive shift of possessions and inhabitation, in which ownership considerations remained secondary.[16] Survivors settled where they could, leaving chalk messages on crumbling walls in the hopes of contacting scattered friends and families in a decidedly impermanent and dangerous world.[17] By April 1946, 42,084 provisionally arranged apartments housed 110,000 persons in a variety of locations ranging from garden cottages to temporary shelters on rooftops.[18] Even available apartments were often severely damaged and only marginally inhabitable. For years, apartment walls and windows throughout the city remained covered with cardboard or some other "temporary" repair whose relative permanence helped underscore how this unfinished material state became the normal condition of postwar Berlin (Figure 3). Shattered walls and chimneys even complicated an apparently simple task like building a fire in a stove. The journalist Margret Boveri describes in loving detail her efforts to assemble a small stove from a steel grate, stones, and other materials she painstakingly gathered from remnants of ruined buildings. Although it allowed her to cook even when the gas service was completely cut, every use left her covered in soot.[19]

The nearly total collapse of the water system left Berliners with few options for sewage disposal. Immediately after the fighting stopped, Andreas-Friedrich returned to a house – already ransacked by Soviet soldiers – in which the stink almost overwhelmed those who entered. Berliners' retrospective denunciation of Soviet soldiers' unfamiliarity with toilets is pervasive, but such accounts merit some caution. One woman describes how a Soviet soldier asked her whether she used the toilet to wash her hair. While this statement may reflect the soldier's lack of sophistication, it might also be read as an insult, a possibility that seems not to have registered with the Berliner who took her cultural superiority for granted. In the same vein, a friend of Andreas-Friedrich criticized the "buffaloes" who

[16] Bohleber, *Mit Marshallplan*, 22.
[17] Sibylle Meyer and Eva Schulze, *Von Liebe sprach damals keiner: Familienalltag in der Nachkriegszeit* (Munich: Verlag C. H. Beck, 1985), 53 and Marie Vassiltchikov, *Berlin Diaries, 1940–1945* (New York: Vintage, 1988), 119.
[18] Bohleber, *Mit Marshallplan*, 23.
[19] Boveri, *Tage des Überlebens*, 68–71 and 124. Andreas-Friedrich reports a very similar experience in *Battleground Berlin*, 13–14.

FIGURE 3. Apartment interior in the Tiergarten District (British sector), 1949. Even four years after the end of World War II, war damage remains "temporarily" repaired with pieces of cardboard. These systematic but somewhat ramshackle efforts to make the apartment livable both reflect and counter the assertion of petit-bourgeois respectability literally signified by the towel hanging on the back wall. It reads "to work and to strive are the source of your pride." *Source:* Landesarchiv Berlin.

left their toilet in a state of filth, but his denunciation of the "Mongol" invaders does more to conceal the massive difficulties produced by even a short-term shutdown of large parts of a major city's water supply.[20] For years to come, building ruins served as convenient dumping grounds, but the piles of garbage and human and animal waste created a separate set of sanitation problems that appeared particularly in the summer months. Swarms of flies and mosquitoes plagued the city, an obvious manifestation of the potential health crisis that lingered just beneath the city's surface. Even into 1947 and 1948, district governments issued occasional appeals for campaigns to bury garbage or sprinkle lime over refuse piles.[21] In this, as in much of daily life in the city, survival often depended on an ongoing series of provisional solutions followed by the subsequent need to address the eventual consequences of those preliminary measures.

Since July 1945, the city had been declared off limits for refugees without authorization from occupation authorities. Signs posted at roads and rail stations called on refugees to keep heading westward, and police and civilian patrols kept watch on roads leading into the city, but the waves of refugees, returning evacuees, and former prisoners of war continued to stream into the city.[22] Until 1946 Jewish Displaced Persons (DPs) fleeing Poland used Berlin as a regular transit station en route to the American zone of Germany and eventually to Palestine. At that point, increasing American regulation of that refugee flow forced these refugees to assume a more permanent place in the city, most visibly in DP camps in the Tempelhof and Zehlendorf districts of the American sector. Often decried by Berliners as hotbeds of (foreign) criminal activity, these refugee camps offered both a local reminder of the international effects of the war Germany had just waged and an additional layering of international authority in the midst of Berliners' everyday lives.[23]

---

[20] Andreas-Friedrich, *Battleground Berlin*, 13; Heidi Scriba Vance, *Shadows over My Berlin: One Woman's Story of World War II* (Middletown, CT: Southfarm Press, 1996), 129.

[21] Andreas Dinter, *Berlin in Trümmern: Ernährungslage und medizinische Versorgung der Bevölkerung Berlins nach dem II. Weltkrieg*, Geschichte(n) der Medizin (Berlin: Verlag Frank Wünsche, 1999), 38–44 and 51–9.

[22] Dinter, *Berlin in Trümmern*, 103–9.

[23] Angelika Königseder, *Flucht nach Berlin: Jüdische Displaced Persons 1945–1948* (Berlin: Metropol, 1998), chs. 4–5; Atina Grossmann, "Trauma, Memory, and Motherhood: Germans and Jewish Displaced Persons in Post-Nazi Germany, 1945–1949," in *Life After Death: Approaches to a Cultural and Social History of Europe During the 1940s and 1950s*; Richard Bessel and Dirk Schumann, eds. (Cambridge and New York: Cambridge University Press, 2003), 118–22; and Grossmann, "Home and Displacement in a City of Bordercrossers: Jews in Berlin 1945–1948," *Unlikely History: The Changing*

Throughout Berlin, the individual municipal districts at first functioned as semiindependent fiefdoms of local authorities that the Soviets had installed. This separateness did not reflect any explicitly political process; that is, it was not a product of occupation boundaries or administrative distinctions but rather a phenomenon that rested on the city's sprawling area and the lack of adequate transportation. In this devastated city with several times the surface area of Paris, getting where one wanted to go was often no easy task. Berlin's vaunted public transportation system had been severely damaged in the battle for the city, and its inhabitants faced lengthy waits before having to cram themselves onto overworked and often malfunctioning trains and buses. The fact that on several occasions, persons hanging on the running boards of S-Bahn trains were killed when trains traveling in the opposite direction rubbed them from their perches gives some sense of the hazardous nature of travel within the city.[24] Bicycles, often cobbled together from assorted found parts, were priceless possessions, and their theft entailed real economic hardships and hampered people's efforts to obtain food and other supplies or even to make it to work. Soviet soldiers, many of whom first learned to ride bicycles in Berlin, sought them out with enthusiasm and made them, as a result, one additional source of contentious encounters between Berliners and the city's first occupiers.[25]

For most Berliners, walking remained the principal form of transportation, a fact that certainly complicated lengthy treks to obtain building supplies, tools, or other goods. Even a minor foot injury could dramatically hamper a person's ability to function effectively. Life of any sort in this city of rubble demanded significant and often prolonged exertion and regularly pushed people to complete exhaustion.[26] If in a "whole" city, the

---

German-Jewish Symbiosis, 1945–2000, Leslie Morris and Jack Zipes, eds. (New York: Palgrave, 2002), 72–6.

[24] Archiv der sozialden Demokratie (hereafter AdsD), Nachlaß Otto Ostrowski, box 35: Kommunalpolitik Berlin/SPD Berlin 1946–61, folder 1. For a general description of the poor state of Berlin's S-Bahn system in the immediate postwar period, including passenger figures, see the Report on the Status of the S-Bahn in Berlin from HV Verkehr-Generaldirektion Reichsbahn, dated October 19, 1948, Bundesarchiv, Abteilung DDR (hereafter BA-DDR), DC-15–913, Bl. 63f.

[25] Wladimir Gelfand, *Deutschland-Tagebuch 1945–1946 Aufzeichnungen einse Rotarmisten*, Anja Lutter and Hartmut Schröder, trans. (Berlin: Aufbau, 2005). See the photo of the woman struggling with a Soviet soldier for her bike in Norman Naimark, *The Russians in Germany: A History of the Soviet Zone of Occupation, 1945–1949* (Cambridge, MA and London: Harvard University Press, 1995), 140ff.

[26] See, e.g., the photograph of the anxious crowd gathered around a man who has collapsed on the street in August 1948. Dinter, *Berlin in Trümmern*, 98.

masses of commuters, flaneurs, and other urban inhabitants going about their daily affairs gave the city and its structures only distracted notice, Berliners' interactions with this postwar urban environment demanded much greater concentration. Overcoming exhaustion, exercising caution in the face of occasionally dangerous conditions on streets and around ruins, and noticing potential resources that might appear in the midst of the devastation meant that the material city necessarily demanded Berliners' intimate appraisal.

One woman recalled that it took eight hours to get from the western district of Charlottenburg (British sector) to Treptow, in the south-central part of the Soviet sector.[27] Walking across a city full of rubble and the detritus of battle often left Berliners covered in dust.[28] Heidi Scriba Vance, a young dancer who would later marry an American soldier in Berlin, described the physical demands of a trek across the city just after the fighting had stopped. She, her mother, and her young brother walked to find shelter after their apartment building was destroyed by a German tank. Along the way a woman shared an old stroller from her basement to help the young boy continue on the way. Other groups of people let them into their home and shared food with them. Scriba Vance recalls that these strangers gave her brother three cookies – he ate one and kept two for later, because "[h]e had learned about hunger."[29] While her account asserts her family's victimhood – and Germans' more generally – a bit too vehemently, her description of her walk across the city helps to map out how she began to manage the transition from war to peace, to adapt to these new spatial and material conditions, and to cultivate the often fleeting relationships that would allow Berliners to cope with these postwar conditions.

The effort to clear the rubble in the city began almost immediately. Occupation officials first dispatched former Nazis to these repair efforts, but they soon expanded their recruitment efforts. Most of the work fell to women, and, in the immediate postwar years, women engaged in rubble removal made up 5 to 10 percent of women employed in the city.[30] Yet the iconic figure of the Berlin "woman of the rubble" (*Trümmerfrau*)

[27] Thomas Scholze, "Zur Ernährungssituation der Berliner nach dem zweiten Weltkrieg. Ein Beitrag zur Erforschung des Großstadtalltags (1945–1952)," *Jahrbuch für Geschichte* 35 (1987), 556.

[28] Karena Niehoff, "Die Unverwüstlichen," in *Bomben, Trümmer, Lucky Strikes: Die Stunde Null in bisher unbekannten Manuskripten* (Berlin: WJS, 2004), 102.

[29] Vance, 117–18.

[30] Heineman, "The Hour of the Woman," 375.

runs the risk of concealing the day-to-day implications of this work. The innumerable photographs of lines of women, passing bricks from one hand to the next, imbed these women in a ruinscape for which they served as repair mechanisms. But we should not lose track of these women as agents negotiating their place within the city and seeking to manage the conditions under which they experienced them. As an anonymous diary writer describes, such work both created material opportunity – access to higher rations and to food at the work site – and constrained the options by which these women could confront the existential pressures they faced. The work exhausted the workers and limited their time available for other vital pursuits, especially pursuing possible food sources, but it also created occasional opportunities – for a hearty and warm midday meal or friendly exchanges with fellow workers.[31] As the work gradually became more automated, with narrow-gauge railways used to transport materials from building ruins, the process of clearing the destruction accelerated, but it remained a lengthy one.[32] Even into the 1980s, it was possible to find apartment buildings in which one or more floors remained uninhabited due to unreconstructed war damage, and not just in the neglected regions on the eastern side of the Berlin Wall. A character in a 1982 novel of the city on both sides of the wall noted: "I like Berlin, really, for the ways in which it differs from Hamburg, Frankfurt, and Munich: the leftover ruins in which man-high birches and shrubs have struck root; the bullet holes in the sand-gray, blistered facades; the faded ads, painted on fire walls, which bear witness to cigarette brands and types of schnapps that have long ceased to exist."[33] This residual presence of the past was not just a product of incomplete *re*construction but mattered already in the immediate postwar period, as Berliners wrestled with the material, psychological, and political remnants that they uncovered each day in the city.

For all its horror, the physical destruction of Berlin initially left a surprising amount of Berlin's industrial infrastructure intact or at least reparable, but Soviet dismantling decimated the city's remaining industrial plant, setting back any hopes for a speedy economic revival. Prior to Soviet dismantling, some 65 percent of industrial capacity had survived the war in working order. Berlin's Industry and Trade Chamber later estimated the

---

[31] Anonymous, *A Woman in Berlin*, 212–31.
[32] Bohleber, *Mit Marshallplan*, 106–13.
[33] Peter Schneider, *The Wall Jumper: A Berlin Story*, Leigh Hafrey, trans. (Chicago: University of Chicago Press, 1998), 5–6.

loss of industrial capacity in West Berlin at 85 percent.[34] Soviet records reported that Berlin provided 12.6 percent of the more than 5 million tons of material dismantled from industrial sites in the Soviet occupation zone. More than 8 percent of the total (approximately 429,000 tons) came from Berlin's western sectors, which the Soviets controlled for nearly two months in the spring and early summer 1945.[35] One German political scientist puts the total loss of property (*Volksvermögen*) as a result of wartime destruction, plundering, and dismantling at 42 percent for all of Greater Berlin.[36]

The processes of economic decentralization that had begun during the war and the elimination of Berlin's capital function contributed further to the inertia inhibiting economic redevelopment.[37] Thus, whereas many West German cities could undertake an admittedly arduous process of rebuilding their industrial capacity, many of Berlin's key industries had simply vanished.[38] Postwar production figures dramatically demonstrate this reality. In 1946, Berlin's gross industrial production remained only 37 percent of 1936 levels. Levels in some key industrial branches were significantly lower. For example, the critically important electrical engineering sector managed to produce at only 26 percent of its 1936 levels.[39] As late as 1950, West Berlin's mechanical engineering production had achieved a net production value of only 30 percent of 1936 levels, the electrical industry only 40 percent of 1936 levels. In comparison, the western occupation zones in 1947–8 had already reached 106 percent of 1936 levels in mechanical engineering and 155 percent in the electrical industry.[40]

To some extent this lack of industrial redevelopment resulted from a simple lack of funding. A Soviet order of April 28, 1945 directed Berlin banks to halt all financial transfers and to seal all safes. The full Kommandatura approved this measure when it took up its responsibilities in July. As a result, some 8 billion to 10 billion reichsmark (RM) remained unavailable for economic reconstruction. By contrast, in the American zone occupation officials totally froze only 5 percent of the 54 billion

34 Cited in Arthur Schlegelmilch, *Hauptstadt im Zonendeutschland: Die Entstehung der Berliner Nachkriegsdemokratie 1945–1949* (Berlin: Haude and Spener, 1993), 437. See also Naimark, *The Russians in Germany*, 166–75.

35 Rainer Karlsch and Jochen Laufer, eds., *Sowjetische Demontagen in Deutschland 1944–1949: Hintergründe, Ziele und Wirkungen* (Berlin: Duncker and Humblot, 2002), 50.

36 Bohleber, *Mit Marshallplan*, 29.

37 Schlegelmilch, *Hauptstadt im Zonendeutschland*, 441.

38 Bohleber, *Mit Marshallplan*, 31.

39 Schlegelmilch, *Hauptstadt im Zonendeutschland*, 439.

40 Bohleber, *Mit Marshallplan*, 32.

RM in savings accounts and authorized the unrestricted release of three-quarters of these funds. Similar arrangements in the other western zones meant that approximately 107 billion RM were available for economic reconstruction there.[41] Thus Berlin was at an economic disadvantage from the very outset, and, over the long term, the slow pace of rebuilding in the city underscored the extent to which the interstitial character of the immediate postwar period remained the norm for the former German capital.

Even in the process of reconstruction, Berliners confronted conflicting decisions about renovating damaged buildings or completing the destruction of large chunks of old Berlin.[42] An early postwar slogan, "Berlin is building" (*Berlin baut auf*), seemed to emphasize the newness and future orientation of this postwar construction, but all rebuilding efforts in the immediate postwar years necessarily recycled salvageable remnants of the devastated city.[43] Berliners piled up rubble mountains full of the crumbled remains of their prewar lives only after first refurbishing stack after stack of bricks for use in postwar (re)construction. This literal incorporation of the material past into the production of a postwar future challenges uncomplicated notions of the city's inability to find at least some of the resources it needed to survive. Although the placards declaring the support of American Marshall Plan Aid that later graced construction sites throughout the city's western half reiterated the need for material support from outside the city and beyond Berliners' control, it is not enough merely to accept international aid as *the* necessary precondition for Berliners' postwar survival.[44] Berliners and Berlin material remained

---

[41] Ibid., 33–4.

[42] Karen E. Till, *The New Berlin: Memory, Politics, Place* (Minneapolis and London: University of Minnesota Press, 2005), 41.

[43] The SED initially used the slogan *Berlin baut auf*, but in April 1947 adopted a new slogan, "Berlin must live" (*Berlin muss leben*) in an effort to differentiate their approach from that of other parties in the city. See the Bericht der Organisationsabteilung an das Sekretariat des Landesvorstandes (Berlin), 11.9.1947, SAPMO, DY 30/IV 2/5/223, Bl. 208.

[44] Moving beyond a celebratory understanding of Marshall Plan aid as the single explanation for Western Europe's postwar economic recovery, more recent scholarship on what was officially called the European Recovery Program has emphasized it as one part of a larger mix of forces that brought about "miraculous" postwar economic growth. From this perspective the Marshall Plan served as an accelerant rather than as primal cause. See Michael J. Hogan, *The Marshall Plan: America, Britain, and the Reconstruction of Western Europe, 1947–1952* (Cambridge and New York: Cambridge University Press, 1987) and Alan S. Milward, *The Reconstruction of Western Europe, 1945–51* (Berkeley: University of California Press, 1984).

the key components to an admittedly incomplete rebuilding process in the immediate postwar period. Ultimately, the unrepaired Berlin walls, the fractured housing stock, and the ongoing presence of rubble in Berliners' everyday lives made apparent the growing normalcy of a series of temporary solutions that became increasingly permanent.

The Ration System

On May 5, 1945, the Soviet commander in Berlin, General N. E. Berzarin, issued a proclamation to the city's population: "In order to secure the regular food supply of the Berlin population, the Soviet Military Command has, through the Commandant of the city of Berlin, made sufficient foodstuffs available to the city administration."[45] Berzarin's order and the initial generosity of Red Army field kitchens elicited positive if surprised responses from many Germans, but individual acts of compassion and general assertions of goodwill did not solve the tremendous problems of postwar supply.[46] Previously, Berlin had been the hub at the center of the massive German state's administrative wheel. Now, those administrative ties had been severed, and the former capital's national weightiness diminished. Much of Germany's most productive prewar agricultural land now lay under Polish control and thus remained unavailable for German supply needs. Any hopes that Berliners held that the end of the war would bring about a rapid improvement in material conditions soon proved false. Both at the time and in retrospect, Germans generally saw the postwar period as much worse than even the most horrible of the war years.[47]

---

[45] Dinter, *Berlin in Trümmern*, 72.

[46] See Antony Beevor, *The Fall of Berlin 1945* (New York: Viking, 2002), 409 and Gelfand, *Deutschland-Tagebuch*, 86.

[47] See Willi A. Boelcke, *Der Schwarzmarkt 1945–1948: vom Überleben nach dem Kriege* (Braunschweig: Westermann, 1986), 41. Jens Jäger suggests that the ending of wartime restrictions on producing images of horror, hardship, and death helped to produce a retrospective sense of the post-1945 period as more horrible than the war. Jens Jäger, "Fotografie – Erinnerung – Identität: die Trümmeraufnahmen aus deutschen Städten 1945," in Jörg Hillmann and John Zimmermann, eds., *Kriegsende 1945 in Deutschland*, Beiträge zur Militärgeschichte 55 (Munich: R. Oldenbourg Verlag, 2002), 292. Only very recently have the horrors of German civilian experiences entered prominently into public discussion. Most prominently, see W. G. Sebald and Jörg Friedrichs. Friedrich's decision to discuss the German experience under bombardment in terms that explicitly parallel the Holocaust offer a problematic account that, similar to German assertions of greater *postwar* hardship, runs the risk of too dramatically extracting those experiences from the context of the genocidal war, which was launched by the German state and sustained by the actions of the German population more generally. See the forum "World

In the words of the oft-repeated and bitter popular quip from the last months of the war: "Enjoy the war, the peace will be awful." While the wartime violence may have ended, regular rhythms of social and economic life did not return. Wartime supply practices continued and, for the next four years, the material components of people's lives were marked off in *Dekaden* – the ten-day periods at which most rations were issued.[48] A request that calendars be issued with the ration periods marked as well as the weeks and months made clear the extent to which this system provided a framework within which Berliners' understood even the passage of time.

Rationing was not new for Berliners. Their first tumultuous experience with state-regulated supply efforts occurred during World War I, the inadequacies of these measures evident in recurring bread riots and ingrained into collective memory in the iconic "turnip winter" of 1916–17.[49] This past failure weighed heavily on the Nazi leadership, and it strove mightily to forestall what it feared could be the revolutionary potential implicit in food shortages.[50] To that end, the regime attempted to strictly regulate food provision by means of a centrally organized supply and distribution structure that initially came together under the authority of a single head of both the Reich food and agricultural ministries.[51] The Nazi government ruthlessly exploited occupied territories and forced laborers to sustain basic supply levels throughout the Reich, and although the change in Germany's military fortunes in 1943 made this practice more difficult, the official wartime ration levels never reached the crisis levels of 1917 and 1918. Although the regime reduced ration amounts in 1940 and again in 1942, official levels of German caloric intake remained close to or above the "necessary" figure of 1,700 calories. As late as April 1945, one set of statistics put calorie levels for average consumers (*Normalverbraucher*) at 1,602. Heavy and heaviest workers (*Schwer-* and

War II Bombing: Rethinking German Experiences," H-German (November 2003), http://www.h-net.org/~german/discuss/WWII_bombing/WWII-bombing_index.htm; and the thematic issue of *Central European History* 38, no. 1 (2005).

[48] On ration schedules, see Scholze, "Zur Ernährungssituation," 544.

[49] Belinda Davis, *Home Fires Burning: Food, Politics, and Everyday Life in World War I Berlin* (Chapel Hill and London: University of North Carolina Press, 2000) and Maureen Healy, *Vienna and the Fall of the Habsburg Empire: Total War and Everyday Life in World War I* (Cambridge: Cambridge University Press, 2004).

[50] Detlev Peukert, *Inside Nazi Germany: Conformity, Opposition, and Racism in Everyday Life*, Richard Deveson, trans. (New Haven and London: Yale University Press, 1987), 56.

[51] Wildt, *Der Traum vom Sattwerden*, 13.

Schwerstarbeiter) received even more, 2,252 calories and 2,905 calories respectively.[52]

The Soviet occupiers began to impose preliminary order to the food distribution system issuing the first postwar ration cards in mid-May.[53] In their effort to address the supply needs of the German population, the victorious Allies changed very little of the organizational frameworks within which the Nazis had distributed rations. Under the Nazis, rations had been distributed on a differentiated basis, with age and profession as well as racial categorization determining the amounts of foodstuffs each ration card holder was to receive. Members of the armed forces, even those not at the front, received higher rations than even the most privileged civilians. Among the civilian population, those persons performing the most physical work received higher rations. Most persons fell into the category of normal consumers, and by war's end they were allocated just over half the amount granted to the heaviest workers. Jews, forced laborers, prisoners of war, and concentration camp prisoners all received dramatically less than even nonprivileged "Aryan" ration recipients.[54]

When the occupation began, the Allies maintained the basic components of this differentiated structure, even though they organized ration distribution quite differently at home.[55] While they did rework some of the categories, reducing many former Nazis to the lowest ration category and elevating the status of those whom the Nazi regime had persecuted, they did not dramatically rework the way the system functioned. Berliners, of course, immediately grasped how these evolving categories of identity

---

[52] Corni and Gies, *Brot, Butter, Kanonen*, 562 and 581. Figures for ration levels vary considerably. Elsewhere in their book, Corni and Gies cite official records that note a drop in average rations for *Normalverbraucher* in 1944 to 1945 from 2,435 to 1,602 calories (p. 581). Hans-Joachin Braun tells this as a story of ongoing and difficult decline, but in comparison to the experiences of World War I, the Nazi state's relative success at maintaining a viable ration level is striking. See Hans-Joachim Braun, *The German Economy in the Twentieth Century* (London and New York: Routledge, 1990), 127.

[53] Dr. Andreas Hermes, who would serve as postwar Berlin's first food department head, elaborated the five postwar ration categories on May 11. Senat von Berlin, ed., *Berlin: Kampf um Frieheit und Selbstverwaltung 1945–1946* (Berlin: Heinz Spitzing Verlag, 1961), 53. Andreas-Friedrich's diary mentions on May 17 that the first ration cards have been distributed, *Battleground Berlin*, 28.

[54] Corni and Gies, *Brot, Butter, Kanonen*, 555 and 562.

[55] On various rationing practices, see Ina Zweiniger-Bargielowska, *Austerity in Britain: Rationing, Controls, and Consumption, 1939–1955* (Oxford and New York: Oxford University Press, 2000), ch. 1; Amy Bentley, *Eating for Victory: Food Rationing and the Politics of Domesticity* (Urbana and Chicago: University of Illinois Press, 1998), ch. 1; and Barbara Falk, *Sowjetische Städte in der Hungersnot 1932/33: Staatliche Ernährungspolitik und Städtisches Alltagsleben* (Cologne: Böhlau Verlag, 2005).

mattered for their supply options. Thus one vital component of pursuing "Victim of Fascism" (*Opfer des Faschimus* or OdF) status lay in the access it granted to a higher ration level, a process that shifted the implications of the Nazi past into the material present, even for those persons who really had suffered under the Third Reich.[56]

The highly centralized system in which supply and distribution were closely linked did not translate smoothly into an occupied Germany, divided into four separate zones that were each responsible for providing the resources it needed. The loss of much of the former Reich's most productive agricultural land as well as the generally desperate conditions facing three of the four occupiers at home further muddied the situation. Berlin, part of no single occupation zone but divided into four sectors, proved an even trickier proposition. At Soviet insistence, the Western powers assumed official responsibility for the food and fuel supply of their sectors after entering the city in July 1945 and supplies for each sector were thus to be drawn from the corresponding occupation zone.[57] Berlin, however, lay more than 100 miles inside the Soviet zone, a lengthy supply line in any case, and the more distant French occupation zone lay even further away. The substantial disruption of transportation systems produced by wartime destruction and postwar shortages of fuel and equipment heightened the logistical difficulties, and western occupation officials immediately expressed concerns about the feasibility of such arrangements.[58] During the earliest stages of four-power occupation, only the Soviet sector received officially distributed foodstuffs and other supplies from the agricultural areas immediately surrounding the city (areas that became part of the Soviet occupation zone). The need to ship food and other supplies to Berlin provoked popular outcries in western Germany, fears of somehow being disadvantaged with respect to another city or region intermingling

---

[56] Inge Deutschkron, *Ich trug den gelben Stern* (Munich: Deutscher Taschenbuch Verlag, 1985), 187–8.

[57] For an insightful overview of the conversations that laid the groundwork for the occupation regime in Berlin, see the documents in Hans J. Reichhardt, Hanns U. Treutler, and Albrecht Lampe, eds., *Berlin: Quellen und Dokumente 1945–1951*, 1. Halbband (Berlin: Heinz Spitzing Verlag, 1964), 115–26. Schlegelmilch makes the point that the Soviet decision was driven by a breakdown in its ability to supply the city effectively. *Hauptstadt im Zonendeutschland*, 35. The victorious Allies divided Germany into four occupation *zones* and Berlin into four *sectors*. While there was some blurring in their use, the terms were not interchangeable, and I will carefully maintain that distinction throughout this book.

[58] See the report of the meeting between Allied officials in Berlin on July 9, 1945 in *Berlin: Quellen und Dokumente 1945–1951*, 1. Halbband, 120.

with longstanding antipathy toward the onetime Prussian and German capital. Still, as much as popular protests in these areas may have liked to presume, food shipments to Berlin from Bavaria and other western states were not unprecedented. Immediately before the war, Berlin ranked second among major German cities (behind Mannheim-Ludwigshafen) in receipt of foodstuffs shipped by rail from Bavaria.[59] In the overcharged postwar atmosphere, however, such continuities were harder to stomach as hungry people watched food-laden train cars roll into the distance. Of course, organizing and guaranteeing these shipments posed a more fundamental dilemma. Targeted at halts and slow stretches along the way, hardly any trains arrived in Berlin without having been plundered en route. This transportation and security dilemma marked the first hurdle in the process of efficiently supplying Berliners.

The administration of the food allocation program rapidly passed into German hands. On August 15, 1945, the Kommandatura transferred responsibility to the city Magistrat for the equitable distribution of foodstuffs for the entire city.[60] In reality, a differentiated supply system emerged, in which the sectors enjoyed varying levels of official provision, with the French sector faring most poorly. Even in June 1947, the head of the city's food department, Paul Füllsack, reported to the city assembly that only flour was being distributed in unitary fashion (*einheitlich*) to all occupation sectors.[61] Ultimately, this fact reflected the limitations of the city's ration economy and the substantial gap between the theory and praxis of equitable food supply. A graphic representation of goods circulation, prepared in the fall of 1945, suggests the practical complexities that entered into even well-intentioned efforts to adhere to this mandate. According to this plan, goods arriving from the United States, England, the Soviet Union, or other zones of Germany all entered into the jurisdiction of the various Berlin food departments, dispatched first to the city's food department storage depots (*Läger*) before being sent on to district storage depots or processing industries (both under the jurisdiction of one of twenty district food departments). From there goods moved on to wholesalers or to even more local storage depots (*Ortsläger*) before finally finding their way to retail shops, where they became available for purchase. In an effort to maintain control of the continuing goods transfers, warehousing, and rewarehousing, the food departments marked each

[59] Gries, *Die Rationengesellschaft*, 379 n. 40.
[60] Schlegelmilch, *Hauptstadt im Zonendeutschland*, 443.
[61] *Berlin: Behauptung von Freiheit und Selbstverwaltung 1946–1948*, 244.

move within the system with a bewildering array of color-coded forms, none of which managed to prevent widespread loss, theft, or deterioration of quality along the way.[62]

Almost from the outset, the various occupation authorities took steps that undermined the declared policy of unitary supply. On July 19, 1946, the Soviets ordered a halt to all fruit and vegetable deliveries from the Soviet zone to Berlin's western sectors, denying municipal authorities the opportunity to disperse these foodstuffs as needed throughout the city. All the occupation powers evaded their obligations to subject their supplies to the Magistrat-administered foodstuff pool by means of special distributions in their respective sectors.[63] Employees of the various occupation administrations received a regular hot meal at work, which did not count against their ration, a privilege that only increased the desirability of these positions. CARE (Cooperative for American Remittances to Europe) packages and Soviet *pajoks* (from the Russian word for ration) provided very distinct combinations of supplementary supplies to those fortunate enough to receive them. The first CARE packages arrived in Germany in the summer of 1946. Initially, parcels of surplus U.S. Army rations, CARE packages came to contain an almost luxurious assortment of canned meats, margarine, sweets, and coffee. Totaling about 40,000 calories, a CARE package offered an incredible nutritional windfall.[64] A pair of photos in the weekly *Sie* modeled the receipt of a CARE package. In the first, a well-dressed woman in hat and coat took possession of a box of supplies from CARE officials. The caption notes her mixed emotions, as her sister had only recently died of spotted fever. The second photo showed the woman at home with her three-year-old daughter on her knee as they unpack their "treasures," the cans and packets of foodstuffs that contain enough food to last one person for ten days. As the caption explains, the numerous small packets within the CARE package facilitate the "rational" consumption of the contents.[65]

The pajok, a privilege granted especially to SED party functionaries, intellectuals, and artists, was physically quite large and more "robust" than the CARE package, containing substantial amounts of staples like

[62] "Schematische Darstellung des Warenflusses" (October 1945), OMGUS, Berlin Sector, Records of the Economic Branch, Records of the Central Food Office, United States National Archives (hereafter NA) RG 260/390/48/18/2 box 456.

[63] Schlegelmilch, *Hauptstadt im Zonendeutschland*, 443ff.

[64] See the full contents list at "CARE-Paket," *CARE-Deutschland*, http://www.care.de/care/1carepa.htm (accessed August 30, 2002).

[65] *Sie* (August 25, 1946), 2–3.

lard, flour, and sugar. But CARE packages provided glamorous access to American wealth, a material reality also potently reflected in Germans' encounters with American soldiers in Berlin: the goods that even enlisted men could give away almost carelessly – cigarettes, coffee, gum, chocolate, stockings – had a very high exchange value on the black market and thus a worth far beyond the materiality of the gift.[66] Of course, these soldiers' interests were not restricted to gift giving. One carton of American cigarettes cost soldiers approximately one dollar. With an average price of 5 RM per (American) cigarette, the 200 cigarettes in a carton meant a return of 1,000 RM per dollar. Every day, more than 3,000 cartons of cigarettes arrived by military post for American soldiers in Berlin and the American zone, which, according to one contemporary estimate, produced an annual return of $100 million and a black market profit of 12,000 percent.[67]

A contemporary police report explained that American combat engineers (*Pioniere*) working to build the new Tegel airfield in (West) Berlin during fall 1948 earned thirty dollars each day. At a rate of approximately 12 west marks to the dollar, this meant that this soldier's money would have translated to 43,200 east marks to use locally. When an American sector municipal employee earning 750 east marks each month was able to purchase anything he needed on the black market, it becomes clear that even a portion of this dollar wealth created almost insurmountable

---

[66] Annette Kaminsky, *Wohlstand, Schönheit, Glück: kleine Konsumgeschichte der DDR* (Munich: Verlag C. H. Beck, 2001), 20. Gabrielle Stüber suggests that even beyond the temporary relief they provided from ongoing feelings of hunger, CARE packages coming from abroad provided a psychological benefit, suggesting to Germans that they were not entirely excluded from the international community. Stüber, *Der Kampf gegen den Hunger 1945–1950: die Ernährungslage in der britischen zone Deutschlands, insbesondere in Schleswig-Holstein und Hamburg* (Neumünster: Karl-Wachholtz Verlag, 1984), 630. For a telling eyewitness account from a visitor to Berlin, see Margaret Bourke-White, *"Dear fatherland, rest quietly": A Report on the Collapse of Hitler's "Thousand Years"* (New York: Simon and Schuster, 1946), 151–62. A similar privileged distribution took place already during the war: at Christmas 1942, wounded soldiers or soldiers home on leave were issued a card, valid until May 1943, to obtain a so-called "Führerpaket," which contained 2.5 kg flour, 1 kg sugar, 1.5 kg cereals (*Nährmittel*), 1 kg butter, and 1 kg meat/meat products. Corni and Gies, *Brot, Butter, Kanonen*, 565.

[67] Boelcke, *Der Schwarzmarkt*, 131–2; George H. Weltner, "Millions of Guilty Men," *Harpers* (January 1947), 81–4. On Americans and the black market, see Kevin Conley Ruffner, "You Are Never Going to Be Able to Run an Intelligence Unit: SSU Confronts the Black Market in Berlin," *Journal of Intelligence History* 2, no. 2 (Winter 2002); and Ruffner, "The Black Market in Postwar Berlin: Colonel Miller and an Army Scandal," *Prologue: Quarterly of the National Archives and Records Administration* (Fall 2002), http://www.archives.gov/publications/prologue/2002/fall/berlin-black-market-1.html.

economic chasms between American occupiers and most Berliners.[68] But it also helps to explain the rationale of rationing: privilege or the lack thereof depended on much more than elaborations of relative wealth.

In theory, distribution of food and other goods on the basis of ration cards aimed to distribute scarce resources justly and guarantee adequate food supply for people to undertake the necessary work of reconstruction, but, both as policy and practice, that was not the case. The presumption of the absolute scarcity of goods necessary for Germans' postwar survival found a counter in individual practice, which showed anything – even the most luxurious or extravagant item – could be obtained in the city, for a price. Obviously, occupation forces had conspicuous access to food, fuel, and luxury items (most notably cigarettes), but they were not alone. According to official regulations, some goods, like (real) coffee, were restricted (*beschlagnahmte Waren*). They could only be sold with a permit and at a certain maximum price, but no ration coupon was needed because these goods were not regularly distributed. Other goods were part of regular rationed distribution (*bezugsbeschränkte Waren*) and could only be obtained in exchange for the appropriate ration card (*Bezugskarte/Bezugsschein*).[69] In practice, however, the interaction of differentiated consumption practices, efforts to obtain supplemental foodstuffs, and the unequal distribution of resources and means conspired to subvert this system and produced a much broader supply structure of which open, legal rationing was simply one part.

All Berliners fell into one of five ration categories (Table 1), for which they received individual ration cards. They registered each month and received a nontransferable card onto which they wrote their names and addresses (Figure 4). The basic food ration covered bread, potatoes, cereals (*Nährmittel*), meat, fat, sugar, ersatz coffee, and salt and was issued in

---

[68] The account of workers at the Tegel Airfield is found in a Report from Abt. K to Police President Markgraf, dated October 23, 1948, LAB, STA Rep. 9, Nr. 50, Bl. 357. The report on the Magistrat worker is found in a Report from Abt. K to Police President Markgraf, dated October 7, 1948 (LAB, STA Rep. 9, Nr. 50, Bl. 282). The employee in question received 50 percent of his salary in west marks. Exchanged at a rate of 1:4, this contributed significantly to his 750 east mark total. For more on the operation of two currencies in Berlin following the 1948 currency reform, see chapters five and six.

[69] Karl Kromer, *Schwarzmarkt, Tausch- und Schleichhandel: in Frage und Antwort mit 500 praktischen Beispielen*. Recht für jeden 1 (Schloß Blecked an der Elbe: Otto Meißners Verlag, 1947), 20. A ration certificate (*Bezugsschein*) was used to authorize a one-time purchase of a particular item, e.g., a pair of shoes. A ration card (*Bezugskarte*) covered regular supply of foodstuffs or tobacco and comprised individual coupons as described elsewhere in this chapter.

TABLE 1. *Ration Card Groupings in Berlin as of July 1, 1946*

Ration Card	Recipient	Number
I	Heavy worker	70,937
II	Worker	859,132
III	White-collar worker (*Angestellte*)	671,841
IVa	Child, age 0–6	
IVb	Child, age 7–9	}552,337
IVc	Child, age 10–14	
V	Other	941,965

Sources: Nachlaß Otto Grotewohl, SAPMO, NY 4090/369, Bl. 1 and Andreas Dinter, *Berlin in Trümmern*, 76.

FIGURE 4. A sample "normal consumer" ration card (Card III), February 1948. The card seems to guarantee the holder specific amounts of fats, bread, sugar, and other foodstuffs but spells out some of the many ways that these promises might never be realized. The fine print warns that this card is not transferable and will not be replaced if lost. In an even more explicit reminder for Berliners that calories on paper do not equal calories in practice, the meat/fish coupons bear the designation F/A – meat or an alternative good (*Fleisch/Austauschwaren*). *Source:* U.S. National Archives.

exchange for coupons that Berliners collected at the ration office (*Kartenstelle*) where they were registered. The main ration card was divided into separate sections, which could be cut apart: a grocery card, a meat/fish card, and a bread card, each, in turn, divided into individual coupons that delineated both the amount (in grams) to be drawn and the ten-day ration period (*Dekade*) for which it was valid.[70] At times, when desirable goods were available, many people tried to convince the local shopkeepers to supply their next ration early. Allied and municipal authorities worked to prevent such advance purchases but were not always successful.[71] Supplemental cards or coupons covered special distributions – several months' worth of cellaring potatoes, holiday distributions of real coffee or champagne, or whatever good happened to make an appearance in slight excess (Figure 5). Each time a consumer purchased a rationed food item the retailer was obligated to collect the equivalent coupons and paste them into a sheet to mark the legal sale of the goods the shop had received; all transactions involving a rationed good – for example, from farmer to wholesaler to retailer to consumer – required official authorization and the appropriate exchange of documentation.[72] The system presumed authorities' ability to access all steps in the supply process, subjecting them to rationalizing control in the name both of justice and productivity.

Official food rations, especially at the levels of the lowest ration cards, could not provide adequate levels of nourishment. Even after ration increases in November 1948, the normal consumer (Card III) was still officially slated to receive significantly less than 2,000 calories a day.[73] Until occupation authorities eliminated it in March 1947, Card V subjected nearly a million Berliners to *official* rations of less than 1,500 calories per day. Although its most recognizable holders were former Nazis and housewives, Berliners almost universally recognized the unworkability of a ration that they denounced as the "hunger card."[74] The limits of these low ration levels tell only part of the story, and a ration card, regardless

---

[70] Copy of memo from the Office of Military Government Berlin Sector (OMGBS), Public Works Branch on the use of east marks for vital needs, dated June 26, 1948 (includes list of basic ration items), LAB, Rep. 280, Film Nr. 29, Sta.-Ort. Nr. 6278. Sample ration cards are held in almost all archival collections. For example, in the OMGUS Berlin Sector, Economic Branch, Records of the Central Food Office (1945–9), NA, RG 260, 390/48/18/2, box 458.

[71] See the notice from the Bezirksamt-Neukölln, Ernährungsamt, dated July 1, 1948, LAB, Rep. 280 (LAZ-Sammlung), Film Nr. 52, Sta.-Ort Nr. 11215. See also, Hilde Thurnwald, *Gegenwartsprobleme Berliner Familien: Eine soziologische Untersuchung von 498 Familien* (Berlin: Weidmannsche Verlagsbuchhandlung, 1948), 54.

[72] Kromer, *Schwarzmarkt*, 17.

[73] Deutsches Institut für Wirtschaftsforschung, ed., *Berlins Wirtschaft in der Blockade* (Berlin and Munich: Duncker and Humblot, 1949), 24.

[74] Berlin-Kreuzberg ration figures (March 1946) in Dinter, *Berlin in Trümmern*, 77. Berlin-Steglitz reported the average distribution to a Card V holder during the last week of February 1946 to be 1,088 calories per day (p. 78).

FIGURE 5. Two women pass in the entryway of a Schöneberg (American sector) grocery. Armed with a full shopping bag, the well-outfitted, even stylish appearance of the woman leaving the store (note the stockings, handbag, and pocket handkerchief) suggests a normalization of Berliners' consumer practices. But the chalkboards in front of the shop announcing the current ration period (III. Dekade) and the ration coupons necessary to register for vegetables underscore that rationing remained a normal facet of Berliners' everyday life. *Source:* Landesarchiv Berlin.

of the level, was no guarantee that the holder would actually receive the ration in question. In early November 1946, a memo from the Food and Agriculture Branch of the American Military Government in Berlin reported that only 342 tons of a promised 1,500 tons of late vegetables had been delivered from the American zone to the American sector in Berlin.[75] As this example suggests, foodstuffs were often not available or at best replaced by lower-grade goods. Thus one might receive sugar in place of oil or groats in place of oatmeal – in caloric terms perhaps equivalent, but for anyone hoping to put together balanced meals, hardly an adequate replacement.

Even when the official ration was available, poor quality foodstuffs – margarine or sausage with a high water content, for example – meant

[75] Memo dated November 6, 1946, OMGUS, AG Decimal File 422–30, NA RG 260, 1945–9, box 100.

that the authorized distribution amount (in grams) often contained less than the allotted number of calories.[76] At other times, people faced delays of several weeks before they could obtain that month's rations, although Berliners were not permitted to supplement their purchases to supply the next ration period if stocks were high. Additionally, rationed foodstuffs still needed to be purchased, and although municipal authorities imposed strict price regulations, paying for one's limited rations was not always an easy task.[77] Thirty days' ration on Card V cost Berliners less than 10 RMs,[78] but a contemporary newspaper report described the financial pressures that one worker and his family faced as they strived to obtain adequate supplies. The article's assessment that the family was running a significant deficit each month should be viewed with some caution, but it does provide some sense of the daily costs a family faced in the latter part of 1947. For rationed foodstuffs alone (on the basis of ration cards I, III, IVa, and IVb), this family had to pay a total of 83.90 RM per month. Rationed vegetables and potatoes cost 13 RM and vegetables procured from the union (Association of Free German Trade Unions [*Freier Deutscher Gewerkschaftsbund* or FDGB]) or from surplus produce (*freie Spitzen*) cost an additional 13 RM. The worker's income, including a supplement for his children, was 231.80 RM/month. The article calculated his expenses to be 265.90 RM/month, but this included outlays for newspapers, movies, and other nonessentials.[79] Calculating financial outlays can tell only part of the story. No matter what people spent, ration card allocations and food purchases did not necessarily translate into adequate nutrition.

From the very beginning of the occupation period, the Berlin population showed ongoing signs of hunger. The deputy chair of the Soviet Union's Council of People's Commissars described the women and children he saw in Berlin in May 1945: "Their appearance speaks of hunger and deprivation. They gather like flies at our field kitchens and ask for bread."[80] American reports on (U.S. sector) Berliners' nutritional state reached similar conclusions, even long after the war had ended. A restricted March 1946 Nutrition Summary comparing data gathered

[76] Dinter, *Berlin in Trümmern*, 79.
[77] Scholze, "Zur Ernährungssituation," 544–5.
[78] Boelcke, *Der Schwarzmarkt*, 38.
[79] "Wie lebt der Berliner Arbeiter? Der Inhalt einer Lohntüte und sein realer Wert: Trotz voller Arbeitsleitsleistung monatliches Defizit," *Tribüne* (October 7, 1947) in LAB, STA Rep. 113, Nr. 111. See also the collected reports at the end of Thurnwald, *Gegenwartsprobleme*.
[80] Quoted in Dinter, *Berlin in Trümmern*, 72.

in September and December 1945 and March 1946 described gradual improvement in the level of rations and a decline in the rate of nutritional deficiency symptoms measured and asserted that, when compared to similar figures from other urban areas, body weights and levels of signs indicative of nutritional deficiency diseases had dropped "to levels comparable to those of the U.S. Zone."[81] By October 1947, the chief of the Public Health Branch dismissed these "slight gains." His report began with the grim assessment "that the nutritional status of the German civilian population, in the U.S. sector of Berlin, continues to be unsatisfactory and is deteriorating."[82] The report continued, asserting that this gradual deterioration was most marked among those sixty years and older, moderate in children older than nine and in adults forty to fifty-nine years of age. The least amount of deterioration was measured among adults twenty to twenty-nine years of age, in spite of the high caloric demands placed on persons entering their peak period of economic productivity. But even these privileged workers were, according to American estimates, receiving around 80 percent of their officially rationed calories. In fact, according to these estimates from October 1947, the only segments of the Berlin population actually to receive its full ration were children between two and nine years of age (Table 2).

In response to the question, "How are you making out with food?" posed by American public opinion surveyors in May 1946, no Berliners (in the U.S. and British sectors) responded "well," 21 percent indicated that they "make out," while 79 percent replied "not well, badly" (Table 3). By November, 2 percent responded that they were eating "well," but the number of those replying "not well, badly" also increased to 81 percent. While responses to the question, "Do you get enough food to enable you to do your work well?" were not quite as bleak, only 20 percent of those surveyed in November 1946 replied that they could do their work "well" (Table 4). By June 1947, however, this figure had dropped to 13 percent. In response to both these questions (in April, May, and November 1946,

---

[81] OMGUS Nutrition Summary Report (March 1946), OMGUS AG Decimal File 422–430, NA, RG 260 1945–49, box 100, pp. 4, 10. While the comparison with the U.S. zone is useful, some care must be used when addressing the data presented in this report. The assessment of nutritional deficiency based on observable symptoms was only occasionally supported by lab data. Even the collection of weight measurements took place in a way that allowed a wide range of inaccuracies to enter into the figures. The German officials gathering the data stopped persons on the street and weighed them, fully dressed, during all seasons of the year. See also Dinter, *Berlin in Trümmern*, 92–3.

[82] Report on the Nutritional Status of Berlin Population (October 17, 1947), Admin Services Div., Op Branch, For. (Occ) Area Rpts. 1945–54, Germany (U.S. zone), NA, RG 407, 270/69/23, box 1000.

TABLE 2. *Nutritional Status of Berlin Population, October 1947*

Category of Consumer	Calories			
	Recommended	Official Ration in Berlin	Estimated* Consumption First 7 Months 1947	Remarks on Berlin Ration
1. Children				
0–1 year	1,000	1,786	1,020	
2–6 years	1,500	1,653	1,833	
7–14 years	2,400	See below		
(6–9 years)	See above	1,619	1,728	Includes ¼ liter of milk
(9–14 years)	See above	1,559	1,544	No milk included
15–19 years	2,700	See below		
(14–20 if in school)	See above	1,608	1,287	No milk included. Berlin University students (under Soviet zone control) receive special rations. Caloric content believed to be circa 2,000.
(14–20 other)	See above	According to work performed	1,737	
2. Pregnant and Nursing Women	2,700	2,265	1,737	From 5th month of pregnancy only and includes ½ liter milk
3. Normal Consumer	2,000	1,608	1,287	1,608 since March 1947 only; previously 1,500
4. Workers				
Moderately Heavy	2,700	1,999	1,631	
Heavy	3,200	2,498	2,036	
Very Heavy	3,700	2,498	2,036	

* As determined by a survey of significant samplings of 886 children, 268 pregnant and nursing women, and 3,856 adults.
Source: NA, RG 407, 270/69/23, Box 1000.

TABLE 3. *Responses to the Question: "How are you making out with food?"*

	February 1946		March 1946		May 1946		November 1946		June 1947	
	American Zone	Berlin	American Zone	Berlin	American Zone	Berlin	American Zone	Berlin	American Zone	Berlin
Well	12%	—	7%	—	12%	0%	11%	2%	16%	3%
Make Out	33	—	40	—	24	21	38	17	28	15
Not Well, Badly	45	—	53	—	67	79	51	81	56	82

Source: National Archives, RG 84, 350/57/18/02, Box 261.
Note: The Berlin figures include respondents from the British and American sectors. There were no Berlin surveys in February and March 1946.

TABLE 4. *Responses to the Question: "Do you get enough food to enable you to do your work well?"*

	March 1946		April 1946		May 1946		November 1946		June 1947	
	American Zone	Berlin	American Zone	Berlin	American Zone	Berlin	American Zone	Berlin	American Zone	Berlin
Well	38%	—	27%	18%	28%	9%	46%	20%	29%	13%
Make Out	61	—	72	82	71	88	53	78	69	86
Not Well, Badly	1	—	1	-	1	3	1	2	2	1

Source: National Archives, RG 84, 350/57/18/02, Box 261.
Note: The Berlin figures include respondents from the British and American sectors. There was no Berlin survey in March 1946.

and June 1947), Germans in the American zone expressed a significantly higher level of satisfaction with their food supply situation.

"Satisfaction" with the food situation was, of course, not just a question of amounts or calories. Even in the midst of scarcity, Berliners sought to maintain, at least on occasion, a certain qualitative experience of food – occasional white bread, better cuts of meat, or real coffee. Not only did these practices facilitate efforts to retain some sense of respectability, they also provided a means to connect to traditions and habits that had predated the war. A cartoon from the *Sie* weekly in January 1947 effectively sums up this desire for something more satisfying than mere survival. It portrays a mother cooking over an improvised stove whose pipe goes up into the wall and putting a dish on the table for her son, who responds, "Mother, do we always have to eat calories. Couldn't we occasionally eat a nice piece of cake?"[83]

Berliners reprised similar strategies of demonstrative consumption practiced during the economic crises of the late 1920s and early 1930s.[84] *Sie*'s regular column, "Literary-Culinary" combines brief literary food references with innovative ways to translate extant ingredients into a desirable dish, for example a kind of artificial honey from cooked pumpkin or carrot marmalade (improved if one can "stretch" these recipes with a bit of real fruit). Of course, these suggestions and even the column title recreate the "paper" calories with which Berliners bitterly derided newspaper or ration card promises of available foodstuffs that never actually materialized.[85] Even in the midst of desperate scarcity, *how* people consumed (and particularly how they ate) mattered for how they made sense of their place in postwar society. Faced with the reality of hunger and its implications for their health and ability to work, Berliners also confronted the fact that – out of choice and necessity – different segments of the population enjoyed various levels of available foodstuffs. The presumed equality of the ration system vanished in the face of variations in wealth, connections, and employment status (a fact borne out by variations in weight between working-class and more well-to-do districts of the city). Berliners' decisions about how to pursue the material resources they needed to survive were never just a mechanical respose to the inadequate supplies making

---

[83] "Moellendorff's Zeichenbrett'l," *Sie* (January 26, 1947), 12.

[84] Alf Lüdtke, "Hunger in der Großen Depression: Hungererfahrungen und Hungerpolitik am Ende der weimarer Republik," *Archiv für Sozialgeschichte* 27 (1987).

[85] The examples of carrot marmalade and pumpkin honey appear in "Literarisch-Kulinarisches," *Sie* (September 29, 1946), 11.

their way to them through the official ration system. They also reflected a finely tuned understanding of the evolving cultural significance of these survival strategies.[86]

Surviving in an Economy of "Connections"

Berliners developed various strategies to supplement their "official" supplies, calculating the costs and benefits of these various undertakings as they sought to circumvent limiting regulations and obligations. The regulations governing economic life in postwar Berlin were numerous, and the boundaries between personal initiative, corruption, and illegality remained fluid, not least in people's own assessments of their actions. In the calculus of postwar survival, the black market retrospectively serves as a mythic site, combining seedy criminality and the nascent power of a postwar market economy in the midst of rationings' strict controls.[87] But like most myths, it generally remains casually undefined, something almost too obvious for careful delineation. In practice, the black market occupied a blurred conceptual space that integrated legal definitions, particular physical locations, and shifting moral evaluations. Even in the presumably concrete legal realm, the black market's convoluted iterations defied easy categorization. A 1947 primer sought to make sense of that confusion for a German public that, the book's forward presumed, had at least passing practical experience with the subject.[88] Ranging far beyond hurried exchanges on urban street corners, the economic crimes loosely described as black market encompassed a broad range of public and semipublic acts that ranged from the exchange of "extras" as a necessary precondition for selling a good or service (*Schleichhandel*) to large-scale trade in illicit goods (*Großschieberei*). The nuances of these various definitions depended on the relationship between the distinct types of controlled goods and the ways in which postwar authorities presumed to assert control over their use and distribution (Table 5). But these

---

[86] Dinter, *Berlin in Trümmern*, 85.

[87] On the black market as training ground for the West German economic miracle, see Niethammer, preface to "*Hinterher merkt man, daß es richtig war, daß es schiefgegangen ist,*" 10; more generally, see Kromer, *Schwarzmarkt*.

[88] Jörg Roesler, "The Black Market in Post-war Berlin and the Methods Used to Counteract It," *German History* 7, no. 1 (April 1989), 96. On the critical significance of scarcity for life in postwar Germany, see Manfred J. Enssle, "Five Theses on German Everyday Life after World War II," *Central European History* 26, no. 1 (1993), 1–19.

TABLE 5. *Types of Black Market Behavior*

Crime	Definition	Examples
Underhand Trade (*Schleichhandel*)	Demand for "extras" as a prerequisite for conducting business or carrying out a trade.	A dentist demands a pound of butter before he is willing to make a plate for a patient; a grocer demands 10 cigarettes to distribute farina (*Grieß*) instead of barley-groats (*Gerstengrütze*) on a cereals ration.
Barter/Trade in Kind (*Kompensationsgeschäft*)/Gray Market	Exchange of controlled goods outside of the monetary economy; often takes place in semipublic, e.g., using newspaper advertisements.	A company seeks lathes and offers furniture from its own production in exchange; a cabinet maker offers woodwork in exchange for a 5 h.p. motor (if he offers it in exchange for food, he is guilty of black market trade).
Black Market Trade (*Schwarzhandel*)	Illicit trade in rationed goods or the means to access those goods (ration cards or coupons) in exchange for money.	An individual offers sausage for sale at inflated prices without demanding the requisite meat coupon; a restaurant owner procures ration coupons for customers to permit them to purchase a meal from the menu.
Racketeering/ (*Groß-*)*Schieberei*	*Schwarzhandel* with the intent to enrich oneself; "professional" black marketeering; large-scale black market trade; acts that endanger vital supplies or the functioning of the economy (*Wirtschaftsverbrechen*).	Illicit use/sale of two or more full ration cards

Source: Karl Kromer, *Schwarzmarkt, Tausch- und Schleichhandel: in Frage und Antwort mit 500 praktischen Beispielen,* Recht für jeden 1 (Schloß Bleckede an der Elbe: Otto Meißners Verlag, 1947), 10–12, 24, 30, and 164.

mechanisms did not exist entirely separate from or independent of the *official* postwar economy.

Presumably, the ration card served as each individual's ticket for survival, and municipal officials warned Berliners not to lose them. A 1947 poster urged them to watch out for thieves and pickpockets, because even stolen ration cards would not be replaced.[89] The booming market in ration cards and coupons suggested that such warnings were not successful, and, of course, these documents did not only enter into circulation without their holders' knowledge. Variations in individual demand encouraged willing participation in the ration cards market. Families could trade or sell cards for unwanted or less affordable items in the hopes of gaining more desired items such as larger quantities of lower cost food or extra tobacco.[90] Because nonsmokers also received a tobacco ration, they automatically had a supplemental resource that could be deployed without any real sacrifice on their part. Tobacco proved particularly valuable in urban residents' trade with rural residents, where cigarettes were even more difficult to obtain.[91]

Of course, even though rations were allocated on an individual basis, decisions about their use occurred in concert with others, most often family members. Thus, a housewife receiving a Card V ration would very likely share some of that with her hungry children, reducing even further the meager amount on which she had to live. In such situations, it is not hard to comprehend the decision that some women made to remain in bed as a way to conserve energy.[92] A decision to grant the head of household or the person with the most strenuous work a greater share of the household rations reflected a multifaceted calculation both regarding their daily nutritional needs and an assessment of what those choices about what and how to eat meant, particularly within the tension-filled dynamics of postwar familial power structures.[93] The ways in which Berliners endeavored to fulfill these needs and desires also expressed more than mere material calculation. They had to decide what kinds of strategies were personally acceptable: foraging and trade in kind but not black market purchases; theft from coal trucks or barges but not from grocery stores; enough to "survive" or what was necessary to turn a profit. To assert that everyone

---

[89] "Berliner! Achtet auf Eure Lebensmittelkarten," OMGUS, Berlin Sector, Records of the Economic Branch, Records Related to Rationing 1945–1949, NA, RG 260, 390/48/18/3–6, box 467. Of course, like almost every other postwar supply policy, decisions on replacing ration cards did not function in these absolute terms.

[90] Thurnwald, *Gegenwartsprobleme*, 59. See also Andreas Friedrich, *Battleground Berlin*, 176.

[91] Bourke-White, *"Dear Fatherland, Rest Quietly,"* 157–8. The fact that rations could be redeployed in this kind of trade suggests that some Germans' retrospective claims never to have traded on the black market – because they had "nothing" – should be regarded with skepticism.

[92] Andreas Friedrich, *Battleground Berlin*, 74 and Thurnwald, *Gegenwartsprobleme*, 35–7.

[93] Alf Lüdtke, "Hunger in der Großen Depression," 150–1.

participated in the black market perpetrates a myth of plausible deniability surrounding this vital fringe economy and denies the individual choices that informed Berliners' made in an effort to cope with the scarcity they faced.

By reasserting Berliners' real agency, it is also clear how they participated in shaping the various places within which they negotiated their economic and material survival, including those that remained technically illegal. Those persons who owned small garden plots in or on the outskirts of Berlin supplemented their food supplies with the fruit or vegetables that they could grow there. According to one survey of Berlin households in 1947, 26.5 percent of those surveyed were maintaining some sort of a garden plot (Figure 6). But this practice demanded much effort, not least to defend the fruits of one's labor come harvest time.[94] Friends or relatives who lived in the country could at times help out those living in the city, but this option was only available to a limited number of persons.

For workers with regular jobs it was even more difficult to make the necessary trips in the limited time available outside of working hours. Absenteeism plagued all Berlin companies as workers took time off to bargain on the black markets in Berlin or travel into the surrounding countryside to try to trade, buy, or steal additional foodstuffs. The calculation to skip work to pursue food and other supplies elsewhere reflected the reality that the monetary wages one earned (unless in amounts sufficient to purchase all one needed on the black market) could not compare to the benefits gained in occasional time spent foraging or bartering in the surrounding area.[95] Even the Magistrat's Education Department included foraging (*hamstern*) as a category in a list of reasons for school absenteeism.[96] Such official acknowledgment hinted at the measure of

---

[94] Scholze, "Zur Ernährungssituation," 556. Even during the Weimar Republic, such garden plots helped persons make it through economic hard times. See Erich Schmidt, *Meine Jugend in Groß-Berlin: Triumph und Elend der Arbeiterbewegung 1918–1933* (Bremen: Donat Verlag, 1988), 26. Estimates from the Ruhr industrial era suggest that a small garden plot (*Kleingarten*) produced a supplemental supply of about 100 calories per day per person. Boelcke, *Der Schwarzmarkt*, 71.

[95] Jeffrey Kopstein, *The Politics of Economic Decline in East Germany, 1945–1989* (Chapel Hill and London: University of North Carolina Press, 1997), 21 and Roesler, "The Black Market in Post-war Berlin," 92–107.

[96] Hauptamt Statistik: Erhebung über die sozialen Verhaeltnisse der Berliner Schulkinder, 1947/48, LAB, STA Rep. 120, Nr. 3303. The term *hamstern*, used to describe city dwellers traveling out into the countryside in pursuit of food existed at least from World War I. See, e.g., "Aus Gross Berlin: Das Ende der Hamsterfahrten," *Vorwärts*, March 31, 1917 as cited in Davis, *Home Fires Burning*, 291 n. 43. During the Nazi era, Josef Goebbels in particular sought to promote a negative interpretation of the term. See Boelcke, *Der Schwarzmarkt*, 154.

FIGURE 6. Berlin women cultivate vegetable gardens on apartment floors that wartime bombing exposed to the open air (ca. 1946). A testimony to Berliners' ingenuity and initiative, this unique manifestation of widespread efforts to secure supplemental food sources also demonstrates the demystification of the Berlin ruinscape and Berliners' acceptance of fragmented buildings as a normal part of their postwar everyday life. *Source:* Landesarchiv Berlin.

FIGURE 7. Crammed into the compartments and clinging to any available space on the car, a crowd of "hamsterers" prepares to depart a Potsdam station, just southwest of Berlin. Grinning for the camera, they help to create this iconic image of foragers heading into the surrounding countryside to search for food and fuel. But reducing "hamstering" to a staged snapshot of smiling passengers makes it all too easy to overlook the exertions it demanded: multiday trips, exhausting train travel, and even the risk that goods might be seized by the occasional police raid on "black marketeers." *Source:* Landesarchiv Berlin.

legitimacy that accrued to this sort of survival strategy, but foragers remained the subject of police controls and goods seizures, although the authorities remained ambivalent about how and where to draw the line between legitimate and illegitimate practices (Figure 7).

On some level, Berlin politicians were quite aware of the dire straits facing many in the city and often sought to deploy this "reality" in their rhetorical attacks on their opponents. During the spring 1947 political crisis that led to the dismissal of the first mayor elected after the war (see Chapter 3), city officials on both sides of the issue regularly condemned their opponents for inhibiting actions necessary to deal with the significant material crisis confronting the city. In his report to the city assembly on May 22, 1947, the head of the city's Economic Department, Gustav Klingelhöfer (Social Democratic Party of Germany [*Sozialdemokratische*

Partei Deutschlands or SPD]), noted that problems in the supply of Berlin with potatoes and vegetables were especially serious. He explained that the city had been denied access to the harvest in twelve city-owned farms in the surrounding Soviet zone and therefore was forced to import vegetables from as far away as Thuringia, and these longer transport distances heightened the likelihood of losses along the way. He also referred to the variations in deliveries to the various occupation sectors with the resulting inequalities in foodstuffs supplied to the population.[97] The delegates' discussion of this report raised the point several times that almost all Berliners were forced on occasion to turn to the black market to stave off hunger.

One week later, another member of the economic committee presented a report before the full city assembly on the nature of black marketeering in Berlin. According to the criminal police, 5 to 7 percent of all rationed foodstuffs and 10 to 12 percent of rationed textiles wound up on the black market. Economic experts indicated that black market prices thirty times above officially set prices had led one in two merchants to trade their wares on the black market. According to the report, most of the foodstuffs dealt on the black market came from the Soviet zone of occupation and from the approximately 250 daily break-ins into grocery stores in Berlin. More than a source for illicit trade, losses from local shops also had an immediate short-term impact on their ability to fill the rations of those consumers registered there.[98] At least two murders or serious crimes took place daily in direct connection with black market activities in the city. In general, the report argued that the battle against the black market by means of criminal prosecution had thus far proven itself wholly inadequate, and the committee called on the city assembly to battle the black market more effectively by means of stricter administrative measures and the preparation of new laws.[99] Among the Berlin population, however, the black market was losing some of its criminal stigma. According to one sociologist's investigations in 1946–7, the gradual disappearance of barterable possessions as well as the increasingly difficult material situation brought about by the hard winter of 1946–7 led to a

---

[97] Stenographisches Bericht der 30. Sitzung der Stadtverordnetenversammluung (StVV), May 22, 1947. See also the chronology in *Berlin: Behauptung von Freiheit und Selbstverwaltung 1946–48*, 232.

[98] Kromer, *Schwarzmarkt*, 22.

[99] Report by Assemblyman Josef Orlopp (SED), Stenographisches Bericht der 31. Sitzung der Stadtverordnetenversammlung, May 29, 1947, 52ff. See also the comments in *Berlin: Behauptung von Freiheit und Selbstverwaltung 1946–1948*, 239.

gradual shift from barter with friends and family to greater and more open reliance on black market trade.[100]

But to describe the gradual shift in popular perceptions of the black market in this way implies that it was merely a mechanical response to hunger. That explanation is inadequate. It suggests a threshold of desperation that, once reached, triggered a distinct response (black marketeering), a forced turn to darker survival strategies. But the decision to participate in the black market was never a zero sum game. Postwar Berlin was not divided into two worlds, an upright, moral, legitimate world of rations and public authority and an underground, illicit world of shady deals, crime, and depravity. In the postwar environment, the black market was an interstitial space, a place of ambiguity and messiness, of movement and constant change in which individual Berliners' participation also changed regularly. In reexamining the black market, the point is not just to assert the power of the market (the black market as a kind of training ground for the capitalists of the West German economic miracle) but rather to reiterate Berliners' daily struggles to survive as manifestations of their everyday power to shape their world in spite of occupiers', municipal authorities', and party political leaders' various claims to power (Figure 8).

Although the city's black market was constantly evolving, Berliners always knew where to go to find it. The physical locations were, of course, familiar and readily accessible: for example, the areas around Berlin's numerous train stations, the streets near DP camps in the American sector, and several of the most renowned squares in the city center – the Platz der Republik in front of the destroyed Reichstag building, the Pariser Platz in the shadow of the Brandenburg Gate, and most iconically, the Potsdamer Platz, Europe's erstwhile busiest square, now the intersection of the American, British, and Soviet sectors. This abbreviated listing of a few among the hundreds of regular black market locales in Berlin hints at the ironic reality of these black market sites, located at once in the heart of Berlin but also on its fringes. Train stations remained central points in Berlin districts and neighborhoods but also points of departure, the means to leave the city. The camps housing DPs explicitly provided a place for persons who didn't fit the normal boundaries of Berlin residence. Both the Platz der Republik and the Pariser Platz lay just on the border between the

---

[100] In her detailed analysis of interviews with Berlin families during the period February 1946 through the summer of 1947, Hilde Thurnwald explores the wide variety of methods used by families to cope with ongoing need, including barter and moonlighting (*Schwarzarbeit*) in addition to black market purchases. See Thurnwald, *Gegenwartsprobleme*, 76ff.

FIGURE 8. July 1948: a black market in the upper-middle-class district of Zehlendorf (American sector) blurs lines between participant and bystander. Armed with bags and backpacks – the standard accessory for postwar Berliners out in public – this well-dressed group of men and women watches attentively and seems to be considering an offer invisible to the camera. This collective act of evaluation suggests a common engagement with this fluid market space, but that surface similarity also hides potential differences. Berliner and displaced person (Zehlendorf was also the site of a DP camp), one-time Nazi Party member and "victim of fascism": each brought their own "baggage" to these deals. *Source:* Landesarchiv Berlin.

British and Soviet sectors, and, more than any other site, the Potsdamer Platz, with the sector boundary running through its center, embodied the black market's betwixt-and-between-ness, a place that one entered and exited for short stretches of time, under cover of symbolic darkness (the *black* market) but nonetheless in plain sight. A retrospective description of the street scene around the Brandenburg Gate, on the boundary between the Soviet and British sectors, suggests quite clearly the tension between the overt and veiled nature of black market activity:

The scene was not without humor, since the obvious trade was carried out secretly for all eyes to see. The crowd – Germans, allied soldiers of all four powers, scattered souls from all the lands of the world – pushed past each other, apparently without any goal or purpose, while a whispering half-hissing whir of voices lay in the air. From every direction goods were offered and sought, but what was curious, was that the goods were not offered to a particular interested person but offered up in general. Groups of two came together in the face of military patrols for one, two minutes, before the buyer and seller vanished into the pushing and shoving of the crowd[....] The whole scene was ghostly and not only because the suppliers of the goods were the same allied soldiers that made up the patrols. Even the bazaar-like atmosphere between the pillars of the Brandenburg Gate was unreal; the view passed freely over all the destroyed Tiergarten, past the Reichstag ruin to the silhouettes of the ruins of Moabit and Charlottenburg, a destroyed city, like one only knew from romantic drawings of the ruins of Rome.[101]

Even in this circumscribed location – admittedly a notorious black market venue – its operation was both constantly present and continually absent, part and yet not part of the postwar Berlin cityscape. In a description paralleling this contemporary assertion of conceptual distance, a recent novel imagined Berliners' postwar participation in another market square as a Central European version of a Cairo bazaar, a characterization that at once suggests it as out of place, foreign, and, in a way, no longer part of a modern, Western capital.[102]

[101] Dietrich Güstrow, *In jenen Jahren: Aufzeichnungen eines "befreiten" Deutschen* (Berlin: Severin und Siedler, 1983), 190–1. See also Isaac Deutscher, *Reportagen aus Nachkriegsdeutschland* (Hamburg: Junius Verlag, 1980), 116.

[102] Joseph Kanon, *The Good German: A Novel* (New York: Henry Holt and Co., 2001), 283. The "foreign-ness" of the black market was also evident in the widespread assertion that the principal participants in the black market were DPs. That this assertion, with its undertones of anti-Semitism resonated with Germans and Allied occupation officials, suggests the ways in which even regular participants in the various components of the black market nonetheless sought to shift its evils to outsiders. Even in some of the most thoughtful scholarly work, this assertion has continued to manifest itself fairly uncritically. See, e.g., Boelcke, *Der Schwarzmarkt*, 206. On the identification of black marketeering with DPs, see Laura J. Hilton, "The Black Market in Germany: Interaction

During a September 1948 raid on black marketeers in the Mitte district (Soviet sector), municipal police detained the Police Officer Peter Kaltenborn, holding him overnight in a cell at the district police station. In his statement to police, Kaltenborn asserted that he had been shopping with his wife, in the course of which they several times returned to their apartment. He reported that police asked once to see his identification, after which he went off to do some more shopping. As Kaltenborn described it, he then returned and was waiting outside his apartment building for his wife to come back down with a milk bottle when he was approached by three municipal police officers, who asked him to move on.

A number of police reports describe the scene rather differently. They suggest that Kaltenborn stood in front of his apartment without moving for approximately forty minutes, during which time groups of people briefly gathered around him before moving on. This struck the observing officer as suspicious, and he decided to watch him carefully, "in order to eventually charge him with black marketeering." The reports assert that he must have been engaged in black market activities or at least been warning people about police actions in the area. In particular, the reports emphasized that he was carrying a small packet of sweetener, a point that they argued implicated him in black market activities (Kaltenborn noted in his statement that he only possessed two grams of sweetener that he intended to take to an in-law). According to these police officers, Kaltenborn declared that the police actions in the black market area and the arrests connected with them "would dispense with any legal foundation." The police held him overnight and, in response to his complaint, assembled a detailed file on the incident. Although Kaltenborn's neighbors (called as witnesses for the investigation) generally supported police actions against the black market in their neighborhood and seemed hesitant to cross the police (unlike Kaltenborn, they readily complied with the police order to move along the street), they did acknowledge that he was a good father and often stood or played with his children outside their door.[103]

Whether Kaltenborn's particular actions that September day were by any definition illegal or part of the loosely defined black market is largely

among Jewish DPs, Germans, and Americans" (paper presented at the annual meeting of the American Historical Association, Washington, DC, January 11, 2004) and Königseder, *Flucht nach Berlin*, 181–90.

[103] Kommando d. Schutzpolizei, Abt. 2 – Personalabteilung; Referat 2 c – Disziplinarangelegenheiten, May 1948 to September 1948. LAB, STA Rep. 9, Nr. 277, Bl. 240–54.

immaterial. This compilation of reports reiterates how all parties describing the events in question deployed one particular identifying marker – black market – to construct a set of ambiguous meanings that, in practice, blurred the lines between participants and bystanders, between public and private spaces and served to define and/or justify the attempt to enact certain relationships of power within Berlin: the observing police officer decided to watch Kaltenborn carefully in order to pin a charge of black marketeering on him. The fact that Kaltenborn was a west sector police officer who lived in the Soviet sector (where these events took place) added another, more explicitly political layer of motivation to this confrontation, but what mattered much more was the way in which the events (in both the police reports and Kaltenborn's description) emphasized the simultaneity of the potential meanings these interpreters attached to the actions they sought to describe. Standing on the front step and playing with his children could very well have coexisted with Kaltenborn waiting for his wife to bring down a milk bottle or with the illicit trade in small packets of sweetener. The problem both for the police then and for the historian now lies in imagining the black market as a kind of Rubicon, the crossing of which marked an absolute moral and legal transformation. As much as the awareness of and encounters with the fluid boundaries of acceptable behavior conditioned German civilians' decisions about their survival strategies, personal connections (*Beziehungen*) ultimately mattered much more for individuals' efforts to locate themselves in postwar Germany's ambiguous moral terrain. Even more importantly, such connections provide a way to approach the implicitly political nature of their survival efforts. These efforts were relational – ultimately about contesting power – not just about individual "morality."[104]

Surviving in postwar Berlin demanded almost continuous exertion and, at times, people despaired. Between 1946 and 1948, the annual suicide numbers for Greater Berlin ranged from 1,884 to 1,627 to 1,249. These numbers were substantially lower than the 7,057 suicides in 1945, but nearly 70 percent of those came in April and May, in the midst or immediate aftermath of the brutal battle for the city.[105] For the most

---

[104] Paul Erker, "Revolution des Dorfes? Ländliche Bevölkerung zwischen Flüchtlingszustrom und landwirtschaftlichen Strukturwandel," in *Von Stalingrad zur Währungsreform: Zur Sozialgeschichge des Umbruchs in Deutschland*, Quellen und Darstellungen zur Zeitgeschichte 26 (Munich: R. Oldenbourg Verlag, 1988), 395.

[105] *Berlin in Zahlen 1947*, 158 and Hauptamt für Statistik und Wahlen, Berlin, ed., *Berlin in Zahlen 1950* (Berlin: Berliner Kulturbuch-Verlag, 1950), 38. The 1947 edition *Berlin in Zahlen* offers as a comparison the following prewar figures: 1929: 1,678 suicides;

part, Berliners searched out the means to make it from one day to the next. In this respect, they also maintained a relative degree of independence, seeking to secure their survival regardless of changes in occupation decree or personal employment status. From the very start, occupation forces assumed some obligation to prevent massive starvation (if for no other reason than to prevent mass unrest), a presumption that also rested on the belief that normal market mechanisms could not cope with the extreme conditions facing postwar Germany. Berliners understood this and denounced German and occupation authorities when they failed to deliver as promised. At the same time, they recognized the fundamental lie of a system that alleged to provide an *equitable* distribution of scarce resources. Because the ration system did not provide enough for people to ensure their material survival, they were forced to act on their own behalf. They seized the power available to them and used it – within the constraints of the broader political economy that ostensibly defined postwar Berlin – to discover those means necessary to survive. This effort demanded that they push the boundaries – both legally and morally – and it was these fringe activities rather than direct participation in explicitly political events that most defined everyday Berliners' dynamic power to shape their own social and political environment.

Drawing on interviews with nearly 500 Berlin families in 1946 and 1947, Hilde Thurnwald describes how many persons simply withdrew from any involvement in traditional political activity, both because they were forced to spend so much energy trying to survive and because they blamed the ongoing hardships on the politicians.[106] While she is right that Berliners often decided not to attend party meetings or political assemblies or work on behalf of political campaigns, people did not withdraw from political struggles. But to recognize that fact we must acknowledge the functional power of the alternative political spaces within which they fought their battles to survive. Everyday struggles in the midst of scarcity were fundamentally about battles for power, about coping with, managing, and contesting the inequalities inherent to rationing's flawed claims to just distribution. Whether in the ration office, the grocery store, or the black market, Berliners challenged, worked, and subverted the "system" that presumed to control their daily lives, changing in dramatic if unanticipated ways how these controls operated. While perhaps unsurprising,

---

1932 (at the height of the economic crisis): 2,262; and 1938: 2,108. Of course, the city's prewar population included more than 1 million *more* persons than after 1945.
[106] Thurnwald, *Gegenwartsprobleme*, 173.

these "unofficial relations of power" implicated these everyday activities in much larger questions, most noticeably those tied to issues of who controlled Berlin.[107]

Everyday Berliners found themselves in an ironically powerful position that would dramatically shape their world for years to come. They lived in a *temporary* situation of scarcity, a product of the violence of World War II (although those who wound up in East Germany would endure some degree of scarcity for its entire existence).[108] While temporary, this scarcity was also real. Berliners did die of hunger, and many more died of ailments that stemmed at least in part from severe malnutrition. But deciphering the implications of these "facts" for political outcomes in and around Berlin demands that they do more than just provoke a response *to* people's experience of scarcity. It was not just that hungry people would become anarchists or turn to communism but also that even high politics *depended on* the outcomes of the street-level battles for survival taking place, for the most part, beneath public notice.

The Hebbel Theater in Berlin's American sector presented Brecht's *Threepenny Opera* as its first postwar play. After the opening performance on August 13, 1945, an American control officer bemoaned the sustained applause that greeted the end of the second act, calling for a "weakening" of the refrain so as to restrain the public response.[109] In this song a prostitute and the leader of a gang of criminals offer a broader social context for the actions that have earned them public and even legal condemnation. However, their biting words, "*erst kommt das Fressen, dann kommt die Moral*" (perhaps best translated as "feeding first, morals after") represent much more than a justification for their individual (mis)deeds. They do not seek merely to explain but rather to accuse, to decry the hypocrisy of those who denounce the "immoral" actions of the poor yet participate in a much larger crime that condemns the poor to their poverty. Using John Gay's 1728 *The Beggar's Opera* as its critical lens, Brecht's work, which first premiered in Berlin in 1928, directed its gaze at the conditions of exploitation and inequality that characterized the emerging crisis of the Weimar Republic. Brecht's play did not aim to inspire empathy with his eighteenth-century characters but rather to provoke the audience

---

[107] This term comes from Davis, *Home Fires Burning*, 5.

[108] See Mark Landsman, *Dictatorship and Demand: The Politics of Consumerism in East Germany* (Cambridge, MA and London: Harvard University Press, 2005).

[109] Jürgen Engert, ed., *Die wirren Jahre: Deutschland 1945–1948*, (Berlin: Argon Verlag, 1996), 74.

to political action.[110] But the experience of scarcity that informed the language of this political critique also described the battle for power in the midst of a similar postwar reality. In 1949, four years after the play returned to the Berlin stage, Brecht offered a new final chorus to the song, in which he argued even more pointedly:

> Don't follow the small injustice; soon
> It will freeze up on its own, for it is cold:
> Think about the darkness and the great cold
> In this valley that echoes with lamentation
>
> Take to the field against the great robbers
> Fell them altogether and fell them soon
> They stir up the darkness and the cold
> They cause this valley to echo with lamentation[111]

This concluding chorus articulates both a critique that would have found a sympathetic hearing on many street corners in Berlin during the summer and fall of 1946 and a political language that would prove strikingly familiar to Berliners who sought to make sense of the power struggles in which they now found themselves immersed. As Berlin came to assume an increasingly prominent place in the high political calculations of postwar international relations, Berliners' power within the city continued to grow, even if its most potent exercise occurred in venues that remained an open secret, at once unacknowledged and misunderstood.[112]

---

[110] Bertolt Brecht, "The Modern Theater is the Epic Theater," *Brecht on Theater: The Development of an Aesthetic*, John Willett, ed. and trans. (New York: Hill and Wang, 1964), 33–42 and Walter Benjamin, "What Is Epic Theater?" *Illuminations: Essays and Reflections*, Hannah Arendt, ed. and Harry Zohn, trans. (New York: Schocken Book, 1969), 147–54.

[111] Bertolt Brecht, *Dreigroschenbuch*, 129. See also the comments by Siegfried Unseld, 482–3.

[112] Bergerson, *Ordinary Germans*, 267. He follows Eve Kosofsky Sedgwick, *The Epistemology of the Closet* (Berkeley: University of California Press, 1990).

2

October 1946: Rolling Back Soviet Power

More than 90 percent of Berlin's eligible voters turned out on October 20, 1946, for the city's first free elections since the Nazi seizure of power thirteen years earlier. Before they could cast their ballots, Berliners first had to present their ration cards to be stamped, an explicit reminder that their political future remained intimately tied to the material restraints that postwar life imposed on them, and as they left their polling places that Sunday, most of them faced long and roundabout paths back to windowless homes and inadequate meals. While many of the streets through which they passed had new names – gone were Hermann Göring Strasse and Adolf Hitler Platz – it was much harder to put a fresh face on other physical legacies of Nazi rule and wartime destruction. Only six months earlier, an SPD flyer suggested that thousands of party members had stayed away from a referendum on unification with the Communists because they were "worried about material survival."[1] The writers of that flyer presumed that material crisis got in the way of political activity. On this day, however, its supporters turned out in force, and the SPD emerged the undisputed victor in the contest, winning 48.7 percent of the vote for the city assembly. The Christian Democratic Union (*Christlich-Demokratische Union* or CDU) finished second with 22.2 percent of the vote, followed by the SED with 19.8 percent, and the Liberal Democratic Party (*Liberal-Demokratische Partei* or LDP) with 9.3 percent.[2] In an

---

[1] "Aufruf an die Sozialdemokraten Berlins!" April 15, 1946, LAB, Rep. 280, Sta.-Ort. Nr. 596.

[2] Schlegelmilch, *Hauptstadt in Zonendeutschland*, 363. Other general information on the voting process drawn from Delbert Clark, "Berlin's first election tomorrow expected to go against Russians," *New York Times* (October 19, 1946), 7.

article headlined "Soviet Grip Broken By Berlin Election," the *New York Times* asserted that the vote had "demolished the Russian power in the Berlin administration."[3]

The *Times* was only half right. Although the SED continued to hold numerous positions in the Berlin bureaucracy, its failure to win even 20 percent of the vote, finishing well behind the SPD even in the Soviet sector of the city, did mark it as the biggest electoral loser.[4] Soviet sector and district commanders could still exercise their veto in the Kommandatura and issue direct orders to German officials in their sector, but this resounding defeat also signified the failure of the Soviets' first play for Berlin. Most significantly the electoral result drove home to Soviet and SED leaders a shocking truth that had emerged gradually over the course of the campaign: the political windfall that they hoped to reap from the material and structural advantages that accompanied the Soviet conquest of Berlin had slipped through their fingers. Their fundamental weakness in Berlin was not a product of failed electoral campaigning, and Berliners' power was never limited to the willingness to cast their votes in support of Western-leaning political parties. Although the revived democratic process undoubtedly empowered those Berliners who streamed to the ballot boxes throughout the city, their explicit political gesture cannot be extracted from the power that they had already wrested to themselves in the ruined streets and squares of the former German capital. The vote did not transform the power relationships in the city but rather manifested the deep social sources for the underlying sense of insecurity that both the SED and the Soviet Union presumed to have overcome after 1945.[5]

---

[3] "Soviet Grip Broken by Berlin Election," *New York Times* (October 22, 1946), 1 and 9. See also the accounts in *Der Kurier*, an independent-minded newspaper in Berlin's French sector: "Der Wahlsieg der Berliner SPD: Die Christlich-Demokratische Union an zweiter Stelle: Fast 90 Prozent Wahlbeteiligung," *Der Kurier* (October 21, 1946), 1 and "Die Meinung der Welt zu Berlin," *Der Kurier* (October 22, 1946), 1.

[4] The best general account of the political battles in postwar Berlin is Schlegelmilch, *Hauptstadt im Zonendeutschland*. For more focused examinations of SED and to some extent Soviet engagement in this battle, see Harold Hurwitz, *Die Stalinisierung der SED: Zum Verlust von Freiräumen und sozialdemokratischer Identität in den Vorständen, 1946–1949*, Schriften des Zentralinstituts für sozialwissenschaftliche Forschung der Freien Universität Berlin, Band 79 (Opladen: Westdeutscher Verlag, 1997) and Stefan Creuzberger, *Die sowjetische Besatzungsmacht und das politische System der SBZ*. Schriften des Hannah-Arendt-Instituts für Totalitarismusforschung 3 (Weimar, Cologne, and Vienna: Böhlau Verlag, 1996), esp. pp. 84–110 and 167–76.

[5] For an insightful discussion of the significant role that Soviet insecurity played in the early Cold War that also offers a helpful context for my argument here, see Mastny, *The Cold War and Soviet Insecurity*.

A Presumption of Soviet Control

On election day, the Berlin women's weekly, *Sie*, declared it Berliners' (and especially Berlin women's) duty to vote. While the lead editorial explained this obligation as a way to prevent the rise of another dictatorial party and to defend their newfound liberties, the photograph that filled half the front page tells a somewhat more complicated story. With bare feet extending below his pants, a young boy stands on fallen stones in front of a wall plastered with campaign posters from the four parties competing in Berlin's election. The caption asserts,

We are voting for our children. This boy's father fell in battle. He was forced by the will of a single party to march to his ruin. Today, with her vote in the election, his mother has the chance to make sure her boy grows up in a free democratic state. It is only with our vote that we can stop [...] a party with a lust for power from ever forcing people to march again and [thus] allow our children to experience a happier future.[6]

Carefully composed for editorial effect, this photograph and its caption juxtapose a party-political contest with a shoeless boy in the midst of a mound of rubble in an attempt to tie the overcoming of the material crisis in the foreground to the political choice in the background. The presumption seems to be that a child's future happiness (perhaps most obviously shoes in light of impending winter) depended on a choice of votes. A different reading of the image might discount this causal link and see instead processes whose interactions depended on more than mere proximity. The boy, standing nonchalantly on a stone with his hand in his jacket pocket, might be perfectly comfortable running about the rubble. He might even possess shoes that have been taken off for effect or are being saved for the onset of cold weather. But the paper's implied argument that thinking about being barefoot in Berlin in October 1946 might help convince Berliners to join in fighting the potential rise of a new dictatorship at least suggests a need to unravel the threads that bound material crisis to presumptive political and administrative control.

In May 1945 the Red Army alone captured the German capital and moved rapidly to exploit the economic and political advantages that this privileged position gave it. Even as Soviet soldiers continued their nightly rampages of rape and murder in the weeks that followed the German surrender, the new occupier began – wartime agreements to divide occupation responsibilities among the victorious allied powers notwithstanding – to

---

[6] "Unsere Pflicht," *Sie* (October 20, 1946), 1.

enact Stalin's oft-quoted assertion that World War II would end with the victors imposing their system as far as their armies reached.[7] This effort meant the widespread dismantling of industrial sites, especially in those parts of the city that would eventually fall under the Western Allies' authority, but it also included the first steps to reestablish administrative structures in the former Reich. Following closely on the heels of the advancing Soviet troops, three groups of Moscow-trained German Communists began almost immediately to cultivate political contacts and establish the beginnings of local administrations across the territory that would fall under Soviet administrative control. Anton Ackermann led a group to Saxony and Gustav Sobottka led a group to the eastern state of Mecklenburg-Vorpommern. While these groups' efforts ultimately mattered on a regional level, Berlin held much greater national and international significance.

Responsibility for the German capital fell to a group of ten Communist Party (KPD) functionaries headed by Walter Ulbricht, the former Reichstag member and onetime head of Berlin's Communist Party. The returning exiles sought out surviving Communists and other acceptable "antifascists" to fill slots in the city's twenty district governments, making sure that Communists held the critical personnel posts.[8] Their early focus on personnel organization at the cost of reconstruction or economic recovery efforts suggested that ideologically driven sociopolitical change could come later. Wolfgang Leonhard, the youngest member of the Ulbricht Group, had grown up in the Soviet Union and expressed surprise at this focus. He described Ulbricht's brusque indifference to a surviving party member's offer to provide a list of the most active Communists in the district: "Well, I'm only interested in the administration."[9] Even after the KPD became the first postwar party to earn official approval after the Soviet occupation authorized political parties to form on June 10, 1945, Ulbricht sought to rein in overt expressions of party ritual and rhetoric: "red front" greetings, hammer and sickle flags, and especially

---

[7] Milovan Djilas, *Conversations with Stalin*, Michael B. Petrovich, trans. (New York: Harcourt, Brace and World, 1962), 114.

[8] Gerhard Keiderling, *"Gruppe Ulbricht" in Berlin April bis Juni 1945: von der Vorbereitungen in Sommer 1944 bis zur Wiedergründung der KPD in Juni 1945: eine Dokumentation* (Berlin: Verlag Arno Spitz, 1993), 101–2. See also Wolfgang Leonhard's classic *Die Revolution entläßt ihre Kinder* (Frankfurt am Main: Ullstein, 1962). The English-language edition, *Child of the Revolution*, C. M. Woodhouse, trans. (Chicago: Henry Regnery, 1958) offers a slightly abbreviated version of the German original and is not, therefore, entirely satisfactory.

[9] Leonhard, *Die Revolution entläßt ihre Kinder*, 288.

the independent antifascist committees that had come into existence in the last days of the war all had no place in the returning émigrés' focus on establishing control of the postwar bureaucracy.

The Soviet command issued an order creating the first postwar Magistrat on May 17, 1945. Looking ahead to the eventual arrival of the Western powers in the city, Ulbricht and his expanding organization struggled to find a suitable candidate to nominate to head this administration. He hoped to locate a candidate who was "anti-fascist, bourgeois, and recognizable (*namhaft*)" and eventually stumbled on Dr. Arthur Werner, the sixty-eight-year-old head of a technical training institute in southwestern Berlin, who accepted the post after a late-night interview with the Soviet city commander. Although Werner claimed to have been part of a minor anti-Nazi group (in 1942 the Nazis had closed the institute he headed due to its political unreliability), later investigations by the West Berlin parliament (*Abgeordnetenhaus*) also found that he had joined the Nazi Party in 1932.[10] For Ulbricht, however, he was the perfect candidate. In a 1972 interview, he explained:

> [Werner] was the typical bourgeois politician with refined manners [....] He didn't have much to do with the Nazis, so he counted as an independent (*parteiloser*) anti-fascist. But he did have demands that we had to meet. We kept that quiet. [Karl] Maron cursed the fact that he had to do all the work. Werner had no clue about political problems and decision-making.[11]

Even at the time, few doubted the extent to which this overmatched old man served as little more than a façade to conceal Communist dominance of that first administration.[12] But if Ulbricht's retrospective admission of Communist willingness to meet quiescent politicians' material demands, his courtship of a more formidable political figure helps to clarify his understanding of how the material *quid* might translate into a political *quo*.

In a letter to a Soviet intelligence officer, Ulbricht described a meeting with the former Reich Food Minister and Center Party politician Andreas Hermes. Among those persons on Ulbricht's initial mayoral short list, Hermes proved more politically independent, eventually helping to found the CDU in the Soviet zone. But in his letter to the Soviet officer, Ulbricht described his efforts to recruit Hermes for the Berlin administration, noting "[o]ur task must be to influence Dr. Hermes systematically and patiently, to not shy away from any means to insure his friendship for

---

[10] Keiderling, *"Gruppe Ulbricht,"* 62–3.
[11] Ibid., 64.
[12] A table in the weekly *Sie* made this SED dominance graphically public: "Wer regiert uns in Berlin," *Sie* (September 22, 1946), 3.

the Soviet Union." What this entailed came out even more clearly in the letter's final paragraphs. After discussing Mrs. Hermes's complaint that she had not yet received any bread ration – to which Ulbricht offered to make sure to address the food supply for Hermes and his family – Ulbricht ended his missive with the suggestion that the SED look for a house in the Soviet zone that could be made available for Hermes.[13] From the very outset, the Soviet-supported German Communist leadership perceived a clear link between material crisis and the potential to influence the new administration. The personal and the political remained intimately connected, the individual choices made by hand-selected officials defining the contours of the municipal bureaucracy that would take the first steps to address the ongoing crisis situation in Berlin. Even as it worked to craft an administration throughout the city, the Communist leadership extracted its leading supporters from some portion of the material crisis, setting up many of them in Biesdorf, a comfortable Lichtenberg neighborhood of single family homes, appropriating houses with gardens of fruit trees and supplying these officials with supplemental food and heating material. While these privileges served primarily to support the admittedly strenuous work of trying to administer a city in ruins, they conveyed to other Berliners at least a whiff of dependence, of the potential for obsequious submission to an evolving party line.

Among the papers of Wilhelm Pieck, the longtime Communist leader who became cochair of the SED in April 1946, an undated listing of presumably sympathetic leading officials in Berlin's twenty districts gives striking testimony of the extent to which, in their pursuit of a solid hold on all administrative levels in the city, Communist assessments of political reliability trumped even party designation. For each district the document listed several officials, most followed by an "S" or "K," presumably indicating their SPD or KPD backgrounds, others described as independent (*parteilos*) or without any designation. The assessments that accompany many listings – good, reliable, wavering, capable administrator, questionable – locate each individual's political value somewhere beyond mere ideological commitment.[14] The odd blending of these categorizations – suggestive of the need to adhere to a party line (without wavering) and the

[13] 6. Mai 1945: Walter Ulbricht an Generaloberst I. A. Serow, in Keiderling, "*Gruppe Ulbricht,*" 298–301.

[14] Arbeitsmaterialien d. W. P.: Taetigkeit des Magistrats v. Gross-Berlin, Aug. 1945 – Nov. 1952, SAPMO, NY 4036/742, Bl. 86ff. It's possible that this document may stem from January 1947 in which case the "S" and "K" designations likely refer to previous party membership, the lack of any designation perhaps indicating new SED members, and the *parteilos* designation indicating those outside the SED.

need to run a department effectively – foreshadowed the SED's shift to a mass party of cadres, a process of Stalinization that accelerated over 1947 and 1948 in response to the challenges that manifested most obviously in Berlin.[15]

After the Soviets approved four new German political parties, the members of the first postwar Magistrat sorted themselves into nine Communists, two Social Democrats, two members of the CDU, and five independents.[16] Dr. Werner, the mayor, was an independent, but Karl Maron and other Communist officials positioned themselves to control most of the vital administrative and organizational decisions. When he looked back at that first administration in his speech to the newly elected city assembly on November 26, 1946, the outgoing mayor emphasized its transitional role, suggesting that by securing Berliners' "bare survival" (*nackte Existenz*) and beginning a process to normalize life in the city, this first Magistrat had laid the foundation for the city's future right to self-determination.[17] By claiming both to have secured Berliners' material survival and pursued the return of normal life in the city, Werner simply restated the intentions mapped out in both the Soviet and Magistrat decrees announcing the formation of the new municipal administration in May 1945.[18] From the outset, the Soviets and the SED leadership saw establishing the basis for material success as intimately connected to crafting the necessary foundations for administrative control.

When the Kommandatura took up its work on July 11, 1945, the Western Allies confirmed all the decisions implemented by the Soviets in the two months that they alone occupied the city. Meeting in an unassuming former insurance building in the Dahlem district of southwestern Berlin (American sector), the four city commanders and the various specialized committees of the four-power Kommandatura met to shape policy and manage the occupation bureaucracy for the entire city. Because all decisions in the Kommandatura were required to be unanimous, the Western acceptance of the status quo meant that a Soviet veto could prevent any revision of the personnel and policy decisions that it had set in place.[19] Barring some sort of radical intervention by the Western powers, the

---

[15] Hurwitz, *Die Stalinisierung der SED*.

[16] Schlegelmilch, *Hauptstadt in Zonendeutschland*, 108.

[17] Stenographisches Bericht der 1. Sitzung der Stadtverordnetenversammlung, 26 November 1946, LAB, STA Rep. 100, Nr. 1, Bl. 6.

[18] Keiderling, "*Gruppe Ulbricht*," 358.

[19] For a detailed discussion of personnel politics in Berlin up to 1948, see Michael Faisst, Harold Hurwitz, and Klaus Sühl, "Die Berliner Sozialdemokratie und die Personalpolitik

structural dominance enjoyed by the Soviets and their German partners seemed to ensure them de facto control over the city administration. But the Communist leadership did not count on having to fall back on this structural advantage to secure power in the city, assuming that the Communists would enjoy broad popular support among a Berlin population looking to make a radical turn from failed Nazism. Well into the summer of 1945, Ulbricht and the leaders of the new KPD even rejected SPD proposals to combine the two parties. But by the fall, the KPD faced increasing organizational difficulties – declining popular attractiveness, membership stagnation, and de facto if not de jure restriction to the territory of the Soviet zone – that gradually pushed it to advocate union with the SPD in the fall of 1945.[20]

A December meeting between thirty representatives each from the KPD and SPD convinced Otto Grotewohl and other Social Democrats in the Berlin-based Central Committee to agree to a rapid union with the Communists.[21] But a significant portion of the SPD leadership in Berlin refused to go along with the decision for a union and proposed a referendum for party members in the city. In the western sectors, members of the SPD voted on March 31, 1946 as to whether to join the Communists in a new, unified, socialist party. Of the somewhat more than 33,000 SPD members in the west sectors, 72.9 percent voted in the referendum. By a vote of 19,529 to 2,938, they rejected immediate union with the KPD. Suggesting that earlier hopes for a unified socialized party were not yet dead, 14,660 (opposed by 5,559) voted in support of continued cooperation between the two parties. The Soviets did not permit the referendum to take place in their sector.[22] After some disputes about whether the Americans would permit the new party in their sector of Berlin, a compromise solution allowed the SED only in the Soviet zone and in Berlin. In the Soviet zone, the SPD vanished, incorporated into the new SED;

der Besatzungsmächte," *Internationale Wissenschaftliche Korrespondenz zur Geschicthe der deutschen Arbeiterbewegung* 16, no. 3 (September 1980), 313–46.

[20] Gerhard Keiderling, *Wir sind die Staatspartei: die KPD-Bezirksorganisation Groß-Berlin April 1945-April 1946* (Berlin: Verlag Arno Spitz, 1997), 571.

[21] Weber, *DDR: Grundriß der Geschichte 1945–1990*, 23; Erich Gniffke, *Jahre mit Ulrbicht*, reprint (Cologne: Verlag Wissenschaft und Politik, 1990), 119–22; and Andreas Malycha, *Die SED: Geschichte ihrer Stalinisierung 1946–1953* (Paderborn: Ferdinand Schöningh, 2000), 90–100.

[22] Hans Herzfeld, *Berlin in der Weltpolitik*, Veröffentlichungen der Historischen Kommission zu Berlin 38 (Berlin and New York: Walter de Gruyter, 1973), 85. Of course, the battles between former SPD and former KPD members continued within the SED as well. See esp. Hurwitz, *Die Stalinisierung der SED* and Gniffke, *Jahre mit Ulbricht*.

but in Berlin an independent and increasingly activist SPD continued to exist.[23]

In the months following its founding congress in April 1946, the SED looked forward to the fall elections in Berlin and the Soviet zone with high hopes. Soviet officials, as well, looked forward to the coming elections with great optimism. On June 18, 1946 a secret memo sent by Marshall Sokolovskii to the heads of the Soviet administrations in the five states and provinces in the Soviet zone indicated that the election would prove a success only if the SED won an absolute majority of the votes.[24] While the Soviets worried primarily about how to secure control of their zone, they remained interested in ongoing economic access to the western zones and saw a successful, secure Soviet zone as a basic prerequisite for those goals. The office of the Soviet High Command in Germany explained its hope that this anticipated electoral success would subsequently resonate in the western zones, providing the means to help maintain a Soviet presence in Germany. By contrast, "[a] failure for the SED will harm not only the 'state interests of the Soviet Union' but will also produce a significant weakening of the position of the USSR in Germany."[25]

Building on the administrative dominance they had established in 1945, the Soviets hoped to utilize these elections to entrench the position of their supporters in postwar Germany. Otto Grotewohl, the former SPD leader who became cochair of the new SED, spoke to the Executive Board of the SED Central Committee (*Parteivorstand*) in June 1946 and deployed a similar rhetoric of national appeal across zonal lines in his declaration of the need for a convincing SED victory that fall.[26] Part ritual reference to a wished for ideological project, part assertion of German political autonomy, Grotewohl's statement rested less on concrete evidence of the likely electoral outcome than on a belief that, following the destruction of Nazi Germany, this was how German politics ought to evolve. The Soviets and the SED leadership – including the former Social Democrat Grotewohl, who had left the SPD when it became clear that he would

[23] For a detailed examination of the founding of the SED, see Hurwitz, *Die Stalinisierung der SED*, 19ff. For a discussion of the Berlin SPD and its initial effort to combat incorporation into a unity party, see Hurwitz, *Die Anfänge des Widerstands*, pt. 2 *Zwischen Selbsttäuschung und Zivilcourage: Der Fusionskampf*, vol. 4 of *Demokratie und antikommunismus in Berlin nach 1945* (Cologne: Verlag Wissenschaft und Politik, 1990). For the record of the founding congress, see Vereinigungsparteitag der SPD und KPD, SAPMO, DY 30/IV 1/1/1.
[24] Creuzberger, *Die sowjetische Besatzungsmacht*, 49.
[25] Quoted in Creuzberger, *Die sowjetische Besatzungsmacht*, 52.
[26] Stenographisches Bericht über die 3. Sitzung des Parteivorstandes der SED, 18.-20. Juni 1946, SAPMO, DY 30/IV 2/1/4, Bl. 59.

be unable to supplant Kurt Schumacher as the party's national leader – wanted results, and although they continued to hold to their residual optimism, they also thought it only reasonable to deploy any and every material or institutional advantage that their administrative dominance offered, a process that served only to reinforce their rosy expectations.

Soviet occupation officials agreed to free elections in Berlin only if they came after a first round of elections in the Soviet zone.[27] These preliminary results would, they believed, demonstrate to Berliners that the SED now represented the wave of the future and encourage them, in turn, to support this almost inevitable outcome. In an effort to further ensure the desired results, the Soviets provided every advantage to the SED in their zone, granting it larger supplies of paper and gasoline as well as overt expressions of support, while simultaneously harassing and hindering the efforts of opposing parties. The Soviets harbored no illusions about the role they played in the electoral process in the Soviet zone. In a speech in Weimar on January 10, 1947, the Soviet Commander of Thuringia summed up Soviet involvement:

I remind you [...] how the preparations for these elections went. At every step we intervened in all details with the goal of securing an SED victory. We utilized all manner of economic measures, spread all sorts of rumors, gave various unfulfillable promises, only so as to secure the majority of votes for the SED. And the SED received a significant percentage of the votes in the county and state assembly elections[28] not due to the voters' sympathy [for the party], but rather for the promised hundredweight of potatoes (which, by the way, we have neither given out nor will give out). This "potato-democracy" should not blind us. And when one takes into account that we placed decided limitations on the other parties (LDP and CDU) [...] and, where necessary, did not hesitate even to arrest their leaders and dangerous personalities, then it is clear that the percentage of voters, who supported the SED, does not sufficiently reflect the actual sentiment (*Stimmung*) of the Germans. Thus one can assert that a significant percentage of voters did not give their vote to the SED out of conviction, but rather on the basis of a series of measures taken by us, often with the desire to satisfy the occupation power [the Soviets] with whom the SED enjoys the closest relations [...].[29]

---

[27] Creuzberger, *Die sowjetische Besatzungsmacht*, 85.

[28] County assembly elections (*Kreistagswahlen*) were held in September. State assembly elections (*Landtagswahlen*) were held simultaneously with the elections in Berlin on October 20.

[29] Creuzberger, *Die sowjetische Besatzungsmacht*, 106–7. For a description of the Soviet harassment of the SPD in Berlin, see Hurwitz, *Die Stalinisierung der SED*, 152ff. See also Naimark, *The Russians in Germany*, 332ff. In spite of these efforts, the SED did not achieve nearly the successes they had hoped for. For reactions from SED leaders, see the discussions in the Parteivorstand following the elections, SAPMO, DY 30/IV 2/1/10 and DY 30/IV 2/1/12.

Although the SED received more votes than any other party in the zone, the surprising strength of the two opposition parties in the Soviet zone, the CDU and LDP, meant that, in most instances, it failed to achieve the desired absolute majority.[30]

The fact that the voters' support for the SED remained much weaker than this strangely optimistic yet cynical retrospective analysis suggested, pointed to the limits of a "potato democracy." The connections between presumptive material controls and electoral results proved much more tenuous than either the Soviet or the SED were prepared to acknowledge, even after they began to perceive the likely outcome of the election in Berlin. Beginning in late summer 1945, the Communist leadership spoke increasingly of a "special situation" in the city as opposed to the "normal case" of the Soviet zone,[31] but the fall 1946 election results highlighted how the common experiences of material scarcity shaped a political location that transcended occupation boundaries but also constrained occupation power. Berlin never remained isolated from the Soviet zone, but ultimately, this "special" case highlighted the extent to which even "normal" postwar conditions precluded effective top-down management or unambiguous high political control.

Campaigning for Berlin – The SED in the 1946 Municipal Election

In Berlin the basic political arrangement differed substantially from that in the Soviet zone. The city's four occupation sectors, although not cut off from each other, functioned somewhat independently. Even taking into account Communist preeminence in city and district offices, citywide municipal elections could not be controlled wholly by any one occupier. Each occupier sponsored its own German-language newspaper and to varying degrees could constrain political assemblies in its sector. Yet, in most respects, Berlin represented a site where, in 1946, free and direct competition could take place between the four, approved political parties: the two "socialist" parties, the SPD and SED, the broadly confessional CDU that included both conservative members of the middle class and former (Catholic) trade unionists, and the LDP, the one party firmly committed to maintaining a free market, capitalist economic system. Soviet officials accepted this essentially free and open contest for two principal reasons: First, the Soviets believed that an open electoral competition was the best way to gain the other occupiers' acceptance of the SED as

[30] Weber, *DDR*, 33 and Malycha, *Die SED*, 180–8.
[31] Keiderling, *Wir sind die Staatspartei*, 576.

a legitimate German political party; in so doing, they sought to ensure a broader reach for the one force that they saw as readily able to promote Soviet interests in Germany. Second, the Soviets clearly hoped and believed that the SED would win – an absolute majority in the Soviet sector and a relative majority in the western sectors. In addition to the subtle and not-so-subtle influence and coercion that they were able to exert within their sector, the Soviets saw traditionally working-class districts, such as Wedding and Neukölln, as likely to drive support for the SED in the western sectors.[32]

Soviet leaders seemed implicitly to believe that Berliners felt the weight of Soviet military might that could potentially come crashing down on a city located 100 miles into the eastern zone. The head of the Berlin section of the Soviet propaganda division noted that the rest of the Berlin population could be influenced by Berlin's dependence on the Soviet zone: "For the Berliners [. . .] know only too well that they are materially dependent on the decisions of the SMA [Soviet Military Administration] and the Central Soviet Military Command."[33] Thus, in spite of the Western presence in Berlin, much of the Soviet Military Administration (*Sovetskaia Voennaia Administratsia v Germanii* or SVAG) leadership (especially in the propaganda division) felt that if push came to shove in the electoral contest, the material advantages of Soviet dominance in and around the city would ultimately sway the Berliners' votes. At the same time, these leaders continued to believe that an overt deployment of these structural advantages would not be necessary. Even after the Berlin SPD's rejection of the unity party, they could not accept as possible the fact that the city as a whole could reject the party. This belief rested on two profound misconceptions: First, while Berlin did remain dependent on economic and supply contacts with the surrounding Soviet zone, these contacts functioned largely independent of any "official" Soviet authorization or control. Second, Berliners' negative experiences with Soviet power and especially of SED links to that power proved a much more powerful political motivation.

Like the Soviets, the SED also focused on the material crisis and made the party's supposed ability to resolve it a principal element of its appeal to the Berlin voters, but its understanding of potential popular support

---

[32] Creuzberger, *Die sowjetische Besatzungsmacht*, 86 and 180. After the election, SED analyses of the election in terms of the votes the Communists had received during the Weimar Republic helps to explain the source for this belief. Leading up to the election, even the *New York Times* speculated about the "sentiment of 'Red Berlin'." Clark, "Berlin's First Election Tomorrow," 7.

[33] Cited in Creuzberger, *Die sowjetische Besatzungsmacht*, 86.

derived more from an optimistic sense of its future political role than any sense of an ability to coerce the Berliners into supporting its candidates with threats of future (Soviet) restrictions. For SED leaders, the Berlin campaign demanded an extension of the principles and strategies of the campaigns in the Soviet zone, this time deployed in a more competitive setting. Thus the SED emphasized its role in beginning to set up a "new order" in Germany and reestablishing normalcy in everyday life. A July poster excerpted an SED proclamation about the upcoming district elections in the Soviet zone, emphasizing the party's leadership in overcoming three great dangers accompanying the reconstruction effort: the lack of housing, hunger, and unemployment.[34] In Berlin, the party now trumpeted its ability to reinvigorate and transform the Berlin economy. A large poster dated June 15, 1946 proclaimed: "[The] SED is the motor of reconstruction in our capital."[35] Given its dominant position in the city administration, the SED did indeed see itself in a position to direct Berlin's reconstruction and renewal efforts. In spite of the relatively poor living conditions in the capital, the SED still believed that its position of administrative authority, especially its ability to distribute largesse and material benefits to the population, would positively impact its electoral campaign.

This initial optimism gradually gave way to a sense of foreboding, at least among party members in Berlin. On September 18, the joint chairman of the Berlin SED, Hermann Matern, reported to the Parteivorstand that the SED's emphasis on its material accomplishments was not eliciting the anticipated positive reaction. As one example, he described how spectators in Berlin movie houses greeted SED promotional films and their heady claims with derisive whistles. For Matern this vigorous and very public rejection of SED claims resulted from people's desire to claim for themselves some role in the reconstruction efforts: "And what about us? Have we done nothing?" The Berlin party leader summed up the danger he saw in the SED's celebratory approach:

If, in our agitation, we act as though the party has done everything, the natural reaction is: we are responsible for everything. But, to be responsible for everything today means that we are from the outset in an altogether awkward position. We must portray things as if we are not at all responsible, that we are not at all pleased with the current situation, that of all the dissatisfied people, we are the most dissatisfied and have the greatest right to be dissatisfied.[36]

[34] Poster, LAZ-Sammlung, Sta.-Ort 1371, LAB, Rep. 280.
[35] LAZ-Sammlung, Sta.-Ort 1368, LAB, Rep. 280.
[36] Stenographisches Bericht der 5. Parteivorstandssitzung d. ZK d. SED, 18–19 September 1946, SAPMO, DY 30/IV 2/1/8, Bl. 85f.

Matern's willingness to cynically abandon programmatic assertions in the hope of achieving greater electoral successes shines through in this comment, but he still saw the errors as primarily tactical. For him it remained a question of finding the appropriate way to address Berliners.

Matern was not alone in his critical assessment of the situation. In a presentation to party officials preparing for the Berlin election, Anton Ackermann voiced similar concerns. Ackermann, who had headed one of the three Communist party groups to enter Germany with the Red Army, was at that time still the ideological voice of the party. Most famously, he formulated the idea of a German path to socialism, a policy that the SED would reject in 1948 when the Soviet Union became the sole acceptable model for the rest of Europe following Tito's break with Stalin. In his speech at the Karl Marx Party Academy on the outskirts of Berlin, Ackermann worried that the party had failed to effectively link the "stomach question" to important political issues and that there was little indication of a real transformation of the political climate in Germany.[37] The expectation that such a political transformation would take place had driven Soviet, KPD, and later SED thinking since the end of the war.

These Communist leaders all anticipated that the destruction of Nazi Germany marked a turning point in the political fortunes of the German left. From their perspective, the material crisis was one further component that would drive Berliners to support the most "radical" departure from a failed past – in other words, SED political leadership. While the SED correctly recognized that material issues dominated people's daily lives, it misread the antagonistic context in which its electoral campaign was taking place and failed to understand the political and material continuities that still dominated life in Berlin. Although they never expressed their convictions in those terms, Soviet and SED leaders fell prey to an illusory belief that 1945 represented a "zero hour," a new beginning for German politics that would necessarily produce a different, more desirable outcome than that realized in the hotly contested battles during the Weimar Republic.

By late summer, some Soviet authorities began to recognize the lack of strong support for the SED. An independent report submitted to Soviet Central Committee member Mikhail A. Suslov on September 2 described the situation in bleak terms. A Lieutenant Colonel Konstantinovskii, who was not attached to the SVAG, discussed Berliners' generally indifferent

---

[37] Preparations for October 20th Elections in Abt. Organisation, Presse, and Schulung und Werbung, October 1946, SAPMO, DY 30/IV 2/1.01/19, Bl. 6.

attitude toward the SED election program as well as the party's lack of progress in winning the support of women and of working-class sections of the Berlin population. He noted that SED members lacked effective political engagement and a sound doctrinal training. His report reached the conclusion that the SED could anticipate a catastrophic defeat in the October election. Granted, Konstantinovskii argued that the situation could be remedied with a large-scale deployment of Moscow-trained party activists, but his unflinching assessment of the critical political situation faced by the SED in no way underestimated its problems.[38]

To a large degree, the SED campaign squandered the material advantages inherent in wholehearted Soviet support of its efforts or, perhaps more accurately, it suffered as a result. In June 1946, the SED in Neukölln called on its members to visually transform the district, giving it a May Day feel in its agitation on behalf of the party. The detailed directive called for new "banners, posters, flags, slogans, and insignias," for the decoration of train and subway stations, party offices and meeting rooms, and factories (inside and out). There was little letup in the SED's propaganda efforts in the lead-up to the Berlin election.[39] Given the extreme shortage of paper, the never-ending flood of SED posters, flyers, and brochures provoked widespread derision. Berliners of all political persuasions observed the SED's propensity to cover the Berlin cityscape with its election propaganda and more often than not simply reduced these efforts to the butt of biting wit.[40] A letter written by a party member in Prenzlauer Berg (Soviet sector) after the election noted: "With rage, the comrades scratched off the posters on Tuesday after the election. Passersby remarked spitefully, 'Well now, we didn't paste [posters] but still won!'"[41] A 1949 party education report argued even more pointedly that the excessive enthusiasm for posters and printed agitation produced popular misgivings and allowed other parties to compare the SED election

---

[38] In Creuzberger, *Die sowjetische Besatzungsmacht*, 90–1. For more on the Konstantinovskii report, see Naimark, *The Russians in Germany*, 327–8.

[39] Memo from SED Neukölln, Abt. Werbung u. Schulung regarding visual presentation of the SED, dated June 3, 1946, SAPMO DY 30/IV 2/5/5010. In an effort to expand party lists, the memo also called on members to appeal to like-minded persons in their apartment building, trade unionists, newspaper readers, and relatives (excluding former Nazi Party members).

[40] See Anton Ackermann's October 1946 comment about popular impressions that the SED was simply wasting paper, SAPMO, DY 30/IV 2/1.01/19, Bl. 20.

[41] Briefwechsel mit dem Landesvorstand Berlin, DY 30/IV 2/5/223, Bl. 24. See also DY 30/IV 2/5/223, Bl. 30.

FIGURE 9. In the run-up to the October 1946 election, a veritable sea of SED campaign posters covers shop walls in Berlin's Prenzlauer Berg district. The Cyrillic lettering on the street sign in the foreground indirectly makes visible the Soviet role in supplying their German supporters with such massive amounts of scarce paper and reminds passersby of the extent to which the Soviet presence has become an entrenched part of everyday life in Berlin. *Source:* Landesarchiv Berlin.

strategies to Nazi propaganda efforts (Figure 9).[42] In comparison to the near omnipresence of SED posters, the Soviet-sponsored press often had problems reaching the population. Regular complaints reached central SED leaders that on many mornings the party newspapers arrived too late to have any impact. By the time *Neues Deutschland* or other party papers made it to the newsstand, Berliners, even party members, had turned to the *Tagesspiegel* or other western sector papers for their daily news.[43]

Other SED attempts to drum up popular support went equally awry. Except for those of the top party leaders, speeches by party functionaries generally garnered tepid responses, and even the party stars did not always live up to expectations. The police in Neukölln (American sector)

[42] Instrukteurberichte, 1949–51, SAPMO, DY 30/IV 2/5/1194, Bl. 12–13.
[43] See Informationsdienst Nr. 23 from the Berliner Presse- u. Informationsdienst (IPD), LV d. SED Gross-Berlin, Abt. Presse u. Information, dated August 3, 1946, Nachlaß Otto Grotewohl, SAPMO, NY 4090/383.

reported that two speeches that featured Walter Ulbricht and Max Fechner respectively each garnered only about 800 attendees, far below the
3,000 and 1,500 expected.[44] The party's efforts to convince exhausted
workers, whose shoes were very likely falling to pieces, to make their way
through streets that were often unlighted and occasionally dangerous to
attend meeting after meeting or rallies at their factory, housing block,
or at a neighborhood "fair" taxed the political will of all but the most
committed persons.[45] Between September 1 and October 20, the SED
held 3,649 political assemblies, 2,500 alone in the working-class district
of Prenzlauer Berg. In comparison, the SPD held only 428 assemblies in
that same period; the other parties held even fewer gatherings. Although
the SPD's assemblies had a higher average attendance than those of the
SED (438 persons versus 131 persons), the fact that the SED held a large
number of courtyard meetings in apartment blocks makes it difficult to
use crowd size as a measure of enthusiasm. It is important to note that
the SED held more assemblies than any other party in the western sectors
as well as in the Soviet sector.[46]

At a session to plan strategy for the upcoming election, district party
leaders discussed the practical hurdles facing their efforts to organize political meetings, especially in residential housing blocks. One party official
from the working-class Prenzlauer Berg district (Soviet sector) noted that
it was impossible to set up assemblies before seven o'clock in the evening,
which meant that they didn't begin before half past seven. With darkness
coming by eight o'clock as well as the advent of fall's bad weather, people
had little inclination to linger in apartment courtyards to continue political discussions. In response, party sections began holding movie evenings,
distributing half-price tickets to residents in an effort to encourage attendance. Following the newsreel, an SED party member would speak to the

[44] Weekly activity report from the Polizei-Inspektion Neukölln, dated June 22, 1946, LAB,
STA Rep. 9, Nr. 86, Bl. 262.
[45] *Der Kurier* reported that the parties had held 675 assemblies in the weeks leading up to
the election. This figure did not include the "Hof-Versammlungen" of the SED. "Berlin
am Vorabend der Wahl," *Der Kurier* (October 19, 1946), 1. It is worth remembering that
many workers still had to walk great distances to get to and from their work. On the general problem of convincing hungry and exhausted persons to pursue political activities,
see the report in Thurnwald, *Gegenwartsprobleme*, 172–3. According to this account,
an additional factor contributing to this unwillingness to undertake political activity was
an underlying fear of future reprisals at the hands of some "political opponents."
[46] Full assembly figures by district in monthly activity report (October) from the Kommando
d. Schupo to the Police President, dated November 2, 1946, LAB, STA Rep. 9, Nr. 87,
Bl. 133f.

crowd. While this official proclaimed this approach a success, arguing that 130 such evenings had reached 45,000 persons in the district, it's not hard to believe that weary Berliners desperate for culture accepted a brief political harangue as an acceptable trade-off for cheap movie tickets.[47] One need only recall the derisive whistles that greeted some SED newsreels to recognize that attendance alone did not make film audiences passive receptors for a political message.

In a letter to Franz Dahlem, the longtime Communist and head of the SED's organization section, another SED member from Prenzlauer Berg drove home the extent to which the party's propaganda efforts did not necessarily convey the intended message. Although she noted a few exceptions, she generally described the party's great difficulty convincing people to purchase the party's printed materials. This lack of success also made it increasingly difficult to convince party members to take on vital functionary roles and the associated exertions: climbing stair after stair to knock on apartment doors to try to convince Berliners to buy the SED literature. Even those persons who did spend 20 pfennig for a pamphlet often did so, she argued, simply to get rid of the bothersome functionary, who was in any case more interested in selling the literature as a way to eliminate the district party's debt rather than out of any ideological conviction. Whether writing from personal experience or on the basis of accounts she had heard in the district, the letter writer provocatively suggested that a beleaguered housewife, when handed "Lecture-Disposition No. 11: The New Five-Year Plan in the USSR" would see this mysterious "disposition" as completely irrelevant and use the pamphlet to hold the sooty pot she'd just taken from the stove.[48]

It would be easy to read a gendered divide into this set of experiences, and even *Sie* noted ironically that although there were sixteen female voters in Berlin for every ten males, political assemblies nonetheless tended to be dominated by men. The caption beneath a photograph of a crowd listening to a campaign speaker reads: "A woman prefers to make judgments only on the basis of everyday experience (*Lebenspraxis*), whereas a man tests himself in the competition of discussion. Moreover, a woman is generally occupied with household affairs when [political] assemblies are

---

47 On the issue of declining attendance at party events, see the discussion at a conference at the Karl-Marx Party Academy on October 1–2, 1946, SAPMO DY 30/IV 2/1.01/19, Bl. 49.
48 Letter from a Genossin in Prenzlauer Berg to Franz Dahlem, October 29, 1946, SAPMO, DY 30/IV 2/5/223, Bl. 22–30.

held."[49] The writers for *Sie* celebrated the fact that women voters could, on their own, elect a two-thirds majority in Berlin's municipal assembly. But it also worried that these women would not take on their "duty to vote" (*Wahlpflicht*). In fact, nearly 1.4 million, or 92.4 percent, of Berlin's eligible women voted on October 20, and they played a decisive role, particularly in rejecting the SED.[50] But reducing women's ability to shape social and political conditions in Berlin to their votes alone fails adequately to consider the blurring of lines between these arenas or to recognize the extent to which the household remained a center of power in the city.

In the face of ongoing shortages that made a political tract more valuable as a potholder than as a source of information, the SED's ongoing efforts to address the material crisis and its continued failure to recognize how and why it failed effectively summed up the course of its electoral campaign in Berlin. Most Berliners found little appeal in ongoing reiterations of the material progress achieved or proposed by the SED. Some even saw the election as a futile exercise in light of the ongoing hardships people faced in their daily lives. A typesetter noted in August 1946:

Of what value are the finest [election] promises, if one is still going under. Black marketeers and business people are living the good life, but a worker can't even afford a glass of beer. Everyone is talking about sinking worker morale. Give people enough to eat, and they'll work. The cigarette dealer on the black market earns more in a quarter of an hour than I do in an entire week.[51]

This complaint proved difficult for many SED leaders to comprehend. In an effort to reach what were, to their eyes, explicitly political goals, they often made the mistake of measuring material achievement in terms of posters produced or assemblies held. Even reconstruction efforts or economic development meant more as an instrument of political success than as a means to address individual persons' material needs.

For a party that purported to focus on the material as the root of the political process, the SED proved rather ham-handed in its efforts to derive electoral benefit from its attempts to address the material crisis in the city. In January 1946 one Berlin woman, Agnes Papke, wrote to the mayor's office to complain about the material crisis and claimed for herself the identity of a "German woman and mother" while simultaneously

[49] "Frauen: 1.5 Millionen," *Sie* (October 13, 1946), 3.
[50] Hauptamt für Statistik von Groß-Berlin, *Berlin in Zahlen: 1947* (Berlin: Berliner Kulturbuch-Verlag, 1949), 424.
[51] Monatsbericht über Stimmen der Bevölkerung (August 1946) provided to Otto Winzer by the Presseamt, dated September 10, 1946, LAB, STA Rep. 120, Nr. 3245, Bl. 88.

reiterating that she had never been a Nazi Party member. In mid-October, one of the leading SED candidates, Elli Schmidt, published an open letter offering assessments that roughly paralleled Papke's explanatory framework. Addressing her missive to the "women and mothers of Berlin," Schmidt blamed the material crisis on the "Nazis and war criminals." Schmidt's letter proposed a solution that would seem to appeal to women like Papke, women who "labored out in the cold on the [city's] construction sites." Speaking for the SED, she celebrated the improvement in food supply that land reforms in the Soviet zone would permit, called for the elimination of the lowest ration level (Card V), and promised an additional hundredweight of potatoes per person in comparison to the previous winter. Similarly, she emphasized the need to address the coal supply and make preferential clothing supplies available for working women. Summing up, she guaranteed: "Thus the SED will help you women along with your children to live better."

In contrast, Agnes Papke appealed for a reduction of the ration period from ten to seven days and for lower penalties for bakeries that give out bread on the next ration card before that ration period has started.[52] Instead of calling for new, improved food supplies, Papke essentially argued for authorities to turn a blind eye to the ongoing, personal negotiations into which Berliners entered in an effort to meet their food needs. As much as she and other Berliners wanted more food and fuel, they remained most interested in officials crafting conditions in which they could pursue these supplies on their own. Essentially, even in appealing for a shift in official policy, Papke claimed for Berliners the ability to manage their own survival: they did not require that the supplies be delivered to them but rather needed only the space to pursue them on their own. The SED, however, saw a straightforward denunciation of the black market as an obvious means to appeal to Berliners' sense of outrage at those who profited from illegal trade, and the party integrated these claims into its campaign publications and posters (Figure 10).

In its plans for the 100 days before the election, the SED in Berlin's Weissensee district proposed a series of pamphlets to be issued each week. The district party leaders proposed to launch the campaign with a pamphlet elaborating SED demands for household fuel supplies, followed by a second pamphlet calling for a "struggle against the fruit and vegetable

---

[52] Open letter from the SED Spitzenkandidat, Elli Schmidt, 15.10.1946, LAB, Rep. 280, Nr. 1225. Letter from Agnes Papke to Dr. Werner, 30.1.1946, LAB, C Rep. 101, Nr. 115: Sekretariat des OB, Beschwerde- u. Beratungstelle: Beschwerden u. Eingaben d. Bevölkerung sozialer Natur, 4.2.1948 – 25.11.1948.

FIGURE 10. Large-format SED campaign posters trumpet the party's claims to legitimacy as a voice against militarism, corrupt privilege, and the black market. In an appeal to Berliners to "vote for list 2," the unintentional triptych created by the three most visible posters maps out the party's idealized path from the past to the future: a caricatured version of "war criminals and war profiteers" segues into an image of "corruption and black marketeering" that – in a present of scarcity – obscenely fills an illegally supplied table to overflowing. Finally, a hopeful scene of a transformed Germany imagines making "recreation centers out of lords' palaces." *Source:* Landesarchiv Berlin.

black marketeers."[53] Agnes Papke was much more ambivalent about the black market; her comments about purchasing rations in advance at least demonstrated a more nuanced understanding of the moral ambiguities of illegal market activity. In contrast to SED campaigns, she did not see the answer in strict criminal enforcement, suggesting instead that "punishment should be like salad, with more oil than vinegar."

While the contrast between this one woman's perspective and the SED's campaign slogans helps to explain the ineffectiveness of Soviet and SED supply initiatives in the run-up to the fall election, the fact that most high-ranking party officials faced no substantial material concerns further explains the party leadership's tendency to separate everyday scarcity from a functional evaluation of material need and achievement. The popular

[53] SED Kr. Weissensee: Program for assemblies and events leading up to the election, dated July 11, 1946, LAB, BPA IV L-2/5/202.

impression that Soviet material support permitted SED party leaders to live in relative luxury meant that the party came in for particular criticism. Even party members complained about the isolation of the party's high-level functionaries, noting that their wages were ten times the maximum salary of a simple party worker.[54] Although it did not seem to alter their behavior, even the highest-ranking party officials took some notice of the outrage that such inequalities produced. A report sent from the party's Berlin press and information service to SED cochair Otto Grotewohl argued that the SED looked out for its party functionaries but was content to let everyone else go hungry. One account from a district just to the south of Berlin complained that leading employees in the municipal offices and central administration continuously received special distributions, not only of foodstuffs and tobacco, but also of clothing and fuel. Even more viscerally, it described how some school officials publicly consumed rolls generously covered with oil-packed sardines, refusing to stop the practice even when outraged colleagues complained to the local mayor. The report, which Grotewohl or someone else in his office marked with an X in the margin, noted that such examples went on and on.[55] Postwar Germans repeatedly expressed desires for more and higher quality fats, because of all rationed goods they were most often in shortest supply. For the writer of this report, a piece of bread dripping with oil must have exerted an allure bordering on the obscene, and the sense of outrage evoked by disproportionate access to such sensual luxuries resonated broadly.

In his memoirs, a former member of the SED Executive Committee described the shock of SPD members (including himself) when they discovered in 1945 that the meals served by the kitchen in the KPD headquarters varied depending on one's party rank. The party secretaries received a multicourse meal with wine, the section heads received a somewhat more modest meal, and the normal party workers received only a bowl of stew (*Eintopf*).[56] In a scathing attack on the Berlin SED leadership's conspicuous consumption, a letter sent to the editor of the British sector newspaper, *Telegraf*, described the massive amounts of coal and wood delivered by trucks to the homes in Berlin-Biesdorf (Soviet sector) that had been appropriated for these SED leaders. The letter writers claimed that the heating materials that continued to arrive at the houses in late 1946 and even into

---

54 Kritische Bemerkungen über d. subjektiven Ursachen unseres Mißerfolges bei den Gemeindewahlen in Berlin, LAB, BPA, IV L-2/13/436, Bl. 96–7.

55 Informationsdienst Nr. 23 from the Berliner Presse- u. Informationsdienst (IPD), LV d. SED Gross-Berlin, Abt. Presse u. Information, dated August 3, 1946, SAPMO, NY 4090/383, Bl. 74.

56 Gniffke, *Jahre mit Ulbricht*, 59.

January 1947 surpassed the amounts the previous owners used to heat the homes before the war. Writing on behalf of residents whose homes had been appropriated by these municipal and trade union officials and explicitly hoping that the letter might be published to exert pressure on these officials to give up these houses, the letter writer sought to paint an extravagant picture of life among the SED elite. Accounts by former SED officials do little to undermine such assertions.[57] While the Soviets were not the only occupier to "award" their supporters and employees with additional foodstuffs and other goods (American CARE packages have undoubtedly enjoyed a much more lasting reputation), the perception of SED privilege produced a greater level of popular dissatisfaction and served explicitly to define the shortages and material difficulties that ordinary people faced every day.

A 1946 flyer carried a bitter poem that appeared in various versions throughout Berlin and the Soviet zone, the texts evoking well-known tunes in a subversive linkage of material crisis and political shortcoming. Thus, the German national anthem became:

Deutschland, Deutschland, ohne alles	Germany, Germany, lacking all,
ohne Butter, ohne Fett	Lacking butter, lacking fat
und das bißchen Marmelade	And the little bit of marmelade
frißt uns die Verwaltung weg.	Is devoured by the administration.
Hände falten, Köpfe senken,	Fold your hands, bow your heads,
immer an die Einheit denken.	Think of unity instead.

If the first verse reduced this nineteenth-century vision of expansive Germanic identity to an abbreviated list of shortages and an ironic suggestion of the limited appeal of Socialist unity, the poem's second stanza made a more provocative association, deploying the Nazis' "Horst Wessel Song" to denounce elite privilege:

Die Preise hoch,	The prices up,
die Läden dicht geschlossen,	The stores all closed and shuttered,
die Not marschiert mit ruhig festem Schritt.	The crisis marches on with quiet stride.
Es hungern nur die kleinen Volksgenossen,	Only little national comrades hunger,
die grossen hungern nur im Geiste mit.	the great ones just hunger on in spirit.

Not only does this text use the most famous Nazi anthem as the medium to convey its critical message, it claims for ordinary Germans suffering the privations of postwar hunger an explicitly Nazi identification of "national

---

[57] Letter forwarded (by Kurt Mattick) to Johannes Stumm with a copy to Otto Ostrowski, dated January 10, 1947, AdsD, Nachlaß Otto Ostrowski, box 41. Cf. Gniffke, *Jahre mit Ulbricht* and Leonhard, *Die Revolution entläßt ihre Kinder*.

comrade" (*Volksgenosse*). The third stanza then turns to a well-known German table prayer to direct its animosity most explicitly toward the SED leadership and its material privileges:

Komm, Wilhelm Pieck, sei unser Gast	Come Wilhelm Pieck, be our guest
und gib, was Du uns versprochen hast.	and give us what you promised.
Nicht nur Rüben, Kraut und Kohl,	Not only turnips, kraut, and cabbage,
sondern was Du ißt, und Herr	but what you eat, and Herr
Grotewohl.	Grotewohl.

The content of these material desires as well as the nostalgic recollection of the various pasts in which such desires had been normal comes out in the final verse:

Zu Kaisers Zeiten war's fein,	In the Kaiser's time it was fine,
da hatten wir unser Schwein.	then we had our pork.
Als wir den alten Hindenburg hatten,	When we had Hindenburg,
gabs ab und zu auch Braten.	we got a roast from time to time.
Bei Hitler und bei Göring,	With Hitler and with Göring,
hatten wir wenigstens noch 'nen Hering,	at least there was still herring,
aber bei der jetzigen Leitung	but under the current leadership
steht alles nur in der Zeitung.[58]	it's all only in the paper.

Supported by numerous police, occupation, and political party reports on the lack of any popular expectation of rapid improvement in the material scarcity that they continued to face, this final line suggests that the German population recognized the inherent emptiness of any claims to total solutions. While Soviet and SED leaders seemed to believe that their promises of a "potato democracy" would prove enough to convince Germans to support the party, they found that even the successful distribution of foodstuffs and other goods did not translate into the desired political and ideological result. Their efforts instead proved yet another example of their inability to control how ordinary Berliners made sense of their world and the powers at work in it.

On September 4, 1946, the SVAG issued an order – allegedly in response to SED appeals to improve the food supply and to counter speculation in foodstuffs – to permit the off-ration purchase of vegetables from farms that had already fulfilled their delivery quotas. In order to facilitate their access to these additional vegetables, major cities (including Berlin) were to be linked to specific agricultural areas, the connections

---

[58] SAPMO, NY 4090/641, Arbeitsmaterialien des O. G.: Verleumdungen rechter Fuehrer der SPD gegen die SED, 1946–8., Bl. 12. A similar set of texts appears in NY 4036/640: [on microfilm FBS 93/1118] Schaffung d. Einheit der Arbeiterklasse – Verleumdungen der rechten Fuehrer der SPD gegen die SED und leitende Funktionaere der SED, April 1946 – September 1952, Bl. 101.

managed by the central (zonal) administration for trade and supply and the FDGB. The FDGB was to receive 65 percent of all vegetables procured per this order, a measure clearly designed to heighten the appeal of the SED-dominated trade union organization.[59] A report from the Berlin food office described the massive scale of Soviet vegetable deliveries to the city, deliveries that both surpassed Soviet delivery obligations and far outstripped what the three Western powers managed to supply to the city. In September, more than 13 million kilograms of vegetables came to Berlin from the Soviet zone; a month later the Soviets provided more than 15 million kilograms. Together, the three Western powers delivered only 1.5 million kilograms in September and 3.6 million kilograms in October.[60] In conjunction with an August Kommandatura directive that consumer goods (*Verbrauchsgueter*) be distributed only in the sector paralleling the zone or occupier that provided them, these measures seemed likely to create a decisive impression that material supply for Berlin could only be realized in association with the Soviet zone.[61]

The German population interpreted these efforts quite differently. Even if the expanded supply of vegetables seemed less crass than marking coal briquettes with the slogan "Vote SED" or the distribution of 30 million cigarettes in the week before the election,[62] Germans in both Berlin and the Soviet zone perceived the supply improvements that emerged during fall 1946 as unsubtle efforts to sway the election. An August report from the Berlin SED's Presse and Information Service described current topics of conversation in Spandau (British sector): "When Germans speak about the food situation today, they naturally come to talk about the improvements in the Russian zone. Among the indifferent women, there is only one opinion: the Russian (*der Russe*) is improving rations only because elections are coming up, and [he] is trying to influence the population."[63] The

---

[59] Copy of an order from the Oberster Chef der SMA d. Oberbefehlshabers der Gruppe d. sowjetischen Besatzungstruppen in Dtld (Sokolovskii) to Presidents of the Provinces and the Dt. Verwaltung f. Handel u. Versorgung, dated September 4, 1946, LAB, STA Rep. 113, Nr. 63.

[60] Memo from Füllsack to Zentralkommandatur, 13.2.1947, LAB, B Rep. 010–02, Nr. 394: Supply of Berlin w. Fruits/Vegetables, 1945–8/1968.

[61] Copy of an allied directive regarding the transport of goods between sectors in Berlin, dated August 23, 1946, LAB, STA Rep. 6, Nr. Nr. 205: Stadtrat: Zusammenarbeit mit der DWK, July – October 1947, Bl. 7.

[62] Clark, "Berlin's first election tomorrow," 7.

[63] Informationsdienst Nr. 23 from the Berliner Presse- u. Informationsdienst (IPD), LV d. SED Gross-Berlin, Abt. Presse u. Information, dated August 3, 1946, SAPMO, NY 4090/383, Bl. 77. The SED cochair Otto Grotewohl, or at least someone in his office, marked this passage with an X.

report writer's optimistic sense of the Soviet zone's inherent appeal came out in his assertion that people talking about the food situation "*naturally*" discuss the Soviet zone. But even more telling is his appropriation of the singular form to identify the Soviet occupier. "The Russian," whether adopted verbatim from the women, about whom he was reporting or simply his own imposition, encoded the Soviet occupier with an individual identity, one that for the women of Berlin carried a potent accusation of their collective encounters with the individual soldiers who repeatedly raped them in the days and weeks that followed the fall of Berlin. Thus, while attempting to maintain a positive slant on Soviet occupation efforts (improved food supply in the Soviet zone) that is undermined by Western propaganda efforts, the writer unintentionally referenced the fundamental defining experience with which the Berlin majority female population explained its relationship to the Soviet forces: postwar sexual violence.

For women in postwar Berlin, the centrality of this common experience of rape cannot be overestimated. An anonymous diary writer – a young woman in 1945 – describes the "standard question" with which a conversation between women began in the weeks following the end of combat in the city: "How often did they ... ?"[64] While the shock of their encounters with these acts of violence was different than it would have been in peacetime – there was no report of any crime, no investigation, no report in the newspaper – the collective nature of this experience also enabled these Berlin women to approach it differently as well, at least initially. In the days and weeks after the war ended, "[a]ll the women help each other by speaking about it, airing their pain, and allowing others to air theirs and spit out what they've suffered. Which of course doesn't mean that [some of them] won't fall apart or suffer for the rest of their lives."[65] In their diaries and memoirs, these individual women found very different ways to give voice to this experience. The anonymous diary writer mentioned in the preceding text is striking for the laconic, matter-of-fact tone with which she describes the repeated sexual assaults she endured at the hands of numerous Soviet soldiers; but she also describes how she gradually seized partial control over these encounters, selecting her protectors and eventually even integrating them into a postwar language of provision. Thus, "sleeping for food" became "a new concept with its own

---

[64] Anonymous, *A Woman in Berlin*, 163. On the lasting impact of rape and the way it colored one woman's understanding of the events that came after, see Vance, *Shadows over My Berlin*, especially the prologue and the opening sections of each of the following chapters.

[65] Anonymous, *A Woman in Berlin*, 147.

vocabulary, its own specialized jargon, just like 'my major's sugar,' 'rape shoes,' plunder wine,' and 'coal-filching'."[66] To the extent that this evolving vocabulary also prefigured the moral ambiguity with which Berliners, especially Berlin women, approached their postwar survival strategies, this collective experience of sexual violence provides a crucial backdrop for these historical actors' readiness to cultivate their own strategies for survival.

As the violent upheavals of late April and early May 1945 receded into the background, Berliners' discussion of these rapes also began to move below the surface of public attention. As husbands, fiancés, and other male friends and relations returned to the city, they found it difficult to accept many women's brutally frank discussion of rape and their collective battle for survival.[67] One woman's fiancé returned from his service at the front, and after a few days back in Berlin he bitterly declared, "You've all turned into a bunch of shameless bitches, every one of you in the building. Don't you realize?"[68] Thus it is not surprising that efforts to wrestle with the implications of this collective experience of violence necessarily took place in a kind of coded language, while it still remained an important physical and psychological component of women's everyday life in postwar Berlin. Even writing in her diary during the last days of the war, the artist Hannah Höch used more abstract language to describe "visits from the Russians" (*Russenbesuch*). While this sense of distance may have reflected both the fact that Höch was not raped as well as a political desire not to condemn the Soviets, it nonetheless spoke in terms that remained readily decipherable.[69]

Although less visible than in the early summer of 1945, the topic still remained close to the surface of Berlin everyday life. As late as December 1948, a public forum organized by the SED-led Society for the Study of

---

[66] Ibid., 190.

[67] On this evolving view of women and their postwar experiences, see Heineman, "The Hour of the Woman," Grossmann, "Trauma, Memory, and Motherhood," and Andrea Petö, "Memory and the Narrative of Rape in Budapest and Vienna in 1945," in *Life after Death: Approaches to a Cultural and Social History of Europe during the 1940s and 1950s*, Richard Bessel and Dirk Schumann, eds. (Cambridge and New York: Cambridge University Press, 2003), 129–48.

[68] Anonymous, *A Woman in Berlin*, 259. When this diary first appeared in Germany in the late 1950s, the author was denounced for besmirching the honor of German women. See Constanze Jaiser, "Review of Eine Frau in Berlin. Tagebuchaufzeichnungen vom 20. April bis 22. Juni 1945," H-Soz-u-Kult, May 12, 2003, http://hsozkult.geschichte .hu-berlin.de/rezensionen/2003-4-138. See also Gelfand, *Deutschland-Tagebuch*, 79–80.

[69] In zur Nieden, *Alltag im Ausnahmezustand*, 169.

the Culture of the Soviet Union to speak about Germans' relationships to the Russians wound up focusing on rape, even if the discussion took place using coded language in which repeated reference to the theft of a bicycle was clearly understood by the audience as the means to conduct a halting conversation about the pervasive experience of rape.[70] In a postelection assessment, an SED functionary in Charlottenburg (British sector) made the link even more overtly:

The most effective slogan that also ran in other districts: "Do you want *zapperzapp, Frau komm, Uri, Uri,* rape of women, murder and killing, horror," then vote for the SED, the agency of Mongolian culture.[71] These and similar texts were often glued to our posters. The popular mood reflected them as well. A brief example: I was stopped on the street in a loudspeaker truck; as a largish crowd stood and listened, a man rode by on a bicycle and called out: "It started with Uri, Uri." Immediately, there was loud laughter, and the crowd dispersed. An older woman called us Russian pigs (*Russenschweine*) and said: "As long as you have your party ration to feed on, we can go ahead and starve." In a discussion, some people explained to me that they would vote for the SPD, because the SPD was a German party and took a German position on the question of the [eastern] border. When I noted what Comrades Pieck, Grotewohl, and Fechner had said [on the border question], one said: "You just did that as an election maneuver; you'd most prefer to climb up the Russians' backside."[72]

In effect, this account gave indirect voice to the ambiguous assertion made in *Sie* a week before the election that women in Berlin made their voting decisions on the basis of their practical experiences, and, more than anything else, Berliners voted to reject the SED.

The SED's failure to define itself effectively as something other than the German arm of the Soviet occupation meant it could not escape association with Berliners' brutal experiences when Soviet soldiers arrived in the city. In a resolution submitted to the SED's Central Committee following

---

[70] See Naimark's insightful discussion about the ways that this coded language enabled all present to discuss the real issue: rape. The fact that a subsequent forum was much more rigidly controlled suggests that the SED leadership understood this subtext as well. Naimark, *The Russians in Germany,* 134–40.

[71] The expression *zapperzapp* was a euphemism for theft. Although here it refers to thefts by soldiers, the expression is not altogether negative. In the words of Andreas Friedrich, "'To go zapp-zarapp' means to take what one needs no matter where it comes from." In *Battleground Berlin,* 43. "Frau komm" and "Uri, Uri" refer to Soviet soldiers' broken German commands: "Woman, come" and "Watch, watch" (reflecting these soldiers' propensity to collect stolen wristwatches).

[72] Report from Herbert Winkler, Abt. Werbung u. Schulung, SED Kreis-Charlottenburg, stamped 5.11.1946, DY 30/IV 2/5/223, Bl. 30. During the election campaign, SED leaders suggested that they did not see the Oder-Neisse border as permanent.

the Berlin election, a party functionary conference in the Tiergarten District (British sector) distanced itself from official SED characterizations of the SPD victory as the product of a general protest vote or simply as a response to inflated SPD promises of increased food and coal supplies. Instead, these functionaries noted that in an election that saw two-thirds of the voters supporting "socialist" parties, the decision *not* to vote for the SED could not be so superficially explained away and instead reflected a broad failing to find any "spiritual" link to the population. In an effort to explain this shortcoming, the functionaries singled out the SED's inability to recognize popular antipathy to the Soviet occupiers.[73] In his memoirs, Wolfgang Leonhard describes the shock that settled over the SED on the night of October 20 as the election results came in. Even for those who had anticipated a less than optimal result, the resounding defeat came as a brutally public humiliation. In the end, he summed up the vote's outcome, "The election result was the logical consequence of our dependence on the Soviet occupiers."[74]

SED efforts to address popular perceptions that it was nothing more than a "*Russenpartei*" often wound up referring more to the recent German past than to any hoped for German future. A memo to top SED leaders on August 30 points to the knee-jerk reaction with which many in the SED (especially those coming from the KPD) greeted this uncomfortable reemergence of a history in which the Communist role was not unambiguously positive. The memo describes a poster allegedly being prepared by the SPD in which the names of the top three SED leaders, Grotewohl, Pieck, and Ulbricht, were arranged so that the first letters of their last names spell out "GPU." In response to this play on the acronym of the Soviet security forces, the memo writer suggested that an appropriate retort could be made with a poster that tied the SPD to the Nazis, assembling the names of that party's leaders ("Neumann, Swolinsky, Dahrendorf, etc.") into the heading NSDAP, the German acronym for the Nazi Party.[75] Otto Grotewohl, however, warned against "sectarian" sentiments within the SED, linking them specifically to the Communist paramilitary organization of the Weimar Republic, the Red Front Fighters' League (*Rotfrontkämpferbund*); but he also warned against "SPD-tendencies."[76]

---

[73] Copy of the resolution made by the Functionary Conf. of the 2. Kreis Tiergarten on 30.10.1946 (sent to the ZK d. SED), LAB, BPA, IV L-2/13/434.

[74] Wolfgang Leonhard, *Die Revolution entläßt ihre Kinder*, 452.

[75] Nachlaß Otto Grotewohl, SAPMO, NY 4090/383, Bl. 36.

[76] Stenographisches Bericht der 6. Parteivorstandssitzung der ZK der SED, 24–25 October 1946, SAPMO, DY 30/IV 2/1/10, Bl. 34f.

In June 1946, he had warned that the SED must counter popular impressions of the party as a "branch of the Russian occupation." Instead, he claimed rather self-righteously, "We are rather a German party and a socialist party and must turn a corresponding face to the population."[77] Ironically, the effort to return to a more German political tradition imbedded the SED in the tortuous conflicts of prewar "socialist" politics. Instead of moving beyond the political divides of the Weimar Republic, the SED wound up falling back on much of the old KPD rhetoric and initiating an effort to refight the battles lost in the 1920s and 1930s.

Hermann Matern made this comparison overtly. Speaking to the SED Parteivorstand following the county party convention (*Kreisparteitag*) elections in September, he called on the SED to paint a clearer picture of its enemy, emphasizing its assault on the workers' movement and the working masses and in its attempt to undermine the SED's leadership efforts:

Today, this is happening in the same way it happened to the worker and soldier councils in 1918–1919. Today, the antifascist forces that, since May of last year have borne the responsibility and taken a heavy load on their shoulders, are being defamed and dragged through the dirt, just like the worker and soldier councils in 1919. In this history repeats itself, and the reaction tries to travel the same path again.[78]

Matern claimed for the postwar SED the same persecuted identity of the post–World War I revolutionaries who ultimately failed when SPD leaders deployed paramilitary *Freikorps* troops to crush the Spartacist uprisings. Their claim to iconic martyrs such as KPD founders Karl Liebknecht and Rosa Luxemburg – murdered in Berlin in January 1919 – and the workers killed by SPD-led police during widespread May Day violence in 1929 rested at the heart of the Weimar-era KPD's self-identification and, more importantly, served to define its principal opponent: the SPD. In 1946, the SED, like its KPD forerunner, failed to understand the diverse material and experiential motivations for Berliners' voting decisions and increasingly located the source of its own failings in the same party the Communists had attacked so vigorously two decades before.

Noting that the lottery to decide ballot list number in Berlin had awarded List 1 (traditionally held by the SPD during the Weimar Republic)

77 Stenographisches Bericht der 3. Parteivorstandssitzung des ZK der SED, 18–20 June 1946, SAPMO, DY 30/IV 2/1/4, Bl. 140.
78 Stenographisches Bericht der 5. Parteivorstandssitzung des ZK der SED, 18–19 September 1946, SAPMO, DY 30/IV 2/1/8, Bl. 87.

to the "splinter-SPD, the smallest party in Berlin," Matern emphasized the need to contest any sense that the SPD was heir to the tradition of German socialism. Instead, he called on the SED to prove, in its campaign and in its actions, that

we are the old Social Democracy from the period before 1914, not they; they have nothing to do with it and do not carry on the traditions of the German workers' movement; to the contrary, they have totally distanced themselves from it and stand entirely to the side; in Berlin they promote a politics as far to the right as one can imagine, much farther right than the bourgeois parties.[79]

Little separates this rhetoric from the KPD's denunciation of the SPD in the Weimar Republic as "social fascists" who were even more dangerous than the Nazis.[80] At the SED's Parteivorstand meeting on February 22 and 23, 1947, Otto Grotewohl addressed the party's failure to rally workers (especially Social Democrats) to its banners and warned that the party was undoubtedly doomed to failure if the SED sought to speak the same language that was spoken by the KPD in 1930.[81] Yet, as the new administration emerged in Berlin, the shadows of Weimar loomed over all its decisions. The radical break with the German past that the Soviets and the SED hoped to achieve with the October elections had not materialized.

After the Election – Relocating the Struggle for Berlin

Two weeks after the elections in Berlin, one Berlin editorial writer expressed the hope that, with the end of the war now almost two years past, the "postwar period" might evolve into real peace. This vision notwithstanding, the article acknowledged that Berliners were "still walking on temporary bridges (*Notbrücken*), practically and spiritually."[82] Theoretically, the vote on October 20 and the forming of a democratically

---

[79] Ibid., Bl. 89. Matern went so far as to speak of a "Nazi" faction (*nazistische Agitationsgruppe*) at the Social Democratic newspaper, *Telegraf*.

[80] During the "Third Period" (1928–35), the KPD included the SPD (the "social fascists") as a principle opponent of their "antifascist" struggle. The theory of "social fascism" was renounced by the Comintern at its seventh Congress in 1935 when it espoused the policy of the "popular front." On the Comintern resolution, see *A Documentary History of Communism*, rev. ed., vol. 2, *Communism and the World*, Robert V. Daniels, ed. (Hanover and London: University Press of New England, 1984), 103–4. More generally, see Heinrich August Winkler, *Der Weg in die Katastrophe: Arbeiter und Arbeiterbewegung in der Weimarer Republik 1930 bis 1933* (Berlin and Bonn: Verlag J. H. W. Dietz Nachf., 1987), 148–54.

[81] Stenographisches Bericht der 8. Parteivorstandssitzung d. ZK d. SED, 22–23 February 1947, SAPMO, DY 30/IV 2/1/14, Bl. 131.

[82] "Soll und Haben," *Sie* (November 3, 1946), 1.

elected municipal government marked a critical first step on a path toward this goal of peace and an end to the unsettled nature of life in Berlin. But rather than resolving the contest for political and administrative control of the city, the defeat of the SED served only to escalate the conflict.

The extent to which electoral "democracy" had proved a less effective lever than SED leaders had hoped only underscored their conviction that pursuing their "progressive demands" depended on cooperation of an array of forces that would, ultimately, transcend the limits of a parliament.[83] This version of democracy sounded more like that pronounced by Walter Ulbricht to Wolfgang Leonhard and other young Communists in 1945 as they began to set up the first district administrations in the city: "It's got to look democratic, but we must have everything in our control."[84] Attempting to explain how things had slipped away from the SED, Berlin party chief Hermann Matern explained the electoral result as a "protest vote" against existing conditions, for which voters blamed the SED.[85] As he saw it, because the Berlin voter thus was not explicitly rejecting the SED, the SED's strategy could not rest solely on a programmatic vision of the future but must focus on counteracting the enemy arrayed against it. "We are faced with the reality that the reaction still holds on to its positions of power here; the main content of our work must be, in addition to the struggle for the improvement in the lot of the working population, to destroy the reaction's positions of power."[86] The SED leadership acknowledged the party's political defeat at the hands of the SPD, which, similar to the KPD in the Weimar Republic, it branded as a force for reaction. But the SED still failed to grasp the much broader challenge to its presumed power, the unofficial structures of power that Berliners continued to develop in which the Social Democrats' electoral victory was only one component.

A letter to the editor of *Sie* in mid-November portrays hierarchies of power in the city using very differing categories. The letter describes the situations of three cleaning women in the city. The first worked for Berlin's public transportation company and earned 0.72 marks/hour. The second worked for one of the occupying powers and, like the first, earned 0.72 marks/hour. But she also received something extra "for the stomach."

---

[83] Stenographisches Bericht der 5. Parteivorstandssitzung d. ZK d. SED, September 18–19, 1946, SAPMO, DY 30/IV 2/1/8, Bl. 120, 133–4.

[84] Leonhard, *Child of the Revolution*, 303.

[85] Stenographisches Bericht der 6. Parteivorstandssitzung der ZK der SED, October 24–5, 1946, SAPMO, DY 30/IV 2/1/10, Bl. 41.

[86] Ibid., Bl. 47.

By contrast a third cleaning woman working for the municipal hospital received only 0.60 marks/hour with no supplemental supplies. The letter writer sought to deploy these examples as the means to promote a change in official policy. That is, she saw in this disparity an opportunity for the municipal administration to intervene and grant these hospital workers an increased wage or at least a supplement for hazardous work. In particular, she emphasized that many of the women in this third category served as the lone provider of food for their families and suggested that this injustice demanded administrative intervention.

On the same page, another letter evaluates the material conditions facing Berliners in terms that are at once more explicitly physical but also psychologically potent. A worker on a construction site, the writer described how her dirty and sweaty work challenged the most basic demands of personal hygiene. Although she occasionally managed to purchase a sliver of soap, it was too expensive for her to buy regularly, and going without left her quite often disgusted by her own body. In the end, she noted that it would be a "blessing" if there were more soap and soap powder.[87] The two letters pose slightly different assessments of the necessary response to the material crisis facing Berliners. The first suggests the need to recategorize some Berliners to permit them to access available supplies. Even in issuing its public appeal, the second letter detaches the hope for material improvement from any official action, the passive construction of her wish for the "blessing" of more soap[88] an expression of the extent to which conditions of personal hygiene operated in a space quite distinct from that of political rhetoric that characterized the new municipal administration.

Addressing the first session of the newly elected Berlin City Assembly on November 26, 1946, its SPD speaker, Otto Suhr, laid claim to a new democratic vision for the city: He thanked the Allies for reestablishing Berlin's political independence and granting the population the opportunity once again to determine its own future by selecting a new city administration. Yet he also expressed the desire for a certain independence from those occupation authorities: "[...] we ask that the allies now also trust the democratic parties, within the framework of the boundaries which they have set, to deal independently with Berlin affairs in the future."[89] In the coming months, this claim to self-determination would increasingly

---

[87] "Briefe an die Herausgeber," *Sie* (November 17, 1946), 4.
[88] The German subjunctive mood is quite explicit here in expressing this counterfactual wish: "Es wäre also schon ein Segen, wenn es endlich für Menschen etwas mehr Seife und Pulver geben würde."
[89] Stenographisches Bericht der 1. Sitzung der StVV, LAB, STA Rep. 100, Nr. 1, Bl. 10.

characterize the SPD's approach to the new city government. At this moment, however, it proved somewhat overoptimistic and also suggested a clarity of purpose that had not yet crystallized within the party or its leadership. Substantial limitations still constrained the municipal government's political and administrative independence as well as the Social Democrats' ability to direct the administration's actions. Major pieces of legislation required unanimous approval of the Kommandatura as did the appointment or dismissal of "leading figures" in the city administration.[90] Additionally, while the restrictions of occupation policies limited the ability of all German parties in Berlin to pursue their political agendas, Soviet willingness to intervene regularly in municipal affairs (through the Kommandatura and its local commanders) meant that the minority SED emerged as a more powerful force than implied by its limited voting numbers. Just as the battle against the Social Democrats had largely defined the SED's approach to the October election, the continuing need to combat SED efforts to exert material control over the city and its administration would help redefine the SPD.

Even after its October victory, it was not easy for the SPD to completely renounce any associations with its "socialist" counterparts in the SED. After all, the March 1946 vote in which Berlin Social Democrats had rejected an immediate union with the KPD had also given overwhelming support for continued cooperation between the two "worker" parties,[91] and in spite of the heated election campaign, some hope remained that the new municipal government could function in a general spirit of cooperation. With the exception of the LDP (with only 12 of 130 seats in the city assembly), all the parties espoused some sort of a "socialist" solution to the political and economic problems confronting Berlin, a situation that suggested at least the possibility of common approaches to the material crisis facing the city as winter approached.

But the transfer of power to the new administration did not go smoothly. In the weeks following the election, the principle point of contention lay in competing interpretations of the balance of power between

---

[90] This requirement elaborated in Article 36 of Berlin's provisional constitution proved the basis of much conflict over the nature of municipal power and its relationship to the occupation authorities. Schlegelmilch, *Hauptstadt im Zonendeutschland*, 113.

[91] In his memoirs, a former CDU deputy mayor povides a critical view of continued friendly relations between the two "socialist" parties even after the formation of the new Magistrat. Ferdinand Friedensburg, *Es ging um Deutschlands Einheit: Rückschau eines Berliners auf die Jahre nach 1945* (Berlin: Haude und Spenersche Verlagsbuchhandlung, 1971), 141.

the city administration and the Kommandatura as set forth in the city's provisional constitution. Central to this tension was the SED desire to maintain as many positions in the new administration as possible. The provisional constitution guaranteed all authorized parties a spot in the new Magistrat. Although the SED was not able to achieve the prominent portfolios to which it initially laid claim, it did fight a rearguard action to delay the new Magistrat's assumption of power and, more significantly, to hold onto subordinate posts as a means of trying to limit the impact of the new department heads.[92] Eventually, the assembly did elect a new Magistrat headed by the SPD mayor (*Oberbürgermeister*), Otto Ostrowski. The SPD's nomination of this party moderate and former mayor of the Wilmersdorf district (British sector) for the post reflected a decision to take the middle path between the unabashed pursuit of traditional socialist reform goals in association with the SED and a decided anti-Communist position in association with the CDU and LDP. As such, it reflected some measure of uncertainty as to the precise direction that the party should take but suggested the continued centrality of a program of crisis management, the same basic approach espoused by the SED.[93]

In some ways, Ostrowski seems an odd choice for mayor of the former German capital. Before 1933, he had been mayor of the Berlin district of Prenzlauer Berg and active in the *Reichsbanner Schwarz-Rot-Gold*, the SPD's paramilitary organization. When the Nazis came to power, they forced him from office, and he moved back and forth across the hazy boundary of illegality during the years of the Third Reich. After the war, he resumed his activities in the SPD (initially outside of Berlin) before taking the district mayor post in Wilmersdorf in May 1946. Ostrowski did not enjoy national prominence. A poor public speaker, his chief qualification for the post seemed to be his administrative expertise.[94] Thus in a city that

[92] The protocols of the last sessions of the old Magistrat give testimony to this rising tension. See LAB, Rep. 280, Sta.-Ort. Nr. 3501/37 to Nr. 3501/48. See also the Stenographisches Bericht der 4. Sitzung der StVV, December 9, 1946.

[93] See Arthur Schlegelmilch, "Otto Ostrowski und die Neuorientierung der Sozialdemokratie in der Viersektorenstadt Berlin," *Jahrbuch für die Geschichte Mittel- und Ostdeutschlands* 42 (1994), 59–80, esp. 61–4. This is the only significant analysis of Ostrowski, a figure who, as I will argue in the following text, must figure prominently in any effort to understand the evolving nature of the postwar battle for Berlin.

[94] For a very flattering summary of Ostrowski's career, see "Unsere Spitzenkandidaten," *Der Sozialdemokrat* (October 8, 1946) in AdsD, Nachlaß Ostrowski, box 31. Some other materials in Ostrowski's papers suggest the need for caution with respect to any claims to heroism during the Nazi Era. See especially the papers in box 24. See also the critical comments by Deutschkron, *Ich trug den gelben Stern*, 147–9.

has assumed iconic status for its postwar political battles, the SPD's first choice for mayor targeted less the political than the material crisis. As mayor, Ostrowski's political view tended more in the direction of Social Democratic/Communist cooperation á la SED cochair Otto Grotewohl, a reflection of his sense that the effort to address the problems facing Berlin needed to be above politics. His rather naive belief that the situation in Berlin could be reduced to a purely administrative problem complicated his management of the diverse political participants in the Magistrat.[95] More significantly, Ostrowski failed to grasp that the interactions between the municipal administration and occupation authorities also demanded more than a bureaucratic relationship. These failures of vision drove both his personal political failure and the evolving self-confidence of his party, the SPD.

In addition to Ostrowski as mayor, the three top parties each garnered one of the deputy mayor posts. Of the fourteen city councilors (*Stadträte*) selected on December 5, seven belonged to the SPD, three to the CDU, two to the SED, and two to the LDP.[96] For the most part, the city assembly adopted the new Magistrat members without dissent. Only in a few cases did the SED object to the other parties' proposals. It accused the CDU nominee for city treasurer, Dr. Ernst, of supporting the Nazis in his earlier banking position and cited the LDP nominee for head of the Postal Department for having ties to "conservative-reactionary forces" and the Stahlhelm.[97] The Kommandatura eventually rejected both these nominees and only provisionally accepted the SPD's Ernst Reuter as head of the Department of Transportation and Supply Enterprises.[98] These preliminary challenges did little to disrupt the functioning of the new administration but did hint at the way with which the SED hoped to utilize the Soviet ability to control and limit personnel decisions to help counter its loss in the October election.

---

[95] In this regard see Schlegelmilch, *Hauptstadt in Zonendeutschland*, 215ff. For additional accounts of Ostrowski's personality and his failure to succesfully manage the Magistrat, see Friedensburg, *Es ging um Deutschlands Einheit*, 140–2 and Willy Brandt and Richard Löwenthal, *Ernst Reuter: Ein Leben für die Freiheit* (Munich: Kindler Verlag, 1957), 375–7.

[96] Stenographisches Bericht der 3. Sitzung der StVV, December 5, 1946, LAB, STA Rep. 100, Nr. 3, Bl. 20ff. Consultations ahead of time had allocated various portfolios to different parties.

[97] LAB, STA Rep. 100, Nr. 3, Bl. 22ff. The Stahlhelm (steel helmet) had been a right-wing paramilitary organization during the Weimar Republic.

[98] See Herzfeld, *Berlin in der Weltpolitik*, 173. Also Stenographisches Bericht der 5. Sitzung der StVV, December 12, 1946, 3.

On December 9, 1946, the city assembly met in special session to consider the question of when and how the new Magistrat should assume
its duties from the old. Legalistic wrangling over the precise meaning of
Article 34 of the provisional constitution took up most of the session, but
more fundamental conflicts seethed just beneath the surface.[99] While the
SED certainly hoped its parliamentary delaying tactics would allow its
members to hold on to administrative authority as long as possible, the
rhetoric that cloaked this debate largely reflected the broader issues within
which this legal detail was imbedded. Kurt Landsberg (CDU) denounced
the SED's reading of the provisional constitution and suggested that its
behavior recalled obstructive parliamentary tactics in the period prior
to 1933, a time in which such behavior helped enable the enemies of
democracy so easily to exclude the parliament from power. At this point,
calls of "Article 48!" and "Enabling Law!" from SED ranks interrupted
his speech, both pointed references to authoritarian policies that undermined parliamentary authority during the Weimar Republic.[100] Karl Litke
(SED) even more explicitly linked the CDU's predecessor to the collapse
of republican authority that led to Hitler's rise, suggesting, "It was Herr
von Papen, who belonged to the [Catholic] Center Party."[101] Otto Winzer
(SED) noted that everyone desired that the city administration possess the
right to self-determination, "but only political children can assert that in
Berlin and in Germany today power is located anywhere but with allied
officials." Instead, he accused the other parties of seeking to play off the
Allies against each other for their own benefit, concluding:

Such politics has already led Germany to ruin once before. (Renewed strong indig-
nation, disquiet, and catcalls from the SPD, CDU, and LDP: Monstrous! – the bell
of the speaker.) That is hardly so monstrous. Historical experience teaches that
this is how it once was in Germany and that some persons have not learned the
least bit from this historical experience.[102]

---

[99] Article 34 of the provisional constitution states: "Die beim Inkrafttreten dieser Ver-
fassung bestellten oder zugelassenen Organe der Stadtgemeinde Groß-Berlin in der
Hauptverwaltung wie in den Bezirksverwaltungen üben als Organe von Groß-Berlin die
verfassungsmäßigen Befugnisse bis zur Bestellung der Neuorgane aus." StVV, December 9, 1948, 5. The SED suggested that the new Magistrat had not yet been appointed
(*bestellt*) and called on the city assembly to assume all legal responsibilities (to the Kommandatura) that would result from the decision to permit the new Magistrat to begin
its work (p. 4).

[100] Article 48 refers to that article of the Weimar constitution that enabled the Reich Chancellor to rule by presidential decree, without the support of parliament. The enabling law
was passed by the Reichstag in March 1933 and facilitated the Nazi seizure of power.

[101] Reichskanzler Franz von Papen (1932). These remarks from Stenographisches Bericht
der 4. Sitzung der StVV, December 9, 1946, 9.

[102] Ibid., 19.

The SED's rhetorical posturing did nothing to sway delegates' votes, and the majority carried the day, adopting an SPD proposal that the Magistrat should assume power as of its election and swearing in. Even more important than the administrative result, this debate underscored the continued resonance of political experiences from the Weimar Republic and the deep political divides that separated the SED from the other parties in the assembly.

Despite these early conflicts, the city assembly moved ahead with a number of major policy undertakings, for the most part concentrating on efforts to address the material crisis facing the city but also endeavoring to make use of that crisis situation to help usher in a dramatic sociopolitical transformation. The centerpiece of these efforts was a proposed "socialization law" that hoped to transform industrial ownership in Berlin. On December 12, the SPD proposed a law to transfer the property of large trusts and other businesses to collective (public) ownership, explaining that such a step would help alleviate the economic injustice and promote democratization among the German population. The SED initiated a similar measure that aimed to expropriate Nazis and war criminals. In the discussion of the expropriation question and proposals to reorganize the Berlin economy, the SPD argued that in the interests of social order and promoting democracy, a new method of economic organization was needed. The SED based its proposal on the explicit recollection of the Nazis' rise to power. It desired to return Germany to international respectability by removing forever the roots of this rise that it saw in the "capitalist" forces that thrived after World War I. Gustav Klingelhöfer warned that socialization should not be used to punish war criminals. Alternatively, Joachim Tiburtius (CDU) emphasized traditions of Christian Socialism and cautioned that the pursuit of justice should come before efforts to prevent economic poverty; he also warned that it must consider the other zones as it tried to formulate economic policy for Berlin. While the motivations to support socialization varied considerably, only the LDP opposed any socialization measures, noting that the danger of monopolies was best solved by independent market forces.[103]

After further discussion in committee, the measure received its second reading and was eventually adopted by the city assembly on February 13, 1947. In its final form, the law designated monopolies and dominant firms

---

[103] Stenographisches Bericht der 5. Sitzung der StVV, December 12, 1946, 8–42. Even before the October election, the SPD critiqued the SED's effort to link socialization to the expropriation of war criminals. See the SPD Pamphlet: "Entmachtung der Konzerne" published in Berlin, October 1946 (before the election), LAB, C Rep. 101, Nr. 1921, Bl. 3ff.

to be transferred into public ownership. War criminals and Nazi activists were not to receive any compensation for their expropriated property.[104] Only the LDP voted against the measure. While never to be approved by the Kommandatura, this socialization law demonstrated the extent to which the German municipal government in Berlin was indeed able to marshal broad support in order to undertake major legislative measures.[105] But the debate over the socialization law also highlighted tensions within the SPD between its pursuit of effective municipal government – including efforts to address the immediate material crisis – and its advocacy of democracy in Berlin.

This tension had emerged implicitly in the SPD's campaign leading up to October 20. Speaking to the Berlin SPD on August 18, Franz Neumann laid out a program that emphasized both the particular importance of Berlin as well as the desire to pursue a program in which socialism and democracy were equal components of an effort to rebuild Germany. He claimed for Berlin the status of a fifth zone. "It is clear that Berlin is that site where probably more than anywhere else in the world perspectives and opinions stand starkly opposed to and in combat with each other." Neumann particularly sought to distinguish his party from the SED, for whom democracy was only a "tactical demand of the moment." Additionally, he explained the SPD's efforts to cooperate with the "bourgeois" parties (CDU and LDP) as part of the party's commitment to democracy. This would, he suggested, not compromise the SPD's dedication to socialism. Indeed, he suggested that a "socialist order" was a necessary part of the "spiritual reorientation" required for material recovery. Neumann even went so far as to suggest that socialism could also be reached from a starting point of the Sermon on the Mount.

Ultimately, Neumann suggested that the successful resolution of these problems depended on a single issue: "We live as it were in a passive democracy; the power of the state rests in the hands of the allies. Our goal as Germans is active democracy: state power will proceed from the

---

[104] Stenographisches Bericht der 15. Sitzung der StVV, February 13, 1947, 8–9.
[105] The French, British, and especially American authorities greeted the law with some skepticism. Nonetheless, while the Americans cautiously played for time and the Soviets fought to exclude Soviet Joint-Stock Companies (SAGs) from any socialization proposals, discussions continued in various allied bodies. A British compromise solution proposed in the spring of 1948 was never realized. Discussion of the law was dropped from the agenda of the last Allied Kommandantura meeting (June 16, 1948), and later developments, especially linking West Berlin to the U.S. European Recovery program, made further discussions moot. See Schlegelmilch, *Hauptstadt in Zonendeutschland*, 399ff.

people."[106] But Neumann also acknowledged the material foundation on which this effort to construct socialism must also build. The starting point, he suggested in a September speech, must first be to meet "people's bare survival needs (*nackte Lebensnotdurft*)": better food, a dry apartment, a warm room, and necessary clothing. When Germany was rich, he argued, the German people did not want socialism. Now, the material crisis could serve as the means to a larger ends.[107]

Faced with Berlin's postwar devastation, the SED also perceived a unique opportunity to construct a new social and political order on grounds swept clear of failed political alternatives. Even after more than a year of "normalization" efforts, the SED's Karl Maron could emphasize in the city assembly that "we still do not live in normal times."[108] Yet the SED failed to grasp that this continued lack of normality ultimately empowered Berliners to seize control of their own material fate in ways that did not depend on any one party's political or administrative vision. As the "temporary" postwar conditions assumed a kind of permanence, ordinary Berliners – in contrast to most political leaders – understood their improvised survival strategies as a new normality in which the municipal administration was but one among many variables. Their decisions about how to vote on October 20 certainly drew on their experiences of navigating Berlin's altered social and economic terrain, but did not depend on the SED's or any other party's ability to manage their material supply in and around the city.

It is not enough, however, to declare that Berliners were the agents of their own material conditions without also considering the ethical implications with which they invested, explained, justified, or contested their own survival strategies. Pointing out the extent to which staying alive in these postwar conditions necessitated a compromise of principles, an editorial one month after the elections asserted: "Today, a person's survival is proof that he circumvents laws, ignores regulations, and practices economic respectability only from time to time, in certain situations drops it altogether."[109] Every transaction from repairing shoes to

[106] "Berlin und die deutsche Politik," Referat von Franz Neumann auf dem Parteitag der SPD [Berlin] am 18.8.1946, AdsD, Nachlaß Otto Ostrowski, box 6.
[107] Rede Franz Neumanns auf dem Parteitag des Landesverbandes Gross-Berlin der Sozialdemokratischen Partei Deutschlands am 14.9.1946 in der "Neuen Welt;" title: "Wo stehen wir – wohin wollen wir?" AdsD, SPD-LV Berlin, 3/BEAB000003: Organisation Sekretariat, 3. Parteitag des SPD LV Groß-Berlin (17./18.8.1946).
[108] Stenographisches Bericht der 4. (Außerordentlichen) Sitzung der StVV, 9.12.1946, 11.
[109] "Backschisch," *Sie* (November 24, 1946), 1.

replacing window glass requires something "extra" – cigarettes or raw materials – before the craftsman will take on the job. Seeing in this break-down of the normal payment structure a return to "primitive" practices that prewar Berliners encountered only on their trips to "southern lands," the editorialist urged readers to rein in these "malevolent habits" and take steps toward respectability (*Anstand*) that would solidify a foundation for democratic political life. The large photo paired with this editorial shows a woman chosen as the "typical American housewife" by British and American journalists. Walking down a London street in a stylish suit, hat, and corsage, she has come to Europe to discuss "problems facing housewives" with her English colleagues. The photo's caption concludes, "Today, even housewives' problems wind up directly in international politics" but leaves unelaborated the process by which these presumably small problems made their way onto the grand stage of international affairs. The problems facing Berlin women were not, however, easily negotiated in a suit and a corsage. Surviving in Berlin remained a dark and dirty business, which helps to explain how these practices remained beneath the surface, even when they took place out in the open. In her memoir, Heidi Scriba Vance recalls a catchphrase from the brutally cold winter of 1946–7, "Let's get dressed and go to bed."[110] While this phrase effectively captures the physical implications of living and sleeping in unheated apartments that often remained partially open to the elements, it also moves the act of surviving indoors, domesticating it into a simple act of endurance that does not require any interrogation of its moral ambiguity.

---

[110] Vance, *Shadows over My Berlin*, 179.

3

June 1947: Berlin Politics in the Shadow of the Black Market

Writing to the Berlin Magistrat on June 26, 1947, a Berlin mother bemoaned the horrendous state of the city's food supply and criticized the politicians for putting party concerns above the material crisis facing the population:

Please go ahead and live only three months on nothing more than the employee ration card [Card III] with no money to buy anything on the black market; and you try, in addition to your work obligations, which are very strenuous, to care for a home and two children; then and only then will you learn what hunger means! You can believe me that then all your party nonsense (*Parteigewäsch*) would be of no matter to you.[1]

For two pages, this one woman wrote "in the name of many Berlin mothers," to denounce city officials' failure to take the necessary steps to alleviate the crisis. She held no doubts that the material catastrophe could be mastered with the proper policy; after all, she noted, in exchange for valuables offered up in trade, one could get *anything* from the farmers around Berlin. This mother called on Berlin authorities to confiscate foodstuffs from those farmers and to distribute them to the Berlin population before the goods could make their way to the black market. "Give us more to eat, and the black market will come to an end!" For this frustrated woman, there was little doubt about whom to hold accountable: "We Berlin mothers blame you [the Magistrat] when our children become sick and weak." Her letter goes on to elaborate this

---

[1] Letter to the Magistrat der Stadt Berlin, dated June 26, 1947, LAB, STA Rep. 101, Nr. 119. It is signed only "H. P."

moral shortfall more concretely: decrying the scant allocations that prevented her from satisfying the hunger of her fourteen-year-old, nearly six-foot tall son, she suggested that they were all likely to contract tuberculosis. The only ones who would escape this fate, she argued, were "you ladies and gentlemen [of the Magistrat] and the black marketeers." Even more bitterly, she wrote that rather than daily face their children's desperation, she and many other mothers would rather have been struck by a bomb.

This mother's scathing critique rested on the simultaneous assertion of her (and other Berlin mothers') weakness and the municipal authority's power – a power that it had neglected to deploy effectively. But even this single letter manages to subvert her claims of powerlessness. Although the writer initially claimed to have neither the means nor the inclination to participate in black market trading – "we who take our jobs seriously cannot leave our workplace to trade with the farmers for something 'extra'" – a few lines later, she describes how she managed to get by.

Now, with this food situation – since there are no potatoes, the bread is already long gone – everyone, and I mean everyone who wants to survive – and we mothers want to and must do so – must now and again, with a heavy heart, buy bread on the black market, so that our children don't starve.

In her oblique admission that she, like most Berliners, continued to search out the means to survive – even if that meant trading on the black market – she nonetheless condemned politicians for their failure to connect with ordinary Berliners' material concerns.

This letter is one among hundreds sent by Berliners in the first four years of the postwar period and now found in the files of the mayor's office. Ranging from proposals for developing a "mayonnaise-like" bread spread to complaints about a lack of reimbursement for homes seized by occupation forces to one woman's request for a CARE package on the occasion of her husband's eightieth birthday, these letters give voice both to Berliners' sense of the ongoing material hardships they faced and their hope that someone in the municipal government might be able to offer some sort of material aid. After Louise Schröder took over as acting mayor in April 1947, many in the city – especially women – seemed to believe that a female mayor might be particularly open to their appeals for official help. Her office – and quite often Schröder – replied to most letter writers, even those who wrote repeatedly, and while many responses incorporate fairly standard language about the need for individuals to turn to district officials to process their requests, the willingness of the mayor's office to take seriously these petitions (and occasionally even to intervene) offers a compelling account of moments in which political officials interjected themselves quite explicitly into ordinary Berliners' efforts to remake the conditions in which they endured life in postwar Berlin. In this particular case, Schröder's assistant asked the police to help find this anonymous letter writer, but they failed to do so.[2] Although this official acknowledged that the woman's criticisms seemed at least somewhat justified, the motivation behind his desire to "answer" those charges remains unclear. Was this an effort to intervene to ameliorate this woman's particularly difficult situation or did he seek to offer an alternative interpretation of the situation the woman described, one in which the authorities' efforts faired more positively?

Over the course of 1947 – a year generally identified with iconic Cold War starting points: the Truman Doctrine, the Marshall Plan, and the founding of the Cominform – municipal and party officials in Berlin engaged this interface between high politics and the continuities of scarcity in Berliners' everyday lives in ways that also help to explain the evolving contours of the postelection battle for Berlin. Otto Ostrowski, the mayor selected after the October 1946 elections saw material crisis as a management problem that depended, in particular, on interventions by the occupying powers. For Ernst Reuter, whom the municipal assembly selected as mayor in late spring 1947, the slippage remained clear between Berliners' material struggles and the political and symbolic battle for freedom that he increasingly emphasized in his public discourse. Indeed, for Reuter, that was precisely the point. Responding to critics who suggested that his emphasis on the political battle for freedom was misplaced ("people can't live on freedom"), Reuter asserted, "Well, a fish doesn't live on water, but it lives in water. A person doesn't live on freedom, but they can only live in freedom."[3] The methods they then used to survive (to live) remained, presumably, up to them. More than a reprise of wartime appeals to hold out (*Durchhalten*),[4] Reuter's perspective depended on Berliners doing much more than just passively surviving. That they did so would help to explain Reuter's and the SPD's political successes in the city.

---

[2] Memo to Polizei-Inspektion Tiergarten, dated July 2, 1947, LAB, STA Rep. 101, Nr. 119.

[3] The German original runs, "Nun der Fisch lebt auch nicht vom Wasser, aber er lebt im Wasser. Der Mensch lebt nicht von der Freiheit, aber er kann nur in der Freiheit leben." Quoted in Brandt and Löwenthal, *Ernst Reuter*, 374.

[4] "Durchhalten," *Sie* (January 19, 1947). See also Davis, *Home Fires Burning*, 63.

Hunger Winter

The 1946–7 winter has entered popular recollection as particularly difficult, especially in contrast to the mild winter that immediately followed
the end of the war. Mean daily temperatures from December 1946 to
March 1947 remained far below normal. On only eleven January days
did the temperature climb above freezing; during a brutal February, there
was not a single day on which the temperature reached 32 degrees.[5] Initially, municipal officials expressed only little concern. In a meeting with
members of the SPD's city assembly delegation on January 14, Gustav
Klingelhöfer reported that a recent warm spell had eased the situation.
He explained that the demand for coal had lessened and that even on
the coldest days, public warming halls had not been used as much as
officials anticipated.[6] But as the cold wave deepened in February, the
sense of popular desperation figured more and more prominently in press
accounts and public discussion, and pressure grew for an official response.
Following frantic discussions in the city assembly, city authorities ordered
a wide array of emergency measures to cope with the continuing icy cold.
As of February 15, all usable spaces, including air raid shelters, hospitals, and other heated rooms were to serve as warming halls; theaters,
music halls, and cinemas were to remain open to the public until one
hour before the start of all performances. All luxury venues and dance
halls were to close and public carnival events were prohibited. The Food
Department arranged to provide old and sick Berliners a warm meal at
no cost in municipal cafeterias (*Volksgaststätten*). Louise Schröder, the
deputy mayor and head of the Magistrat's emergency committee set up to
deal with the winter crisis, asked police officers to begin immediately to
check all houses for persons at risk.[7] By the end of the month, even those
responsible for public welfare (and thus receiving higher rations) began to
feel the pinch: the Berlin fire department warned of personnel shortages
because so many of its firemen were out with flu or other cold-related
ailments.[8] The Soviet sector newspaper, *Berlin am Mittag* described the
ongoing cold wave as the "hardest winter of [Berliners'] lives."[9]

---

[5] *Berlin in Zahlen 1947*, 47–8.
[6] Protokoll d. Fraktionssitzung am 14.1.1947, dated January 16, 1947, AdsD, SPD-Fraktion
des Abgeordnetenhauses von Berlin, Lfd. Nr. 563.
[7] The cold crisis figured prominently in city assembly sessions on February 13 and 14, 1947.
On the various measures proposed and adopted, see *Berlin: Behauptung von Freiheit und
Selbstverwaltung 1946–1948*, 149–51.
[8] Ibid., 158.
[9] "Gerüchte um Dr. Ostrowski," *Berlin am Mittag* (February 22, 1947), AdsD, NL
Ostrowski, box 22.

According to a June 1947 report by the city's Department of Social Welfare, 1,142 persons froze or starved to death during the 1946–7 winter, three-quarters of them older than sixty.[10] Nonetheless, the impression of absolute desperation demands a measured assessment. While the 1946–7 winter was undoubtedly much colder than the preceding year's winter, the number of overall deaths dropped significantly. From December 1945 through February 1946, 29,852 Berliners died; in the same months one year later, only 21,628.[11] While his report admittedly came before the real cold wave hit in February, Klingelhöfer's description of underutilized warming halls, even on the coldest days, suggested that Berliners did not depend only on municipal benevolence to survive the harsh weather. When Mayor Ostrowski made his report to the city assembly on February 13, he emphasized that some 200 persons had committed suicide during January, an apparent indication of the levels of desperation felt in the city. In fact, suicides for the three winter months dropped from 480 in 1945–6 to 451 in 1946–7. The monthly figure for January did not differ greatly from prewar levels, suggesting that Berliners' responses to the cold wave were not limited only to total despair.[12]

Restricting Berliners' experiences in the second postwar winter merely to passive suffering (freezing, starving) at the hands of brutal forces of nature reduces them to objects dependent on municipal or occupation benevolence and – just like the failure to acknowledge their ability to impact political structures aside from the October election – refuses to admit how their multifaceted actions coped with and indeed shaped the difficult material conditions in which they found themselves. Even in the midst of the extreme cold, Berliners sought out opportunities to reassert their humanity and do more than just survive. Ruth Andreas-Friedrich described sitting in an apartment with friends bundled up in hats and coats listening to one of them recite poems by Goethe. "And when you think about it, they seem even more beautiful at twenty degrees below zero, without electricity or coal."[13] Another woman reported that her daughter remembered those days without electric light or a warm apartment as

[10] *Berlin: Behauptung von Freiheit und Selbstverwaltung 1946–1948*, 261. A preliminary report to the city assembly on February 13, 1947 noted that between December 1, 1946 and February 5, 1947, 134 Berliners froze to death and 500 persons were admitted to hospitals with acute cold-related conditions; some 60,000 persons were treated on an out-patient basis. Schlegelmilch, *Hauptstadt im Zonendeutschland*, 449 n. 243.

[11] *Berlin in Zahlen 1947*, 137.

[12] Ibid., 159. The final suicide figure for January 1947 was somewhat lower than the 200 initially reported to the city assembly and at 172 only two more than in January 1946.

[13] Andreas-Friedrich, *Battleground Berlin*, 147.

the best of times, crowded into the kitchen while the mother read aloud to the children by candlelight. Even accepting a certain degree of retrospective romanticization in such accounts (although some high school boys – average age, sixteen – also reported at the time that rolling blackouts [*Stromsperre*] helped families hold together),[14] these moments of pleasure also helped bring into relief the tremendous work necessary to make them possible, to obtain enough fuel to warm even one room of an apartment or to husband a few swallows of brandy for friends coming in from the cold, exertions that remain beneath the surface even in these personal accounts. For individual Berliners, the important *how* of their everyday actions too often gets lost in both negative and positive recollections of their experiences of cold and hunger.

But by concretely elaborating the physical and material details of some of these basic practices – heating, water procurement, and basic hygiene – the multilayered complexity of the Berlin location more generally also comes into focus and provides the necessary context for an analysis of the politics that presumed to control the city. During the winter months, sociological investigators visited 154 families in Berlin. Of the 135 for which they had effective data, six families survived the winter without any heat, and 85 families survived with inadequate heat (less than 55 degrees Fahrenheit), although in the face of ongoing cold, many families tended to assess lower temperatures as adequate and temperatures of 55 or 57 degrees as warm. In most instances (82 of 135) families heated only one room in an apartment; in only five instances did central heating function regularly.[15]

Trying to keep warm in their porous, war-damaged apartments, Berliners faced more obstacles than mere fuel shortages. Even when they could obtain coal or wood, the lack of window glass and other structural damage meant that heat often just escaped outside.[16] For those buildings that did not depend on heat from in-room tile stoves, frozen water pipes often made it impossible to produce steam to warm their radiators.[17] This lack of running water also forced Berliners more than two years removed from the end of the war to reprise their time-consuming trips to public pumps

---

[14] Thurnwald, *Gegenwartsprobleme*, 217.

[15] Ibid., 44–5.

[16] On the lack of window glass, see "Berlin und die deutsche Politik," Referat von Franz Neumann auf dem Parteitag der SPD am 18.8.1946, AdsD, NL Ostrowski, box 6: SPD-Berlin (1945/1946).

[17] Sylvia Conradt and Kirsten Heckmann-Janz, *Berlin halb und halb: Von Frontstädtern, Grenzgängern und Mauerspechten* (Frankfurt am Main: Luchterhand, 1990), 20.

for water by the bucket; nor could they escape the need once again to carry small packets of human waste to drop into nearby ruins each time they left their homes.[18] Mothers with small children in constant need of diaper changes faced an especially arduous winter task: washing dirty diapers (a scarce item). One mother described how she tossed dirty diapers into a bucket of water, which froze overnight. The next morning, she hacked apart the frozen diapers and heated the bucket on the stove. When the diapers thawed, she used her bare hands to rub the diapers clean in water just above freezing temperature.[19] The necessarily repetitive cycle of diaper-changing offers a potent example of the process by which the winter's extraordinary challenges entrenched themselves as part of Berliners' evolving repertoire of postwar routine. One social worker reporting on the conditions among the families she observed noted, "Every now and then, the hard-working men and women offer up a discouraged sigh or shrug their shoulders in resignation at their lot. Most live like a horse in a harness."[20] Never-ending exertion and living constantly "in harness" thus proved a subtext to even moments of relaxation and amusement, and in the face of these never-ending energy demands, the continued lack of food remained a potent force in Berliners' everyday lives.

Hunger was still the norm. In one extreme case, a forty-five-year-old Berlin worker killed a colleague for his ration card, later justifying his action with the explanation that he had eaten only a few slices of dry bread in the days before his crime. The month before he had lost his ration card, and the limited replacement card, he argued, did not allow him to obtain any more to eat. In December 1947, a Berlin court accepted the strain of hunger as a mitigating circumstance when issuing its decision in the case.[21] Of course, as we have already seen, purchased rations were hardly the only route by which food reached Berliners, and these unofficial supply structures continued unabated through the winter.

A late January letter from the district Soviet military commander to the head of the District Food Department in Pankow noted the dramatic increase in break-ins and thefts from stores selling rationed goods in the district. He ordered store owners to insure that all windows and doors were fitted with iron bars, install alarm systems, and supply night watchmen. Given his suspicions that shop owners were using reported break-ins

[18] Andreas-Friedrich, *Battleground Berlin*, 147.
[19] Meyer and Schulze, *Von Liebe sprach damals*, 103.
[20] Thurnwald, *Gegenwartsprobleme*, 179.
[21] Dinter, *Berlin in Trümmern*, 101.

as a way to funnel their goods to the black market, the district commander declared store owners to be financially liable for the value of all stolen
goods at current market prices.²² Whether the break-ins that so concerned the Soviet commander reflected shop owner corruption or merely
a potentially violent criminal underside to illicit food trafficking, their
prevalance certainly suggested that in the face of winter hardships and
the inadequacies of official supply, Berliners had little choice but to turn
to the black market. A CDU delegate to the city assembly described a sign
that appeared at a cemetery in the district of Wedding (French sector) in
late 1946: "Whoever isn't lying here by New Year is a black marketeer"
(*Schieber*). She then challenged her colleagues, "I ask you, whoever lives
on rations alone, is that person still alive?"²³

The focal point for popular outrage about inadequate rations remained
ration card five, the so-called hunger card that officially allotted its holders
less than 1,500 calories a day. In January 1947, nearly 1 million Berliners
continued to receive rations at that level.²⁴ On October 22, 1946, the first
postwar Magistrat had forwarded to the Kommandatura an SED proposal to eliminate ration card five for certain groups of people, including
housewives, invalids, pensioners, older persons incapable of work, and
sick persons during the period of their convalescence.²⁵ The Kommandatura eventually ordered the elimination of ration card five in its meeting on February 28, and all recipients were incorporated into group three,
beginning March 1.²⁶ Speaking on Berlin radio that day, Mayor Ostrowski
emphasized the concrete benefits that this decision would bring for thousands, especially for housewives and older Berliners. Interestingly, he also
admitted that the improved rations would help those who had avoided
work and "obtained their often extravagant food supply by means of
shady dealings on the black market."

Ostrowski's description of the material improvements achieved by
municipal authorities at least implicitly emphasized the need to combat these threatening forces. Mostly, though, his remarks underscored

---

²² Copy of order from Militär Kommandant Bezirk Pankow to the Leiter des Ernährung-
   samts Bezirk Pankow, 25.1.1947, AdsD, NL Ostrowski, box 30.
²³ Stenographisches Bericht der 30. Sitzung der Stadtverordnetenversammlung, May 22,
   1947, 35. More generally on the almost universal participation in the black market, see
   Roesler, "The Black Market in Post-war Berlin."
²⁴ Dinter, *Berlin in Trümmern*, 76.
²⁵ Minutes of Magistrat Session on Tuesday, October 22, 1946, LAB, LAZ-Sammlung, Rep.
   280, Sta.-Ort. Nr. 8501/37.
²⁶ *Berlin: Behauptung von Freiheit und Selbstverwaltung 1946–48*, 163 and 165.

the practical implications of the ration increase, that it would necessitate a substantial increase in foodstuff allocations from the occupying forces, nearly 19,000 hundredweight (*Zentner*) per month. From his perspective, the policy shift and the supply adjustments that must follow depended on the effective cooperation between the municipal government and occupation authorities. He expressed supreme confidence in his own ability to manage this cooperation, suggesting that his vision offered the best hope for improved conditions in the city. But his ongoing conviction that Berlin remained essentially a management problem to be solved also contained the seeds of his own political failure.[27]

The Ostrowski Crisis

The elimination of the lowest ration category was Otto Ostrowski's greatest administrative success and evidence of the progress to be made in coping with the difficulties facing postwar Berlin. But he failed to grasp the evolution of the city's sociopolitical conditions in which the dynamic tension between continued material hardship and symbolic stagings of battles for democracy simultaneously constrained German officials' room for maneuver and offered new opportunities for political breakthroughs. As the winter crisis continued to worsen, the increasingly self-confident SPD, under the vigorous leadership of Otto Suhr and Franz Neumann, pursued an aggressive effort to distance itself from the SED. Turning their back on the March 1946 referendum in which the party rank and file (at least those in the west sectors who were permitted to vote) had expressed the optimistic desire to cooperate with their Communist fellows, SPD leaders worked vigorously to extract themselves from most connections to their SED opponents. Throughout the winter months, a principle target for their efforts continued to be SED holdovers in subordinate positions in the municipal and district administrations. But such efforts faced explicit challenges from Soviet authorities, who in most instances forbade dismissals without their approval, and in some cases insisted that dismissed personnel be reinstated.[28] The SED party organ denounced the "totalitarian" aspirations of the new SPD leadership, suggesting that the alleged

---

[27] Otto Ostrowski on the Berliner Rundfunk, 1.3.1947, AdsD, NL Ostrowski, box 27. Also, Schlegelmilch, *Hauptstadt im Zonendeutschland*, 215–16.

[28] See orders from district commanders to district SPD officials in AdsD, Nachlaß Otto Ostrowski, box 30: Kommunalpolitik Berlin (1946–51). More generally, see David Barclay, *Schaut auf diese Stadt: der unbekannte Ernst Reuter* (Berlin: Siedler Verlag, 2000), 215–17.

effort to eliminate incompetent officials concealed an attempt to get rid of the antifascists that had been installed in 1945.[29] Under pressure in the Western press to deny undue subservience to Soviet demands but also committed to his vision for an administrative resolution to Berlin's problems, Ostrowski nonetheless proved ready to make political concessions in exchange for possible administrative change. Rather than marking a desire to travel a third way, which would have mediated between competing Soviet and Western occupiers, this approach reflected his long-established conviction that Berlin's problems required first and foremost a nonpolitical manager. Ostrowski was thus less the "Ost-westrowski" that a newspaper mockingly described later that spring – a play on the German word for *east* (*Ost*) – than a bureaucrat who failed to understand how Berliners and Berlin politicians now found themselves helping to craft a symbolic location that resonated far beyond the city.[30]

On February 22, the SED leaders Karl Litke, Hermann Matern, and Karl Maron met with Mayor Ostrowski and his fellow SPD-member, Johannes Stumm, to discuss "the resolution of municipal political and certain personnel questions related to the Berlin city administration." At the conclusion of their conversation, all five signed a typed text summarizing the content of their "non-binding discussion." Ostrowski repeatedly emphasized the informality implicit in that dismissive characterization, but the document's rather formal style belied that description. As summarized in the document's three points, SED leaders indicated that they would withdraw two deputy department heads from their positions in the city administration. Litke and Matern suggested that they would be prepared to withdraw two further deputies from the administration if, during the next three months, the two parties embarked on a cooperative political program and halted all polemical attacks in the press and in public speeches. Finally, the undersigned declared (this particular formulation, *erklären*, implied a level of participation for all signers that runs counter to Ostrowski's claims of informality) not to release any reports of this conversation to the press without first clearing it with the SPD and SED delegations to the city assembly.[31] This discussion presented the possibility of a radical shift in the political constellation in Berlin. But

---

[29] "Dr. Ostrowski vor der Presse: Die Berliner haben andere Sorgen als ihr Oberbürgermeister," *Neues Deutschland* (February 9, 1947).

[30] Pasquill, "Es bürgermeistert in Berlin," *Berlin am Mittag* (27.5.1947?), AdsD, NL Ostrowski, box 10.

[31] A typed original of this protocol with the five signatures can be found in LAB, BPA, IV L-2/10/384.

while the three top figures in the Berlin SED conducted these negotiations, the SPD leadership only learned of the conversation after the fact.
Although Stumm would go on to head the west sector police in 1948, this
act of independence proved the final blow that severed Ostrowski from
the continued support of his party leadership and unleashed a storm of
protest.

After receiving a report of the conversation, SPD leaders reacted
quickly. On February 25, Otto Suhr and Franz Neumann dispatched a
letter to the SED State Executive Committee (*Landesvorstand*) in which
they distanced the Berlin SPD from any close association with the SED or
any other party. While expressing support for an end to unsubstantiated
attacks in the press, the two SPD leaders emphasized that negotiations
for any sort of agreement with their party could only be conducted by
the executive board of the Berlin SPD.[32] This rebuke marked more than
a personal repudiation of Otto Ostrowski. It suggested that the SPD was
now firmly distancing itself from the compromise path that led it to nominate Ostrowski in the first place. Under the dynamic leadership of Suhr,
Neumann, and, increasingly, Ernst Reuter, the party seized this chance to
reinterpret its view of the parameters defining Berlin politics. Ostrowski's
actions, while perhaps reflecting a naive disregard for his own party, were
not grounds for the SPD to abandon him. Rather, the SPD's vigorous
reaction must be viewed as a response to the evolving politics in the new
administration in general, and the political strategies pursued by the SED
specifically.[33]

In his almost daily reports to the SPD leadership in Hanover, the
western zone SPD's liaison to Berlin, Erich Brost, initially made little of
the Ostrowski discussion. In his report of February 25, he referred to
Franz Neumann's assessment that Ostrowksi's readiness to cave into SED
demands had resulted from "personal weakness." Brost suggested that
Neumann was attempting to smooth over the situation by some means
or other.[34] Two days later, the situation appeared more serious. Brost
described a dinner with a number of American officials, who bombarded
him with questions about the Ostrowski affair. He reported that he told
them that should "something dramatic change in Berlin," the Americans

---

[32] Letter from Suhr and Neumann to the SED Landesvorstand Gross-Berlin regarding SED
conversations with Stumm and Ostrowski, dated February 25, 1947, LAB, BPA, IV lL-
2/10/384.

[33] See Schlegelmilch, *Hauptstadt in Zonendeutschland*, 212ff.

[34] Erich Brost, Tätigkeitsbericht Nr. 5, 25.2.1947, AdsD, Bestand Kurt Schumacher, Mappe
165.

should "certainly restrain themselves," a comment that provocatively turned on its head easy notions of Germans as passive recipients of occupation orders. Later, Brost wrote that a meeting of the SPD Magistrat delegation and Berlin Landesvorstand had reached no conclusion regarding Ostrowski, but he offered a clear sense of the direction he saw the situation heading. "In this matter, Neumann appears to continue to push my view, namely that Ostrowski must be toppled [. . . .] As far as Ostrowski's successor goes, Reuter is naturally the first choice. But it's still not clear whether he'll accept."[35] Thus, two days into the crisis, the outcome seemed predetermined. Yet it dragged on for more than a month.

The extent to which American officials or Ernst Reuter played a role in forcing Ostrowski from office remains unclear. As Brost's report indicates, American officials were at the very least concerned about the affair. In retrospect, an embittered Ostrowski blamed American intrigues, focusing his animosity in particular on a Captain Ulrich Biel, whom he accused of passing word to SPD leaders that the mayor had made a 180-degree turn and now functioned as a Communist "Trojan horse" in the party. In this account, his "sworn enemy," Ernst Reuter, used these accusations to push for the SPD to drop Ostrowski as mayor.[36] As he grew older, Ostrowski launched a series of legal proceedings in an effort to obtain a pension at a higher level as well as to seek public repudiation of persons whom he saw as having defamed him. Although he never left the SPD, his pride and unrealistic sense of his own abilities clouded his recollections and fueled his almost paranoid sense of betrayal. His efforts to regain the stature he briefly enjoyed as *Oberbürgermeister* achieved a certain pathos and more than anything else point to Ostrowski as the premier example of a problem that plagued Berlin in the immediate postwar period: aside from a very few exceptions, the city found itself forced to cope with second-tier political leaders.[37]

Despite the growing opposition within his party, Ostrowski continued to hold out and resist efforts to convince him to step down voluntarily. He remained convinced of his ability to work with all the occupying forces (including the Soviets) to address the material crisis in

---

[35] Erich Brost, Tätigkeitsbericht Nr. VII, 27.2.1947, AdsD, Bestand Kurt Schumacher, Mappe 167.

[36] Otto Ostrowski letter to Strick (February 15, 1961); Otto Ostrowski letter to Heinrich Albertz (May 15, 1962), AdsD, NL Ostrowski, box 12. British reports seemed at least to support the assertion that Biel had been rapidly informed about Ostrowski's conversation. Barclay, *Schaut auf diese Stadt*, 218.

[37] Andreas-Friedrich also makes this point, *Battleground Berlin*, 165.

Berlin.[38] At this point, however, it didn't really matter what actions Ostrowski undertook. The SPD's antipathy toward the mayor rested less on the explicit political failings he may have exhibited than on a renunciation of the very principles that led the party to select Ostrowski in the first place. On March 5, Ernst Reuter informed Brost that he had been calling for Ostrowski's ouster for a month already.[39] The party's sense of a "democratic" mission increasingly centered on Reuter. Reuter had returned to Berlin from Turkish emigration in late December 1946.[40] Although not an active participant in the party's early postwar struggles, Reuter came more and more to give voice to the SPD's symbolic stature as a source of political strength in the city. After returning to the Magistrat post he held in the 1920s, Reuter worked ceaselessly and proved effective at managing his department's efforts to begin to rebuild the city's transportation and utility systems. The Magistrat, however, increasingly frustrated Reuter, and he seethed at some officials' combination of incompetence and political intransigence.[41] The Ostrowski affair brought these sentiments to a head and helped them coalesce within the party more broadly.

In a special session of the city assembly on April 11, the delegates considered an SPD proposal calling for the resignation of the entire Magistrat and its reelection in a form that truly reflected the outcome of the October election. Although speakers from the three Western parties expressed various opinions about the changes necessary for the Magistrat to work effectively, only the SED argued that the Magistrat could continue to function in its current state. In the end, however, the debate centered on Ostrowski's role in the city government and his overture to the SED. Franz Neumann (SPD) denounced Ostrowski for ignoring the duty of his office to administer its affairs in a nonpartisan fashion.[42]

---

[38] For Ostrowski's retrospective assessment of his actions, see the commentary he wrote in 1958 [?] in response to an article in *Der Tagesspiegel* (Berlin), "Der Fall Ostrowski," AdsD, Nachlaß Otto Ostrowski.

[39] Brost, Tätigkeitsbericht Nr. XI, 6.3.1947, AdsD, Bestand Kurt Schumacher, Mappe 165.

[40] Brandt and Löwenthal, *Ernst Reuter: Ein Leben für die Freiheit* (Munich: Kindler Verlag, 1957), 368–9. During his lifetime, Reuter was relatively well known in the United States, but, following his early death in 1953, Reuter has largely vanished from the American public and even scholarly attention. Although an American scholar wrote the best recent biography of Reuter, it appeared only in German: Barclay, *Schaut auf diese Stadt.*

[41] Ibid., 218.

[42] Herzfeld, *Berlin in der Weltpolitik*, 177. Of course, this statement is rather ironic given the fact that the SPD leadership was essentially denounced (at least within the party) for a perceived *lack* of party discipline. See Schlegelmilch, "Otto Ostrowski."

Long Ostrowski's supporter in the SPD leadership, Neumann's decision to turn on the mayor struck Ostrowski as a friend's betrayal. Essentially, Neumann accused the mayor of casting his lot with the SED and suggested that the SPD's concern about the SED's ongoing ability to affect the city administration more decisively motivated the decision to move at this time. Josef Orlopp (SED) argued that an overture by Ostrowski to the CDU or LDP would not have produced such a political furor, and, although he was perhaps right, his argument was really beside the point.[43] The assembly voted eighty-five to twenty with one abstention to support a measure of no confidence against Dr. Ostrowski.[44] When even the LDP gave up its neutral position and threw its support behind the vote of no confidence, Ostrowski left his place among the members of the Magistrat and demonstratively took a seat among the SED delegates.[45] Six days later he resigned.[46] This symbolic rejection of his own party highlighted the personal bitterness that would plague Ostrowski for the rest of his life. Much like Otto Grotewohl, his pride in his own abilities could not cope with his party's decision to reject his leading role. But unlike the first head of Berlin's postwar SPD, Ostrowski continued to nurse his grudge within the party, his liaisons with the SED never progressing beyond the half-hearted flirtations of a spurned lover hoping to recapture past attentions.

At the height of the crisis, the SED's Berlin cochair received a memo describing a conversation on a subway in the working-class Kreuzberg district (American sector):

A woman is reading the [SPD newspaper] Telegraf. In response to the question, "anything new in the Berlin Magistrat?", she answers: "A vote of no confidence has been introduced against Dr. Ostrowski." The person who asked the question asserts [with typical Berlin sarcasm], "great (*toll*), I'd like to know when they'll start working." To which the woman responds, "I can tell you: never! Dr. Ostrowski's actions were entirely correct. He has to establish a good relationship with the occupation powers; after all, we're dependent on them for many things. Dr. Ostrowski is the one person in the entire Berlin Magistrat that

---

[43] Stenographisches Bericht der 25. Sitzung der StVV, 11 April 1947, 50.

[44] Ibid., 58.

[45] "Zieht Dr. Ostrowski die Konsequenzen? Die Hintergründe des Misstrauensvotums – Die heutige Amtshandlung," *Der Kurier* (April 12, 1947), 1.

[46] See Stenographisches Bericht der 26. Sitzung der StVV session, April 17, 1947. Ostrowski read a brief, twelve-line statement. Under pressure from his party, he did not present a lengthy speech, which he had prepared in an effort to justify his actions. "Umstrittene Nachfolge Ostrowski: Verkürzte Abschiedsrede – Zweifelsfragen über die Stellvertretung," *Der Kurier* (April 18, 1947).

recognized that and also the only one who wanted to work. But they have no use for people who work; you see, no method is too low to give that kind of person the sack."

The report continued, noting regretfully that at that point the train pulled into a station, and the questioner had to get off. The other passengers, the writer observed, did not express any opinion or even react to this exchange. "One had the impression that they had no interest whatso-ever."[47] Although a British intelligence officer also attested to Berliners' general apathy about the Ostrowski affair,[48] the memo about the U-Bahn conversation suggests more than anything the SED's continuing desire to invest Berliners with a particular political mood. If a woman reader of an SPD newspaper could (as reported here) see through the SPD's politi-cal schemes and acknowledge the need to cooperate with the "occupation powers" – a shorthand for the Soviets striking only in its lack of subtlety – then there seemed some hope for coming political transformation. Even the report's wry comment on general apathy wishes and hopes for that possibility: if the woman's interlocutor had not had to get off, perhaps then the other passengers might have reacted. Lost in the report is the physical reality of travel in cramped, underheated, and often dilapidated subway cars, the crowding made even more unpleasant by the stench of unwashed passengers and the so-called bread cough that fouled the air as bodies struggled to cope with low-quality food that was not easily digested.[49] For years after the war, a dank smell lingered in the tunnels, a by-product of the tragic decision by Nazi security forces to flood the main S-Bahn tunnel as Soviet troops entered the city and a pervasive reminder of how difficult it was for Berliners to escape the aftereffects of wartime violence.[50]

For all the hardships that they personally faced, municipal politicians with their privileged food supplies could not but seem far removed from Berliners in the midst of these trying daily commutes. The even more privi-leged occupying powers with whom these politicians necessarily cultivated relationships remained even more distant. For most Berliners, the Soviet occupier likely mattered most when, for example, it announced a special distribution of sugar for the Easter holiday. But even here, there were limits. The Magistrat planned to make the sugar available for children

[47] LAB, IV L-2/10/380: Vors. Hermann Matern: Rpts./Info. on SPD, 1946–8.
[48] Barclay, *Schaut auf diese Stadt*, 219.
[49] Andreas-Friedrich, *Battleground Berlin*, 160. See also Gisela R. McBride, *Memoirs of a 1000-Year-Old Woman: Berlin 1925–1945* (Bloomington, IN: 1stBooks, 2000), 572.
[50] McBride, *Memoirs*, 573 and Beevor, *The Fall of Berlin 1945*, 371–2.

up to age fourteen and for hospital patients. An additional 60,000 kilograms of fruit preserves were to be made available to institutions housing children, old persons, and the blind as well as to hospitals, but amounts proved insufficient to make these distributions to the general population.[51] In the midst of the evolving Ostrowski crisis, this reported distribution highlighted the unevenness of top-down interventions in Berlin's material conditions, ultimately making clear the inability of such efforts to transform the fundamental reality of scarcity in the city. Even as he headed toward his own political demise, Otto Ostrowski failed to grasp this fact and suggested that two years after war's end, the occupying powers remained ultimately responsible for conditions in Berlin. He pointed to the upcoming foreign ministers' meeting and called for dramatic changes; otherwise, he suggested, Berliners would not make it through another winter.[52]

Coping with the Lack of International Resolution

From March 10 to April 25, 1947, the foreign ministers of the victorious World War II powers met in Moscow to attempt to resolve some of the outstanding questions on the future of Germany.[53] Leading up to the conference, there was indeed hope that the Allies would adopt some kind of agreement, and the press presented fairly optimistic previews of the meetings.[54] In Berlin, too, the gathering of the occupation powers renewed anticipation that concrete steps would be taken toward a peace treaty and the resolution of the economic crisis confronting the country. Ruth Andreas-Friedrich recorded in her diary: "The Moscow Conference temporarily upstages even the problems of hunger, cold and coal shortages. In the same way that a drowning person clutches at a straw, the people

---

[51] "Rund um die Osterfeiertage," *Der Tagesspiegel* (April 3, 1947), AdsD, NL Ostrowski, box 22.

[52] "Was erwarten wir von Moskau," AdsD, NL Ostrowski, box 27.

[53] The conference also discussed Austria. For a summary of the postwar peace treaties, see the chronology in David Reynolds, ed., *The Origins of the Cold War in Europe: International Perspectives* (New Haven and London: Yale University Press, 1994), 224ff. For complete records of the two 1947 CFM meetings, see United States, Department of State, ed., *Foreign Relations of the United States 1947*, vol 2, *Council of Foreign Ministers; Germany and Austria* (Washington, DC: U.S. Government Printing Office, 1972), 139–576 and 676–830.

[54] See the article headlined, "Big 4 Parley Opens Today; Marshall Reaches Moscow, Confident of Agreements," *New York Times* (March 10, 1947), 1.

of Berlin put all their hopes in it, confident that 'things will come out all right.'"[55] This hope vanished rapidly.

Soviet Foreign Minister Viacheslav Molotov opened the conference with a speech calling for the question of developments in China to be added to the agenda.[56] This opening immediately suggested a shift away from a focus on concrete measures to address specific German or even European issues. From that beginning, the sessions realized only minimal practical gains and did little to address the larger issues of the German situation. Indeed, Western representatives increasingly came to believe that the Soviets felt no sense of urgency to reach any resolution of the political and economic problems facing Germany. Charles Bohlen, an advisor to U.S. Secretary of State George Marshall, describes a meeting between himself, Marshall, and Stalin in which Stalin indicated that if the Allies did not reach any agreement at this meeting, they would at the following, or perhaps the one after that. Bohlen asserts that this conversation played a significant role in convincing Marshall that the Soviets were looking to exploit the economic and social upheaval in Europe and that significant American steps were now necessary to stabilize the chaotic situation there.[57]

The lack of stability in Berlin nonetheless produced opportunities for those willing to undertake occasional risks and exploit the breakdown of normal economic relationships. Young people, in particular, proved more adept than their parents at illicit trade.[58] For persons used to purchasing goods at a set price, the need to barter and haggle often proved a tricky proposition. One mother admitted her incompetence and left these negotiations to her son instead. She traveled first to farmers in the surrounding communities and asked what they needed. At that point she dispatched her eleven-year-old son who took the family's cigarette ration or its milk card to the black market, where he brokered the necessary deals to exchange it for nails or yarn or whatever else their rural trading partners desired.

---

[55] Andreas-Friedrich, *Battleground Berlin*, 165.

[56] See *Tägliche Rundschau* (March 11, 1947), 1.

[57] Bohlen, *Witness to History*, 263. Following his return from the conference, Marshall organized the new Policy Planning Staff under the direction of George F. Kennan. This body formulated the recommendations that evolved into the Marshall Plan. See also George Kennan, *Memoirs 1925–1950* (Boston and Toronto: Little, Brown and Co., 1967), 325.

[58] Sebastian Haffner makes a similar point in discussing the opportunities that the inflationary period in the early Weimar Republic offered enterprising young people, opportunities (and risks) that their more conservative parents proved unable to take. Sebastian Haffner, *Defying Hitler: A Memoir*, Oliver Pretzel, trans. (New York: Picador, 2003), 56.

His black market competence allowed his mother to bring home potatoes or vegetables far beyond the amounts their rations allotted them. As the woman explained, "I was no great black marketeer (*kein großer Schieber*) but an advanced forager (*ein gehobener Hamsterer*)."[59] Her open-ended assertion might be reiterating her earlier point about her incompetence on the black market, but it also contains a moral evaluation of her actions: she was no *großer Schieber* – not the much despised big-time black market criminal that Berliners continually contrasted with the unfortunate small-scale *hamsterer* that always seemed to get caught in police nets. The implications of this desire to keep one's moral distance played out even more clearly for another boy in the city whose father, "a straight-laced civil servant," preferred to "starve [rather] than trade on the black market." *Therefore* (and this term is explicitly present in the boy's retrospective account), he headed out to various black market venues in Berlin – the Brandenburg Gate, Stresemannstrasse, and Potsdamer Platz. He started with a metal box of Stabilo brand pencils, which, by a series of trades, he turned into cigarettes. Aided by his ability to steal coal, wood, and scrap metal, he managed to make a bit of money, at least some of which undoubtedly helped support his father who, of course, had absolutely nothing to do with the black market.[60]

Even if police records captured only a portion of these practices, the dramatic upsurge in youth criminality in Berlin in late 1946 and early 1947 testified both to the evolving material conditions in the city and developing strategies to cope with that material need. A preliminary report for the Police President described that from October 1945 to August 1946, incidents of youth criminality (involving persons between ages fourteen and eighteen) remained between 150 and 190 cases per month. After that they increased dramatically: in November 1946 there were 539 cases; in January 1947, 637 cases; and in May 1947, 928 cases. By August 1947 the number had dropped again, but only to 593 cases.[61] Whether Berliners perceived them as young hooligans or as vital components of familial supply networks, the presence of these young figures on Berlin's street corners confronted the city's inhabitants with their complicity in the morally ambivalent practices on which their postwar survival depended.

---

[59] Meyer and Schulze, *Von Liebe sprach damals keiner*, 100–1.
[60] Conradt and Heckmann-Janz, *Berlin halb und halb*, 22.
[61] Memo from Abt. K. (Erdmann?) to Markgraf regarding information about the activities of the police for a talk by Bgm. L. Schroeder, dated September 12, 1947, STA Rep. 9, Nr. 1, Bl. 287. See also, Hauptamt für Statistik, *Berlin in Zahlen*, 383–5.

Accepting the implications of such practices was not always easy, not least because it forced Berliners to reconsider their comforting claims to be either wartime victims or energetic rebuilders.[62] For "respectable" Berliners, it was much more palatable to explain black market criminality as a by-product of a corrupting foreign presence in the city. Polish and Yugoslav military missions and especially DP camps offered easy and, in contrast to the four occupying powers, less threatening targets. But in the evolving semipermanence of the postwar, the hazy dividing lines between occupier and occupied, foreign and local, reinforced the mutual interdependence of these diverse residents in Berlin and their collaborative production of postwar Berlin's ambiguous moral economy. Russian and American cigarettes remained the principal source for Berlin's black (and thus illegal) market, and occupying soldiers' legal "gifts" helped sustain their German *fräuleins*. More than any other postwar relationships, these liaisons – especially between American men and German women – made explicit just how tricky it was to draw hard and fast moral lines in postwar Berlin.

American officials' concerns about innocent American boys succumbing to the seductive allures of a Nazi temptress mirrored German unease with reputable girls being turned into a soldier's "Veronika," enticed by chocolate and silk stockings.[63] But even Hollywood's portrayal of these iconic relationships makes clear the limits of such absolute condemnations. In Billy Wilder's *A Foreign Affair* (1948), Marlene Dietrich plays Erika von Schlütow, a singer in an underground nightclub whose Nazi past has been suppressed with the aid of her American lover, Captain Pringle (John Lund). More than any other Hollywood production of its generation, *A Foreign Affair* accessed deep personal knowledge of Berlin, both before and after the war. Wilder, the Viennese Jew who emigrated to Hollywood by way of Weimar-era Berlin collected much of the film's exterior footage while back in the city during the American occupation in 1945. Dietrich, whose leap to international fame started in Berlin's

---

[62] See esp. Heineman, "The Hour of the Woman," 354–95.

[63] Emily S. Rosenberg, "'Foreign Affairs' after World War II: Connecting Sexual and International Politics," *Diplomatic History* 18, no. 1 (Winter 1994), 61–3; Petra Goedde, *GIs and Germans: Culture, Gender, and Foreign Relations, 1945–1949* (New Haven and London: Yale University Press, 2003); and Maria Höhn, *GIs and Fräuleins: The German-American Encounter in 1950s West Germany* (Chapel Hill and London: University of North Carolina Press, 2002). The German population also adopted the American nickname for fraternizers, which stemmed from a U.S. Army paper's unsubtle warning against association with "Veronika Dankeschön" (VD). See Heineman, "The Hour of the Woman," 381 and Goedde, *GIs and Germans*, 93–4.

Schöneberg district, returned there in 1945 to visit her mother who had survived the war's end in the German capital. Her evocative songs steal the show, and both their lyrics and music bear poignant witness to Berlin, past and present.[64] In her first song, she sings about the black market "just around the corner, Budapester Strasse" (British sector). Her sequined gown sparkling in the spotlight, she sings in a way that seems to offer ample ammunition for both German and American moralizers: "To you, for your K-Ration, compassion, and maybe an inkling a twinkling of real sympathy. I'm selling out, take all I've got, ambitions, convictions, the works!"

But more than these songs, her character's small gestures create nuanced connections to the human experiences on the ground in Berlin. On a street outside a local police station, von Schlütow frankly explains her survival strategy to an American congresswoman (Jean Arthur) in Berlin to investigate the moral condition of American troops. At first von Schlütow's account seems to reinforce the viewer's sense of her calculating ruthlessness, but even this defiant proclamation comes after a request that the congresswoman try to imagine what it was like to be a woman in Berlin when the Russians entered the city. Although her reference to the experience of rape remains oblique, Dietrich's character more explicitly locates her story and her apartment in a destroyed city, "only a few ruins from here." Von Schlütow has just obtained the two women's release after they were seized in a police raid, and as they are leaving the police station, she makes sure to slip a few cigarettes to the policeman processing their papers and requests that he also release the nightclub's waiters. Because this bit of dialogue occurs only in German, the film's American audience would likely have seen it only as a bit of extra atmosphere, but it effectively, if perhaps unintentionally, captures the way that almost all relationships in Berlin – professional and personal – operated in a network of material negotiations.

In the same way that it remained difficult to make clear moral judgments about the relationships between occupation soldiers and German women, it also proved tricky to draw clear distinctions between the trades, purchases, and deals with which Berliners sought to supply their material needs. On August 10, 1946 American officials created the "Berlin Barter Center" in their occupation sector. Until the center closed in May 1948,

---

[64] Dietrich's songs were written and accompanied by Frederick Hollander (Friedrich Holländer), who had also performed with her in the 1930 Josef von Sternberg film, *Der blaue Engel.*

Berliners could bring in goods to sell and for which they then received
certificates in the amount of the sale price to be used to obtain other
goods at the Barter Center.[65] This kind of institution formalized the barter
arrangements that dominated Berliners' initial postwar supply arrangements, and similar barter markets (*Tauschmärkte*) existed in other sectors. Such exchanges remained only slightly removed – in either spatial
or practical terms – from the black market. A monthly police report from
November 1946 describes the profusion of black market activity near the
official barter markets in the Lichtenberg district (Soviet sector).[66] On
July 13, the weekly *Sie* illustrated its front page with a drawing of a Berlin
street scene. Playing on the implicit color coding of the "black" market
(and the expanded adjectival properties of the German *schwarz*), the illustration proposed to show readers what would come to light "If we could
see, what we have that is black [illegal] . . . ." On a scene drawn in gray,
the illustrator uses black to make visible how much Berliners depended
on illegal trade. Grey roofs are repaired with black shingles; black glass
fills most windows; the policeman on the corner wears black shoes; and
every cigarette is conspicuous in its inky darkness.[67]

Berliners' everyday encounters with the workings of the black market
regularly reminded them of the personal compromises necessary for their
material survival but also confronted them with the ability of unscrupulous individuals to profit from that need. They took part in an ongoing
debate about the advisability and efficacy of occupation and municipal
authorities' effort to combat or regulate illicit trade in the city. On some
level at least, this discussion offered a context in which to debate how to
assign blame for the ongoing material crisis, but as occupation officials
and German politicians struggled to conceptualize Germany's postwar
future, it also framed a broader dispute on zonal boundaries and economic
development. The Potsdam agreements had called for the victorious Allies
to treat Germany as a single economic unit, but this had been proved a
fiction already by 1946. In December 1946, the British and Americans
decided to link their two zones as of January 1, 1947.[68] The creation of

---

[65] NA, RG 260 390/50/25/4 box 117: OMGUS, Records of the Berlin Command, The Berlin
Barter Center: Correspondence, 1946–8.
[66] Monthly activity report (November) from the Kommando d. Schupo to the Police President, dated December 2, 1946, LAB. STA Rep. 9, Nr. 87, Bl. 170.
[67] *Sie* (July 13, 1947), 1.
[68] On the creation of the Bizone, see Kleßmann, *Die doppelte Staatsgründung*, 101. More
extensively, see John Gimbel, *The American Occupation of Germany: Politics and the
Military, 1945–1949* (Stanford: Stanford University Press, 1968), 80–129.

the "Bizone" resonated across Germany, suggesting a new permanence to the zonal divides. For Berlin, as well, the Bizone raised new questions about the city's economic and political position within Germany, questions that proved especially potent for the SED.

Speaking to the SED Landesvorstand in Berlin, Hermann Matern criticized developing ties between Berlin and the bizonal economic council in Minden (near Frankfurt am Main in the American zone), explicitly warning that these connections threatened Berlin's material supply and the future shape of the German state. From this perspective, any move that privileged Berlin's ties to one zone over another risked dividing the country. He condemned SPD leaders in particular for – as he described it – encouraging some Berliners to try to exploit the Soviet zone population.

What is the reason that they so strongly support the fact that everyone can go out from Berlin into the Zone in order to forage (*hamstern*) there? This has two aspects: the first is to disrupt and disorganize the economy in the Soviet zone; the second aspect is to agitate the [members of the] population against each other, to bring the Berlin population to a wholly antagonistic view of its broader surroundings. In reality, what is the flood of tens of thousands into the Soviet zone of occupation? It is an individual exchange of goods. Not all Berliners can travel out of the city, and not all have goods to trade; that is and will remain a small segment; but it is a wild action which the Berlin Magistrat must, along with the central bureaus in the Soviet zone of occupation, control according to a plan. But the Magistrat has no ties to the central administrations. But they go and sit in Minden; Minden is closer than Leipziger Strasse and after all, they can bring more back from there! [But n]ot for Berlin![69]

For Matern's symbolic geography, the Magistrat's growing cooperation with the Bizone's Central Economic Bureau – located in Minden, near Frankfurt am Main in the American zone – meant that it was turning its back on the administrative structures physically located in Berlin – the Soviet zone's central administrations located in Hermann Goering's former Air Ministry building on Leipziger Strasse. Building on this image, he tried to invest his criticisms of Berliners traveling into the Soviet zone with a trace of the populist dissatisfaction at elite privilege and inveighed against "wild" and unscrupulous actions in need of more rigid controls. In his eyes, the Berlin Magistrat had traded in its ability to cope with exploitative black marketeering for privileged connections to the evolving western zones. Although he embedded this critique in his pointed

---

[69] Protokoll d. Landesvorstandssitzung, June 28, 1947, LAB, BPA, IV L-2/1/18, Bl. 17–18. The Deutsche Zentralverwaltungen were the central administrative bureaus set up for the Soviet zone on July 27, 1945. See the chronology in Weber, *DDR*, 284.

denunciation of the SPD and the Berlin Magistrat, he could not conceal his real uneasiness that there were tens of thousands of Berliners heading out into the Soviet zone to enter into individual exchanges outside of any official control. For Matern and for the SED more generally, the debate over Berlin's economic ties to the various zones of occupation reflected the implicit tension between its rhetoric in support of German unity and the growing evidence of its inability to master the material situation, even in the zone almost wholly under its administrative control.

The Munich Conference of Minister Presidents and the Marshall Plan

As the economic turmoil in Germany dragged on without any indication of an imminent solution coming from the occupying Allies, German politicians, too, began to attempt to find a way to help overcome the negative economic impact of zonal division. They also sought to find a way to end the international political vacuum in Germany that continued to exist more than two years after the end of World War II. Following failed attempts by the CDU leader, Jakob Kaiser, to organize a national meeting of German political party representatives, the Bavarian Minister President, Dr. Hans Ehard, invited his counterparts from all of the German states to meet in Munich on June 6 and 7.[70] This meeting proved the first and last between German governmental heads from all zones of Germany. The decision by Soviet zone minister presidents to walk out of the conference marked the open declaration of competing eastern and western visions of the path toward a German state. As the following text will show, it also provided a clear indication of Soviet efforts to exert heightened control over the officials and policies in the Soviet zone, not least among the leadership of the SED.

Ehard sent out the initial invitation to the conference on May 7, and while it emphasized economic issues, it also called for "cooperation of all German states (*Länder*) with regard to economic unity and future political fusion."[71] Throughout May, preliminary discussions between

---

[70] On the Munich Conference of Minister Presidents, see Rolf Steininger, "Zur Geschichte der Münchener Ministerpräsidenten-Konferenz 1947," *Vierteljahreshefte für Zeitgeschichte* 23, no. 4 (October 1975), 375–453. On its impact on developments in the Soviet zone, see Jochen Laufer, "Auf dem Wege zur staatlichen Verselbständigung der SBZ: Neue Quellen zur Münchener Konferenz der Ministerpräsidenten 1947," Jürgen Kocka, ed., *Historische DDR-Forschung: Aufsätze und Studien*, Zeithistorische Studien 1 (Berlin, 1993), 27–55.

[71] Rolf Steininger, "Zur Geschichte der Münchener Ministerpräsidenten-Konferenz 1947," 378.

representatives of German administrations and political party leaders in the western zones gradually narrowed the focus of the conference agenda so that on June 2, Ehard indicated before the Bavarian ministerial council that the planned conference had only two goals: to determine how our people (*Volk*) can be brought through the next winter and to establish clarity and truth about the situation of the German nation.[72] While broadly conceived, these goals represented a significant undertaking, marking a potential shift in the locus of emerging German political power from the competing party leaderships to the elected political administrations.

For the SED, Ehard's invitation represented a significant tactical dilemma and brought to light conceptual divides that continued to exist within that party's leadership. Erich Gniffke, a member of the SED central Secretariat who fled to the west in October 1948,[73] notes that the initiative unleashed heated discussion in the SED's central Secretariat. He writes that the members of that body debated whether this was an entirely German proposal or whether the Americans stood behind it. Furthermore, they wondered whether the offer pointed to American interest in organizing an all-German government on the basis of minister presidents. Walter Ulbricht immediately reacted negatively, denouncing Ehard as nothing more than an American "agent."[74] Other participants in the discussion, including some former KPD members, were less certain, arguing that regardless of the underlying motivations, this opportunity to pursue some sort of all-German politics was worth undertaking.[75] After initial discussions between Ehard and the Saxon Minister President, Dr. Rudolf Friedrichs, the SED sent the Bavarian leader a telegram

---

[72] Ibid., 411. For a detailed assessment of the rather ambiguous views of Kurt Schumacher and some other SPD leaders with regard to a broader conference agenda (esp. with the participation of the SED), see 395ff. To some extent, Schumacher questioned the competency of the minister presidents to address all-German issues, noting that the minister presidents spoke for the states (*Länder*), but the parties spoke for all of Germany (p. 409). The French military government gave the minister presidents from its zone permission to attend the conference only on May 28 but indicated that they expected the minister presidents to deal exclusively with economic issues (p. 383).

[73] Erich Gniffke had been a member of the SPD before accompanying his friend Otto Grotewohl in the 1946 union with the KPD and joining the leadership of the SED.

[74] In this assertion he clearly reflected SVAG views. See Laufer, "Auf dem Wege zur staatlichen Verselbständigung der SBZ," 41, esp. n. 59. Laufer quotes a report by Sergei Tiul'panov, the head of the SVAG's propaganda section: "The Conference was a maneuver by American officials to evade the agreements of the Moscow Conference with the goal of solidifying the[ir] federative efforts."

[75] Gniffke, *Jahre mit Ulbricht*, 236f.

proposing that representatives of the parties and trade unions be included in the conference. The telegram also called for the creation of German economic and political unity to assume the central position in the agenda and for the site of the conference to be moved to Berlin.[76]

These "compromise" negotiations belied real tensions within the Soviet zone between the SED and the minister presidents and even between the SED and Soviet occupation officials. SVAG opposition to the conference was strong from the outset, but the presence of substantial German support for Soviet zone participation, especially among former Social Democrats in the SED, forced the process of "rejecting" the Western offer to drag out much longer than anticipated. The increasing SED demands to modify the organization of the conference were designed in no small part to force a Western rejection, thus placing the onus for the collapse of the all-German conference on western German politicians.[77] In Soviet eyes, the SED did not pursue this effort with the appropriate vigor or dedication. Marshall Sokolovskii's deputy, Ivanov, reported on May 25: "We are of the opinion [in the SVAG] that neither Pieck nor Grotewohl grasp the principal side of this question, and precisely this explains their wavering."[78] Thus, increasingly, the outcome of the Munich Conference mattered less as a means to achieve substantial steps on a path toward German political union than as an indication of the level of political instability within the Soviet zone and even in the SED.

At the preliminary discussion of the agenda held in Munich on June 5, Dr. Wilhelm Höcker (minister president of Mecklenburg in the Soviet zone) proposed on behalf of the other Soviet zone participants that the following topic be added to the agenda as point one: "Creation of a German central administration through an agreement of the democratic parties and trade unions for the purpose of forming a unified German state."[79] The western minister presidents refused to adopt the proposal, and the Soviet zone representatives indicated that they would no longer participate in the conference.[80] Reporting to the city assembly, Berlin's participant at

---

[76] Steininger, "Zur Geschichte der Münchener Ministerpräsidenten-Konferenz 1947," 407.
[77] Laufer, "Auf dem Wege zur staatlichen Verselbständigung der SBZ," 45.
[78] Quoted in ibid., 45.
[79] In Steiniger, "Zur Geschichte der Münchener Minister-Konferenz 1947," 425.
[80] Ibid., 437. Much of the argument against including the point proposed by the Soviet zone representatives could be found in the strict limitations placed on the participants from the French zone by French military government authorities. See also the articles under the headline "Müchener Konferenz von der Ostzone gesprengt," *Der Kurier* (June 6, 1947), 1. For his account of last-ditch efforts to facilitate a compromise that would have brought at least some of the Soviet zone minister presidents back to the conference,

the conference, Acting Mayor Louise Schröder (SPD), expressed regret for the departure of the Soviet zone minister presidents, but hoped that the conference represented a beginning from which to overcome the isolation of Berlin and further the socioeconomic recovery of Germany as a whole.[81]

The gathering of minister presidents proved to be neither the instrument for overcoming the ongoing economic crisis nor a basis for reestablishing a unified German state. It chose a commission on economy and food supply and designated a four-person committee (including Louise Schröder) to report on the current situation to the ACC.[82] Limited by restrictions imposed by the occupying powers and the unwillingness on the part of some party leaders to cede political authority to elected representatives, the Munich Conference never had a real chance to do any more than discuss the situation. Yet, its outcome managed to exert pressure on the internal situation within the Soviet zone. It significantly weakened the hands of those leaders (especially former Social Democrats) within the SED who had supported taking part at Munich and further constrained the freedom of action of the minister presidents and state (*Länder*) governments in the zone.[83] Thus the conference's outcome provided substantial impetus to those in the SED around Walter Ulbricht promoting the centralization of control within the party and throughout the Soviet zone. The announcement of the American Marshall Plan only heightened Soviet and SED leaders' sense of urgency about the need to secure their position in their zone in the face of competing economic and political measures being developed and promoted by the West.

Even before the announcement of the Marshall Plan, the SED leadership seemed to sense a real threat in the promotion of independent (i.e., non-SED-dominated) economic development in Germany, not only to its national aspirations but to its position in the Soviet zone. Speaking to the May meeting of the SED Parteivorstand Otto Grotewohl claimed that the United States required a weak and divided (federal) Germany for its economic policies in Germany and its expansionist policies in

---

see Friedensburg, *Es ging um Deutschlands Einhei*, 165–73. Although Friedensburg's rather self-righteous account must be treated cautiously, his assessment of the ambivalent feelings, especially of Minister President Rudolf Paul (Thüringen), are worth noting. Paul later fled to the West. See Hurwitz, *Die Stalinisierung der SED*, 403.

[81] Stenographisches Bericht der 33. Sitzung der StVV, July 12, 1947.

[82] See the summary in *Berlin: Behauptung von Freiheit und Selbstverwaltung 1946–48*, 246. The Soviet zone minister presidents sent their own delegation to report to the ACC.

[83] Laufer, "Auf dem Wege zur staatlichen Verselbständigung der SBZ."

Central Europe.[84] Thus, the refusal to permit the SED in the western zones reflected American fears that the party was a threat to the capitalist goals of "dollar imperialism." Given this sense of insecurity, he argued, the Americans were willing to take even the most extreme measures to suppress any segments of the German population that opposed them. Most provocatively, Grotewohl referred to an American colonel who had threatened to impose martial law and allegedly even the death penalty on strikers in Wiesbaden in the American zone.[85]

Although the American Military Governor, General Clay had already repudiated this declaration, Grotewohl used it as a rhetorical device to characterize the American approach to German economic recovery. For the SED, he asserted, such comments by representatives of the American occupation forces demonstrated their moral stance on the German question: "if the economic difficulties cannot be removed by other means, they will be removed with armored cars and bayonets." He wondered sarcastically whether the Americans would use the death penalty as a tool to solve the food problem – the survivors could then receive higher rations.[86] Even in this bitter jab at the Americans, Grotewohl nevertheless depicted the "food problem" as a single dilemma that awaited the proper policy to be resolved. The irony that Germans were addressing (if not solving) their own personal food problems each day played little role in this political calculus.

On June 5, one day before the start of the Munich Conference, American Secretary of State Marshall gave his renowned Harvard speech in which he outlined a proposal for U.S. aid to help rebuild the economies of Europe. In terms of real impact on the situation in Europe, this pronouncement had a much greater significance than the elaboration of the Truman Doctrine three months earlier.[87] Initially, Secretary Marshall

---

[84] Stenographisches Bericht der 11. Parteivorstandssitzung der SED, May 21–2, 1947, SAPMO, DY 30/IV 2/1/20, Bl. 123ff. The equation of "federal" with "divided" is quite significant. SED leaders regularly distinguished between a "federal" and a "central" government. In its external rhetoric, but certainly within the party as well, the SED attacked "federalism" as an effort to divide and weaken a future Germany.

[85] Of course, the ongoing Soviet measures in the Soviet zone, including kidnappings, arrests, and deportation to labor camps lent an underlying if unintentional irony to these criticisms. Such assaults on the German public garnered increasing attention even within the ranks of the SED. See Gniffke, *Jahre mit Ulbricht*, 260–2.

[86] Stenographisches Bericht der 11. Parteivorstandssitzung der SED, May 21–2, 1947, SAPMO, DY 30/IV 2/1/20, Bl. 125.

[87] For a brief, critical overview of the Marshall Plan, see Milward, "The Reconstruction of Western Europe," 241–70.

expressed some concerns about the potential Soviet reaction. He wondered whether they would accept the American aid offer, a possibility that would likely have doomed the measure in the increasingly anti-Soviet American Congress. Marshall's advisors, most notably George Kennan and Charles Bohlen asserted that the Soviets were unlikely to accept an aid program that required American verification of the use of aid. This proved to be the case. Soviet representatives initially attended the Paris exploratory meeting on the Marshall Plan in July but withdrew after the rejection of Molotov's proposal that aid be given to countries without any conditions.[88] All the other Eastern European countries rejected the plan as well. Although in the case of Czechoslovakia, its leaders had to be called on the carpet in Moscow to quell initial interest in the plan. It would be 1948 before Marshall Plan aid began to arrive in Europe, but its announcement made an immediate impact on the beleaguered European population. Even in Berlin, which was initially excluded from the program, it was grounds for renewed optimism.[89]

For the SED leadership, the Marshall Plan and the Munich Conference operated as part of a joint assault on its political and economic strategies. Speaking to the SED Parteivorstand, Walter Ulbricht described the Marshall Plan as an American effort to use its economic strength as a weapon. He argued that such American efforts could only be undertaken with the assistance of German politicians who were ready to assist in the division of Germany, a process he saw at work during the Munich Conference.[90] In the same session, Otto Grotewohl drew similar conclusions about the links between material conditions and high political developments, noting: "For us, the struggle for German unity is not only a political

---

[88] See Kennan, *Memoirs*, 342 and Charles Bohlen, *Witness to History*, 263ff. At the July session of the SED Parteivorstand, Walter Fisch, a KPD member from Frankfurt am Main (U.S. zone) used Molotov's attendence at the Paris meeting as an example to criticize the refusal of Soviet zone minister presidents to attend any of the sessions at the Munich Conference. Wilhelm Pieck rejected the comparison, claiming that the Munich Conference was nothing more than a front for an American scheme. Stenographisches Bericht der 12. Parteivorstandssitzung der SED, July 1–3, 1947, SAPMO, DY 30/IV 2/1/22, Bl. 122, 135.

[89] See the remarks in the entry for June 5 in *Berlin: Behauptung von Freiheit und Selbstverwaltung 1946–1948*, 245. See also the remarks in Andreas-Friedrich, *Battleground Berlin*, 175 and the article, "Marshall für Initiative Europas," *Der Tagesspiegel* (June 6, 1947), 1.

[90] Stenographisches Bericht der 12. Parteivorstandssitzung der SED, July 1–3, 1947, SAPMO, DY 30/IV 2/1/22, Bl. 98–9. Interestingly, Ulbricht's talk was entitled: "The party in a struggle against federalism and for the creation of a central German administration."

(*staatliches*) problem; it is not only of decisive significance for the development of socialist principles but is at the same time, seen from today, the foundation of the struggle against hunger, want, and cold."[91] Under pressure from the Marshall Plan and the Munich Conference, Walter Ulbricht pointed to the links between German unity and the "struggle for democracy" and emphasized that such conditions held true for Berlin. Over the course of the summer, this effort to consolidate "democratic achievements" in the Soviet zone consisted of tightening control over the SED's rank and file, establishing new structures for economic and security control, and cultivating extragovernmental political arenas as an alternative basis of political authority.

Trying to Master Berlin

On June 11, 1947, the Kommandatura issued a directive in which it accepted Ostrowski's resignation and instructed the city assembly to choose a new mayor. After selection by the assembly, this person would then be subject to allied approval. Until that time, Deputy Mayor Louise Schröder was to serve as acting mayor.[92] Less than a week later, the city assembly selected Ernst Reuter to fill the post. The SED opposed Reuter, arguing that the onetime leader of a Soviet Republic and a KPD Central Committee member who had turned his back on that party in 1921, now rejected working-class party unity. It denounced his election as a step that would increase the tension and level of crisis in the city. Still, the vote endorsed the onetime Communist by an overwhelming margin. In a secret ballot, Reuter received eighty-nine votes with seventeen opposed and two abstentions.[93] Max Fechner (SED) later claimed that the SPD was well aware that the Soviets would not approve Reuter but had selected him as its candidate anyway.[94] For the SED, Reuter's election represented an attempt to directly challenge the authority of the occupation regime and was a clear indication of the SPD's efforts to exclude the SED from the circle of elected power. In mid-August, the Kommandatura announced that it had been unable to approve Reuter as *Oberbürgermeister*.[95] The

---

[91] Ibid., Bl. 39.

[92] Allied Kommandantura Order BK/O (47) 145, June 11, 1947, LAB, Rep. 280 (LAZ-Sammlung), Sta.-Ort.-Nr. 1461.

[93] Stenographisches Bericht der 36. Sitzung der StVV, June 24, 1947, 51.

[94] Stenographisches Bericht der 37. Sitzung der StVV, July 11, 1947, 26.

[95] Communique Nr. 71 of the Allied Commandatura, Berlin regarding election of Reuter to Lord Mayor, August 12, 1947, LAB, Rep. 280 (LAZ-Sammlung), Sta.-Ort. Nr. 1463.

immediate power struggle for control of the city administration thus ended in a draw.

In his report to the Parteivorstand, Karl Litke, the cochair of the Berlin SED, emphasized the extremely difficult state of affairs facing the SED in the four-sector city. As he described it, the assault on the SED had not let up in any way since the October 1946 elections. It rested largely on the support of thousands of "agents" and a horde of journalists who continuously targeted the SED. While he described some growth in party membership, Litke noted that the Berlin SED suffered from a lack of young and, especially, active members.[96] Only 30 to 40 percent of the membership typically attended full-member assemblies. Even at the party's city convention to elect delegates to the Second Party Convention, a number of delegates failed to appear. In trying to explain this apathy, Litke noted that one could say that the Landesvorstand does not have sufficient authority or that the members' material concerns take precedence. "Tens of thousands work to obtain additional nourishment, and one comrade told me: You must understand one thing, Karl; at the moment a carrot is more important to me than a pretty speech that is held at your members' meeting! That's not how people should speak, but that's how it is."[97]

Near the end of his remarks, Litke emphasized that the party's work in Berlin remained under the shadow of the city assembly. Its debates filled the next day's papers and exerted significant influence on the city population, including SED members.[98] This comment, slipped in between more general critiques of the situation *within* the SED is actually quite telling. It suggests the difficulties faced by the SED in a competitive political environment where political accountability (to the voter) coincided with administrative authority. In the context of the general effort to exert more rigid controls over the SED's rank and file throughout the Soviet zone, it also hints at the real threat that the SED's instability in Berlin represented to the whole party.

Wilhelm Pieck also mentioned the political struggles in Berlin in his opening remarks to the Parteivorstand. Referring especially to the SPD and its decision to remove Otto Ostrowski and elect Ernst Reuter as mayor, Pieck explained: "Behind [the SPD] stand foreign powers, especially Americans, who have an interest in gaining total control over the

---

[96] For a detailed look at developments in the SED membership, see Hurwitz, *Die Stalinisierung der SED*, 271–311.

[97] Stenographisches Bericht der 13. Parteivorstandssitzung der SED, August 20–1, 1947, SAPMO DY 30/14 2/1/24, Bl. 94.

[98] Ibid., Bl. 99.

policies of Berlin's Magistrat and directing them against the Soviet occupying power."[99] Although cloaked within a globalizing rhetoric of an American-backed enemy, the threat that Pieck perceived should be seen less in the specific politics of Western parties in the Berlin Magistrat than in the extent to which the party's need to remain engaged in municipal politics strained the cohesion of the SED, both within and beyond the city. For this reason, the political and administrative shape of Berlin assumed special importance for the SED leadership and for its Soviet patrons.

On November 2, 1947, Dieter Friede, a journalist with the west sector newspaper, *Der Abend*, vanished after a phone call lured him into the Soviet sector. It was not until June 1948 that the Soviet-licensed news service, ADN, announced that he had been arrested for spying on behalf of American and British intelligence services.[100] In the intervening months, the case became a focal point for public outrage over the general sense of insecurity within Berlin. The city assembly discussed the case and the general problem of abductions in its session on November 13. In his denunciation of the police handling of the Friede case, an SPD deputy blamed the police for the disappearance of 5,413 people in Berlin.[101] Mayor Ferdinand Friedensburg (CDU) defended the actions of the police and seemed to suggest that the reality of disappearances was an unfortunate by-product of the unsettled legal situation in occupied Germany. This response elicited heated criticism, even from members of Friedensburg's own party. Franz Neumann (SPD) asserted that even under the

---

[99] Ibid., Bl. 11–12. Wilhelm Pieck also noted that the SPD's policies in Berlin and its failure to solve the ongoing material crisis in the city presented the SED with a real opportunity to mobilize the Berlin population on its behalf.

[100] *Berlin: Behauptung von Freiheit und Selbstverwaltung 1946–1948*, 342–3 and 499. Along with a number of other German prisoners, Friede was released from imprisonment in the Soviet Union in 1955. "Berlin reporter freed by Soviet," *New York Times* (October 12, 1955), 3.

[101] Deputy Lehnert (SPD) did not indicate the period of time over which these disappearances took place. A bit later, Franz Neumann (SPD) explained that the number, 5,413, was reached on the basis of individual reports submitted to the SPD in response to a public request to do so. Stenographisches Bericht der 47. Sitzung der StVV, November 13, 1947, 70 and 83. This caveat should not be taken as refuting the serious problem of abductions, arrests, and disappearances in postwar Berlin. On the extent of kidnappings and arrests and the nature of Soviet concentration camps in the Soviet Zone of Occupation (*Sowjetische Besatzungszone* or SBZ), see Naimark, *The Russians in Germany*, 376–94. For a discussion of an SED leader's concern about the extent of arrests, see Gniffke, *Jahre mit Ulbricht*, 260ff. For a discussion of postwar abductions that explores them almost entirely in the context of international espionage operations in Berlin, see Arthur L. Smith Jr., *Kidnap City: Cold War Berlin*, Contributions to the Study of World History 100 (Westport, CT and London: Greenwood Press, 2002).

Nazis, persons had possessed the right to send word to their family members from the concentration camps; now, Berliners disappeared without any trace.[102] Ruth Andreas-Friedrich described the situation in Berlin as a "dance on the edge of a volcano." Referring to the case of Dieter Friede, she noted that occasionally "the crater opens up and swallows one dancer or another."[103] This image effectively captures the sense of helplessness felt by many Berliners in the face of the ongoing threat of arbitrary arrest or detention. With the Soviet occupation out of reach except for the force of popular disdain, the public criticism centered increasingly on the Berlin police and especially on police president, Paul Markgraf.

Following its debate on November 13, the city assembly adopted a resolution stating that the police president no longer enjoyed its confidence. Most of the critical debate centered on a sense that the police remained under the SED's domination.[104] In response to critique of his initial comments in defense of the police, Friedensburg indicated that it was wrong to speak of the police as the instrument of a single party (the SED). He noted that the deputy police president and the head of the municipal police (*Schutzpolizei*) were SPD members and that the SPD received by far the largest representations in elections for worker councils.[105] While these statements were accurate, they likely understated the SED's ability to exert influence within the police. In comparison to its percentage of the Berlin population, the SED was overrepresented in the police ranks, especially in the upper echelons.[106] The SED was quite aware of that fact

---

[102] Stenographisches Bericht der 47. Sitzung der StVV, November 13, 1947, 70ff. Neumann's assertion is somewhat problematic. In many respects it reflects the tendency among many postwar socialist leaders (even those who were arrested by the Nazi regime) to restrict their representation of concentration camps to the experience of political ("antifascist") prisoners. Jeffrey Herf, "German Communism, the Discourse of 'Antifascist Resistance,' and the Jewish Catastrophe," in *Resistance against the Third Reich, 1933–1990*, Michael Geyer and John W. Boyer, eds. (Chicago and London: University of Chicago Press, 1994).

[103] Andreas-Friedrich, *Battleground Berlin*, 193.

[104] Stenographisches Bericht der 47. Sitzung der StVV, November 13, 1947.

[105] Ibid., 89. Friedensburg's assertion about the worker councils was challenged by the SED report cited in n.106.

[106] See the file Otto Winzer – Berliner Polizei, 1947, LAB, STA Rep. 120, Nr. 3249, Bl. 26. An SED report dated November 29, 1947 asserts that 18 to 20 percent of all policemen belonged to the SPD. In contrast to Mayor Friedensburg's assertion in the preceding text, this report notes that twenty of thirty-two members of the *Gesamtbetriebsrat* as well as 85 percent of the police *Betriebsgewerkschaftsleitungen* belonged to the party. In October 1946, SED members comprised 4.5 percent of the Greater Berlin population over age fourteen; in December 1948, however, this was only 4.3 percent. See the table in Hurwitz, *Die Stalinisierung der SED*, 275.

and not altogether unoptimistic about the possibilities that this provided. More significantly, though, the substantial SED presence in this critical city department reflected one of the venues in which the SED could continue to access the means of political control in the city.

SED influence within the police assumed a sinister character for individual policemen as well, serving at the least as a continuous, invasive presence that closely monitored their actions. An incident from late 1947 demonstrated this intrusiveness and hinted at even more threatening possibilities looming ominously in the background. Two reports sent to the police presidial section (to Markgraf's office) described instances of police officers who had been approached by Soviet officials about serving as informants and subsequently fled to the west sectors. The first, the copy of a lower-level report forwarded by the station chief in Lichtenberg (Soviet sector) described how the officer in question, Budack, supposedly claimed that the Soviets had ordered him to provide them with a list of all SED members, all nonmembers (presumably within the police station), and "all forces that are working against the police." When he was unable to meet the deadline for this "important assignment," Budack apparently felt threatened by the Soviet Command and reported to the police's American liaison officer. The American liaison then indicated that this was not the first such case, citing the death of one policeman and the disappearance of another that had occurred under "the same circumstances." Here it is worth mentioning that this report had been passed up the police ladder in spite of various individuals' requests that it be kept confidential and not used in any official context.[107]

In an accompanying memo, the station chief described a conversation with another policeman who had joined Budack in fleeing to the west. The officer, Liebmann, explained that he had joined the force in Lichtenberg with the expectation that his knowledge of the Russian language would allow him to advance rapidly. He soon discovered, however, that his failure to commit to the SED would prevent him from getting ahead. After he had worked in the department for some time, he was ordered to report to the Soviet liaison officer, who questioned him in detail about a medal awarded him during World War II. At a second meeting, Liebman was told that he had only received that award "because he had many Russians on his conscience" and as a result should face arrest and removal to a penal camp. Forty-five minutes later, the Soviets offered him a way out: if he

---

[107] Copy of a Report from Pietrowski to Inspektionsleiter Klepsch (Lichtenberg), dated December 8, 1947, LAB, STA Rep. 9, Nr. 89, Bl. 153.

would report which of his colleagues in the police held anti-Russian views, he could demonstrate his loyalty. After being accosted by the liaison officer's deputy in a public square and urged to take on an expanded role as an informant, Liebmann turned to the head of the Berlin Municipal Police, Hans Kanig. Kanig advised him to call in sick and no longer return to the Soviet sector.[108] The willingness of west sector police officials to find jobs and even apartments for those fleeing Soviet-sector police work earned the growing ire of eastern police officials. Both sides possessed a clear sense of opposing forces within the police administration, intensifying competition for the city's police officers even before the department split in the summer of 1948.

Other Soviet interventions were much more public, direct challenges to the ability of Berliners and their elected officials to manage their city's affairs. On December 9, the Soviet-licensed newspaper, *Tägliche Rundschau*, announced an order from the Soviet city commander dismissing Ella Kay (SPD), the district mayor of Prenzlauer Berg, for "sabotage of wood procurement efforts and provocatory behavior."[109] Less than two months earlier, the SPD district mayor of Friedrichshain had been dismissed under similar circumstances.[110] In both instances, the Soviets designated SED deputies to assume the district mayors' responsibilities. On December 11, the city assembly considered Kay's dismissal in a heated and embittered debate. Here, the resolution adopted by the majority, calling on the Magistrat to obtain an explanation of the dismissal from the Kommandatura is of much less significance than the tone of the biting polemics unleashed by both sides of the debate. Kurt Mattick (SPD) denounced the attacks on Ella Kay in SED-sponsored demonstrations and in the Soviet-licensed press:

The insults expressed there remind us all of the days, I would like to go ahead and say, of May 1929.[111] The only thing missing is the caption: strike the social-fascists

---

[108] Copy of a report from the P.-I. Lichtenberg (Klepsch) to the Polizeisektor-Assistent f. den sowj. Sektor, dated December 8, 1947, LAB, STA Rep. 9, Nr, 89, Bl. 154.

[109] *Berlin: Behauptung von Freiheit und Selbstverwaltung 1946–1948*, 364. Neither Ella Kay nor the acting mayor of Greater Berlin received this command (which was dated December 8, 1947) prior to its publication. For an account of Ella Kay's defense of her actions before international press representatives, see "Ella Kay berichtet," *Der Tagesspiegel* (December 11, 1947), 6.

[110] *Berlin: Behauptung von Freiheit und Selbstverwaltung 1946–1948*, 334.

[111] Mattick was referring to the bloody clashes on May Day 1929 in which police battled Berliners in several working-class sections of the city. The events were characterized by bitter rhetorical exchanges between the Communists and the Social Democrats. See Thomas Kurz, *"Blutmai": Sozialdemokraten und Kommunisten im Brennpunkt der*

wherever you find them. Then we'd have the old tone again. Instead of seeking a way, to carry out work cooperatively [...], a mass psychosis has apparently developed.

After noting that the Soviet Command dutifully supported the SED in Berlin, Mattick accused his opponents of acting to divide Berlin because they had proved unable to achieve their ends by democratic means.[112] In response, the SED's Otto Winzer gave a bitterly antagonistic speech in which he decried the SPD for neglecting the material interests of the Berlin population in the face of a catastrophic winter. He noted that more brown coal was coming into Berlin (from the Soviet zone) than before the war, and that the lack of hard coal could only be addressed by a decision of the Western powers. At the end of his remarks, he pointed to a legacy of "antifascism" and suffering under the Nazi regime to claim for the SED a level of moral superiority in the current political debates:

In our delegation sits Ottomar Geschke, who for 12 years was dragged through all the tortures and suffering of Hitler's concentration camps. Here sits Bruno Baum, who narrowly – (Prolonged catcalls and great disquiet.) escaped, and this faction, in which there is hardly any member, who did not suffer under Hitler; this delegation cannot be insulted by the members of a delegation, whose head is a beneficiary of Hitler's [anti-] Jewish legislation.[113]

The SPD response was equally sharp. Curt Swolinsky condemned the attacks on the various SPD district mayors, suggesting that their actions had been exemplary under the circumstances. He then unleashed a direct assault on the nature of SED politics:

I assert: we are not far from the catastrophe of 1929/30 that put Hitler in the saddle, if we allow these methods to develop further. (lively agreement from the SPD and the CDU.) Therefore, my appeal to all civilized (*gesitteten*) persons in Berlin: (applause from the SPD and the CDU) don't take part in these things; don't look only at their muzzle, look at their paws! If the émigrés[114] come and want to

Berliner Ereignis von 1929 (Berlin and Bonn: Verlag J. H. W. Dietz Nachf., 1988) and Pamela Swett, *Neighbors and Enemies: The Culture of Radicalism in Berlin, 1929–1933* (Cambridge and New York: Cambridge University Press, 2004), 120–36.
[112] Stenographisches Bericht der 50. Sitzung der StVV, December 11, 1947, 11f.
[113] Ibid., 14ff. Winzer was referring to Curt Swolinsky. The SPD leader had purchased a store from a Jewish acquaintance, who then emigrated. Swolinksky explained the case of his dealings with the storeowner (named Levy), noting that he bought the store so that his acquaintance could emigrate, expanded it, and later offered to give him a store of equal size with 20,000 RM in goods and cash. According to Swolinsky, Levy declined because he would otherwise not be master of his own affairs (p. 35).
[114] Here, referring to the German Communists who spent the years of Nazi rule in emigration in the Soviet Union.

demonstrate to us that they are the real representatives of the Berlin population, then I must say: "You could have proved that already in Hitler's time," regardless of which deserter from the front of the honest working class will speak following me. In any case, you brought on misfortune back then and then folded; and now you will do something similar. In an irresponsible fashion, you agitate the people against the functionaries of the working class, and if it winds up getting dangerous, then you'll fold just like you always have.[115]

Based on the response of the assembly's speaker who was repeatedly forced to ring his bell in a vain effort to restore order, this speech unleashed stormy applause not only among the deputies but among the crowd gathered in the balcony at the back of the hall. The head of the SED faction, Karl Litke, offered up a more calculated response to the criticisms of his party and its Soviet patrons. He pointed out that in November, the district of Weissensee brought in 9,000 cubic meters of wood with only seventy workers, but Prenzlauer Berg, with 250 to 260 persons, brought in only 8,699 cubic meters.[116] Although he admitted that Weissensee's successes came under the direction of an SPD district mayor, Litke seemed implicitly to argue that the ultimate measure of political success in the city was still to be taken in material terms, terms in which he believed the SED would eventually come out ahead.

This relative optimism likely reflected both an awareness of the continued material hardships facing Berliners and the hope that recent Soviet initiatives presented new opportunities for socioeconomic engagement outside of the structures of the city government. On October 9, the SVAG issued its Order No. 234, designed to improve industrial productivity. Among its notable initiatives was the expansion of incentive-based piece wages, the provision of a warm noon meal in selected factories, and measures to improve worker training. In Berlin, Soviet Commander General Kotikov issued a fourteen-point plan to improve the material and legal situation of workers in the city, an effort that sought to extend the material benefits of Order No. 234 to some workers in Berlin.[117] Adolf Deter, a former member of the KPD who spent the Nazi era in American exile, explained SED efforts to promote Kotikov's Fourteen Points in Berlin by

---

[115] Stenographisches Bericht der 50. Sitzung der StVV, December 11, 1947, 40.

[116] Ibid., 46.

[117] See *Berlin: Behauptung von Freiheit und Selbstverwaltung 1946–1948*, 325 and 339. Soviet Order No. 234 did not realize productivity improvements to the extent hoped for. Control reports indicated that often measures to ease working conditions were being carried out without the accompanying measures to stimulate production. See the reports submitted to the Sekretariat Lampka, BA-DDR, DC-15-764. On the contents of the Kotikow-Essen, see LAB, IV L-2/3/100.

concentrating on building worker support in the factories, but he noted that many workers reacted apathetically. They failed to see the need to rally broad support for a program that would be supported or rejected by the Soviet Command in the city. In their view, popular action was relatively immaterial.[118] In some circles at least, reaction was even more negative. Deter referred to SPD members denouncing Soviet Order No. 234 with the slogan "piecework is murder" (*Akkord ist Mord*).[119]

For the SED leadership, however, vocal popular advocacy of these new programs was critical as it sought to mobilize German workers in broad-based support of Soviet and SED economic initiatives (or at least to create the impression of such support), thereby strengthening their hand to act outside of the structures of elected government. To this end, the SED also organized supplementary citizen patrols (*Volkskontrollen*) under the administrative auspices of the FDGB to assist the police in targeting black marketeers and other criminal economic activity.[120] The planning documents emphasized the need to represent this movement as a spontaneous popular initiative: "By all means we must avoid the appearance that this initiative of the working population required official inspiration or tutelage," but any such claim concealed the careful guidance being provided by SED and Soviet officials.[121]

Yet as the London meeting of the Council of Foreign Ministers approached, SED leaders tried to burnish a facade of popular support for the party as it faced continued animosity toward its policy proposals. A report from Thuringia described even party functionaries as recognizing that "the masses don't want political speeches but rather a bearable existence." In response to pleas for more foodstuffs, fats, and clothing, the functionaries reportedly replied: "There is nothing there; only German unity can save us."[122] A report from Berlin was even more to the point. It indicated that the low point in party morale in the city could be explained by two primary factors: 1) the failure to supply local party secretariats

---

[118] See the comments by Adolf Deter in Stenographisches Bericht der 3. (17.) Parteivorstandssitzung d. ZK der SED, November 12–13, 1947, Bl. 107.

[119] See Hurwitz, *Die Stalinisierung der SED*, 392.

[120] Of course, around the same time Soviet authorities forbade the Berlin police to seize black market cigarettes of Soviet make and ordered them to return to the previous owners those already collected. See the memo from the *Gewerbeaußendienst* to the Presidial Section, dated August 25, 1947, LAB, STA Rep. 9, Nr. 223.

[121] Bemerkungen zum Entwurf über Vollkskontrolle, dated November 21, 1947, SAPMO, DY 30/IV 2/6.02/67, Bl. 19.

[122] Auszug aus den Informationen Thüringen vom 23.9.47, SAPMO, DY 30/IV 2/9.02/44, Bl. 40.

with any heating material for the winter, and 2) these same secretariats' inability to provide their employees with a supplementary warm soup.[123] Writing to the Hanover SPD in September, Erich Brost reported renewed fears about the coming winter. While praising American Military Governor Lucius Clay for doing everything possible to increase food deliveries to the city, he suggested that achieving a regular ration of 1,550 for the coming months would be a significant accomplishment.[124]

Two months later, the Berlin SPD convened an economic-political conference that voiced further concern about the ongoing material and economic crisis facing the city and called for the party to speak out more forcefully about its dissatisfaction with allied efforts to address the crisis. Focusing in particular on the problem of dismantling, these SPD officials cited worker complaints that, following initial dismantling in 1945, they had managed to cobble together production facilities out of materials that they rescued from the rubble only to see them once again targeted by occupation officials.

In his presentation, Willi Kressmann argued that the SPD needed to explain to the occupiers that the costs of the Nazi past could not just be loaded on the backs of German workers. To sustained applause, he suggested that before 1933 the SPD would not have stood idly by in the face of such actions, but now the party had become too hesitant. Referring especially to coal deliveries from British and Soviet zones, Kressmann argued that this was a problem not only for Berlin, but for Germany as a whole. But he also warned that the SPD in the British and American zones remained ambivalent about the situation in the city. "They have already written off Berlin as a Bolshevik horror. I say loud and clear: in the British and American zones, we Berliners are simply seen as 'finished'; they don't even bother to ask whether the national comrades (*Volksgenossen*) in Berlin are just starving to death (Hear! Hear!)." Although his use of the Nazified term *Volksgenosse* marked at least a striking, if unintentional, holdover from everyday practice during the Third Reich, he did appeal for maintaining German unity. He argued that tearing Germany apart undermined reconstruction and that unity was a prerequisite for any effort to reshape Berlin. In phrasing that prefigured Lucius Clay's well-known remarks in April 1948, Kressmann emphasized, "But it always seems to

---

[123] Memo from the Org.-Abt. to Franz Dahlem, et al., October 22, 1947, SAPMO, DY 30/IV 2/5/223, Bl. 257.

[124] Brost, Taetigkeitsbericht Nr. 64, 12.9.1947, AdsD, Bestand Kurt Schumacher, Mappe 165: Berliner Sekretariat des SPD-Parteivorstandes: Erich Brost-Berichte Nr. 4–84 (February 1947–January 1948).

me that, both in our own party and beyond Berlin in Germany as a whole, we have to make one thing clear: whoever abandons Berlin, abandons Germany, and if Germany is abandoned, the question of war is only a question of months or of the ongoing development in Europe."[125]

Implicitly, this characterization of Berlin's international significance also suggested that Berliners did not really control their own destiny, and that the city's economic recovery depended on shifts in great power policies. Concerned primarily about the extent to which, more than two years after war's end, the city's economy still did not function normally, most conference delegates suggested that they remained imbedded in a great power politics for which Berliners mattered only little. A few speakers suggested that whatever economic development was taking place in the city depended on the illicit deal making that workers and managers undertook to gain necessary raw materials and arrange trading contacts, but the conference as a whole rejected even tacit acceptance of an illegal (black or gray) economy. For the speakers, that, too, was tied to the realities of life under occupation control.

Kressmann referred in particular to the circulation of illegal tobacco products in the city, a problem he described as "the plundering of the Berlin economy on a scale not seen before." He explained that most of these untaxed tobacco products bore no revenue stamp and came from the Rasnoexport firm offering brands of Russian cigarettes by now familiar to Berliners: Drug, Stella, Caucasus, and others. The firm explained its sales to the price bureau, noting that Rasnoexport did not provide any cigarettes for sale in reichsmarks. For Kressmann, such sales strived only to absorb illegally circulating dollars and Swiss francs. "Rasno-Export sells a thousand cigarettes for two dollars and individual cigarettes for 1,20 M, in other words at an exchange rate of 600 reichsmark to the dollar."[126] In his wrap-up following the discussion, Kressmann expressed ambivalence about accepting Marshall Plan aid without German controls and underscored the fundamental need to pursue a unified Germany. None of the SPD leadership attended the conference, and although their discussions made clear the participants' connections to popular dissatisfaction in the city, their distance from the policy formulations of Neumann, Suhr, and Reuter was also clearly evident.

---

[125] Stenographischer Bericht: 2. Wirtschaftspolitische Konferenz d. SPD Gross-Berlin, 16.11.1947, AdsD, SPD-LV Berlin, 3/BEAB000503.

[126] In an effort to explain how dollars made their way into Berlin, Kressmann blamed a "foreign" firm, whose principal "agents" were DPs. See also Hilton, "The Black Market in Germany," and Königseder, *Flucht nach Berlin*, 181–90.

An October report to the Berlin SED attempted to describe popular sentiments toward the Russian occupiers and offered a more concrete example of the ways in which Berliners' everyday experiences intersected with broad political frameworks. After some introductory comments discussing Berliners' negative views of continued Soviet factory dismantling and their desire that the SED, too, support accepting Marshall Plan aid, the report described an SED member traveling by train to the western zones and his vigorous reaction to his fellow passengers' expressions of enthusiasm for the economic conditions there. In response to their assertions that goods were cheap there and would not be seized from them on trains, the party member protested vehemently but earned only laughter in return. When, shortly before reaching the zonal border, two Soviet soldiers came and took his watch at gunpoint, he hardly dared say anything more.[127] On the one hand, this incident underscored the limitations of the "discussions" that SED leaders repeatedly called on party members to initiate in an effort to change their opponents' political viewpoints; but it also teased out the multiple layers across which such everyday encounters necessarily functioned. At once a material loss (the watch), an interjection of (wartime) violence into the postwar period, and an explicit, physical refutation of the political and economic assertions that this SED member was making to the other travelers in his car, this incident drove home a point that the SED leadership never seemed able to grasp: the significance of ongoing material crisis never lay in its materiality alone but in the ways that postwar Germans explained what it meant.

While this moment of personal embarrassment demonstrated how everyday experience could undermine party political explanatory assertions, the SED – more even than the other parties in the city – agonized over its ability to seize control of precisely that sort of highly individualized and personal incident. In the December 2 issue of the Social Democratic paper, *Telegraf*, a brief notice announced the suicide of a student, Günther Wolf, after he had supposedly been interrogated by Soviet authorities at their headquarters in Karlshorst. Coming only a month after the disappearance of Dieter Friede, this mention was one small gesture in the SPD's campaign to highlight the risk of abduction in the city. For the SED, however, this small notice unleashed a series of investigations that highlighted

---

[127] Bericht ueber die Stimmung der Bevoelkerung der russischen Besatzungsmacht gegenueber, dated October 10, 1947, LAB, IV 4/6 – 403: Stimmungsberichte Bd. 2, January 1947 – May 1952.

a very different and more expansive kind of insecurity. Already that same morning, SED officials undertook the first efforts to gain further insights into the "Günther Wolf Case." A first call seeking information uncovered that a second student had joined Wolf in committing suicide at the Oberspree S-Bahn Station (the exact details were never reported). While Wolf is described as an SPD member, his companion is depicted as the daughter of an "SED-family" and a member of the Free German Youth (*Freie deutsche Jugend* or FDJ). The report writer explains that "according to rumors in the area" the student had received orders from the SPD to "disappear (like in the Friede case)." The next day, a phone call to the police in Treptow (Soviet sector), the district where the suicide took place, did not produce much additional information other than to report that the student's mother, who had also been in the hospital following an alleged suicide attempt, had recently been released from the hospital and questioned by the police. More striking was the report writer's comment that the investigating police officer's lack of knowledge about the *Telegraf* article meant that he failed to recognize the case's potential political fallout. A subsequent report prepared for Karl Mewis, a protégé of Walter Ulbricht in the Berlin SED, described a conspiratorial claim that Wolf had made to officials in the Wedding district (French sector) about an interrogation at Soviet headquarters in Karlshorst and an eventual escape from armed persons driving him off in an unknown direction.[128]

The most expansive account of the incident came in an interview with another student (an SED member) who identified himself as Wolf's best friend and explained the suicide as the result of a personal financial and emotional crisis. His friend described Wolf as a member of the SED who left the party for "personal reasons." After flirting with a Social Democratic student group, Wolf supposedly became politically "indifferent" and a few weeks before his death apparently confessed that he desperately needed money to repay debts he owed.[129] In the end, this seems to have been a story of personal tragedy and material desperation, but in the hypercharged ideological atmosphere of late-1947 Berlin, no political party hesitated to take on this sort of human interest story in the hopes of making a political point. For the SED in particular, the fear that its opponents might exploit any material crisis that it failed to master created an

---

[128] SED, Landesverband Groß-Berlin, Abteilung Werbung, Presse, Rundfunk, LAB, STA Rep. 120, Nr. 3249, Bl. 47–50.
[129] Protokoll, December 3, 1947, LAB, STA Rep. 120, Nr. 3249, Bl. 45–6.

almost obsessive motivation to try again and again to assert its political influence over the material terrain through which Berliners moved. Instead, material crisis provided the means with which Berliners framed their participation in the high political contest for the city, and the SED found even many of its scripted demonstrations of political power subject to frames of reference imbedded in everyday practices that remained beyond its reach.

4

March 1948: Berlin and the Struggle for the Soviet Zone

March 18, 1948 dawned cold and rainy in Berlin. Although the city government had proclaimed the 100th anniversary of the 1848 revolution an official holiday, Berliners awoke to a day that seemed ill-made for personal or political celebrations. One century earlier some 900 persons had died on Berlin's barricades, the dramatic challenge to the Prussian crown only a momentary triumph that came to symbolize the failure of German democratic possibility.[1] Commemorating that sacrifice, the Social Democratic speaker of Berlin's city assembly, Otto Suhr, began the day by unveiling a new memorial at the graves of those killed in the March 1848 revolt, emphasizing in his speech at the gravesite that this celebration marked the first time that a Berlin government had officially acknowledged those revolutionary events. A short time later, some members of the municipal government, foreign guests, and German representatives from the western zones gathered at the Städtische Oper in Berlin's British sector to listen to Paul Löbe, a Social Democrat and the former president of the German Reichstag, claim that the German people didn't need a congress or a national referendum to assert its desire for national unity.[2] The immediate object of his scorn, the People's Congress (*Volkskongress*), which the SED had organized in an effort to legitimate its claim to speak for all of Germany, was meeting in the *Admiralspalast* in the city's Soviet sector to debate the organization of a referendum on German unity and to formulate a new People's Council (*Volksrat*) that would eventually issue an East

---

[1] Hans Joachim Hahn, *The 1848 Revolutions in German-Speaking Europe* (Harlow and London: Longman, 2001), 93–4.
[2] *Berlin: Behauptung von Freiheit und Selbstverwaltung 1946–1948*, 434.

German constitution. Still cloaked by mutual protestations of German unity, the unfinished skeletons of two new German states lingered just under the surface of the day's events.

A gloomy afternoon saw competing mass demonstrations – that of the SED at the gravesite in Friedrichshain and that of the three Western parties (SPD, CDU, and LDP) in front of the ruined Reichstag building in Charlottenburg (British sector). The Standing Berlin Committee for Unity and a Just Peace – the local arm of the SED-sponsored People's Congress movement – called on workers to assemble throughout the city at 9:30 A.M. and march to a demonstration at the *Gendarmenmarkt* in the city center before continuing to the graves, farther east in the city's Soviet sector.[3] The Volkskongress interrupted its deliberations to allow delegates to participate in the event, but, according to SED Executive Committee member Erich Gniffke, most SED leaders drove to the ceremonies because of the bad weather, an ironic touch given earlier SED criticism of SPD officials' plans to reach the gravesite by car.[4] Around noon, SED cochair Wilhelm Pieck addressed a large crowd there, denouncing American monopoly capitalism and its "national socialist methods."

The Western parties' demonstration in front of the Reichstag suffered due to its separation from the actual commemorative site, but a substantial crowd attended, huddled under a sea of umbrellas, to hear speeches by leaders of the Berlin SPD, CDU, and LDP.[5] Ernst Reuter both opened and closed the event, praising the thousands assembled in the rain as evidence of Berliners' willingness to battle for freedom. He argued that their "iron will" meant the city would not succumb to the Communist tide that he described sweeping from Finland to Prague.[6] Trying to convey

---

[3] See the flyer, "Heraus zur März-Demonstration," LAB, Rep. 280 (LAZ-Sammlung), Sta.-Ort. Nr. 1230.

[4] Gniffke, *Jahre mit Ulbricht*, 298. On SED criticism of SPD plans for March 18, see the comments of Berlin SED cochair, Karl Litke, Stenographisches Bericht der 6. (20.) Parteivorstandssitzung des ZK der SED, January 14–15, 1948, SAPMO, DY 30/IV 2/1/38, Bl. 168.

[5] See Tusa, *The Berlin Airlift*, 101–2. The Tusas put the crowd at 30,000. Peter Auer asserts that there were 80,000. He notes that free public transportation and early work dismissals in municipal offices helped swell the crowd at the rainy, 4 P.M. assembly. Peter Auer, *Ihr Völker der Welt: Ernst Reuter und die Blockade von Berlin* (Berlin: Jaron Verlag, 1998), 144. In her diary, Andreas-Friedrich at least somewhat metaphorically reports equal crowds of 50,000 at the eastern and western assemblies, *Schauplatz Berlin: Tagebuchaufzeichnungen 1945 bis 1948* (Frankfurt am Main: Suhrkamp, 1984), 218–19. See also the photographs of the crowds in *Sie* (March 28, 1948), 3.

[6] "Schlußwort auf der Kundgebung der demokratischen Parteien vor dem Riechtsagsgebäude am 18. März 1948," in Ernst Reuter, *Schriften, Reden*, vol. 3, *Artikel, Briefe, Reden 1946 bis 1949*, Hans J. Reichhardt, ed. (Berlin: Propyläen Verlag, 1974), 368–9.

popular reactions to the SED-led march, one participant described for party officials an almost universal spirit of enthusiasm, even though participants came out of the experience completely soaked. The report writer argued that the unpleasant conditions contributed to the marchers' positive assessment of the event: they were amazed that so many were willing to take part in spite of the rain. "I believe that the powerful demonstration helped strengthen the confidence and belief in the party a thousand-fold."[7] That this explanation so neatly paralleled Western assessments of the Reichstag demonstration points to the ways in which leaders on both sides presumed that simply showing up produced the desired political outcome, but a confrontation among spectators listening to speeches in front of the destroyed German parliament building emphasizes the extent to which the day's speeches did not fall unchallenged on waiting ears, and the contests for and about their meanings took place well beyond any official controls.

Two members of the SED-controlled FDJ reported to the SED bureaucracy on their experiences among the crowd gathered for the demonstration in the British sector. They narrated the antagonistic responses that their commentary and even their presence provoked but, more significantly, described a scene comprised explicitly of contestation and competition. After arriving at the square in front of the Reichstag, they noted a group of about twenty persons, where one trade unionist sought to "open the eyes" of the surrounding group belonging to the Independent Trade Union Opposition (*Unabhängige Gewerkschaftsopposition* or UGO), the SPD-sponsored opposition within the central union. When they moved toward the Reichstag and began to listen to the speaker addressing the crowd, one of their group felt obligated to clarify a point – in the second sentence they heard. The comment purportedly produced a reaction from a nearby spectator, "When your elders are speaking, you should be still; if you want to agitate (*provozieren*) you'd be better off getting lost; we should smack these rascals in the chops." The report described the escalating threats that confronted these FDJ members' efforts to argue their points but also implied that they managed to exert some appeal. When three women who were about to leave noticed their FDJ badges, another bystander explained that the young people had come only to

---

Czechoslovakia's Communists had seized control of its government in a coup on February 25, 1948.

[7] Observations from the demonstration on March 18, 1948 (copy March 31, 1948), SAPMO, DY 30/IV 2/5/974, Bl. 35.

agitate, to which the women then replied that they would stick around a while longer. The report offers no comment as to whether these women sought to stand in solidarity with the youths or to witness a potentially explosive confrontation. At the end of the speech, the speaker declared that there were undoubtedly a few among the crowd that had attended the morning SED demonstration and had been sent here to disrupt the event. Two of those standing near the three FDJ members pointed them out, an acknowledgment that the report writer seemed to view with pride. Indeed, the account celebrated their accomplishments: dedication to the SED line, willingness to argue on its behalf, and fearless efforts to provoke its political opponents.

But this coding of their actions demands scrutiny. The report writer and his friends reached their decision to attend the Reichstag demonstration on the spur of the moment: "Even though it was already 17:00 hours, we thought we'd pay a visit to the Platz der Republik." This description implied that, as much as an opportunity for political activism, they sought an entertaining way to finish off their day. In their characterization of the verbal clashes with the rest of the crowd, there is an undercurrent of youthful exuberance, a kind of perverse joy in the opportunity to goad their older interlocutors. The point for the three FDJ members seemed less to change their opponents' minds than to offer a mocking perspective on their enraged responses to the youths' effective provocation.[8] It seems clear that these three youths had attended the SED demonstration that morning. Because they came from the Schöneberg district in the American sector, they spent the day moving back and forth across the sector boundaries, their efforts to make sense of the competing claims to the political symbolism of 1848 thus not imbedded in any single place. Indeed, it was precisely in their moving back and forth that the contours of the evolving contest for the city took shape.

March 1948 tends to figure as the opening scene in the act that will see the final collapse of allied cooperation in Germany and the open eruption of the Cold War in Berlin: the Soviets walked out of the ACC and a "creeping blockade" increasingly threatened Berlin's west sectors with isolation. Rather than marking a hardening of boundaries, these steps also functioned in a context of ongoing boundary crossing, and it was precisely that fact that most unnerved Soviet and especially SED officials.

---

[8] Bericht von FDJ-Genossen von der Kundgebung der SPD auf dem Platz der Republik (copy from March 31, 1948), SAPMO, DY 30/IV 2/5/1080: Reports on SPD / UGO (West Berlin), October 1947 – December 1949, Bl. 81.

Even for supporters like the three FDJ members who attended the Western demonstration on March 18, the very means with which they practiced their everyday politics reiterated just how much of that everyday eluded SED control. In its increasingly desperate efforts to reassert its authority over the terrain through which Berliners like these moved, the SED kept hoping for some kind of international *deus ex machina* to drop in and stabilize the fluid situation in and around the city. That was not to be.

A Last Chance for Resolution: The London CFM

Five months earlier, on October 17, 1947, the front page of the American sector paper, *Der Tagesspiegel*, bore the headline, "Last Chance Conference." Referring to remarks made on the current international situation by the French Foreign Minister Georges Bidault, the paper reported that on the eve of the London CFM, the Great Powers' negotiating positions were no closer.[9] In early November, James Riddleberger, an American State Department official in Berlin, presented his discussion of potential Soviet policy developments in the Soviet zone under the assumption that the London conference would fail to break the deadlock over Germany.[10] Although the diplomats crafting foreign policy held out little hope for success, the conference opened on November 25, and the delegates gathered to retread the issues over which they had stumbled so often before.

Some German leaders were working to introduce a German voice to the deliberations, and on November 9, following preparations by Berlin Deputy Mayor Ferdinand Friedensburg (CDU), a number of politicians and public figures including the former Reichstag President, Paul Löbe (SPD), met to discuss the formation of a "Forum of national representation."[11] The gathering decided to publish a political program calling for German economic unity, a central government, the drafting of an occupation statute, and the admission of German representatives to

---

[9] "'Konferenz der letzten Chance': Bidault zur internationalen Lage," *Der Tagesspiegel* (October 17, 1947), 1.

[10] Telegram from Berlin (Riddleberger) to SecState; No. 3530, November 7, 1947, in Decimal File 1945–9 from 862.00/11–147 to 862.00/2–2848, NA, RG 59, 250/38/12/4–5, box 6685.

[11] Friedensburg's memoir explicitly emphasizes the central place that the pursuit of German unity played in his political efforts. See his *Es ging um Deutschlands Einheit: Rückschau eines Berliners auf die Jahre nach 1945* (Berlin: Haude und Spenersche Verlagsbuchhandlung, 1971).

the preparatory discussions on a German peace treaty at the London Conference.[12] Löbe's efforts in particular earned him a biting rebuke from Kurt Schumacher and the SPD leadership in Hanover and Berlin, and Friedensburg's apparent willingness to compromise with the SED provoked suspicion from both inside and outside his party. SED-sponsored efforts to promote a united appeal to London from the "antifascist block" of all parties in the Soviet zone also failed when the Soviet zone CDU chief, Jakob Kaiser, refused to participate without the support of the German parties in the western zones.[13] He suggested that such competing efforts would more likely present an image of German division rather than of a unified German political will. SED cochair Wilhelm Pieck noted that opponents' attacks on the Volkskongress proved beneficial for its organizers, as it brought the event even greater publicity than it might otherwise have garnered.[14]

For the SED, the ongoing uncertainty and the lack of a German settlement also hurt the party's organizational efforts. Two months after the party convention in September, Franz Dahlem described to the party's *Parteivorstand* the real contradiction between the enthusiasm and dedication demonstrated by the convention delegates and the generally subdued mood in the rank and file. "We find, in the face of the calamity, the hunger, the material scarcity among our membership, which represents a significant part of the people, much depression and pessimism, doubt to the point of disbelief whether the party is in a position to solve the survival questions of the nation, disappointment over unkept promises."[15] In the face of such continued instability within the party, the SED again moved to broaden its base of action, looking to co-opt potential opposition (within and outside the party) as a means of defending its own access to power.

On November 26, a special session of the Parteivorstand called for the First German People's Congress for Unity and a Just Peace to meet in Berlin on December 6 and 7. Otto Grotewohl identified this undertaking as a seizure of national initiative from the "haggling bourgeois parties [.... T]he working class is picking up the national interests of Germany that are lying on the street and have been abandoned by everyone, in order to realize them for the German nation and to form a new

---

[12] *Berlin: Selbstbehauptung von Freiheit und Selbstverwaltung 1946–1948*, 346.
[13] Ibid., 350 and 354. See also Hurwitz, *Die Stalinisierung der SED*, 393.
[14] Opening remarks to the fifth meeting of the SED Parteivorstand (December 8, 1947), SAPMO, DY 30/IV 2/1/36, Bl. 14.
[15] Stenographisches Bericht der 3. (17.) Parteivorstandssitzung der SED, November 12–13, 1947, SAPMO, DY 30/IV 2/1/32, Bl. 20.

democratic Germany."[16] Although all German parties, along with "mass organizations" (FDGB, FDJ, etc.) could be represented in this new movement, the democracy in the Volkskongress was to be carefully controlled. Wilhelm Pieck noted that this decision did not represent a turn from the *Blockpolitik* in the Soviet zone in which all parties cooperated in a single "antifascist block," but rather strengthened it by establishing closer links to the working-class members of the block parties.[17] As this comment suggested, the increasingly Stalinist SED leadership (especially Wilhelm Pieck and Walter Ulbricht) sought to overcome the differences between the parties, to draw them into a single organization that, under not very subtle SED direction, would work to promote its version of a Soviet line in Germany.[18] The organizers of the Volkskongress paid careful attention to the balance of speakers and the proposed candidates for the presidium in an effort to inhibit any *impression* of SED dominance. At the same time, they endeavored to prevent the emergence of any expression opposed to the SED line. The Volkskongress voted to send a delegation to the London CFM to express the desires of the German people for "unity and a just peace" and selected a standing congressional committee to monitor the implementation of its resolutions.[19]

In Berlin, SED public opinion surveys on the Volkskongress elicited varied responses. Often people expressed only limited optimism that the new movement could prove successful and criticized the SED as a dictatorial force. They saw the idea of the Volkskongress as something positive, but only as long as it was truly an all-party undertaking. In a broader context, opinion reports about the London Conference indicated that most people saw little hope of any agreement; some spoke of the impending division of Germany, a few of a coming war.[20] For the most part, though, people continued to struggle in the midst of material conditions that showed few signs of easing. Ruth Andreas-Friedrich described how "thieves" took flowers and a small Christmas tree that she had left at the grave of a friend. The need for fuel did not even stop at cemetery walls, and international conferences did not change that fact.[21]

---

[16] Stenographisches Bericht der 4. (außerordentlichen) Parteivorstandssitzung der SED, November 26, 1947, SAPMO, DY 30/IV 2/1/33, Bl. 12.
[17] Ibid., Bl. 13.
[18] Hurwitz, *Die Stalinisierung der SED*, 396–402.
[19] Berlin (West Berlin) Landesarchiv, *Berlin: Selbstbehauptung von Freiheit und Selbstverwaltung*, 363.
[20] SED Landessekretariat (Berlin): Information on Volkskongress Movement/National Front, 1947–52, LAB, BPA, IV L-2/13/441.
[21] Andreas-Friedrich, *Battleground Berlin*, 197.

Any hopes that the CFM would accept a Volkskongress delegation proved illusory. On December 12, the British government denied entry visas to the seventeen delegates selected by the Volkskongress, noting that the CFM had not come to any agreement on the question of German representation to the council.[22] It was unable to agree on much else either. Three weeks into the conference, *Der Tagesspiegel* blamed the Soviets and their insistence on excluding the Soviet zone from the economic union emerging in the western zones because "now the struggle over the reunification of Germany has stepped from the realm of deceptive phraseology into the open field of hard economic competition."[23] At face value, the lack of a compromise on the issue of reparations proved the ultimate stumbling block in the foreign ministers' discussions, but the issue of forming a provisional German government loomed large.[24] On Monday, December 15, Soviet Foreign Minister Molotov called on the council to discuss the possibility of hearing the delegation from the Volkskongress. The Western ministers refused, drawing attention back to the issue of reparations on the agenda and asserting that the Volkskongress was not representative of the German people as a whole. By that evening, it had achieved no further progress on the reparations question and the council was adjourned with no future meeting scheduled.[25] The diplomatic path to German unity or even to a German peace treaty seemed thus to be decisively closed.

For the SED, the failure of the London Conference brought an end to the brief wave of optimism that some party members had derived from the first Volkskongress. Once again, the party found itself faced with the reality of its limited political reach. Karl Mewis asserted that many in the party had, as in October 1946, deluded themselves with overoptimism. He blamed this failure on the lack of clarity within the party on the issue of German unity and posed the rhetorical question: "Should we withdraw to one part of Germany or should we continue our policies in the Zone but unfold the banner of a struggle for national liberation in all of Germany?"[26] But this question posed a kind of false dilemma,

---

[22] Berlin (West Berlin) Landesarchiv, *Berlin: Selbstbehauptung von Freiheit und Selbstverwaltung*, 367.

[23] "Der Umweg zur Einheit: Sonderbericht für den Tagesspiegel," *Der Tagesspiegel* (December 14, 1947), 2.

[24] See Gunther Mai, *Der Alliierte Kontrollrat n Deutschland 1945–1948: Alliierte Einheit – deutsche Teilung?* Quellen und Darstellungen zur Zeitgeschichte 37 (Munich: R. Oldenbourg Verlag, 1995), 453.

[25] See "London vertagt – auf unbestimmte Zeit," *Der Tagesspiegel* (December 16, 1947), 1.

[26] Cited in Hurwitz, *Die Stalinisierung der SED*, 402.

as the SED struggled to maintain control even in its own zone, regardless of what decisions the occupiers made about reconstituting German unity.

The Collapse of Four-Power Administration in a Soviet Zone Context

Two days after the demonstration on the Platz der Republik, the ACC gathered in the former Prussian Supreme Court Building just a few miles to the south. Six months later, demonstrators would march south from the same square, heading down Friedrich Ebert Strasse and Potsdamer Strasse to deliver a petition to the three Western powers still remaining in the ACC. On March 20, the Soviet Military Governor, Marshall Vasilii Sokolovskii, started the last meeting he would ever attend by demanding that his Western colleagues provide him a full accounting of the ongoing London six-power talks on Germany. Since February 23, officials of Britain, France, and the United States, along with representatives of the three Benelux states, had been meeting to formulate new economic and political strategies for Germany's western zones.[27] When the Western military governors replied that they must first consult with their governments, Sokolovskii read a brief statement, declared the meeting adjourned, and led his delegation from the room.[28] In his remarks, Sokolovskii noted that the actions of the Western Allies underscored that the "Control Council no longer exists as an organ of ultimate authority in Germany."[29] Although the ACC's coordinating committee continued to meet and the four military governors would later gather to discuss the evolving Berlin crisis, the Soviet walkout marked the de facto end of the ongoing four-power administration in Germany.

More than a miscalculated effort to forestall the formation of a West German state (which, according to this line of reasoning, was quickly followed by the blockade as a truly last gasp effort), this walkout offered Western occupiers a welcome opportunity to proceed with plans for a

[27] The London Conference continued in two sessions until June 1948. Its decisions included such critical steps as the acceptance of the western zones into the Marshall Plan and the determination of an international agency to control the Ruhr industrial area. Most important, however, was its recommendation to proceed with the creation of a West German state. Shlaim, *The United States and the Berlin Blockade*, 33–4. See also Kleßmann, *Die doppelte Staatsgründung*, 166.

[28] See Shlaim, *The United States and the Berlin Blockade*, 113ff. For a detailed and insightful examination of the ACC in Germany, see Mai, *Der Alliierte Kontrollrat*.

[29] For the text of Sokolovskii's remarks, see Ministerstvo Inostrannykh Del SSSR, *Sovietskii Soiuz i Berlinskii Vopros (Dokumenty)* (Moscow: Gospolitizdat, 1948), 22–5.

separate West German state and currency without having to shoulder public blame for dividing Germany.[30] But this perspective runs the risk of focusing too much on developments pointing toward the creation of West Germany and neglecting the situation facing the Soviets and their German allies on the ground in the eastern zone.[31] For the SED, the ACC's collapse did not come as a total surprise. In January, SED leaders discussed the impending demise of the ACC and tried to decipher the political context in which such a rupture would occur. Speaking to the SED Parteivorstand, Otto Grotewohl specifically linked the situation in Berlin to a paralyzed ACC. He referred to an article in *Tägliche Rundschau* that called for Berlin no longer to be "an object of the politics of division and a focus of intrigues."

Grotewohl suggested that the question of Berlin reflected a broader symbolic debate on the future shape of Germany under allied occupation: "Is Berlin a territory under four-power occupation and the capital of Germany according to the occupation regulations or a city in the Soviet zone of occupation?"[32] Berlin's presumed connection to the Soviet zone explained its importance for the SED's continued imaginings of a unified German future. Grotewohl optimistically concluded his remarks by asserting that the fate of Germany did not lie in the hands of the ACC. Rather, he claimed for the SED the role of speaking "the decisive word for the future of Germany."[33] These remarks implicitly expressed the SED's confidence in its ability (with Soviet assistance) to formulate the power structures of postwar Germany and underscored the importance of Berlin for these plans. The ACC's collapse accelerated the erosion of German-wide political opportunities and suggested that the SED's struggle to assert control over the Soviet zone now mattered even more.

Almost immediately, the *international* resonance of the Soviet walkout seemed to matter most. Two days after Sokolovskii's abrupt departure from the ACC, the independent-minded Berlin newspaper, *Der Kurier*, ran a banner headline across its front page, "Berlin and Trieste – Focal

---

[30] American Military Governor Lucius Clay countered suggestions that the Western powers offer to reconvene the ACC by emphasizing that they were unlikely to receive a better opportunity to exit the body without significant political damage. See Mai, *Der alliierte Kontrollrat*, 469.

[31] Carolyn Eisenberg very effectively elaborates the lack of any real American or British interest in pursuing a unified Germany. See Eisenberg, *Drawing the Line*, 485ff.

[32] Stenographisches Bericht der 6. (20.) Parteivorstandssitzung d. ZK der SED, January 14–15, 1948, SAPMO, DY 30/IV 2/1/38, Bl. 35–6.

[33] Ibid., Bl. 40.

Points of World Politics."[34] The next day, the same paper wondered about the specific motivations for the Soviet action. Citing American sources, the paper suggested that the Soviet action was either a pretense seeking to force a stop to Western plans to consolidate the three western zones of Germany or a prelude to Soviet plans to create a separate eastern German state. We should be cautious about too quickly conflating these two motivations. If we fail to take seriously the real crisis facing Soviet and SED control efforts within the Soviet zone, we risk subordinating all actions undertaken east of the Elbe to a set of Western initiatives that ultimately serve as the primary explanatory reference. The article continued in the same vein, noting that these American sources presumed that the Soviets would exert every effort to force the Western Allies from Berlin. But the motivations for these new control measures should not be reduced to that single goal.[35]

Beginning on April 1, a series of new Soviet directives went into effect to further regulate transportation in and out of Berlin as well as between Berlin and the western zones. Attention has most often focused on the rather sensational cases of American and British military trains that were halted on the zonal border and the battle over Soviet access to check the passengers and freight carried by these trains.[36] Certainly, these inflammatory incidents merit attention, as do allied debates about the proper response. It *is* accurate to view such steps as intentional harassment of the Western Allies' access to Berlin and as at least symbolic challenges to the Western occupational presence in the city.[37] Nevertheless, these control measures functioned even more significantly to shape the Soviet zone and *its* relationship to Berlin.

The announcement to the western military governors (very late on March 30) of "supplementary regulations" on traffic between Berlin and the western zones was not the only new measure introduced by the Soviets.[38] District military commanders in Berlin's Soviet sector issued oral directives to the district mayors to carry out expanded controls on traffic across sector boundaries. Although these controls lasted only forty-eight

---

[34] "Berlin und Trieste – Brennpunkte der Weltpolitik," *Der Kurier* (March 22, 1948), 1.

[35] "Vorwand oder Vorspiel?," *Der Kurier* (March 23, 1948), 1.

[36] See, e.g., Tusa, *The Berlin Airlift*, 106ff and Haydock, *City under Siege*, 125–7.

[37] See the positive Soviet assessment of the impact that these restrictions were having on the German population's view of the Western powers discussed in Mikhail Narinsky, "The Soviet Union and the Berlin Crisis, 1948–9," Gori and Pons, eds., *The Soviet Union and Europe in the Cold War, 1943–53*, 64.

[38] Although in most accounts it often seems to be. See Tusa, *The Berlin Airlift*, 106ff.

hours (April 1 and 2), they produced significant shock among Berliners.[39] The Soviets also ordered police in the state of Brandenburg to carry out similar controls on goods being transported into and out of Berlin.[40] In its description of the impact of the various new measures, *Tägliche Rundschau* wrote of an "expansion of interzonal traffic."[41] At the same time, Soviet zone officials expressed dismay about the scope of interzonal contact already taking place, contacts that quite explicitly escaped their administrative control. Prior to the announcement of new control measures, the Soviet-licensed press had denounced the invasion of the Soviet zone by hungry hordes from the western zones and the illegal removal of an industrial plant from Berlin. Yet, this rhetoric of the "plundering" of the Soviet zone appeared not only in the press but in internal correspondence. The Brandenburg police order to expand the scope of the vehicle checkpoints that comprised the "Ring around Berlin" explained this step as necessary to guarantee the food supply for the Soviet zone.[42] This order referred not to isolated acts of harassment or short-term shows of force but to an essentially permanent regime of control measures designed to (re)assert control over trade to and from the Soviet zone. In this sense, the *Tägliche Rundschau* headline of April 1 was not wholly inaccurate. The political and economic organs of the Soviet zone did desire expanded trade relationships with the western zones if for no other reason than to help support its sputtering economic development.[43] However, it was absolutely critical that these contacts take place under close supervision of the responsible official bodies and, hence, under the tight control of the SED.

---

[39] See the city assembly debate of this topic, Stenographisches Bericht der 64. Sitzung der Stadtverordnetenversammlung, April 15, 1948, 12ff.

[40] MdI Brandenburg, Abt. Polizei: Befehl Nr. 2 – Aktion Ring, 1.4.1948, Brandenburgisches Landeshauptarchiv (BLHA), Ld. Br. Rep. 203, VP, Nr. 102, Bl. 148.

[41] "Erweiterung des Interzonenverkehrs: Zusätzliche Bestimmungen zum Regime an der Demarkationslinie und an den Verbindungswegen zwischen den Zonen," *Tägliche Rundschau* (April 1, 1948), 1.

[42] Volkspolizei Operativstab, Tagesmeldungen, BLHA, Ld. Br. Rep. 203, VP, Nr. 51, Bl. 462. This point counters somewhat American assessments of these descriptions as merely a "propaganda campaign." See the secret memo from Robert Murphy to the Secretary of State (April 1, 1948) in U.S. Department of State, *Foreign Relations of the United States 1948*, vol. II, *Germany and Austria* (Washington, DC: U.S. Government Printing Office, 1973), 884.

[43] Naimark, *The Russians in Germany*, 193 and Wolfgang Zank, *Wirtschaft und Arbeit in Ostdeutschland 1945–1949: Probleme des Wiederaufbaus in der Sowjetischen Besatzungszone Deutschlands*, Studien zur Zeitgeschichte 31 (Munich: R. Oldenbourg Verlag, 1987), 18–29.

A series of April reports for the district office of the SED in Prenzlauer Berg emphasized the intensity with which the new control measures were being discussed in the population. One party member who worked for the Berlin transportation authority reported that his colleagues did not support the new restrictions, seeing in them a step toward hardened borders and the ultimate division of Germany. Most significantly, the report emphasized that it was impossible to make clear to these persons that the new control measures were directed only against "reactionaries and black marketeers."[44] An SED member with the city gas works reported that workers there welcomed the intensified border controls. They saw them as an "effective means to combat the black market" and "secure democracy in the eastern zone."[45] A chauffeur agreed, asserting that something had to be done to "defend Berlin from being plundered." But a student reported that twenty-six of the thirty-two students at Berlin's Municipal Building Academy saw the Soviet measures as a "provocation."[46] Moving beyond these broad evaluations that – whether positive or negative – seemed to accept at face value the assertion of rigorous new controls, some other comments offered a more nuanced assessment of the control mechanisms. An SPD member from Reinickendorf (French sector) suggested that the measures had impacted the black market but also the economy more generally, which largely depended on black market purchases of scarce materials. Another person admitted that black marketeers had received an initial shock but that their prices had shot up and they had sought out new routes to move their goods.[47]

In these reports, any positive sentiment about combating the black market found its counter in a thread of outrage and insecurity, a belief that control measures often became instruments of injustice. For one report writer, the complaints and sense of outrage reflected the fundamental problem that people see everything "solely from the perspective of the cooking pot."[48] Thus some SED members pointed to recent press reports about the seizure of 580 hundredweight of potatoes in the state of Brandenburg, reacting with particular outrage to the fact that the potatoes were subsequently handed over to farmers at no cost to be used for seed – in effect

---

44 SED Kreisleitung Prenzlauer Berg, Report of April 5, 1948, LAB, BPA IV, 4/6/402.
45 SED Kreisleitung Prenzlauer Berg, Undated report, LAB, BPA IV, 4/6/402.
46 Stimmen der Bevölkerung zu den Massnahmen der SMA (April 9, 1948), LAB, BPA IV, 4/6/402.
47 SED Kreisleitung Prenzlauer Berg, Reports April 15, 1948, LAB, BPA IV, 4/6/402.
48 "Abzug der Westmächte aus Berlin etc. Stimmungsbericht aus Sachsen" (Berlin, April 4, 1948), LAB, BPA IV, 4/6/403.

rewarding the same people who had earned high black market profits by selling them in the first place. Similarly, a critique of the *Volkskontrollen* in Brandenburg compared them unfavorably to those in Thuringia and Saxony, which lacked the "draconian and robber-like" flavor of actions that Berliners encountered in the areas surrounding the city, thereby investing with a criminal flavor the SED-organized measures whose ostensible goal was to rein in the illicit behavior of black marketeers.[49]

This popular inversion of licit and illicit behavior assumes even greater significance to the extent that it puts at least some blame for this threatening behavior at the feet of the Soviet occupiers. In trying to explain the general antipathy toward the Soviet occupiers and the tendency of most people – even in the Soviet zone – to hold the Western occupiers in high regard, one report emphasized that the "side effects" of the arrival of Soviet troops cannot be forgotten. In many locales, the onset of darkness forced people from the streets. Nighttime attacks and robberies were still the norm, and "even if in most cases no members of the Russian occupation forces were involved but rather German civilians or Germans in Russian uniforms, people still claim, it was the Russians!"[50] Widespread discussions of new Soviet troop deployments in the areas around Berlin only heightened this sense of insecurity. One report writer explained how the dominant popular view described these troops as "Mongols" and emphasized new rumors about the rapes that these troops had already carried out. "It is just like it was during the attack on Berlin."[51]

American military government officials did not convey this sense of the events in their reports to Washington. For them, it was not the Soviet zone but the Western Allies that remained the focus of Soviet policy. In an April 8 airgram to the secretary of state, the U.S. Political Advisor to Germany, Robert Murphy, drew a portrait of an intense international struggle centered on Berlin. He reported that the Soviet Commander of Berlin, General Kotikov, allegedly stated following the last ACC meeting on March 20 "that 'the battle for Berlin has begun.'" He supposedly added "that the day would soon come when the western Powers would be in Berlin 'only as tolerated guests.'" Murphy's source also claimed that "Soviet-Communist circles" spoke of Berlin as a "political Stalingrad" but given the "uncertain attitude of the Americans, [. . .] it [was] still not

---

[49] "Stimmungsbericht! Meinungen unserer Genossen!" SED Kreisleitung Prenzlauer Berg (April 26, 1948), LAB, BPA IV, 4/6/402.

[50] "Abzug der Westmächte aus Berlin etc. Stimmungsbericht aus Sachsen" (Berlin, April 4, 1948), LAB, BPA IV, 4/6/403.

[51] "Stimmungsbericht aus der Öffentlichkeit!" (April 26, 1948), LAB, BPA IV, 4/6/402.

entirely clear who [would] win the battle."[52] Nonetheless, this source indicated, the SED believed that the Western Allies would be forced to retreat from Berlin. Murphy went on to assert "that the new Soviet regulations to control traffic between Berlin and the western zones should be interpreted against this apparent background of Soviet-Communist ambitions and expectations"; that is, they reflected "Soviet-Communist" strength. Earlier in his assessment, Murphy offered a somewhat more nuanced take on these same transportation restrictions. He explained them as part of an effort "to render Berlin untenable for the western Powers" but also suggested that they were conceived "to help seal off the [Soviet zone] from the 'reactionary' influences of the [western zones]."[53] While this additional motivation remained almost entirely absent from the broad conclusions Murphy drew in the latter portion of this airgram, it offered a more accurate picture of the extent to which, even in the Soviet zone, political and especially economic affairs still eluded Soviet and SED control.

Trade Union Elections in Berlin

In Berlin, the SPD's refusal to join the Communists in the SED in April 1946 and the SED's decisive defeat in the election the following October challenged Communist leaders' 1945 assumptions that they would be able to translate their early access to the municipal administration and sweeping Soviet support into a decisive position of political power. Faced with this lack of popular electoral support, the SED sought to defend what its leaders had thought to be the structural preconditions for political power: a powerful presence within the municipal administration, control of the countryside surrounding Berlin, and control of the trade unions. Given the trade unions' role in distributing additional sources of food and clothing to its members, the SED's dominant place in union leadership provided it access to more than political influence or even economic bargaining power. It provided a direct channel to the mechanisms that oversaw many of the supplemental material supply networks on which union workers

---

[52] The image of Berlin as a new Stalingrad appeared again later that summer in a photograph caption in the SED party organ. Around a photograph of a dead horse in front of a bombed out building, the paper suggested that the destruction of Stalingrad in 1943 would be the result of SPD calls to defend "German freedom" in Berlin. The article directly equated the pronouncements of SPD leader Ernst Reuter to those of Josef Goebbels at the time of the Battle of Stalingrad. See *Neues Deutschland* (July 14, 1948), 4.

[53] Airgram from U.S. Political Advisor for Germany; No. A-269; April 8, 1948 (mailed 4/14/48), NA, RG 84 350/57/18/02, box 215.

depended. While these supplemental disbursements of fresh vegetables,
potatoes, and other scarce goods did not necessarily translate into control
over workers, even the SED's opponents viewed this control as a critical
element of SED power in the city, a fact that helps to explain the attention
union voting received from Western politicians and occupation officials.

Trade union elections took place in Berlin throughout March. With
the aid of convoluted voting methods, the SED had been able to maintain
ongoing dominance of the central trade union organization, the FDGB,
in Berlin as well as in the Soviet zone.[54] In this round of voting, however,
the SED felt its supremacy more seriously challenged. The SPD-led UGO
had emerged as a formidable force especially in some of the city's largest
industrial unions. Hermann Schlimme, one of the FDGB leaders in Berlin,
reported to the SED Executive Committee that the three Western occupiers
were actively supporting an open and aggressive campaign against the
SED.[55] He explained this support by stating: "The trade union election
is after all not just a union affair but has become a great international
political question; now in Berlin, the great dispute will be settled to prove
to what extent the SED has influence among the workers. We have, I
would like to say, already anticipated to some degree the struggle for
German unity." At the very least, Schlimme suggested that the trade union
elections served as a shorthand assessment of SED political potential that
might also resonate beyond the city. More broadly, he denounced the
Marshall Plan – which the United States Senate had endorsed just a few
days earlier – as a worldwide assault on trade unions and warned that
its material promises could provide some enticement to trade unionists,
but he continued to express confidence that the SED would retain the
absolute majority in the trade union councils.[56] The Soviet-licensed press
also expressed confidence in light of early returns, anticipating that the
UGO would receive only 15 percent of the vote. According to the *Tägliche
Rundschau*, daily resolutions of support had been pouring in from worker

[54] The SPD's complaints about unfairness of the election procedures centered on two
components: the lack of direct elections (representation was selected by a multitiered
delegate system) and the failure to permit the party designation of candidates on the ballots. See Schlegelmilch, *Hauptstadt in Zonendeutschland*, 237–42. For the election rules
for the March elections, see Vorstandssitzungen d. FDGB (Groß-Berlin): Materialien,
1947–50, SAPMO, DY 34/21738.
[55] Stenographisches Bericht der 8. (22.) Parteivorstandssitzung der SED, March 20, 1948,
SAPMO, DY 30/IV 2/1/42, Bl. 49. Schlimme especially noted the creation of "new newspapers" that had been formed to combat the SED in the trade unions. Here, he was
referring to the UGO paper *Das Freie Wort – Wochenzeitung für Gewerkschafts- und
Sozialpolitik*, which began publishing on March 5.
[56] Ibid., Bl. 49ff.

assemblies around the city, suggesting that the UGO would face a debacle that put the lie to its claims to popular support.[57]

The actual results did not reflect this optimism. In spite of huge obstacles presented to opposition candidates in the city's Soviet sector, the UGO managed to win 280 of the 573 delegates.[58] Although SED loyalists thus managed to maintain an overall majority of delegates to the district union convention, the UGO made major inroads in some of the most important unions as well as in district councils in the western sectors. Berlin FDGB head, Roman Chwalek, sent a gloomy assessment of the results to Wilhelm Pieck and other SED leaders. In his report, Chwalek explained the UGO's successes not as the result of anti-SED propaganda but rather as a product of widespread weaknesses in the SED's work in the unions and in the factories in general. Almost universally, he asserted, SED trade union leaders radically underestimated UGO strength in their firms, often claiming that *no* UGO members could be found there. Particularly disturbing for Chwalek were telegraph workers that prior to 1933 had comprised Communist bastions but now gave the UGO an overwhelming majority of their votes.[59] That even the most "radical" centers of Weimar-era trade union activism increasingly rejected SED direction underscored the party's widespread lack of appeal. Although the SED would manage to hold onto its leadership positions at the FDGB delegate conference in May, Chwalek described the SED position in critical unions as one of disorganized retreat. At that citywide delegate conference in May, the UGO proved unable to overcome the entrenched SED forces in the leadership positions, and, after several futile attempts to challenge the makeup of the union's ruling board, the opposition forces left the assembly. This step marked the definitive rupture of the unified trade union and the first split of a postwar institution into two halves, one westward and one eastward leaning.[60]

When trade union voting in Berlin came up for discussion in the SED Parteivorstand, Franz Dahlem linked the party's failures in Berlin to its

---

[57] "Starke Mehrheit für gewerkschaftseinheit: Nur 15 Prozent UGO-Stimmen in Berlin," *Tägliche Rundschau* (March 11, 1948), 2.

[58] Detlev Brunner, *Sozialdemokraten im FDGB: von der Gewerkschaft zur Massenorganisation, 1945 bis in die frühen 1950er Jahre* (Essen: Klartext Verlag, 2000), 276. See also Ulrich Gill, *Der Freie Deutsche Gewerkschaftsbund (FDGB): Theorie – Geschichte – Organisation – Funktionen – Kritik* (Opladen: Leske und Budrich, 1989), 158–60.

[59] Vorläufige Einschätzung der Gewerkschaftswahlen (dated April 13, 1948), SAPMO, NY 4036/728, Bl. 208. For an initially (and inanely) positive assessment of the elections, see the report by Karl Fugger, SAPMO, DY 30/IV 2/5/32.

[60] The stenographic record of the conference provides a gripping account of the rhetorical battle fought on the conference floor. Stenographisches Bericht der 3. Delegierten-Konferenz des FDGB Gross-Berlin am 21., 22. und 23. Mai 1948, SAPMO, DY 34/2226.6.

shortcomings in the Soviet zone.[61] Berlin served as the point at which the Western occupation powers – and perhaps even more importantly, the SPD – most directly confronted Soviet and SED politics and rhetoric but also the one site in which the SED could directly compete against its political foes. Recognizing the seriousness of the challenge, the SED sought to deploy its version of this contest in an explanatory framework that it hoped would resonate far beyond the city.

On March 12, *Tägliche Rundschau* carried a story on its front page headlined, "Hitler Methods of USA-Officials: Fear of German Unity: Military Police Occupy SED Offices in the Berlin Districts of Kreuzberg, Tempelhof, and Neukölln – Protest in the City Assembly." The article went on to describe how American military police (MPs) temporarily closed SED party offices in these three districts of the American sector. According to the article, these authorities made copies of much material, especially that having to do with the trade union elections and the movement for German unity.[62] The American officials were apparently searching for a pamphlet titled "Gangsters at Work" that contained offensive assertions about the U.S. military government.[63] This incident most likely represented little more than a minor escalation in the ongoing clash between the American military government in Berlin and a party that it saw as a Soviet instrument, but the SED sought to deploy it as a much more public issue and utilize it as a device to mobilize popular support behind its initiatives. For the party leadership, the American decision to raid the

---

[61] Stenographisches Bericht der 10. (24.) Parteivorstandssitzung der SED, May 12–13, 1948, SAPMO DY 30/IV 2/1/46, Bl. 98.

[62] "Hitlermethoden der USA-Behoerden: Angst vor der Einheit Deutschlands: Militaerpolizei besetzt SED-Büros in den Berliner Bezirken Kreuzberg, Tempelhof udn Neukölln – Protest in der Stadtverordnetenversammlung" and "Eigenartige Motivierung Oberst Howleys," *Tägliche Rundschau* (March 12, 1948), 1. An interesting exchange took place within the Kriminalpolizei in response to criticism that German policemen participated in these raids. Apparently, two German police officers had been requested to accompany an American officer. Documents from the Kripo assert that they did not actively participate and had no knowledge ahead of time as to the nature of the operation, an assertion that points quite tellingly to the need of all German organs in Berlin to juggle their obligations to competing occupation officials. LAB, STA Rep. 9, Nr. 243, Bl. 166ff.

[63] The pamphlet in question, "Gangster am Werk," can be found in English translation in a letter from Robert Murphy to Charles Bohlen (March 19, 1948), NA RG 84 350/57/18/01, box 9 (Dept. B). The *Tägliche Rundschau* sought to legitimize the existence of this pamphlet in a brief article a few days later. It argued that the pamphlet was based on reports of American journalists and not (as Radio in the American Sector or RIAS reported) lies. It referred to a report from Tom Agoston (International News Service) about the murder of the "red-haired queen of the German underworld" and the accompanying scandal for U.S. military forces. See *Tägliche Rundschau* (March 17, 1948), 1.

SED's offices helped to validate its assertions of relevance and power: if American occupation officials felt it necessary to target the party's offices, these leaders seemed to argue, the SED and its ongoing endeavors must have constituted a real threat – a perspective that ironically paralleled the alarmist assessments of many American anti-Communists.

The same day as the raids on the party offices, Berlin SED heads Hermann Matern and Karl Litke sent a letter to Soviet Commander Kotikov outlining their version of events; the other commanders also received a copy at the next day's Kommandatura meeting. *Tägliche Rundschau* reported an open resolution from the employees of several major firms who protested the allegedly close link between these police raids and the upcoming People's Congress.[64] While undoubtedly organized by the SED, such a declaration at least provided the facade of popular support to the party's protests. The city assembly unanimously adopted the SED's proposal criticizing the U.S. search of SED offices in the American sector but only after adding an amendment calling for an end to all measures that hampered the work of the democratic parties in the Soviet sector. In response to this addition, the SED refrained from voting on the final measure.[65] The party's effort to translate the event into political capital had, not surprisingly, slipped from its control. For a party that Berliners continued to link to the brutal excesses of the Soviet forces that took the city at the end of the war and, more recently, with arrests and abductions in the city and the reestablishment of concentration camps in the Soviet zone, SED critiques of American MP "terror" had only limited traction.

In a radio interview on March 12, Litke and Matern sought to reposition the event in the popular imagination, noting that the U.S. action was likely due to the incoming results of the trade union elections or perhaps even in response to the ongoing city assembly debate on the political control of the police. They emphasized that the Berlin population would provide a rousing response to the Americans when it turned out for a

---

[64] Letter from the SED Landesvorstand Gr.-Berlin to the AK (Kotikov) regarding U.S. raids on SED offices in Tempelhof and Neukölln, dated March 11, 1948, LAB, BPA, IV L-2/10/410. Also "Gegen Polzeiterror im US-Sektor: Jelisarow fordert Bestrafung der Schuldigen – Massenprotest der Berliner Werktätigen," *Tägliche Rundschau* (March 13, 1948), 1.

[65] Stenographisches Bericht der 58. Sitzung der Stadtverordnetenversammlung, March 11, 1948. The *Tägliche Rundschau* reported only a unanimous vote of protest against the American searches. "Hitlermethoden der USA-Behoerden," *Tägliche Rundschau* (March 12, 1948), 1.

massive demonstration on March 18. The *Tägliche Rundschau* repro-
duced Matern's argument that Berlin workers possessed a "keen sense for
the fact that police actions are first directed against left-leaning parties in
order to later turn on the entire working class."[66] Thus, he equated the
American actions to those of the Weimar Republic in the period leading
up to the Nazi seizure of power and, in this vein, called upon Berliners to
join in the March 18 commemorations (and by extension in the People's
Congress Movement). An editorial in the same edition of the *Tägliche
Rundschau* that reported the interview drew the link even more overtly:

In recent days the nerves of the power holders in the American sector have apparently frayed altogether. We don't know whether the People's Congress or the trade
union elections are to blame, or whether it's the general political development that
is causing it; thanks to the Anglo-American politics, the Control Council is becoming more and more of a shadow entity, a fact that naturally must have a fundamental and readily perceptible impact on the situation in Berlin. It is possible that all
of this worked together to cause them to take off the kid gloves but also to ignore
the most elementary legal guarantees and the obligations assumed in the spirit of
four-power administration and to carry out attacks in true gestapo fashion on the
SED's district offices in the working class districts of the American sector.[67]

This linking of American forces to the gestapo marked a rhetorical high
point in ongoing Soviet and SED efforts to equate events in Berlin to
those of the recent Nazi past. Yet, the Soviet-controlled paper's compar-
isons pointed to something more than mere propagandistic flourish. It
consciously juxtaposed Berlin, German, and international forces at work
in this single incident, making a case for an interconnected chain of cau-
sation, for which Berlin politics were much more than an object of larger
battles. For the SED, this rhetoric helped to define a space that moved
beyond the constraints of occupation authority but also pointed to the
international significance of the party's efforts in Berlin. To the extent
that these assertions of (local) power transcended the definitions of occupation authority (the claim to have elicited a Nazi-like response certainly
imbedded the party's power struggles in an expanded temporal but also
German-specific context), these public framings helped to position the
SED in a battle for power that did not operate only according to the stip-
ulations of four-power occupation. But these assertions of broad influence
proved illusory.

---

[66] "Litke und Matern über die Hintergründe," *Tägliche Rundschau* (March 13, 1948), 1.
[67] "Thema des Tages," *Tägliche Rundschau* (March 13, 1948), 3.

The SED Campaign for the Soviet Zone

While SED leaders depicted the Volkskongress as a means to build on a general desire for greater "German" participation in allied efforts to craft a postwar settlement, those outside the SED had only criticism for a measure they decried as a thinly veiled front for an SED effort to hijack the real popular desire for a unified and independent German state. More significantly for the SED, the Volkskongress came at a point of growing disillusionment within the party, and many SED members – in both the leadership and the rank and file – perceived the effort as an attempt to move beyond merely defensive political survival tactics and hoped that it might foreshadow a possible movement for democracy both in the party and beyond.[68] On December 8, 1947, one day after the first Volkskongress, the SED Parteivorstand discussed the steps necessary to build on the "successes" of the gathering. Franz Dahlem, the onetime political head of the International Brigades during the Spanish Civil War, warned that these initial successes would unleash a propaganda offensive from their opponents and called for decisive efforts to help the SED stay on the offensive in order to act aggressively to influence the shape of political struggle within Germany:

[...] we adopted the line at the Congress that the working class, represented in the eastern zone by the SED, must assume and maintain leadership; in the face of the opponents' attacks and opposition, we cannot isolate ourselves but must penetrate deep into the other parties. I would like to refer to the example of the penetration of [other] parties' ranks in the eastern zone to demonstrate the current task to the responsible comrades in the West.[69]

Here, Dahlem outlined an approach that encompassed much more than party politics, emphasizing the SED's need to fight its battles not just in legislative bodies or public forums but *within* competing parties. He especially singled out the SPD in Berlin and the industrial Ruhr area as important targets for such efforts. By this time, the "independence" of the "bourgeois" parties in the Soviet zone had largely disappeared. Both the CDU and the LDP existed in the Soviet zone but found their room for maneuver strictly constrained by Soviet authorities. Following their refusal to

---

[68] Hurwitz, *Die Stalinisierung der SED*, 393–5.
[69] Stenographisches Bericht der 5. (19.) Parteivorstandssitzung d. ZK der SED, December 8, 1948, SAPMO, DY 30/IV 2/1/36, Bl. 43–4. On the CDU in particular, see Norman M. Naimark, "The Soviets and the Christian Democrats: The Challenge of a 'Bourgeois' Party in Eastern Germany, 1945–1949," *East European Politics and Societies* 9, no. 3 (Fall 1995), 369–92.

support the People's Congress movement, the CDU leaders Jakob Kaiser and Ernst Lemmer were dismissed in late December 1947. The death of LDP leader Wilhelm Külz in April 1948 insured that that party's leadership also stood ready to cooperate with the SED.[70] Because the SPD had ceased to exist in the Soviet zone following its forcible union with the Communists in April 1946, only in Berlin did the two "socialist" parties find themselves in direct competition.[71] Dahlem's remarks suggested that the SED's pursuit of political control within the Soviet zone offered a model for its evolving assault on the SPD in Berlin. But the struggle in Berlin also mattered – both symbolically and materially – for SED efforts in the Soviet zone.

Richard Weimann, an SED member from Berlin, emphasized the importance of that city for the "national" movement the party sought to unleash. He called for the People's Congress to utilize the 100th anniversary of the 1848 Revolution to help mobilize support for German unity. In this he urged it to differentiate between the March anniversary of the uprising in Berlin and the May anniversary of the Frankfurt Assembly.[72] He sought thus to distinguish not only 1848's revolutionary component from its parliamentary component but to contrast emerging western German political structures (centered in Frankfurt) and those sponsored by the SED in Berlin. Although the SED contributed financially to the May anniversary celebrations at the Paulskirche in Frankfurt am Main, the party essentially asserted that 1848 meant 1848 *in Berlin*.[73] In the same way, it claimed Berlin as the defining location of 1948 Germany. Given the SED's tenuous position in the city, this assertion was not without risk.

Speaking to the Executive Committee at its January meeting, Otto Grotewohl suggested that the division of Germany was no longer in doubt. Reiterating the party leadership's optimistic vision that the Volkskongress

[70] See Weber, *DDR*, 27–9.

[71] On the competition between the SPD and the KPD and later the SED, see Harold Hurwitz, *Demokratie und Antikommunismus in Berlin nach 1945*, vol. 4, *Die Anfänge des Widerstands* (Cologne: Verlag Politik und Wissenschaft, 1990); Beatrix Bouvier, *Ausgeschaltet!: Sozialdemokraten in der sowjetischen Besatzungszone und in der DDR, 1945–1953* (Bonn: Dietz, 1996); and Malycha, *Die SED*.

[72] Stenographisches Bericht der 5. (19.) Parteivorstandssitzung d. ZK der SED, December 8, 1948, SAPMO, DY 30/IV 2/1/36, Bl. 49.

[73] Stenographisches Bericht der 10. Parteivorstandssitzung d. ZK der SED, March 26–7, 1947, SAPMO, DY 30IV 2/1/18. For eleven months beginning in May 1848, a German national assembly met in the Frankfurt am Main Paulskirche. See, e.g, James J. Sheehan, *German History 1770–1866*, Oxford History of Modern Europe (Oxford: Clarendon Press, 1993), 672–91.

might set the national agenda for German political life, he asserted, "We are faced with the fact that we as a party must reach decisions [...] that make the issues of the national movement we have initiated the issues of the German people."[74] To this end, Grotewohl emphasized that the Volkskongress was the body most representative of the German people and its desire for national unity. This programmatic assertion of support for German unity cannot conceal the underlying reality of the Volkskongress, that it was an instrument of SED power and brooked no challenge from "opposition" forces. Referring to a proposal by the CDU delegation in Saxony-Anhalt (Soviet zone) that called for the ACC to convene a consultative assembly made up of representatives from the state governments throughout Germany, Otto Grotewohl underscored the SED leadership's unwillingness to tolerate such alternatives. A step such as the one proposed by the Saxony-Anhalt CDU would, he indicated, constitute a direct threat to the People's Congress. Instead, he argued that the SED had "seized the right to decide on the future development of Germany" and thus claimed for the SED both a successful recent past and a future legitimated by those achievements.[75]

Grotewohl's remarks aggressively described a set of "democratic" principles that did not operate along any narrow, legal definition but rather encompassed a broad set of party and extraparty actors (the ostensibly independent "mass organizations" in the Soviet zone and Berlin that operated under the party's watchful eye) and superceded any limiting factors, such as electoral defeats or parliamentary competition. In the context of the rapidly evolving arena of German politics, the SED leadership reiterated its prerogative to direct and control the development of centralized political structures. This assertion seems to have contained equal parts delusional hubris and calculating cynicism: For all the setbacks that SED efforts had encountered, many leaders still seemed to believe that it would simply be a matter of time before the mass popular support their program deserved essentially fell into the party's lap. At the same time, they suffered few qualms about using the most ruthless measures to manipulate the processes in which they "competed."

SED party cochair Wilhelm Pieck outlined the proposed agenda for the Second People's Congress. He noted that it would be held under the central slogan of German unity but would also campaign against the Frankfurt

---

[74] Stenographisches Bericht der 6. (20.) Parteivorstandssitzung d. ZK der SED, January 14–15, 1948, SAPMO, DY 30/IV 2/1/38, Bl. 36.
[75] Ibid., Bl. 38, 39–40.

agreements,[76] the Marshall Plan, and consider measures to create central German administrations, guarantee the food supply, implement a unitary currency reform, and clarify reparations obligations. More importantly, he indicated that the Congress would convene a People's Council and take steps to organize a referendum on German unity. The extent to which the People's Congress fell wholly under SED direction came out clearly in the cautionary words with which Pieck began his remarks: "What I am about to say about the Secretariat of the Standing Committee is for the time being to remain as confidential information for the Parteivorstand, because we cannot preempt the decrees of the Standing Committee and must rather permit them to formulate and publish corresponding decrees."[77]

The SED had organized the first Volkskongress in only ten days, and its programmatic "success" came less as a product of carefully exercised control than of good fortune.[78] As the second congress approached, the stakes for the SED were rising. In the western zones, the concrete steps leading toward a West German state (and hence toward a rival claimant to a German national voice) continued to move forward. The end of four-power control as it had existed to that point seemed to be fast approaching. Even more importantly, SED dominance in the Soviet zone was not evolving as seamlessly as the SED leadership had anticipated. For this reason, the SED sought to direct the organization as well as the outcome of this session much more rigidly. Its call for careful, central direction and a refusal to tolerate any alternative proposals reflected the SED leadership's recognition of uncertainty, disillusionment, and a lack of motivation among the party's rank and file. Fred Oelßner noted that many party members wondered about the value of a campaign for "German unity" when SED leaders were, at the same time, denouncing the formation of a western state. He called on the leadership to counter this sentiment in the party and make clear to their comrades that the battle for German unity had not lost its significance.[79]

[76] In February 1948, western officials expanded and reorganized the Economic Council in the western zones. They doubled the number of representatives (to 104), recast the executive council (*Exekutivrat*) as a States' Council (*Länderrat*), and endowed its administrative branch with greater personnel and authority. These steps substantially increased German participation in the expansion of the independent political organization of the western zones. See Kleßmann, *Die doppelte Staatsgründung*, 186.

[77] Stenographisches Bericht der 7. (1.) Parteivorstandssitzung der SED, February 11–12, 1948, SAPMO, DY 30/IV 2/1/40, Bl. 8, 10. (Bl. 8).

[78] See Hurwitz, *Die Stalinisierung der SED*, 390ff.

[79] Stenographisches Bericht der 6. (20.) Parteivorstandssitzung der SED, 14.-15.1.1948, SAPMO, DY 30/IV 2/1/38, Bl. 62.

On its first day of deliberations (March 17), the Second Volkskongress adopted the SED measures creating the new Volksrat and authorizing a referendum (*Volksbegehren*) on German unity, electing 400 members to the new People's Council the next day. In his speech to the Volkskongress, Deputy Party Head Walter Ulbricht reiterated the rhetoric of German unity but spoke extensively about the economic and political structures being developed in the Soviet zone, positioning them both as a model for and an enticement to the rest of Germany: "We are convinced that the example of development in the Eastern Zone will encourage the working people of western Germany so that the working people in western Germany will respond to the colonization measures with the national resistance that has become necessary," but the structural measures underpinning the People's Congress as well as the economic and political concepts to which it appealed were strongly anchored in the Soviet zone.[80] Although Otto Grotewohl later asserted that the SED had erred in its Volkskongress rhetoric by too strongly holding up the Soviet zone as a model for the western zones, the party did little to change this approach. Indeed, in this same speech, Grotewohl emphasized that the drive for German unity would most likely last for years and thus necessitated strong, independent political and economic structures in the Soviet zone.[81]

The belief that the proper argument could carry any policy proposal underlay much of the optimism held by SED leaders in the face of other obstacles. In a series of reports on public opinion (*Stimmungsberichte*) submitted to the SED's party organs section, party officials described a mixed popular response to the People's Congress movement but also suggested an ongoing belief in the power of effective political arguments. One report described how a Russian representative from the Soviet Central Command in Berlin countered a whole series of negative questions posed by students at a school assembly. Questions about the relative truthfulness of Berlin newspapers and why the SPD was not allowed in the Soviet zone seemed in particular to reflect the competitive nature of political discourse in the city. Even more pointedly, the students asked what had happened to young people who had disappeared in the Soviet zone. Although the report writer criticized the official for giving the same speech used for adult factory workers and not connecting it to any particular youth concerns, he emphasized the Soviet official's willingness to

---

[80] Stenographisches Bericht d. 2. Deutscher Volkskongreß, SAPMO, DY 30/IV 2/1.01/83, Bl. 150.

[81] Stenographisches Bericht der 8. (22.) Parteivorstandssitzung d. ZK der SED, March 20, 1948, SAPMO, DY 30/IV 2/1/42, Bl. 22, 24.

accept any and all challenges from his student listeners. When the school director sought to bring an end to the questions, the official encouraged students to ask all their questions, because, in the words of the report writer, "we were for democracy, and everyone has the right to express his opinion." Nevertheless, the fact that the students' second question asked why the school administration had forced them to attend this assembly hinted that these young Berliners held no illusions about the purpose behind this information session.[82] Another report writer detailed a conversation with a colleague at work. Over the course of the conversation, he asserted, he was able to recognize his colleague's arguments as based on a brochure published by the American sector paper, *Der Tagesspiegel*. The SED member's well-reasoned elaborations (at least as he reported them) about the benefits of the socialist economic structures being introduced in the Soviet zone allegedly swayed his colleague and overcame the Western information with which he had been supplied. For the SED leadership, these experiences reiterated exactly what they wanted to believe, that it was still possible to overcome the party's political opponents, even in Berlin.[83]

At its opening session on March 17, the Second People's Congress also called for a referendum (*Volksbegehren*) on German unity and a just peace to be held from May 23 to June 13. It aimed to gather signatures from all zones of Germany in support of the program elaborated by the Congress. In describing the organization of the *Volksbegehren* to the SED Executive Committee, Otto Grotewohl emphasized that it was taking place in a period of intense political struggle in which the party must choose its tactics carefully. Thus, the People's Council (*Volksrat*) decided not to place "Deutscher Volksrat" across the top of the initiative forms. It felt that such a heading would be an invitation for prohibitions in the western zones. He went on to appeal for an effort to transform collecting signatures into some sort of grand expression of popular will on behalf of the German *volk*.[84] From its inception, the People's Congress sought to combat the notion that it was merely an SED front organization, emphasizing that it

[82] Bericht von einer Schülerversammlung des Bezirks-Friedrichshain am 16.1.1948, SAPMO, DY 30/IV 2/5/974, Bl. 4. The report indicated that this assembly was one of a series arranged by the Soviet Central Command in cooperation with directors of middle and upper schools in Berlin.

[83] Stimmungsbericht, February 15, 1948 (copy of April 1, 1948), SAPMO, DY 30/IV 2/5/974, Bl. 20.

[84] Stenographisches Bericht der 8. (22.) Parteivorstandssitzung d. ZK der SED, March 20, 1948, SAPMO, DY 30/IV 2/1/42, Bl. 20. Note the similarity to his remarks in January.

was voicing the view of almost all Germans in support of German unity.[85] The preliminary text of the petition read:

The undersigned German men and women desire a plebiscite (*Volksentscheid*) for a unified democratic German republic in which the states are to receive the rights as allocated them in the Weimar Constitution.

Grotewohl explained that this formulation, referring back to the states' rights in the Weimar Republic, would make it difficult for many among the bourgeoisie as well as for the Social Democrats in the western zones to speak out against the initiative.[86] This phrasing also implicitly drew upon the political experiences of the Weimar Republic in which plebiscitary campaigns figured prominently. Grotewohl expressed high hopes for this new campaign: "The scope of signature collection must become the decisive breakthrough for the German people in the question of German unity. The people must be so deeply gripped and moved that no one in Germany or in the world can any longer ignore this expression of [popular] will."[87]

Grotewohl's remarks suggested that with the breakup of the ACC looming on the horizon, the German party political arena as defined by quadripartite rule would be radically revamped. Based on his comments in that day's session (prior to the ACC meeting) and their similarity to Sokolovskii's declaration at the ACC, there is some reason to argue that Grotewohl (and presumably the other SED leaders) knew about the Soviet walkout in advance.[88] While this potential transformation implied little change in the SED's dominant position in the Soviet zone (the structures of its political control), it did suggest that a new method would be required to translate these politics for the broader population. The *Volksbegehren* represented a first step in that direction, but it could not overcome the extent to which the continued resonance of the material conditions in

[85] This fact served as one of the principal arguments for Volkskongress opponents as well. They suggested that Germans' support of national unity was self-evident and did not require any artificial movement to express it. Paul Löbe (SPD) made this point in his speech on March 18, 1948. See *Berlin: Behauptung von Freiheit und Selbstverwaltung 1946–48*, 434.

[86] Stenographisches Bericht der 8. (22.) Parteivorstandssitzung d. ZK der SED, March 20, 1948, SAPMO, DY 30/IV 2/1/42, Bl. 20. The final text of the initiative was slightly different. It called on the occupying powers to either pass a law or permit a plebiscite on a law with this wording: "Germany is an indivisible democratic Republic, in which the states should be granted rights similar to those contained in the constitution of the German Reich of 11 August 1919." See the copy of a signature form in Nachlaß Wilhelm Pieck, SAPMO, NY 4036/762, Bl. 159.

[87] Ibid., Bl. 22.

[88] Note especially Grotewohl's comments beginning on SAPMO, DY 30/IV 2/1/42, Bl. 18. On this issue see also, Tusa, *The Berlin Airlift*, 103.

Berlin and elsewhere in Germany trumped this sort of effort to restrict politics to a purely symbolic realm.

In early spring 1948, the SED asked a number of persons in the Treptow district to respond to the question, "What do you think of the current political situation, and how do you assess its further development?" The respondents generally emphasized the fact that the occupiers had shown that they were no longer capable of working together and expressed uncertainty about the possibility of any positive developments. One worker saw little reason to hope that the People's Congress would be able to accomplish anything to achieve German unity: "There will be a western and an eastern state; then we will see who can better manage [the state] (*wer besser wirtschaften kann*)." An administrative employee (*Verwaltungsangestellte*) sounded a similar material theme, indicating that his main concern was whether there was enough to eat. Perhaps most telling were the remarks of a shoemaker. He asserted that it was best not even to bother thinking about politics because none of the occupation powers gave any thought to the Germans. In the end, he simply hoped that there would not be another war.[89]

A late-March report from a locomotive repair plant in the Soviet sector expressed a similar mixture of concerns about political and material issues. According to one locomotive mechanic, the majority of workers there viewed German economic and political unity as an absolute necessity. Nonetheless, they were hesitant to support the People's Congress, calling it "Russian theater." The planned introduction of piece rates at the plant seemed to elicit even stronger reactions. Workers decried the decision as nothing more than an "imitation of Nazi methods." None of these sentiments seemed to promote a great deal of political activism. The report noted that at the last meeting of the party factory group, only five of sixty-three members even bothered to attend.[90]

Faced with such indications of political apathy, even among SED members, the *Volksbegehren* campaign seemed ill-equipped to mobilize a mass popular movement, especially given the certain opposition of the Western occupation administrations and most members of other parties. But before signature gathering started, the SED leadership reformulated its assessment of the political context in which the *Volksbegehren* would

---

[89] Stimmungsbericht über die Stellungsnahme der Bevölkerung zur Frage: "Was halten Sie von der gegenwärtigen politischen Lage und wie beurteilen Sie ihre Weiterentwicklung?" in Treptow (copy April 6, 1948), DY 30/IV 2/5/974, Bl. 50.

[90] Ibid., Bl. 39.

take place. At the May meeting of the SED Parteivorstand, Wilhelm Pieck presented a "Report on the strategic change in our struggle for unity, democracy, and a just peace." He announced that the division of Germany into two parts necessitated a "change in our strategy and in the role of our party." While he condemned the emerging West German state as a territory wholly dependent on the Western powers with an economy subject to American dictates, Pieck asserted that the Soviet zone was developing as an independent state entity. He tied together the SED's rise to power in a new state with securing the Soviet zone and improving people's living conditions.[91] Transforming the SED into a "Party of the New Type" (*Partei neuen Typus*) also required significant political steps for the Soviet zone.

Pieck indicated that zonal elections would most likely have to be postponed from the coming fall to spring 1949 in order to allow two newly created parties to establish a basis for electoral participation and, more importantly, to address any structural transformations that division might entail.[92] Next, Franz Dahlem issued a call for intensified party discipline to counter the ideological and tactical failings in the SED. He appealed for a "steeling of the body of functionaries" in the effort to develop the SED into a "party of struggle" (*Kampfpartei*).[93] In their vapidity, these open declarations suggested that the *Volksbegehren* had ceased to play anything but a self-justifying role.

The collection of signatures for the *Volksbegehren* began with much fanfare on May 23. Although banned outright in the American and French zones (and sectors), the *Tägliche Rundschau* reported that on the eve of the initiative fires were to be lit on the mountains along the western boundary of the Soviet zone to shine far into the western zones and recall the national will for unity.[94] Attempts to gather signatures in the French and American sectors of Berlin resulted in a number of arrests. The *Tägliche Rundschau*

---

91 Stenographisches Bericht der 10. (24.) Parteivosrtandssitzung d. ZK der SED, May 12–13, 1948, SAPMO, DY 30/IV 2/1/46, Bl. 61–2.
92 See Hurwitz, *Die Stalinisierung der SED*, 416. The two parties to which Pieck referred were the Democratic Farmers' Party of Germany (*Demokratische Bauernpartei Deutschlands* or DBD) and the National-Democratic Party of Germany (*National-Demokratische Partei Deutschlands* or NDPD). The DBD was established on April 29, 1948 and the NDPD was established on May 25, 1948. Both parties were wholly subservient to the SED. See Weber, *DDR*, 28 and 287.
93 Stenographisches Bericht der 10. (24.) Parteivosrtandssitzung d. ZK der SED, May 12–13, 1948, SAPMO, DY 30/IV 2/1/46, Bl. 96ff.
94 Prof. Dr. Kastner, "Das Deutsche Volk hat das Wort: Der Sinn des Volksbegehren," *Tägliche Rundschau* (May 23, 1948), 3.

reported that one person collecting signatures at the Friedenau S-Bahn station in the American sector was beaten bloody.[95] British officials did not ban the collection of signatures but indicated that they felt the process was superfluous and did nothing to promote German unity. Furthermore, they believed that the signatures gathered would be misrepresented as support for the People's Congress.[96]

Even in the Soviet sector, however, the decision to sign the referendum often derived from motivations other than heartfelt ideological commitment. A report for the district SED on the gathering of signatures in one fire station in Prenzlauer Berg helps to clarify this process. The report writer and another party member in the station agreed to begin collecting signatures. The two of them signed first before presenting the list to all the higher ranking officers (*Vorgesetzten*) and works council members present. Only after these higher-ups had signed did the two organizers circulate the list to the remaining firemen on duty in the station. Only one of the ranking officers initially refused to sign. An earlier entry in the report had quoted this same officer's response to a poster supporting the Volksbegehren in the window of the cooperative grocery store across the street, "they should rather give us more to eat." Still, the report writer described him as someone "sympathizing with the SED," and after he was presented with the list of all those who had already signed, he too put his name on the list.[97] While this report writer sought to cast a positive light on his organizational efforts as compared to the SPD member who showed decidedly less enthusiasm in trying to drum up signatures during the fire station's other shift, he cannot conceal the ways in which party and professional hierarchies likely exerted significant pressure on individuals' decisions to put their name to a list circulating in public within the fire station. As this example suggests, the actual process of gathering signatures was much more mundane and too carefully directed (and manipulated) to suggest that it in any way represented a spontaneous upswelling of popular support.

[95] "Der erste Tag des Volksbegehrens: Starke Beteiligung in der Ostzone und Berlin – Sabotageversuche der Einheitsgegner in der Berliner Westbezirken," *Tägliche Rundschau* (May 25, 1948), 1. The fact that the S-Bahn system was controlled by the Soviet zone (under the auspices of the German Reichsbahn) gave stations in the western sectors a strange kind of extraterritoriality that would continue to play an important role in the political and economic conflicts in years to come. See ch. 6.

[96] Copy of British Statement on "Volksbegehren" in Berlin, 21.5.1948, LAB, STA Rep. 101, Nr. 170, Bl. 2b.

[97] "Bericht!" (May 26, 1948), SED KL Prenzlauer Berg, LAB, BPA IV 4/6/402.

In his report to the SED Executive Committee on June 30, 1948, Paul Merker noted that the highest levels of eligible voters signed the *Volksbegehren* in the states of Mecklenburg and Saxony but that no state in the Soviet zone reported a signature rate of less than 95 percent of eligible voters. In Berlin, however, the figures were much lower; about 34 percent of eligible voters signed the referendum. Even in the Soviet sector only 79.3 percent supported the appeal. Altogether, the campaign gathered approximately 14.5 million signatures, all but 1.5 million from the Soviet zone.[98] When Berlin's city assembly banned the collection of signatures in official city buildings, the Soviet deputy commander issued an order directing that this resolution not be carried out in the Soviet sector.[99] In some respects, this decision overshadowed any other significance of the signature-gathering campaign.

Writing to the Kommandatura on May 28, Deputy Mayor Ferdinand Friedensburg (CDU) argued that this decision set a disturbing precedent, implying that the pronouncements of the duly elected city assembly and Magistrat could unilaterally be declared invalid in one sector by one occupying commander. He viewed this intervention as a significant disruption of the unified government and administration of the city and suggested that this incident could have a detrimental effect on the development of democracy among the people, as they would see that an elected body's decrees possess only minimal value.[100] While the course of the referendum in Berlin underscored the extent to which even the SED's most public success stories depended on manipulation and the support of the Soviet "friends," its relative failure in Berlin – achieving nowhere near the levels of support reached in the Soviet zone – offered a hint of the tenuous support that an honest assessment of the SED's position there might also reveal. In the Soviet zone, the final push for centralized economic and political control and the eventual establishment of East Germany

---

[98] Stenographisches Bericht der 11. (25.) Parteivorstandssitzung d. ZK der SED, June 29–30, 1948, SAPMO, DY 30/IV 2/1/48, Bl. 238. Some western officials challenged the validity of the count, claiming that they were able to sign signature lists multiple times without hindrance or asserting that signatures were acquired under false pretenses (e.g., on a list of persons claiming their homes to be vermin-free). For some of these critiques, see the discussion in the Stenographisches Bericht der 69. Sitzung der Stadtverordnetenversammlung, May 25, 1948, 24ff.

[99] See the city assembly debate from April 29, 1948, Stenographisches Bericht der 66. Sitzung der Stadtverordnetenversammlung. Also, LAB, Rep. 280 (LAZ-Sammlung), Sta.-Ort. Nr. 8503/25.

[100] Friedensburg letter to the AK on Volksbegehren decision, May 28, 1948, LAB, STA Rep. 101, Nr. 170, Bl. 2j-2k.

overshadowed the continued existence of spaces, such as the multifaceted black market, that (from the SED perspective) at best eluded and at worst directly challenged the control to which the party aspired. In Berlin the multiple levels of slippage between assertions and realization of power that also marked conditions in the Soviet zone simply remained more visible. Thus, from this perspective at least, Soviet and SED claims that Berlin was part of the Soviet zone were not inaccurate.

The German Economic Commission

On February 12, 1948, Soviet Order No. 32 dramatically expanded the powers of the German Economic Commission (*Deutsche Wirtschaftskommission* or DWK). Founded in June 1947 to address shortcomings in the civilian central administrations that the Soviets had first established to manage the civilian administration in the Soviet zone, the DWK initially proved only slightly more effective at establishing centralized control structures. Reacting to ongoing concerns about this body's inability to direct the Soviet zone's economic affairs effectively (most notably due to the states' unwillingness to cede significant power to the DWK), this order concentrated zonal administration in the hands of an expanded bureaucracy and gave the DWK the right to issue binding orders to all German organs in the Soviet zone, at least as related to the "peacetime economy" and questions of reparations delivery.[101] Nearly all the Soviet zone's existing central administrations were incorporated into the new administrative structures of the DWK as main administrations (*Hauptverwaltungen*); only the interior, education, justice, and health administrations were

[101] Creuzberger, *Die sowjetische Besatzungsmacht*, 164. Although the development of the planned economy in East Germany has garnered significant attention, the DWK remains a decidedly underresearched component of political and economic development in the SBZ. There is one rather unsatisfactory book-length analysis: Bernd Niedbalski, "Die Deutsche Wirtschaftskommission (DWK) in der sowjetischen Besatzungszone Deutschlands und ihre Bedeutung für die Herausbildung neuer zentraler Strukturen beim Aufbau von Wirtschaft und Staat" (PhD diss., Freie Universität Berlin, 1990). More usefully, see Wolfgang Zank, "Wirtschaftliche Zentralverwaltungen und Deutsche Wirtschaftskommission (DWK)," in *SBZ-Handbuch: Staatliche Verwaltungen, Parteien, gesellschaftliche Organisationen und ihre Führungskräfte in der Sowjetischen Besatzungszone Deutschlands 1945–1949*, Martin Broszat and Hermann Weber, eds. (Munich: R. Oldenbourg Verlag, 1990), 265–6 and André Steiner, "Die Deutsche Wirtschaftskommission – ein ordnungspolitisches Machtinstrument?" in *Das letzte Jahr der SBZ: politische Weichenstellungen und Kontinuitäten im Prozeß der Gründung der DDR*, Veröffentlichungen zur SBZ/DDR-Forschung im Institut für Zeitgeschichte, Dierk Hoffmann and Hermann Wenkter, eds. (Munich: Oldenbourg 2000), 85–105.

initially excluded. Brandenburg's Economic Minister, Heinrich Rau (SED) assumed control of a body that also included two deputy heads, the presidents of the central administrations, three representatives of the FDGB, two from the Association for Mutual Farmers' Assistance (*Vereinigung für gegenseitige Bauernhilfe* or VdgB), as well as representatives of the five states in the Soviet zone. At the head of the DWK was a nine- (later ten-) person Secretariat including (among others) Rau and the heads of the FDGB and VdgB. In mid-1948, approximately 5,000 persons worked for the DWK; by 1949, this number swelled to 10,000.[102] From the outset, the new administration emerged as a powerful bureaucratic force, and, under SED direction, it came to wield increasing political power.

The Soviet decision to expand the DWK came at least partially in response to the Western Allies' steps to increase the powers of the Economic Council in the Bizone.[103] But this should not conceal the extent to which the expanded DWK fundamentally was part of broad efforts to shape and control political developments in the Soviet zone during early 1948. In December 1947, the head of the SVAG propaganda administration, Colonel Sergei Tiul'panov, asserted that the DWK had proven itself no more effective in dealing with the economic and political organization in the Soviet zone than the earlier central administrations. In response, he called for the DWK and the central administrations to function as a stable, powerful force for German self-administration.[104] The primary motivation for an expanded DWK should be seen not as a countermeasure to Western steps to expand the German administration in Frankfurt, but as a proactive means to assert control over the political and economic situation within the Soviet zone, a situation that, similar to the SED's presumably secure position in Berlin's trade unions and municipal administration, seemed increasingly wobbly.

Due to its unique four-power status, Berlin occupied an uncertain economic position, often finding its traditional economic networks disrupted (at least in official channels) by the vagaries of competing occupation bureaucracies. Yet, owing to its geographical location in the midst of the Soviet zone, officials in both the city and zonal administrations expressed real interest in developing and solidifying economic links between the two. Following the initial creation of the DWK in June 1947, the Berlin FDGB appealed to the DWK to promote greater economic ties between the Soviet

---

[102] Zank, "Wirtschaftliche Zentralverwaltungen," 265–6.
[103] Ibid., 265.
[104] Cited in Creuzberger, *Die sowjetische Besatzungsmacht*, 163.

zone and Berlin, especially its Soviet sector. A letter it sent to the DWK
in July complained that the Berlin Magistrat – specifically the Economic
Department – saw its obligations realized in the promotion of economic
contacts to the western zones alone. In response, the letter called on the
DWK to incorporate the Soviet sector in economic planning, especially in
the areas of raw materials, energy, and industrial production.[105]

These complaints notwithstanding, municipal officials were by no
means uninterested in economic contacts with the Soviet zone. Klingelhöfer sought to have the Berlin Magistrat included in the DWK's economic discussions. In a letter to DWK deputy head Bruno Leuschner,
dated August 13, 1947, Klingelhöfer expressed hope that the Magistrat's
Economic Department could be incorporated into the zone's Economic
Commission as soon as the states were included. Ten days later, Leuschner
coolly replied that the DWK was not organized on a "federal" basis and
that the states were not represented on the commission.[106] One month
later, another official from Berlin's Economic Department sent a letter to
Leuschner suggesting that because the Soviet sector of Berlin was generally
treated as an economic part of the Soviet zone, heightened cooperation
was needed between the economic bodies of Greater Berlin and the SBZ.
The letter suggested that such cooperation take place along similar lines
to that taking place with the administrative office of the unified zones (the
western Bizone). Leuschner again responded rather coolly, acknowledging
the need for close cooperation but questioning how this could specifically
take place.[107] In spite of potential economic and organizational benefits,
it is not difficult to understand Leuschner's hesitancy to engage the Berlin

[105] Letter from Rossignol, FDGB Groß-Berlin, to the DWK, July 22, 1947, BA-DDR, DC-
15–479, Bl. 5.
[106] Letter from Gustav Klingelhöfer to Bruno Leuschner, dated August 13, 1947; Letter
from Leuschner to Klingelhöfer, dated August 23, 1947 in Organisation der Wirtschaftsplanung in Groß-Berlin und Einbeziehung in der Planung der SBZ, October 1946–
September 1949, BA-DDR, DC-15–479, Bl. 8–9.
[107] Letter from W. Kressmann (Magistrat, Abt. f. Wirtschaft) to Bruno Leuschner (DWK),
dated September 20, 1947; Letter from Leuschner to Magistrat Abt. f. Wirtschaft,
dated October 10, 1947 in Organisation der Wirtschaftsplanung in Groß-Berlin und
Einbeziehung in der Planung der SBZ, October 1946–September 1949, BA-DDR, DC-
15–479, Bl. 10–11. In this context it is worth noting that during the summer of 1948
(i.e., during the blockade), Berlin's Deputy Mayor, Ferdinand Friedensburg (CDU), held
conversations with the DWK about establishing closer ties to Berlin. Such efforts to
continue to work with the Soviets and the SED earned Friedensburg the ire of his SPD
counterparts in the municipal government who saw him as too conciliatory. For a summary of Friedensburg's contacts as well as a report on how they were received by Reuter
and other members of the Magistrat, see the account by the deputy head of the DWK,
Fritz Selbman, in Nachlaß Walter Ulbricht, SAPMO, NY 4182/906, Bl. 2–8.

Magistrat more fully in the DWK. If the state administrations in the Soviet zone had proved a hindrance to DWK administrative efforts, the competitive and contentious municipal government in Berlin could only prove worse. A rise in influence by a democratically elected body would have run counter to the centralizing, SED-dominated control to which the DWK aspired.

Soviet and SED leaders sought to draw a clear distinction between their efforts and the measures being undertaken in Germany's western zones, denouncing the former as decisive steps to divide Germany and set up a separate western state. Speaking before the SED Executive Committee on March 20, the former SPD official Max Fechner emphasized that the DWK was not seeking to establish a separate (East) German state but was rather a "coordinating measure in the economic sector."[108] But if one takes Tiul'panov's assertions seriously – that the DWK should provide a solid basis for German self-administration – it is difficult to perceive the DWK, even in early 1948, as anything less than a German proto-state for the Soviet zone. The SED, or at least persons sympathetic to the SED program, occupied all positions of real authority in the expanded DWK. Of the ten Secretariat members, only two even nominally belonged to parties other than the SED (one each from the CDU and LDP). The remaining eight, including the ostensible representatives of "independent" organizations (such as the FDGB) belonged to the SED.[109] Of the seventeen main administrations, fifteen were headed by an SED member, and one each by a CDU member and an independent. In both those cases, the deputy head belonged to the SED.[110] Thus, it was clear from the outset that, within the DWK, the SED line reigned supreme. Buttressed by the expanded powers of Soviet Order No. 32, the DWK moved quickly in an effort to realize this control throughout the economic and political life of the Soviet zone, a proposition that proved much more difficult than pushing through bureaucratic dominance within the DWK. While black

---

[108] Stenographisches Bericht der 8. (22.) Parteivorstandssitzung der SED, 20.3.1948, SAPMO, DY 30/IV 2/1/42, Bl. 7. A draft history of the DWK found in the Nachlaß Heinrich Rau (and written around 1960) calls the DWK an "offensive response" to the Frankfurt Economic Council. SAPMO, NY 4062/77, Bl. 56.

[109] It is worth noting that of the eight SED members in the DWK Sekretariat, all but one had previously been members of the KPD. This assessment is based on the Secretariat of June 1948. Zank, "Wirtschaftliche Zentralverwaltungen," 266 and 282. Zank emphasizes the DWK's subordination to the SED by referring to a resolution of the SED Central Secretariat in which "Die DWK ist zu beauftragen..." (cited on p. 266).

[110] Besetzung der leitenden Funktionen in der Deutschen Wirtschafts-Kommission (dated April 2, 1948) in Wilhelm Pieck Papers, SAPMO, NY 4036/687, Bl. 1–3.

market trade and widespread foraging and bartering by urban residents traveling from Berlin and other cities into the Soviet zone countryside proved massively difficult to rein in, even the "legal" activities that fell under DWK jurisdiction remained slippery.

In its session of April 14, the DWK Secretariat issued a decree in which it suggested to the SVAG that the DWK be granted the power to issue directives that would be binding for the German population in the Soviet zone. The Soviet administration approved the proposal less than a week later.[111] This centralizing process continued throughout the spring. On April 23, the DWK assumed control of the largest People's Factories (*Volkseigene Betriebe* or VEBs), removing them from the jurisdiction of the states. That same month, the VdgB also came under the DWK's direct administrative control.[112] With these two steps, the DWK assumed supervisory control over many of the zone's most important industrial enterprises and firmly inserted itself into the direction and management of agricultural production. While such steps did much to promote the desired consolidation of economic authority, the DWK did not limit its expanding control structures only to questions of economic production.

In March, the DWK had started to discuss plans to introduce a new supervisory body, the Central Control Commission (*Zentrale Kontrollkommission* or ZKK). According to the initial decree, this body was designed to "guarantee order and punctiliousness (*Sauberkeit*) in the economy and administration and to regulate the democratic rights, as guaranteed by the state constitutions, and the people's control of public administration."[113] This wording suggests the implicit desire to control not just the administration of economic production but also to direct popular engagement in political and economic affairs. The nature of the ZKK as eventually authorized on May 29, 1948 reiterated this intention. According to this directive, the members of the ZKK were to be chosen by the DWK Secretariat in conjunction with the German Administration for the Interior.[114] Subordinate to the ZKK were five state commissions; they in turn supervised local, volunteer control commissions whose duty it was to ensure the fulfillment of economic plans, combat black marketeering, and counter bureaucratic obstacles to economic development. These local

---

[111] DWK Beschluß S 15/48 in SAPMO, DY 30/IV 2/6.02/114, Bl. 18. See also Zank, "Wirtschaftliche Zentralverwaltungen," 266.

[112] Part of the motivation for assuming control of the VdgB lay in an effort to counter the influence that owners of large and well-to-do farms continued to exert within that organization. See Zank, "Wirtschaftliche Zentralverwaltungen," 267.

[113] DWK Beschluß S8/48, SAPMO, DY 30/IV 2/6.02/114, Bl. 9.

[114] Zank, "Wirtschaftliche Zentralverwaltungen," 269–70.

commissions had the authority to initiate criminal and judicial investigations and worked in conjunction with local police.[115]

During the first half of 1948, the DWK continued to expand its jurisdictional reach, eliminate state governments from important administrative functions, and consolidate its power under the careful direction of the SED and the SVAG. Yet, for all the resources put at its disposal, the DWK's march toward centralized control of the Soviet zone did not progress without interruption. In fact, the DWK's organizational methods faced competing constituencies with often divergent political and economic interests, and these forces challenged the straightforward control measures that the DWK sought to implement. At no point was this more apparent than in the convoluted relationship between the DWK and the city of Berlin.

Technically, even the Soviet sector of Berlin did not come under the DWK's jurisdiction, but this did not mean that the DWK intended, as a matter of course, to exclude itself from Berlin's economic affairs. In a confidential meeting held on May 21, 1948 to discuss the responsibility for trade agreements dealing with Berlin, Georg Handke, a permanent member of the DWK Secretariat, declared:

> [...] that it is entirely clear that the Economic Commission is responsible exclusively for the Russian Zone and thus can neither authorize nor advocate the carrying out of foreign trade deals by the [Berlin] Industry and Trade Office [*Industrie- und Handelskontor* or IHK]. At the same time, it is clear that the current conditions are untenable in the long term.[116]

Handke went on to express concern that any efforts to circumvent the authority of the Kommandatura in Berlin could be perceived as an effort to promote the division (*Spaltung*) of Berlin. Hans Mummert, the head of the Berlin IHK, responded that the Western powers had been authorizing foreign trades under the auspices of the Western Joint Export-Import Agency (JEIA) for months;[117] thus they had already effected the division. He argued that any hesitation by the Russian occupiers to take parallel measures was not justified. This viewpoint carried the day, and the discussants

---

[115] Ibid., 270.

[116] Aktennotiz über eine Besprechung bei der Deutschen Wirtschaftskommission am 21. Mai 1948, LAB, BPA, IV L-2/6/307. Regarding the establishment of the Berlin Industrie- u. Handelskontor, see the memo from Hans Mummert to Stadtrat Klingelhöfer, dated March 18, 1948, LAB, BAP, IV L-2/6/305. Here, it is worth noting that the Soviet *zone* excluded even the Soviet *sector* of Berlin.

[117] The JEIA was the combined export-import body for the Bizone. The final agreement on its establishment was reached on February 3, 1947. See Clay, *Decision in Germany*, 199 and 474.

agreed that the Soviet Central Command (in Berlin) should serve as the responsible authority for approving international trade deals for Berlin's Soviet sector, but a subsequent discussion with officials from the Soviet economic section failed to elicit complete agreement. Instead of supporting the DWK's suggestion that Soviet authorization of international trade deals be provided for the Soviet sector alone, Lieutenant Colonel Nesamaev proposed that the Magistrat should request such authorization for the entire city.[118] Given the political situation in the Magistrat, where the three parties opposed to the SED enjoyed an overwhelming majority, such a request could, of course, lead nowhere.

Its inability to control trade to and from Berlin weighed heavily on DWK and other Soviet zone officials. Throughout the spring of 1948, eastern rhetoric decried the shipment of factories and materiel to the west. In a speech in early 1948, a member of the SED's Berlin Landesvorstand, Bruno Baum, cited a case of a firm (AEG) that had set up a new branch in Augsburg (American zone) and outfitted it with all the technical drawings from its Berlin plant. He claimed that this showed that the firm planned, "at the decisive moment," to block the supply of raw materials to the Berlin plant, effectively shutting it down. According to his account, the AEG leadership as well as the UGO factory council had asserted that "before the iron curtain falls, all [technical] drawings must be in the West." Baum almost certainly exaggerated the level of crisis. At a meeting to discuss the removal of "technical drawings" from Berlin (which included Stadtrat Klingelhöfer as well as an SED official from the city's Economic Department), the participants discussed how copies of drawings were typically submitted along with repair orders, and all present reiterated their desire to maintain AEG production capacity in Berlin.[119] The eastern press still published numerous denunciations of firms shipping valuable machinery to the western zones and thereby "plundering" the Berlin economy. Given the artificial and obstacle-filled nature of the immediate postwar economy in Germany, it is difficult to ascertain the extent to which equipment and personnel transfers were part of "normal" business activity or motivated by fears of changes in the political situation in Berlin.[120]

[118] Aktennotiz über eine Besprechung bei der Deutschen Wirtschaftskommission am 21. Mai 1948, LAB, BPA, IV L-2/6/307.

[119] Sek. f. Wirtschaft Bruno Baum: StV Fraktion d. SED, 1947–8, LAB, BPA, IV L-2/13/452.

[120] See "Klingelhöfer und Magistrat verantwortlich fuer die Ausplünderung Berlin," *Tägliche Rundschau* (April 1, 1948), 1. "Wir fordern Schutz Berlins! Verstärkte wirtschaftliche Kontrollmaßnahmen erforderlich." *Neues Deutschland* (May 23, 1948) in SAPMO, DY 30/IV 2/6.02/81, Bl. 22.

It is nonetheless necessary to recognize that such rhetorical assertions (and even exaggerations) represented more than empty polemics against the West. Among Soviet zone officials, the inability to harness Berlin's economic activity represented a significant threat to its ongoing control efforts – not only with respect to the city but more broadly for the Soviet zone. In mid-April, Bruno Baum reported to the SED economic section that he had received information that an engineering firm in Saxony (Soviet zone) was planning to shift its operations to Berlin's western sectors. The firm's owner had allegedly already purchased an apartment there, and a move seemed imminent. Responding to this report, the responsible SED official appears to have triggered an investigation (*Kontrolle*) of the firm, thereby imbedding it in the very control structures it presumably threatened.[121] On one level, the expanding reach of zonal controls did counter these real and perceived threats to Soviet authority. Yet, at the same time, the greater level of aggressive political and economic intervention, threatened SED efforts to mobilize popular support on behalf of its political projects. For all its institutional and material backing – including the not insignificant aid it received from Soviet authorities – the SED seemed unable to cope with a postwar environment, in which Germans' efforts to survive did not stop at the boundaries of the administrative structures that presumed to contain them.

A report from late January imbedded the efforts of these Volkskontrollen into the "heroic struggle against economic saboteurs" that the state of Brandenburg had been conducting for over two years. In light of an upsurge in large-scale economic crimes, the report suggested that police needed to develop new strategies so as not only to solve this sort of crime but to prevent them from occurring.[122] A February 20 directive to police in the Soviet zone state of Brandenburg, which surrounded Berlin, expressed grave concerns about the transportation of machinery, rails, trucks, and other goods into Berlin and other adjacent states, actions perceived as producing "severe damage to our economy."[123] But the concern for such losses derived not just or even primarily from the fact that they went *to* Berlin or the western zones but rather that they eluded the control structures within the Soviet zone.

---

[121] DY 30/IV 2/6.02/81, Bl. 32–3. See also the internal report addressing the transfer referred to in the preceding newspaper article (Bl. 35).

[122] Bericht über Volkskontroll-Ausschuß (January 29, 1948), BLHA, Ld. Br. 203, VP, Nr. 31, Bl. 209.

[123] Directive from the Landesregierung Brandenburg, Min. d. Innern, Abt. Polizei (February 20, 1948), BLHA, Ld. Br. Rep. 203, Nr. 33, Bl. 260.

The accounts of hamsterer coming from Berlin to cut deals with Brandenburg farmers and Berlin companies obtaining machinery from their
Soviet zone branches cannot be extracted from authorities' more general
complaints about their inability to control economic affairs in the Soviet
zone. Railroad police in Saxony-Anhalt reported that although it counted
preventing coal losses as its primary duty, its officers proved incapable
of making a noticeable dent in these thefts, which continued even as the
weather began to get warmer. At times as many as 600 persons swarmed
train stations in pursuit of coal, and the report writer suggested that the
police could not cope with such "mass plundering."[124] These incidents –
and even more so the police's explanation of them as part of a more
than two-year-long struggle against economic crimes – reflected the continuity of ordinary people's efforts to survive and the extent to which
they remained a fundamental challenge to even the expanded powers of
emerging German authorities.

Currency Reform and the Two-Year Plan

Throughout the first half of 1948, the expectation of an impending currency reform ran as an undercurrent to all economic activity and weighed
heavily on public opinion. Although the unworkability of the existing mix
of devalued reichsmarks, Weimar-era rentenmarks, and occupation scrip
was readily apparent, people looked to the impending currency reform
with unease. Some feared that it would hit workers and low-level employees hardest while the wealthy would emerge with their property and material holdings intact. According to an SED report on the popular mood in
Berlin-Mitte, one worker hoped that it would "clip the wings" of the big
capitalists and the black marketeers. Other respondents and Germans,
more generally, expressed little hope that currency reform could overcome the economic hardships that they continued to face.[125]

In all zones of Germany, the sentiment prevailed that "separate" currency reforms would seal the division of Germany.[126] Regardless of popular views on currency reform, nobody could ignore the rumors, constant

---

[124] Report from the Dt. Reichsbahn RBD Magdeburg to the Minister d. I (S-A) regarding
security situation in RBD-Bezirk Magdeburg, dated April 15, 1948, LHAM, Rep. K3,
Nr. 4161, Bl. 28.

[125] See the report from Berlin (Mitte) dated January 22, 1948, SAPMO, DY 30/IV 2/5/974,
Bl. 7. On American concern about these popular fears, see Clay, *Decision in Germany*,
210.

[126] See the Stimmungsbericht (March 25, 1948), SAPMO, DY 30/IV 2/5/974, Bl. 33.

newspaper speculations, and the general sense of foreboding that accompanied the seemingly endless waiting or avoid the material impact that these discussions had on their daily life. An American report from earlier in May noted that black marketeers had largely stopped selling luxury goods (e.g., nylons or liquor) because they feared being penalized if they had to exchange especially large amounts of old currency into new.[127] People widely believed that shops were hoarding goods in the weeks and months leading up to currency reform, but barring some decision by occupation officials, there was little they could do but wait.[128]

For the previous two years, ongoing discussions between the occupiers had failed to come to an acceptable four-power solution on currency reform. With the establishment of the Bizone in 1947, American and British leaders felt much less pressure to reach a four-power currency agreement. The Bizone made an independent U.S.-British effort both "attractive and feasible."[129] In fact, the finance section of the British administration in Germany received instructions to begin preparations for a separate currency reform in January 1947.[130] American Military Governor Clay had new currency secretly printed in the United States and shipped to Germany before the end of the year.[131] During these ongoing debates, the Soviets did not sit idly by. On December 10, 1947, the USSR Council of Ministers authorized the SVAG to "print new bank notes for the Soviet zone of occupation of Germany."[132] Although negotiations on a four-power agreement continued, January 1948 found both the Soviets and the Western Allies poised to act independently on currency reform. The possibility for compromise seemed slim, and Marshall Sokolovskii's walkout from the ACC on March 20 dashed nearly all hopes for a four-power agreement on a common German currency.

In Berlin, however, the presence of all four occupying powers contributed to a different atmosphere and somewhat different expectations. Even after the breakup of the ACC, the Kommandatura continued to meet in Berlin. Not until June 16 did the Soviet deputy commander, Colonel

---

[127] Letter from American Consulate General, Hamburg (William B. Kelly, American Vice Consul), May 3, 1948, NA, RG 84, 350/57/18/02, box 252, folder 851.7.

[128] On this issue as well as the monumental place that currency reform holds in West German memory, see the account in Kleßmann and Wagner, eds., *Das gespaltene Land*, 174–6.

[129] Mai, *Der Alliierte Kontrollrat in Deutschland*, 288–9.

[130] Ibid., 287.

[131] Clay, *Decision in Germany*, 211. See also Mai, *Der Alliierte Kontrollrat in Deutschland*, 290–1, esp. n. 131.

[132] Cited in Narinsky, "Soviet Policy and the Berlin Blockade," 4.

Jelisarov, abandon the body in response to an alleged sleight by the American commander.[133] Some German leaders in Berlin continued to hold out hope that the dilemmas presented by currency reform in a city with four occupiers could serve as a lever to achieve a single currency reform across all zones. In late May and early June, Deputy Mayor Ferdinand Friedensburg (CDU) sought to make contact with all four occupiers, promoting Berlin's leadership as a way to overcome the currency impasse.[134] While such hopefulness may seem naive in retrospect, for German politicians and the public more generally, the currency situation appeared far from settled.

A confidential memo from Gustav Klingelhöfer described a number of currency solutions that could potentially have been realized in Berlin. He expressed the greatest apprehension about the possibility that all of Berlin could be incorporated into the Soviet zone currency reform. In his view, this would represent a significant economic and political blow to Berlin. Even the continued presence of Western troops in the city could, he asserted, do little to assuage the disillusionment caused by this step. Klingelhöfer suggested that the Berlin administration would much prefer a split currency in the city to complete incorporation into the Soviet zone and would find ways to cope with the economic difficulties that would present. Regardless of these complications, he argued that in the long term, Berlin's economic viability depended on its ability to easily transport its products out of the city.[135] This remark referred especially to the increasing administrative and regulatory difficulties that Soviet officials had been imposing on transportation to and from Berlin throughout the spring. The never-ending demand for new transportation forms to be filled out, new inspection requirements, and other harassment produced a backlog of shipments in Berlin's post offices and freight yards.[136]

---

[133] Colonel Jelisarov asserted that the departure of U.S. Colonel Frank Howley from the session after thirteen hours of deliberation (leaving his deputy to represent him) was an insult to the Soviet delegation and left the meeting. *Berlin: Behauptung von Freiheit und Selbstverwaltung 1946–48*, 506. See also Frank Howley, *Berlin Command* (New York: G. P. Putnam's Sons, 1950), 179–84.

[134] Note of Dr. Friedensburg on Berlin engagement in the question of currency reform, dated May 31, 1948, LAB, STA Rep. 101, Nr. 168, Bl. 17. See also Friedensburg's remarks in the city assembly on June 19. Stenographisches Bericht der 73. Sitzung der Stadtverordnetenversammlung, 25ff.

[135] "Memorandum zum Einbau Berlins in die Währungsreform," (June 9, 1948?), LAB, STA Rep. 101, Nr. 168, Bl. 21ff.

[136] Report from the Magistrat Economic Department, Trade and Supply Section, dated Berlin, April 9, 1948, LAB, Rep. 280 (LAZ-Sammlung), Sta.-Ort. Nr. 7489; Memo from Hauptgruppe gewerblicher Güterverkehr and Transportgewerbe, dated Berlin, April 26,

Following the breakup of the ACC, agreement among the Western Allies on currency reform came fairly quickly. On June 18 the three military governors announced a currency reform for the three western zones. They explicitly excluded their sectors in Berlin from that reform.[137] One day later, Soviet Military Governor Sokolovskii issued a directive forbidding the circulation of the new Western currency in the Soviet zone and in Greater Berlin. Additionally, he ordered a series of "protective measures" that went into effect at 0.00 hours on June 19. These regulations halted all passenger traffic into and out of the Soviet zone and banned vehicle traffic from the western zones into the Soviet zone as well as along the autobahn between Berlin and Helmstedt (British zone). The decree also banned pedestrians from entering the Soviet zone from the western zones and placed significant restrictions and controls on freight train and boat traffic into and out of the Soviet zone.[138] On June 22, last-minute discussions between financial representatives of the four powers failed to reach a compromise agreement on currency reform in Berlin.[139] The next day, Marshall Sokolovskii issued Soviet Order No. 111, which called for a Soviet currency reform in the Soviet zone and all of Greater Berlin. The city's Western military commanders responded with a declaration voiding the Soviet order and ordering a separate currency reform in their sectors of the city.[140] While these decrees radically transformed Berlin's economic and political landscape, it is important to recognize that even these earthshaking changes did not occur in a vacuum. The SED's ongoing Stalinization drive and its efforts to assume more rigid control over the Soviet zone continued without pause. Indeed, they suggest an expanded context for some of the control measures introduced along with the Soviet currency reform.

The *Tägliche Rundschau*'s front-page response to the announcement of the Western currency reform made the three core elements of political

1948, LAB, Rep. 280 (LAZ-Sammlung), Sta.-Ort. Nr. 7491; and Situation Report of the Trade and Supply Section, dated Berlin, June 14, 1948, LAB, Rep. 280 (LAZ-Sammlung), Sta.-Ort. Nr. 7492.

[137] *Berlin: Behauptung von Freiheit und Selbstverwaltung 1946–48*, 508.
[138] "An die Bevölkerung Deutschlands! Aufruf der Sowjetischen Militärverwaltung in Deutschland" and "Unerläßliche Schutzmaßnahmen: Mitteilung der Sowjetischen Militärverwaltung," *Tägliche Rundschau* (June 19, 1948), 1.
[139] See Mai, *Der Alliierte Kontrollrat in Deutschland*, 475.
[140] *Berlin: Behauptung von Freiheit und Selbstverwaltung 1946–48*, 515–16. On May 18, the Soviet government directed the SVAG to introduce monetary reforms in the Soviet zone immediately following such a step in the western zones. Noted in Narinsky, "Soviet Policy and the Berlin Blockade," 11.

and economic power in the Soviet zone clearly evident. Under the banner headline, "Western Powers Complete the Division of Germany: Separate Currency Reform in Trizonia – A Heavy Blow to the Interests of Workers," the front page carried appeals from Soviet Marshall Sokolovskii, the SED, and the DWK.[141] This construction implicitly linked the DWK and its project of economic organization and political administration to the issue of currency reform. Significantly, the DWK's major push to consolidate the administration and control of the Soviet zone economy culminated almost simultaneously with the explosion of the currency crisis. At the June meeting of the SED's Parteivorstand (June 29–30), Walter Ulbricht's announcement of the first two-year plan for 1949–50 marked both a new stage in the Soviet zone's economic transformation and the nearly total victory for Stalinist forces in the upper ranks of the SED.[142]

Ulbricht's report to the party's Executive Board addressed the economic plan for 1948 as well as the first two-year plan to follow. He began by describing the various achievements of the Soviet zone and then went on to discuss these efforts in terms of the conflict unleashed by the currency reform: "Recently, additional difficulties have developed as a result of the separate currency reform and the division of Germany by the London Recommendations. We were forced to take protective measures against the effects of the separate currency in western Germany."[143] Ulbricht focused less on the division of Germany than on the potentially negative impact that such developments could have on the economic and political developments taking place in the Soviet zone. Referring to Western "acts of sabotage," Ulbricht declared that the Soviet zone would nonetheless supply the iron and steel needs of its industry and fulfill the economic plan.[144]

If some defensive measures directed against the separate currency reform harm some members of the Berlin population, we say openly: It is better to have a few victims now in order to force the western allies to turn from their steps that will bring about economic ruin. It seems to me that the principal task for the Socialist Unity Party and for all democratic forces in Berlin is to produce a plan for the economic development of Berlin and to make clear to the population that when the western allies are no longer prepared to assist with the supply [of the city],

---

[141] *Tägliche Rundschau* (June 19, 1948), 1.
[142] On Ulbricht's speech as the ultimate signal of defeat for those in the SED resisting the Stalinization drive, see Gniffke, *Jahre mit Ulbricht*, 318ff.
[143] Stenographisches Bericht der 11. (25.) Parteivorstandssitzung d. ZK der SED, June 29–30, 1948, SAPMO, DY 30/IV 2/1/48, Bl. 19.
[144] Ibid., Bl. 19.

the progressive-democratic forces will assume this task and guarantee an orderly democratic economy.[145]

Ulbricht's economic strategy helps to make sense of the SED's national vision: expanding material control offered the best route to political (territorial) control. While it would be foolish to take Ulbricht's assertions *literally*, it is important to take them *seriously*. In his presentation, Ulbricht focused on the goal of a centrally directed economy and the final transformation of the SED into the (Stalinist) "Party of a new type" needed to serve in the vanguard of such an effort.[146] He viewed the currency problems and the evolving crisis in Berlin in the context of the project to ensure Soviet-directed SED control in the Soviet zone, a project whose symbolic and material framework had already been apparent in March and that still tried to wear the cloak of German national unity. In the end, however, Ulbricht's optimistic (if also cynically calculating) approach failed to address just how much was eluding SED and even Soviet control. The problem that Ulbricht and the SED ultimately faced was that the "acts of sabotage" undermining their plans for expanded economic and political controls were not coming from the West. They were part of those everyday practices with which Berliners as well as Germans in the Soviet zone sought to ensure their material survival.

[145] Ibid., Bl. 32–3.
[146] See Hurwitz, *Die Stalinisierung der SED*, 422–4.

5

August 1948: Battle Lines on the Potsdamer Platz

On August 19, 1948, Soviet sector police twice raided the usual crowd gathered to trade at the black market on Berlin's Potsdamer Platz. During the 1920s, the square, located just south of the main government quarter, had been Europe's busiest intersection, the site of its first traffic light and a focal point for life in a modern, hurried metropolis. In 1948, however, Erich Mendelssohn's steel and glass Columbus-Haus and the elaborate Deutschlandhaus, with its multiple theme-restaurants and massive movie palace, remained heavily damaged, and fuel restrictions kept away most of the cars that had previously navigated the complicated triangular inter-section at the heart of the city. Its central location and established iden-tity as a transportation hub made its postwar emergence as a center of black market activity unsurprising – in addition to the Potsdamer Train Station, both the S-Bahn and subway stopped there, and the square was crisscrossed by streetcar tracks. But postwar occupation arrangements added an additional wrinkle that heightened its importance for the illicit trade upon which most Berliners' material survival depended in the years after World War II: Potsdamer Platz found itself at the intersection of the American, British, and Soviet occupation sectors, a convergence that pro-duced its unofficial designation as Berlin's "fifth sector."[1] For the open, but nonetheless officially illegal, trade that thrived there, this boundary loca-tion allowed black marketeers to melt away across sector lines, eluding

[1] Unlike occupied Vienna, Berlin did not possess a distinct international sector. In the Aus-trian capital, the city's first district inside the famed Ringstrasse fell under joint four-power control, patrolled by jeeps with a representative from each occupying power and made famous in the 1949 film, *The Third Man*.

approaching police forces that were in most instances not authorized to continue their pursuit into the adjacent sectors.

On this summer day, Soviet sector police carried out an initial raid in the midafternoon, following fairly standard police practice: appearing suddenly from several directions, the police sought to surprise the crowd and round up onto trucks those persons who failed to see the arriving authorities and escape in time. According to a West Berlin police report, this raid proceeded without noticeable incident. When the Soviet sector police returned again, around half past six in the evening, they found the black market reconstituted; but this time, they encountered stronger resistance. When police tried to seize some of the crowd, others who were retreating into the American sector began to throw stones, and the police responded by firing their weapons. Witnesses later reported to west sector police that fifteen to twenty shots had been fired and six to eight people injured.[2] The least sensational newspaper assessment of the events on the Potsdamer Platz suggests that the clash resulted when the crowd developed a sense of superiority to the small police force on the square. In the face of what they perceived as a mob, some individual policemen lost their nerve and fired into the crowd. Assuming a more critical tone, the article argues that the evolution of such a mob was possible only because sector boundaries and a divided police permitted people to flee from police pursuit (and in this case to rally themselves for an assault against that police). It discounts claims that this riot was organized and protected by western MPs and criticizes conditions in which criminals could play one police force against another.[3]

While the level of violence present in this August 19 raid was unusual, the raid was not. A year before, *Sie* reported that open-air black market sites handled only the smallest deals. Large transactions, the article asserted, now took place in apartments behind closed doors.[4] Most Berliners, however, did not depend on big deals but rather the small kinds of trades that at least some in the Berlin police described as "black marketeering in self-defense."[5] Thus, not surprisingly, crowds of people continued to gather at the Potsdamer Platz and other regular black market venues. And although well aware that these markets would reconstitute themselves soon after they departed, police regularly staged "surprise"

[2] See reports filed by the police in the Kreuzberg and Tiergarten districts (western sectors), LAB, Rep. 280 (LAZ-Sammlung), Sta.-Ort. Nr. 11054 and 11055.

[3] "Landfriedensbruch," *Die Welt* (August 21, 1948), LAB, STA Rep. 9, Nr. 115, Bl. 81.

[4] "Schwarzmarkt-Schatten," *Sie* (August 3, 1947), 5.

[5] Ibid.

raids, appearing suddenly and walking down the street with arms locked, loading into trucks those caught in their net, and transporting them to a nearby police station for processing (Figure 11).[6] As much as these raids represented a regular risk for anyone trading on the black market, the police seizure of the goods they had obtained marked a significant short-term hardship and while most police raids went offers without significant incident, the popular outrage they produced offers a context of popular discontent for this particularly vigorous response to a police raid. Only the day before, the cochairs of the Berlin FDGB, Roman Chwalek and Hermann Schlimme, wrote to Acting Mayor Louise Schröder, pointing to several recent instances of unrest in black markets and calling for Berlin-wide efforts to combat the "increase in recent weeks of disruptive illegal trade and black markets."[7]

Going beyond an attempt to merely narrate the violent events of that August evening, the various contemporary efforts to explain what they meant present an opportunity to relocate our understanding of the escalating battle to control Berlin. The American Military Commander in the city, Frank Howley, blamed the incident on the Soviet blockade, which prevented goods from reaching the western sectors and forced residents to resort to illegal means to obtain them.[8] The Soviet sector newspaper, *Vorwärts*, blamed "young people in black pants and high boots" who attacked the police with the aid of American MPs and west sector police officers.[9] The paper's broader discussion of the newly crafted west sector police even more explicitly tied this postwar present to a recent "fascist" past.

The day before, *Vorwärts* denounced the west sector police, comparing it to the police under Karl Friedrich Zörgiebel, the SPD police president who had led a brutal crackdown on May Day demonstrators in 1929. The *Berliner Zeitung* denounced new west sector Police President Johannes Stumm as complicit in right-wing political murders during the Weimar

[6] See, e.g., the Operation Directive for a raid on the Potsdamer Platz, February 22, 1949. LAB, STA Rep. 26, Nr. 143, Bl. 54. On evolving police strategies targeting the black market, see the letter from Police Pres. Markgraf to AK Public Saftey Committee, December 4, 1947, Archiv des Polizeipräsidiums, folder 17.
[7] Letter from the Executive Committee of the FDGB Gross-Berlin to Louise Schröder (August 18, 1948), LAB, FDGB 47.
[8] Cited in "Folgen der unmenschlichen Blockade: Oberst Howley zu den Zwischenfällen am Potsdamer Platz," *Spandauer Volksblatt* (August 21, 1948), LAB, STA Rep. 9, Nr. 115, Bl. 94.
[9] "Schwarze Garde organisiert Ueberfall: MP und Stumm-Abteilungen schützen Schwarzhändler und ehemalige SS," *Vorwärts* (August 20, 1948), LAB, STA Rep. 9, Nr. 115, Bl. 71.

FIGURE 11. Berlin municipal police round up people caught in a 1946 raid of a black market. Neither the police nor the crowd waiting to be loaded into the police truck show particular outrage or even exertion. Instead both sides reflect a certain resignation, a sense that for all the individual material hardship such roundups entail, the ritual of the black market raid remains a necessary inconvenience in the workings of Berlin's postwar economics of survival. *Source:* Landesarchiv Berlin.

Republic, suggesting that he was now turning a similarly blind eye to reprised Nazi behavior in postwar Berlin. The article explicitly linked Nazi policies to postwar animosity toward Communism. It described half-grown boys who harassed "Jewish-looking" men and women, calling them "red pigs." Even more pointedly, it claimed that members of what it termed a "black guard," a security force under American jurisdiction, marched through Tempelhof (American sector) singing new lyrics to the Horst Wessel-Lied, "Weapons up, we're shooting at Reds!" (*Die Waffen hoch, auf Rote wird geschossen!*).[10]

This symbolic coding of a very *ordinary* postwar event – a police raid on a known black market venue – suggests one way to relocate a discussion of the summer's events, which generally serve to comprise a crisis

---

[10] "Schmutzige Methoden der Stumm-Agenten," *Vorwärts* (August 19, 1948), LAB, STA Rep. 9, Nr. 115, Bl. 46. Veritas [penname], "Erinnerung für Dr. Stumm: Die Hintermänner der Fememörder/Er wußte und schwieg doch," *Berliner Zeitung* (August 20, 1948), Bl. 52.

that helped to define the Cold War: the Berlin Blockade. Presumably, what mattered during the summer of 1948 was (West) Berliners' gradual transformation from helpless objects of occupation (and especially Soviet) power to heroic fighters for democracy and freedom. But taking August 19 as a starting point from which to examine the events of the escalating Berlin crisis allows us to map out clearer links between the multiple layers that went into making this struggle for Berlin into the first battle of the Cold War.

These two Soviet sector papers' polemical rhetoric offers only limited insight into what actually happened that August day, but its provocative subordination of the city's political conflicts to the battle against the black market offers a powerful if unintentional explanatory frame. For the papers, the battle against black market criminality offered a shorthand for the SED's struggle against Western-leaning political parties and the municipal government in which the SED remained distinctly subordinate.[11] Indirectly, the article rightly points to the black market as an alternative site of Berliners' power but also highlights the black market as the best setting in which to apprehend the SED assault on the municipal government and its place in Berlin's evolving international symbolic stature.

The Stadthaus Demonstration

Nearly two months before the raid on the Potsdamer Platz, a more explicitly political crowd captured Berlin's attention. Faced with conflicting Western and Soviet directives on currency reform in Berlin, the Berlin City Assembly met in a special session on June 23, 1948 to decide how to proceed. The three Western parties (SPD, CDU, and LDP) joined to adopt a resolution that accepted the circulation of both new currencies in the city, but violence overshadowed the day's parliamentary debates. Large numbers of SED-led demonstrators both inside and outside of the Stadthaus delayed the start of the session for nearly two hours, and the crowds attacked several deputies as they sought to leave following the end of the proceedings. Generally, historians have taken these events as evidence of the SED's totalitarian methods and of the ineffectiveness of institutional

---

[11] "Das Zusammenspiel," Vorwärts (August 20, 1948), LAB, STA Rep. 9, Nr. 115, Bl. 52. By equating "Stumm-agents," American MPs, black marketeers, and fascist "terror troops," the paper sketched a rhetorical teleology that integrates the multiple sets of political and material experiences across several decades of life in Berlin.

measures to cope with the emerging Soviet threat to Berlin. By imbedding the demonstration and its moments of violence into a context in which popular power is not limited to face-to-face encounters with political institutions, we can see the SED-led crowd as a sign of weakness and recognize that debates about currency made sense only as part of the ongoing conversation on material conditions in the city, the contours of which depended on actions largely outside municipal or even occupation offices.[12]

In his remarks to open that Wednesday's special session of the Berlin City Assembly, Otto Suhr (SPD) apologized for the nearly two-hour delay. He explained that a number of factory delegations had planned to deliver petitions to the city assembly, and, anticipating the crowds, he ordered that no large groups be admitted to the building. Only delegation leaders were to be allowed entrance so as to deliver their petitions to his office. From one to three o'clock in the afternoon, this took place without incident. At that point, however, crowds of demonstrators pushed aside the doormen and forced their way into the building. They wove through the hallways and up the stairways to occupy the balcony and the back rows of the assembly hall and the back of the building's second floor. In spite of repeated entreaties by Suhr and by Acting Mayor Louise Schröder (SPD), the protesters refused to leave.[13] Only at the request of the SED delegate and Berlin FDGB head, Roman Chwalek, did the demonstrators agree to leave the hall and permit the assembly to begin its deliberations.[14]

Suhr explained his decision to call the special assembly as a response to the Soviet order to introduce a new eastern mark into Berlin. But, he asserted, the assembly faced not just a currency question but a "question of the fate of Berlin's self-administration." From his perspective, the Western orders countermanding the Soviet directive to implement the Soviet currency reform in the western sectors marked the end of Allied cooperation and thus forced new demands on the city administration.[15] Ostensibly about competing currency reforms, the assembly's debate really focused

---

[12] The beating of the Jewish SPD deputy and concentration camp survivor Jeanette Wolff is most often cited to suggest the parallels between an SED-led mob and the Nazis (especially the SA). See, e.g., Tusa, *The Berlin Airlift*, 141.

[13] Stenographisches Bericht der 74. (außerordentlichen) Sitzung der Stadtverordnetenversammlung von Berlin (StVV), June 23, 1948, 3–4.

[14] "Berliner Arbeiterschaft erhebt ihre Stimme: Massenproteste gegen die verräterische Poliik des Mehrheitsblocks vor und im Berliner Stadthaus." *Tägliche Rundschau* (June 24, 1948), 1.

[15] *Stenographische Berichte der Stadtverordnetenversammlung von Berlin*, 4.

on the continuing battle to control the city government and the position that government would assume in the evolving Berlin crisis.

Speaking from a text approved by the Magistrat immediately before the assembly session, Schröder clearly stated the position of the Western majority. She spelled out the specific demands that Soviet and French, British, and American occupation officials had placed on her and outlined the Magistrat's decision to direct all district mayors in the Soviet sector to comply wholly with the Soviet Order No. 111 while calling upon district mayors in the western sectors to adhere to the emergency directives issued by their respective sector commanders. In spite of this divided currency policy, she emphasized that, for the city government, Berlin remained a single administrative unit and the leadership would continue to treat it as such.[16] A resolution adopted by the assembly underscored the majority position. It concluded:

The disruptions and difficulties for the self-administration of Berlin that have increasingly resulted from the joint actions of the occupying powers demand that the constitutional organs of Berlin immediately be granted free self-administration on the basis of the constitution adopted on 22 April and that the occupation powers confine themselves to the supervision and maintenance of their occupation interests.[17]

Even more overtly, Deputy Mayor Ferdinand Friedensburg questioned whether the Kommandatura's "failure" to resolve the currency question had not in fact returned to the German municipal authorities a certain freedom of action to address the crisis.[18] These sentiments reflected the long-running efforts by some members of the city administration to claim a position independent of competing occupiers. But they also denied Berliners a level of agency that they had long since seized in their ongoing efforts to navigate the demands of daily survival.

Gustav Klingelhöfer hinted at the tense situation facing the municipal administration as he addressed the assembly. He saw the fact that the two currencies could now enter into competition with one another in

---

[16] The text of Frau Schröder's speech was approved by a session of the Magistrat meeting immediately before the city assembly session. Minutes of the 101st Session of the Magistrat (June 23, 1948) in LAB, Rep. 280, Film Nr. 41, Sta.-Ort. Nr. 8503/31.

[17] *Stenographische Berichte der Stadtverordnetenversammlung von Berlin*, 9.

[18] Ibid., 35. Friedensburg, who in the past had proposed a variety of different currency strategies for Berlin, including a separate Berlin currency, was ridiculed by the SED Deputy Mayor Heinrich Acker, who noted that he didn't know where he should direct his comments, as with Dr. Friedensburg one never knows whether one should address yesterday's, today's, or tomorrow's point of view (p. 36).

Berlin as a positive development, allowing the two economic systems that had divided Germany to compete directly with each other. "It is good that the dice have been cast; when the blindfold falls from the eyes, then the working person can also finally see what is truth and what is propaganda, what is deed and reality, what is valuable and worthless."[19] The SED deputy and Ulbricht protégé, Karl Maron, also hinted at the Berlin population's important role. Reading from an SED statement, he asserted that the Soviet currency reform offered the only way for Berlin to emerge from the ongoing economic hard times. He warned Berliners that any person who accepted the western "separatist Mark" would lose the means to support themselves. Even more explicitly, he noted ominously that the Berliners' savings and the assets of the social insurance system were kept in the Soviet sector and that these funds would not be "sacrificed to the monopolistic interests of the Western Powers."[20] An unsubtle threat, certainly, but the SED's claim to popular economic fears was tenuous at best and its ability to master material conditions in the city even less than in 1946. A closer look at the crowds outside the building will help to make this clear.

According to the monthly police report, a crowd of approximately 3,000 persons from Berlin factories demonstrated in front of the Neue Stadthaus on June 23. In quite understated terms, it goes on to note that there were disturbances within the building as well.[21] Ostensibly, these demonstrators represented Berlin's factory workers and were protesting the emergence of two currencies in the city. During the session, Otto Suhr read out some fifty resolutions submitted to the city assembly by various factory groups (*Betriebsgruppen*). Of these, one SPD Betriebsgruppe from Marienfelde (American sector) protested against Soviet Order No. 111. The remaining resolutions generally protested against the circulation of two currencies in Berlin; most of them called for the incorporation of Berlin into the Soviet zone or at the very least into its new currency.[22] For the SED, these resolutions served simultaneously as political instrument and ideological wish-fulfillment.

In the short term, these resolutions functioned – along with the demonstrators that accompanied them – as part of an effort to disrupt and intimidate the workings of a municipal administration that increasingly

[19] Ibid., 44.
[20] Ibid., 22.
[21] Activity report from the office of the Polizeipräsident in Berlin, LAB, STA Rep. 9, Nr. 89, Bl. 181.
[22] *Stenographische Berichte der Stadtverordnetenversammlung von Berlin*, 6–9.

relegated the SED to subordinate status. But in the midst of this obvious and growing impotence, resolutions and demonstrations that the party directed came to sum up a level of support that from its perspective *should* have existed. Of course, Berliners *did* want a single currency that was the same as that circulating in the Soviet zone, but that fact could not translate SED-organized assertions of some version of that policy into universal support for the party or its Soviet patron.

Soviet and SED accounts of the events of the day did not differ that much from those of the Western parties. An article in *Tägliche Rundschau*, described SED leaders speaking to the crowd about broad concepts such as a unified Germany and a unified Berlin. In a description that seemed to emphasize the party's authority, the paper portrayed the crowds as leaving the assembly chambers only when requested to do so by SED leaders and responding enthusiastically to those leaders' pronouncements. Yet, if this depiction underscored SED ability to exercise control, it also made no effort to conceal the violence that erupted following the end of the session. It justified the beating of the LDP delegate, Anton Schöpke, and the violent harassment of SPD delegate Jeanette Wolff as products of the workers' dissatisfaction with the "deceivers of the people" (*Volksbetrüger*). The article derided Deputy Wolff as a betrayer of the working class and explains her speeches and actions *within* the assembly as the reason for her mistreatment in the street outside.[23]

A letter from Deputy Schöpke to Otto Suhr characterizes the incidents in much more visceral terms. He described how the mob derided Jeanette Wolff as a "national traitor" (*Volksverräterin*) and an "old Jewish sow." For him these "acts of terror" had less to do with politics than criminality, although his complaint about a lack of any police action (in the Soviet sector) contains an implicit suggestion of police (and by extension the SED's and the Soviets') political culpability.[24] When taken together with SED assessments, however, it suggests a more ambiguous relationship between disputed claims of authority and the independence of popular action.

Speaking to the city assembly, the head of the SPD faction, Franz Neumann, claimed Berliners' real support for his party. He noted that the Soviet Order No. 111 explained itself as a product of the "demands of the

---

[23] "Berliner Arbeiterschaft erhebt ihre Stimme: Massenproteste gegen die verräterische Politik des Mehrheitsblocks vor und im Berliner Stadthaus." *Tägliche Rundschau* (Nr. 145 [950], 4. Jg., Thursday, June 24, 1948), 1.

[24] LAB, Rep. 280 (LAZ-Sammlung), Film Nr. 31, Sta.-Ort. Nr. 6611.

German democratic public," an assertion he rejected. The DWK proclamation of a new currency for Berlin and the Soviet zone had been issued simultaneously with the Soviet Order No. 111, and Neumann denounced any claims that body might make to represent the German public.[25] He moved on to address the unrest that had confronted the assembly as it sought to start the session. Neumann condemned the 600 to 800 persons driven there from the "SAG-Betrieben" (Soviet Joint-Stock Companies) to participate in the demonstrations before the Stadthaus as unrepresentative of the Berlin workers. He dismissed the crowds as organized by the SED and criticized the various SED leaders who had incited the crowd. In his assessment this "theater" served only to highlight the fear felt by those "people from the [DWK]." Offering an alternative to this artificial version of popular support, Neumann concluded his speech with a call for Berliners to gather the next day at the Hertha sports field to demonstrate for "freedom, the independence and autonomy of Berlin."[26]

A flyer announcing that assembly clearly elaborated the SPD's understanding of the situation: In the upper corner, a line proclaimed "About the currency" followed, in large letters, by the slogan, "Berlin free, never communist!"[27] Ernst Reuter spoke to a crowd that the police estimated at 45,000.[28] Developing the themes from his March speech commemorating the 1848 Revolution, Reuter proclaimed Berlin's unwillingness to submit to a "wave of communist dictatorship."[29] With Marshall Sokolovskii's currency proclamation, he argued, the Soviets had openly asserted their claim to all Berlin sectors. Faced with this new stage in the "battle for Berlin's freedom," Reuter called on Berliners to raise their voices to be heard around the world. Although he asserted the Social Democrats' leadership in this battle for freedom, he also recognized that their efforts depended on the particular contours of life in postwar Berlin, contours that still transcended the political and economic lines of the sector boundaries.

Reflecting on the outward cause of the immediate crisis, the competing currency reforms, the future West Berlin mayor focused on a fundamental, common experience that continued to tie all parts of the city together. In

---

[25] *Behauptung von Freiheit und Selbstverwaltung 1946–48*, 515.
[26] Ibid., 26 and 28.
[27] LAB, Rep. 280 (LAZ-Sammlung), Film Nr. 57, Sta.-Ort. Nr. 11763.
[28] Activity report from the office of the Polizeipräsident in Berlin, LAB, STA Rep. 9, Nr. 89, Bl. 181. West Berlin newspapers estimated the crowd at approximately 80,000. See Davison, *The Berlin Blockade*, 101.
[29] Reuter, *Schriften, Reden*, 400.

East and West, he noted, we all know the "fantastic black market prices," and recognize the need for dramatic economic transformations. But if the common experience of material crisis provided a common motivation for change, Reuter saw in Berlin's four-power status a unique opportunity to stake a claim to a form of power that transcended the common material experience. In response to SED assertions that Berlin lay in the Soviet zone and therefore must depend on the Soviet zone for its economic survival, Reuter instead emphasized Berlin's ongoing status as a global metropolis (*Weltstadt*). "Berlin was never just a city in the province of Brandenburg [. . . .] Anyone who now asserts that Berlin belongs only to the Zone that surrounds it destroys Berlin. Berlin cannot and does not want to be a provincial city that would in any case, by the way, have the character of a one-dimensional garrison town." Thus while simultaneously maintaining Berlin's imbeddedness in a common German experience of material scarcity, he also asserted its potential to transcend the limits that other powers sought to impose on the city, claiming for Berliners a unique, symbolic power that remained independent of any attempts to subject the city to the "lash of hunger" (*Hungerpeitsche*).[30] This sort of looming threat did not, however, prove long in coming.

Transport Restrictions, Airlift, and the Battle for Position in Berlin

On June 24, the same day Reuter took the podium at the Hertha stadium, *Tägliche Rundschau* announced that technical problems had disrupted freight and passenger service on the rail line between Helmstedt and Berlin.[31] Perhaps more significantly, in the night of June 23, the Soviet Command ordered that remotely produced current (*Fernstrom*) as well as current produced by the Soviet sector power plants, Klingenberg and Rummelsburg, no longer be provided to the city's western sectors.[32]

---

[30] Reuter, *Schriften, Reden*, 407–8.

[31] "Störung an der Eisenbahnstrecke Berlin – Helmstedt," *Tägliche Rundschau* (June 24, 1948), 1. Although appearing on the front page, this notice is unobtrusively placed beneath another article and easily overlooked. While obviously an empty excuse, it perhaps reflected some underlying insecurities in the Soviet zone as the paper explained that rail traffic could not be rerouted because that would cause an excessive disruption of rail transport throughout the Soviet zone. Actually, traffic from western Germany into the Soviet zone (and to Berlin) was restricted on June 18 in response to the Western currency reform. The Western forces issued no protests as they deemed these steps reasonable control measures. See, e.g., Tusa, *The Berlin Airlift*, 139.

[32] From the Wochenbericht Nr. 157 ueber die Arbeiten der BEWAG vom 21.-27.6.48 in LAB, STA Rep. 114, Nr. 155.

American officials represented these steps as an almost immediate threat to the Berlin population. In a cable to Under Secretary of the Army, William H. Draper, General Lucius Clay estimated that the German population would begin to suffer in a matter of days and that this suffering would become acute in two to three weeks.[33] For the Americans, this threat to Berliners remained fundamentally about the Western powers in Berlin: it sought to force them to withdraw from Berlin or to remain in the city only with a humiliating loss of prestige and privileges.[34] But on June 29, a report for the head of the city Department for Trade and Supply (*Handel und Versorgung*) indicated that supplies for eight major foodstuffs would last at least until late July.[35] During the last days of June, nonairlift food transports continued to arrive in Berlin even after the Soviet transportation restrictions had been imposed.[36]

The American response to the situation developed rather slowly. Uncertainty reigned in Washington as the Truman administration debated the merits of options including sending an armed convoy through the Soviet zone, withdrawing from Berlin, or seeking some kind of renewed currency agreement with the Soviets. American military officials on the ground in Berlin forced the administration's hand.[37] On the afternoon of June 24, the American Commander in Berlin, Frank Howley, promised that the Americans would stay in Berlin, that they would not "stand by and allow the German people to starve."[38] After receiving assurances from Ernst Reuter that the German population would be willing to endure substantial hardships rather than cave in to Soviet pressure, Clay ordered Major-General Curtis LeMay, commander of the U.S. Air Force in Europe, to dispatch all

[33] Clay to Draper, June 25, 1948 in *The Papers of General Lucius D. Clay: Germany 1945–1949*, vol. 2, Jean Edward Smith, ed. (Bloomington and London: Indiana University Press, 1974), 696–7.

[34] Robert Murphy summary to Sec. State (June 26, 1948), *FRUS* 1948, vol. II, 919.

[35] Memo from the Ern. HB. VIII/2, dated June 29, 1948, Hauptamt für Bedarfsdeckung, LAB, STA Rep. 113, Nr. 16. The supplies of these eight foodstuffs were projected to last at least until July 27 (flour, not taking into account existing grain reserves) or as long as until November 22 (sugar).

[36] See the report filed in the Sekretariat des OB: Handakte Dr. Friedensburg zu Fragen der Spaltung, 12.5.1948 – 17.11.1948, LAB, STA Rep. 101, Nr. 169, Bl. 35. The report notes, for example, that 345 train cars arrived from the west from June 24–7. Penciled comments indicate that they arrived on secondary tracks as the main Helmstedt-Berlin line was closed. Robert Murphy reported to Washington on the arrival of various food trains and barges in the last days of June 1948. See Stivers, "The Incomplete Blockade," *Diplomatic History*, 572 n. 5.

[37] One former State Department staffer explained that officials in Washington accused Americans in Berlin of suffering from "localitis." Mautner, interview with the author.

[38] Quoted in Shlaim, *The United States and the Berlin Blockade*, 199.

his C-47s to fly supply runs to Berlin: the airlift was on.[39] These momentous decisions largely determined the course of American (and Western) policy for the next eleven months. The airlift proved a remarkable technical achievement, an innovative use of air power in international affairs. In seeking to assess the nature of this struggle, however, we should not rush to accept too rapidly these decisions as a natural response to the situation on the ground in Berlin or as the sole source of an eventual Western victory in Berlin.

During the last days of June, the situation in Berlin became increasingly tense. Beginning on Thursday, June 24, Berliners started to exchange their old currency for new. While the administrative and political ruptures between the Soviet and western zones had evolved over several years, the currency reforms now set out new lines of division in the midst of Berlin. For some time, the papers in the Soviet zone had been decrying the decision to go ahead with a currency reform in the western zones as the final step in Western efforts to divide Germany.[40] But in Berlin, the rupture was not nearly as radical as these accounts sought to imply. Especially for those in the west sectors (but by no means only for them), the decision to exchange one's savings for one currency did not imply a total rejection of the other. The exchange process encapsulated the multilayered survival practices that Berliners had learned over the past three years: the independent methods they adopted to cope with or even exploit these new developments simply continued.

In a final police report on the currency reform in the Soviet sector, the police sector assistant described how during the first day of the exchange, the conversations among the people lining up at the exchange sites focused primarily on their concerns about the steps to obtain the new currency and speculation about what it would buy them. Black market demand far outstripped supply, as people sought to translate their old money into material goods. The large crowds met police efforts to control black market trade with resistance. Because the amount of old currency that could be exchanged was limited, it was officially impossible to transfer existing wealth into new currency, but enterprising Berliners sought out alternatives. One woman described how persons with less than the allowed exchange amount sold a portion of their allotment to those looking to

---

[39] Ibid., 199–206 for a summary of the course of American decision making at this point in the crisis.

[40] See, e.g., "Westmächte vollenden Spaltung Deutschlands," *Neues Deutschland* (June 19, 1948), 1.

translate larger sums of old currency into new.[41] In some instances strings of subordinates each carried the maximum allowable sum to various exchange sites in return for a share of their patron's new currency.[42]

Rumors abounded about the sale of the stickers with which the Soviet sector financial authorities were transforming the old currency into the new, but the Berlin police reported no arrests in spite of energetic investigations.[43] The previously mentioned Soviet sector police report describes large numbers of West sector inhabitants who gathered in front of the Soviet sector exchange sites on June 29 (the day after the last day of the exchange). Apparently, they only dispersed after loudspeaker trucks announced that no further exchanges would be made and that controls would be carried out to check for possession of west marks. The report clearly implied that these persons were coming to the eastern sector in an effort to obtain east marks after having already received west marks in their home sectors. Soviet sector police checked gatherings, especially in known black market locales, to find persons possessing the new western marks. Anyone found to have the new currency was to be temporarily detained, the money confiscated, and a citation issued.[44] But in spite of Soviet sector efforts to restrict access to and control the value of the new currency, it rapidly took on a life of its own. The currency trade in east and west marks reached substantial proportions almost immediately and provided a new measure of economic activities that continued to cross sector lines.

Two weeks after the currency reform, *Sie* reported results from a survey of shopkeepers in east and west sectors to try to assess its impact on economic life in the city. In the days just prior to the currency reform, it universally reported dramatic sales increases, but the two days immediately after the currency exchange began, June 25 and 26, saw sales drop to almost nothing. By early July sales seemed to be improving slightly, but

---

[41] Birgit Gravelmann and Annette Weickert, *Weibliche Selbständigkeit als Phänomen der Nachkriegszeit? Vier Berliner Frauen berichten über ihren Alltag*, Veröffentlichungen von hervorragenden Diplomarbeiten (Berlin: Fachhochschule für Sozialarbeit und Sozialpädagogik, 1991), 116.

[42] Andreas Friedrich, *Battleground Berlin*, 228.

[43] Final report on the Carrying out of the Currency Reform from the Police Sector Asst. for the SovSector to Oberstleutnant Kotyschew (Central Command), dated June 29, 1948, LAB, STA Rep. 9, Nr. 24, Bl. 127. A report filed with the Brandenburg Criminal Police described how coupons valued at 700 RM were being offered for 1,000 RM in old currency at the train station in Treptow (Soviet sector). Brandenburgisches LHA, Ld. br. Rep. 203 VP, Nr. 127, Bl. 101.

[44] LAB, STA Rep. 9, Nr. 24, Bl. 128.

the respondents' brief narrative comments hinted at the ways that consumers and retailers remained uneasy about the long-term implications of the new currency situation, even as they developed short-term strategies to cope with the changes. West sector retailers reported that they were accepting both currencies but that most people offered east marks.

In the Soviet sector, retailers noted that they were permitted only to accept east marks, although two added the qualifier "officially," and one even asserted "unofficially, of course the D-Mark [west mark], too." An east sector flower seller complained that customers paid only in small coins (*Groschen*), perhaps reflecting their effort to take advantage of the fact that these small coins retained their face value, unlike larger coins that retained only a fraction of their prereform value. While a housewares retailer was the only one of the West sector merchants to express concerns about the blockade, east sector merchants noted that their limited access to western currency would hamper the ability to access necessary products and supplies produced in Germany's western zones.[45] *Sie's* increasingly critical perspective toward the SED and its policies in Berlin and the Soviet zone suggest the need for some caution about its summary of the difficulties facing east sector shopkeepers, but this survey's fragmentary account of postcurrency reform Berlin trade offers a vision of a fluid economic environment that takes seriously the ability of Berliners to shape the operation and significance of the currency reform.

On June 27, a representative of the criminal police in Brandenburg took an information-gathering tour through Berlin. He reported that the black market was currently trading not in goods but in currencies. Near the Zoological Garden station (British sector), he observed a woman selling a man west marks at the rate of one to twenty east marks. Perhaps even more interestingly, though, he described the beginnings of a process of qualitative assessment of the two currencies. In Treptow (Soviet sector) he encountered a crowd of people discussing the currencies. He reported that these people saw the trading of east marks for west marks at the rate of twenty or thirty to one as the work of speculators trying to portray the east mark as worthless, an assertion that fit nicely into SED visions of the underhanded measures that continually threatened its political and

---

[45] "Preise zu hoch, Geld zu knapp, noch keine Waren aus dem Westen: Eine Umfrage der 'sie' bei Geschäftsleuten im Westen und Osten Berlins – Allgemein noch große Zurückhaltung," *Sie* (July 11, 1948), 5. The paper published a table with information on fourteen merchants in seven different trades, each trade represented by one respondent from the western and one from the eastern half of the city. It is unclear whether these fourteen responses constitute the entire survey or merely a representative sample.

economic efforts. Many of those in the crowd reportedly suggested that the east mark would soon be the currency in highest demand. In contrast, the police agent described a crowd at Innsbrucker Platz (American sector) that discussed the worthlessness of the east mark. They only spoke of "wallpaper money," a derogatory reference to the fact that east marks were not new bills but old marks with new stickers attached. Some voices did speak in favor of the east mark, noting that they would need it if they wanted to go into the Soviet zone.[46]

The officer's decision to include this remark in his report is suggestive on a number of levels. To the extent that it accurately describes at least some Berliners' assessment of the situation they faced that summer, it points to their expectation that they would continue to need to depend on their ability to manage supply connections to the surrounding Soviet zone. At the same time, it is difficult not to imagine the report writer's consciousness of the audience within the SED-dominated Brandenburg police for which he was writing. Asserting (West) Berliners' ongoing need and desire to trade with the Soviet zone implicitly argued for its economic strength and its ability to offer desirable goods. For many Soviet zone and SED leaders beset with feelings of insecurity about the Soviet zone's relative economic viability, this depiction would have offered a welcome validation of their economic policies. Yet even in this report, Berliners' multilayered understandings of the new currency are clearly evident. Subsequent appeals to Berliners on behalf of the eastern currency regularly trumpeted the access to economic opportunity that it could provide. Whether such assertions were wishful thinking, cold cynicism, or uncareful deployment of information like that produced in this report, this account offers a useful point of entry into the evolving discourse of economic insecurity that increasingly dominated eastern authorities' views of Berlin.

These early reports of discussions about the new currencies are important in trying to understand the SED's assessment of its policies and the popular responses to them. As evidenced by the previously mentioned report, Soviet zone officials early on sensed a rhetorical assault on the relative quality of the eastern currency. Accounts of west sector newspapers with "propaganda" for the west mark being seized in the Mitte district (Soviet sector) or of "asocial elements making use of the gatherings of people to incite disquiet in the population and to hold political speeches" suggest even more distinctly the creeping inadequacy felt by

[46] Report on an information-gathering trip to Berlin, dated June 28, 1948, BLHA, Ld. Br. Rep. 203 VP, Nr. 127, Bl. 101.

Soviet sector officials in the face of a competing western currency. They lost little time before they addressed this issue and linked it overtly to the broader material insecurities of life in Berlin. On June 24, the day on which the currency exchange began, a headline in the *Tägliche Rundschau* read, "The new Reichsmark will be stable: Expansion of Interzonal Trade desired – Introduction of West Mark splits Berlin – Catastrophic Consequences for the Economy of the West Sectors." The article that followed decried the introduction of the west mark in Berlin as an effort to divide Berlin, regardless of the economic cost to the city, and an open attempt to disrupt the economy of the Soviet zone.[47]

One day later, the paper published an appeal to the German people from the head of the SVAG, Marshall Sokolovskii. In the front-page declaration, he condemned the Western introduction of a separate currency and asserted that the Soviets were undertaking measures to prevent the swamping of the Soviet zone and Berlin with annulled currency. Countering any suggestion that the food supply for the Berlin population could not be secured without the presence of the Western powers, Sokolovskii noted that the Soviets had provided food for Berlin already one day after the capitulation in 1945. He concluded by citing Stalin's remark that Hitlers come and go, but the German people, the German state remains.[48] That same day, a headline in the SED party organ read, "Americans Disorganize Supply."[49] The implication of these two statements should be taken together. First, Sokolovskii suggested that the Soviets had taken some measures limiting access to the Soviet zone but implied that these steps were purely defensive in nature. At the same time, he challenged the need for Western assistance to meet the material needs of the city. The *Neues Deutschland* headline hints at the possibility of material hardship and places the blame squarely on the Americans.

It is hardly shocking that in their communications with their superiors in Washington, American officials in Berlin represented the situation following the imposition of transportation restrictions on June 24 as one in which the western sectors had been cut off from all outside sources of supply, that only the airlift remained to provide the needed food and fuel supplies for that half of the city.[50] It is, however, a bit more surprising to hear some eastern officials buying into this description. At a conference

---

[47] *Tägliche Rundschau* (June 24, 1948), 2.
[48] *Tägliche Rundschau* (June 25, 1948), 1.
[49] *Neues Deutschland* (June 25, 1948), 2.
[50] Stivers, "The Incomplete Blockade," 592f.

of the Berlin FDGB's Central Committee on June 25, Roman Chwalek described the situation:

The four-power administration in Berlin is essentially finished. By means of the blockage of all links to the West, the foodstuff supply of the West Sectors has been interrupted. For the Western Allies, therefore, only the air route is available to supply the west districts. If the French, e.g., after 14 days no longer have any foodstuffs, the possibility exists that the Russians will offer foodstuffs, but only in exchange for the eastern currency. Thus all Berliners will push for the recognition of the eastern currency in order to guarantee their survival.[51]

Here, Chwalek suggested that the Berliners would in a short time turn to the Soviet zone (and by extension to the SED and the FDGB) to overcome the material hardships facing them.

Chwalek's remarks reflected his general optimism about the opportunity to counter the growing strength of the oppositional trade union movement UGO and the possibilities for further integrating the Berlin FDGB into that of the Soviet zone. His optimistic assessment of the supply situation should be understood largely in terms of a belief that Berliners would *interpret* the situation as extreme and less as an accurate reflection of specific material measures or their impact on the city. Indeed, this early confidence in the evolution of public opinion was fundamentally misplaced. The FDGB's interpretation of the emerging economic difficulties as the product of the Western powers' decision to introduce a separate currency in their sectors did not gain broad acceptance, at least not in the version Chwalek was promoting. To the contrary, any perceived increase in economic hardships increasingly led to a rise in anti-Soviet sentiment among Berlin workers.

A series of late-June reports from FDGB officials in the west sectors described the very limited traction that the eastern union's proposals were finding among western workers. Although the report from the heavily working-class Kreuzberg district blamed much of this sentiment on the propaganda impact of RIAS loudspeaker trucks "racing around" the district's streets, the subtext to these accounts of workers' unwillingness to rally behind the FDGB remained that these workers were uninterested in directly challenging any occupying power and more interested in obtaining whichever currency offered the greatest immediate material

---

[51] Protokoll über die Konferenz des geschäftsführenden Vorstandes mit den Sekretären der westlichen Bezirke, 25.6.1948, LAB, BPA, FDGB1681. It is somewhat unclear from the minutes if this is a direct stenographic account of Chwalek's report or only a paraphrase. The latter seems more likely.

benefits.[52] The FDGB leadership's hope that the evolving crisis would lead Berliners to reject the Western powers and turn to the Soviet zone in desperation faced an even more fundamental obstacle: the supply of the western sectors had not been reduced to the airlift alone and the blockade had not been designed to achieve this.

Berliners undoubtedly found the dual currency reforms and the associated impact on daily life in the city disconcerting; they wondered about the value of their newly obtained marks and worried about their ability to purchase the goods they needed, but these material concerns did not differ dramatically from those they had faced for the past three years. Headlines in Western newspapers trumpeted the assault on Berlin's freedom, calling for Berliners to hold firm and for the West to support the city. At the same time, the first flights of the airlift began to buzz their way into Berlin's consciousness, but these supply efforts had, at this point at least, only minimal material impact. Even at this early stage, the Berlin Blockade emerged not primarily as a battle for material control of access to Berlin but as a contest between competing "spin doctors" who sought to shape popular understanding of what was happening.

The American Commander in Berlin, Frank Howley, as well as the Western-licensed press in the city decried the Soviet refusal to supply fresh milk to the western sectors. As they described it, the Soviet decision represented a heartless assault on west sector infants. This rhetoric did not go unnoticed. On June 28, Berlin SED cochair Hermann Matern wrote a letter to the Soviet Commander in Berlin, General Kotikov, and requested that the Soviets lift their ban on fresh milk deliveries. While noting that the Western powers were clearly responsible for the breakdown of four-power administration in Berlin and emphasizing that each occupier was obligated to supply the food for its sector of occupation, Matern asked the Soviets to supply fresh milk from their zone in the interests of the "innocent sufferers" in the west sectors.[53] In this letter, there is a clear sense of the public relations damage being done to the Soviets (and by extension to the SED). The Americans rejected the subsequent Soviet offer to supply fresh

---

[52] Berichte aus den Beziken der westlichen sektoren über die Auswirkungen der Währungsreform in den Betrieben, n.d., LAB, BPA, FDGB 439: FDGB-Bezirksvorstand Groß-Berlin, Vorstandssek. Schlimme/Deter: Währungsreform-Bewegung, June 1948. On July 2, Soviet sector FDGB officials continued to discuss the need to clarify if and when the Western Allies would have to leave Berlin. Minutes of a meeting of the 1. Vorsitzenden and Org.-Sekretäre from the eastern districts on 2.7.1948, LAB, BPA, FDGB 1681.

[53] Letter from Hermann Matern to General Kotikov, dated June 28, 1948, LAB, BPA, IV L-2/3/512.

milk in exchange for western sector goods, a hard line not easy to reconcile with the spirit of Howley's pronouncement that the Americans would not let the Berliners starve.[54] At the same time, the solution proffered by the Soviets does suggest that even at the outset Soviet blockade policy was not willing even to attempt absolute control at the cost of a public relations disaster.

A letter from Marshal Sokolovskii to the British Military Governor Robinson, published in the *Tägliche Rundschau* on June 30, noted the Soviet declaration to reopen border traffic between the Soviet zone and the western zones to persons who possessed interzonal passes issued on the basis of the regulation that existed before June 19. Marshall Sokolovskii regretted that he had to continue temporarily to maintain the restrictions on motor vehicle traffic on the Helmstedt-Berlin Autobahn because he must use all available means to prevent the illegal transport of hard currency (*Valuta*) from the west zones to Berlin. The note continued with the remark that Soviet personnel would do all they could to eliminate the technical difficulties on the Helmstedt-Berlin train line as soon as possible and indicated support for Western efforts to supplement the existing food stocks in the west sectors by air transport. In conclusion, Sokolovskii referred to the British decision to block all freight trains between the Soviet and British zones and urged the British to take immediate measures to end this disruption of the normal course of German interzonal trade that was damaging the German peacetime economy.[55]

This note captures the Soviets' schizophrenic approach to their expanded control measures in and around Berlin, simultaneously open about some Soviet transportation restrictions (on the Autobahn) while continuing the charade about technical difficulties on the Helmstedt-Berlin rail line. More important, though, was its critique of a disruption in interzonal trade. Another article on that same page touched on this motivation and referred to Walter Ulbricht's speech in front of the SED Parteivorstand that outlined the (SVAG-approved) two-year plan for the Soviet zone. This plan deemed interzonal trade vital both for economic development in the Soviet zone and as a means of projecting its influence into western Germany.[56] In this context, the embryonic Western counterblockade measures (as an extension of Western currency reform)

[54] Stivers, "The Incomplete Blockade," 372.
[55] "Wiedereröffnung des Grenzverkehrs: Antwortschreiben Marschall Sokolowskijs an General Robertson," *Tägliche Rundschau* (June 30, 1948), 1.
[56] See ch. 4.

appeared to Soviet and SED officials as an assault on this inter-German trade and, more pointedly, as an assault on the SED-led remaking of the Soviet zone.

Was this, as is most often assumed, simply rhetorical posturing, an effort to cover up the ulterior motives underlying the Soviet blockade of Berlin? In his memoirs Lucius Clay purported to have gained an insight into the "real reason for the blockade" in a July 3 meeting between the three Western military governors and Marshall Sokolovskii. In this meeting, Sokolovskii allegedly explained that the "technical difficulties" producing the blockade would continue until the Western powers had abandoned their plans for a West German government, an assertion that suggested the crisis was not really about Berlin at all.[57] But this *was* a Berlin crisis, and as exemplified by the expanding control efforts of the "Ring around Berlin" and the campaigns against black marketeering in the Soviet zone, the Soviet transportation and supply restrictions imposed in late June did not constitute a radical break with earlier control efforts.[58] Rather than a new policy directed suddenly against the West and its steps to craft a new West German state (culminating in the London Recommendations reached just weeks earlier), the Soviet measures should be taken as part of a more general effort to cope with ongoing Soviet weakness within its zone. The positions elaborated in the public statements on both sides of the crisis project a sense of much greater control over the course of events than actually existed. Neither the Soviets nor the West were in a position to readily translate policy declarations into any definitive result.

Soviet Order No. 80 and the *Handelsgesellschaft Groß-Berlin*

In its reply to the notes protesting the situation in Berlin sent by France, Great Britain, and the United States on July 6, the Soviet Union emphasized that any agreements on administering the city of Berlin or on Western access to Berlin must operate in the context of agreements that addressed broader German questions. Responding to Western accusations that a Soviet blockade was threatening the "safety of the German population"

---

[57] Clay, *Decision in Germany*, 367. This account has served as the basic explanation adopted by most Western historical accounts of the blockade.

[58] Most often these continuities have been explained in terms of a "creeping Blockade," which again denies the particular significance of the Berlin location, suggesting that these expanding control measures only mattered for the grand strategy issues that have come to define the blockade. See, e.g., Keiderling, *Rosinenbomber*, 82–8.

in their sectors of Berlin, the Soviet note asserts: "In this connection, if the situation requires, the Soviet Government would not object to ensuring by its own means adequate supply [in all "essentials"] for all Greater Berlin."[59] Their offer denounced by the British as mere propaganda, the Soviets rapidly responded. East sector newspapers trumpeted the Soviet provision of 100,000 tons of valuable foodstuffs for the city and the Soviets began to set in place structures with which to carry out their proposal.[60] On July 24, Soviet Order No. 80 set up an eastern subsection of the city's Main Food Office to oversee the supply of West sector residents from shops in the Soviet sector.[61] Directed by the former SED mayor of the city's Mitte district, Paul Letsch, this subdepartment occupied a unique locus of Soviet and DWK engagement that highlights their policies' ambiguous but nonetheless destructive efforts to intervene in the municipal administration.

In an assessment for the SED in Berlin's Prenzlauer Berg district (Soviet sector), one report writer described a positive popular response to the Soviet offer but offered curiously unconvincing justifications for his conclusions. He began by describing the enthusiastic response in a district firehouse as a reaction to the firemen's limited expectations of Soviet action. Somewhat surprisingly, he explained those expectations by pointing out that only a day earlier the 10 P.M. news report on RIAS had rejected the offer made in the Soviet note as a "bluff," unconvincing given the ongoing shortages in the Soviet zone. Apparently, only two members of the shift reacted negatively to the announcement, and the report writer made sure to describe them as "stubborn SPD men." But the absolute line he tried to draw – between clear-thinking public servants and their SPD opponents – crumbled somewhat in light of his suggestion that even the supporters of the Soviet offer were getting at least part of their news from the opposition RIAS. In a further challenge to his effort to craft an impression of a propaganda coup opposed only by a few SPD outliers, the second portion of his

[59] Text of Identical Notes from the Government of the U.S.S.R. to the the Governments of the USA, the United Kingdom, and France on the Berlin Situation, July 14, 1948. In Wolfgang Heidelmeyer and Günter Hindrichs, eds., *Documents on Berlin 1943–1963* (Munich: R. Oldenbourg Verlag, 1963), 73.
[60] See "Die Sowjetunion übernimmt Versorgung der Bevölkerung ganz Berlins: Zunächst 100 000 Tonnen Lebensmittel aus der UdSSr für Berlin – Die Bewohner aller Sektoren erhalten ihre Rationen in voller Höhe," *Tägliche Rundschau* (Nr. 167 (972) 4. Jg., July 20, 1948), 1.
[61] See the chronological overview of events affecting the Food Department, LAB, Rep. 280, Sta.-Ort. Nr. 11307.

report cites his son, a twenty-six-year-old student and SED member who saw in the Soviet announcement an effective counter to Western claims that the "Russians will let the people hunger for the sake of their larger goals." It may be that his decision not to look for additional viewpoints outside his own household merely reflected personal laziness, but as it stands, his report cannot avoid some hint of just trying to offer party officials the optimistic interpretation of the situation that he assumed they would want to read.[62]

Soviet and SED officials did view with great optimism their offer to meet Western sector supply needs. Indeed, initial predictions of the number of persons who would take the opportunity to register for their supplies in the Soviet sector were quite remarkable. A district councilor in Berlin Mitte reported that the food supply and ration card distribution in the district was ready to supply an additional 410,000 rations.[63] These high hopes dissolved rapidly. In August, just over 21,000 West Berliners registered to receive their rations in the Soviet sector. The next month, this number more than doubled but was still only 56,444. Even when registrations reached their highest level, in early 1949, they amounted only to about 5 percent of the West sector population.[64] Most accounts of the blockade see this small percentage as an indication of the West Berliners' heroic willingness to hold out in the face of Soviet enticements, to suffer material hardship in defense of their freedom.[65] This ideological explanation for West Berliners' resistance can be accepted at best for a small portion of those who refused the Soviet offer.[66] In fact, even many SED members failed to shift their registration. Hermann Matern accused SED members in the western sectors of not recognizing the high political significance of the step, when they only began to sign up when coal was

---

[62] Stolpe, "Berichterstattung zur Versorgung von ganz Berlin durch die Sowjetische Militärverwaltung" (July 20, 1948). LAB, BPA 4/6/402.

[63] Aktennotiz, 27.7.1948 signed W. Seiffert. LAB, BPA, FDGB 207.

[64] The September and March figures are taken from "Graphic/Statistical Representations of Food Rations in the Soviet Sector, 1948–50," Magistrat v. Groß-Berlin, Abt. Handel und Versorgung, LAB, STA Rep. 113, Nr. 224, Bl. 105. The August figure is taken from a memo from Paul Letsch to Major Klimov (Soviet Central Command), dated September 10, 1948. Letsch notes the September registration figure to have been 66,105. The difference is produced by a variation in the number of registrants listed as coming from the French sector (34,683 vs. 25,022) but is otherwise unexplained.

[65] See Brandt and Löwenthal, *Ernst Reuter*, 436.

[66] William Stivers refers to the results of American opinion surveys in late July in which only 10 percent of those believing the airlift should be maintained in spite of the Soviet food offer (92 percent of all those surveyed) explained their view with expressions such as, "We will not desert to the Russians." Stivers, "The Incomplete Blockade," 576.

made available as well.[67] If even those most closely linked to the SED failed to take advantage of the Soviet offer, it seems likely that a purely ideological explanation is equally inadequate to explain the actions of those who refused to do so.

An understanding of the limited response to the Soviet supply offer as motivated solely by some sort of moral or ideological opposition to the Soviet Union presupposes the offer to be an isolated escape hatch offered up to West Berliners in the face of an otherwise impenetrable blockade. It assumes an either/or proposition: accept the Soviet offer or suffer undue privation. The notion of inherently superior food supplies in the Soviet sector is not borne out by the facts. Complaints about substitution of one item for another (e.g., of sugar for fats) as well as about the generally poor quality of Soviet sector foodstuffs were commonplace. In a letter to Soviet officials, Paul Letsch, the head of the subdepartment per Soviet Order No. 80, remarks that the "complaints about poor quality foodstuffs [in the Soviet sector] know no bounds."[68]

Three years after the end of the war, it was still not an easy task to travel from a distant western district to obtain one's rations in the eastern sector, especially if there was no assurance that the products would even be available for purchase. Even in early 1949, six months into the program of supplying West Berliners' rations, a woman wrote to the Soviet-licensed radio station in the city to complain that daily announcements about the availability of rationed goods in individual stores, the so-called stomach travel plan (*Magenfahrplan*), promised specific goods that then proved not to be available. The radio official who forwarded the letter to the main food office agreed with the letter writer that the Magenfahrplan should refrain from offering detailed information in order not to disappoint the housewives when they try to make their purchases.[69] The combined failure to provide either the goods in question or accurate information summed up the broad shortcomings of the Soviet supply program.

A complaint Letsch directed to his Soviet counterparts on August 30 elaborates a more provocative explanation for the lack of incentive to register for one's rations in the Soviet sector. He cited reports that large

---

[67] Protokoll d. Landesvorstandsitzung, October 2–3, 1948, LAB, BPA, IV L-2/1/39, Bl. 87.
[68] Letter from Letsch to Major Gubisch, dated August 20, 1948, LAB, STA Rep. 113, Nr. 37. See also the Abteilung K, Daily Rport to the Police President, September 6, 1948, LAB, STA Rep. 9, Nr. 241, Bl. 416. In this instance, the foodstuffs in question were various kinds of cereals.
[69] Letter from Frau Irma Bethge (Berlin-Bohnsdorf) to the Berliner Rundfunk, Stadtreporter (March 6, 1949). LAB, STA Rep. 113, Nr. 184.

amounts of vegetables were being trucked in from western zones and noted that these vegetables were being sold at relatively low prices in the western sectors. The report that prompted his letter even suggested that these prices were lower than those in the Soviet sector. Letsch complained that all efforts undertaken with the Berlin police to halt these transports had proven insufficient and requested assistance from the Soviet Command.[70] Although rations in Berlin had proved inadequate even before the blockade, these reports hinted that no *new* need had arisen for west sector residents to draw their rations in the east.

Perhaps even more striking, many in Berlin and even in the Soviet zone viewed the Soviet offer as empty. In a survey of Soviet zone opinions about the Berlin question and the Soviet offer to meet the food needs of the western sectors, most respondents seemed to feel that the Russians were bluffing and indicated that they did not believe that the West would let Berlin slip away. In general, the supply situation in the Soviet zone remained so bad that Soviet zone residents did not perceive Berliner supply concerns as a legitimate issue.[71] Already before the Soviet offer, other states in the Soviet zone had complained about the general shortages and criticized the preferential allocation of supplies to Berlin.[72] Soviet Order No. 80 did nothing to change these views. Among those who were already living under Soviet administration, the material realities of the often quite desperate supply situation in the Soviet zone tended to overwhelm any propaganda value of an offer that presumed to reflect the possibilities of Soviet largesse.

Still, the symbolic significance of West Berliners' decision to draw rations in the eastern sector should not be dismissed entirely, and the SED leadership in Berlin remained quite concerned about the lack of member participation in the distribution program. An even more telling assessment of popular perspectives on those West Berliners who did register in the east came to light in a discussion with "representatives of the West Berlin population" arranged by the FDGB in late November. The meeting's minutes run for more than sixty pages and describe how the crowd – mostly women – gave voice to their dissatisfaction with the material conditions in

---

[70] Letter from Letsch to Major Gubisch, dated August 30, 1948, LAB, STA Rep. 113, Nr. 37.

[71] Report submitted to Otto Meier on August 26, 1948, SAPMO, DY 30/IV 2/9.02/44, Bl. 398ff. More generally, see Koop, *Kein Kampf um Berlin*, 196–7.

[72] See Copy of a Report on the Versorgungslage from the SED Landesvorstand Sachsen, dated June 17, 1948, SAPMO, DY 30/IV 2/6.02/44, Bl. 105.

the city. The generally critical tone, coming from Berliners whose appearance at an FDGB-sponsored event suggested at least that they were not wholly opposed to the SED-led union's political line, forced the officials present to scramble to respond to this disgruntled public.

One woman, Ilse Treue, described the ordeal of purchasing foodstuffs at the cooperative (*Konsum*) on Neue Jakobstrasse: for the first few days of the month, she noted, it was impossible to buy things there without waiting in line for two to three hours; by the seventeenth or eighteenth, though, the store was nearly empty – only butter and sugar available – but butter could not yet be distributed for the next ration period (*Dekade*) before the twentieth. In response to a string of complaints about logistical difficulties facing west sector inhabitants trying to buy food in the Soviet sector, the meeting adopted a resolution calling for food stores in the Soviet sector to remain open past noon on Saturdays. When another woman stood up to defend the quality of the goods they could obtain in Soviet sector shops, many others in the crowd greeted her with catcalls and vociferous disagreement. For this crowd, presumably those who had decided to draw their rations in the Soviet sector, their decision had certainly not translated into unambiguous enthusiasm for the program's sponsors.

A number of women complained about rude treatment of West Berliners in the Soviet sector ration card offices and grocery stores. They perceived this treatment to be the result of ideological animosity directed toward them by Soviet sector inhabitants, because they, the West Berliners, had voluntarily decided to draw their rations in the east.[73] In this instance, lines of antagonism clearly crossed sector boundaries; individual Berliners put a face on these supply decisions and saw the political and symbolic implications of their decisions as part of clear and very much personal choices. Explicitly ideological coding came from a greater distance. Gustav Klingelhöfer took a hard line against persons registering for rations in the eastern sector, and in some instances district officials in the western sectors sought to force them from their jobs or apartments. In contrast to this rhetoric, the Western Allies in Berlin refused to authorize

---

[73] "Protokoll der Aussprache des FDGB Groß-Berlin mit Vertretern der Westberliner Bevölkerung, 27 November 1948," LAB, STA Rep. 106, Nr. 234. Referring to these clerks, one woman noted, "I don't know what political line they adhere to. We certainly know – our colleague Krueger just said the same thing – even in the eastern sector, the idea of class warfare has not been settled (*noch nicht ad acta gelegt*)" (Bl. 27). Dusiska responded to her complaint by asking her to come to his office the next day in order to drive to the location in question and see that the offending staffer be removed from that post.

measures to penalize those drawing rations in the Soviet sector or inhibit their ability to again receive rations in the western sectors.[74]

Regardless of the limited number of persons who accepted the Soviet offer, it remained an option available for residents of the west sectors and thus points to a level of potential choice that a "total" blockade would preclude. In some instances, people even sought to exploit the competition for Berliners' ration card registration. A confidential report delivered to Police President (east) Markgraf in September described a conversation in which a woman was overheard explaining that she would draw her rations in the Soviet sector only until she received her delivery of coal, at which point she would reregister in the west. The report also cited a worker in a Steglitz (American sector) ration card office who claimed that many people who registered for rations in the eastern sector were reporting their western card lost, thereby receiving a temporary card, which they then registered in the American sector.[75]

The sectors' competition for Berliners' ration cards lent itself to manip-ulation in the pursuit of material gain, a point that undermines any easy coding of West Berliners' failure to draw rations in the east as a "sym-bolic" gesture of defiance in the face of Soviet pressure. Nor should reg-istration in the east be assumed to represent an endorsement of Soviet or SED politics. One woman in Wedding (French sector) allegedly regis-tered in the Soviet sector to lessen the material burden on the airlift and allow more supplies to be stored up for Western troops in case of war.[76] West Berliners who refused to register eluded Soviet sector economic con-trol structures and offered yet another indication of how Berlin and its inhabitants vigorously challenged presumptions of totalizing control in the Soviet zone and even within the SED. More importantly, the lack of a *need* to register for the Soviet supply offer reflected the extent to which material conditions in Berlin continued to be shaped by circumstances independent of the blockade and airlift.

[74] See Stivers, "The Incomplete Blockade," 577f. See also Hallen and Lindenberger, "Frontstadt mit Lücken," 193f. Ration registration may have become an easy short-hand with which to define Berliners' allegiances. However, at this point at least, such coding was oversimplified. See also Katherine Pence, "Herr Schimpf und Frau Schande: Grenzgänger des Konsums im geteilten Berlin und die Politik des Kalten Krieges," in *Sterben für Berlin: Die Berliner Krisen 1948: 1958*, Burghard Ciesla, Michael Lemke, and Thomas Lindenberger, eds. (Berlin: Metropol Verlag, 2000), 185–202.
[75] Report from Abteilung K to Police President Markgraf, dated September 25, 1948, LAB, STA Rep. 9, Nr. 50, Bl. 217.
[76] Report from Abteilung K to Police President Markgraf, dated September 28, 1948, LAB, STA Rep. 9, Nr. 50, Bl. 226.

In a dramatic meeting on July 19, Marshall Sokolovskii met with two leading officials from the DWK to explore solutions to their dilemma: in spite of all the restrictions that they had introduced, Berlin's economic life continued to elude their control. After noting the Soviet decision to provide 100,000 tons of grain for the city, they discussed their plans to offer electric current and foodstuffs to the western sectors and eventually incorporate all of Berlin into the administrative structures of the DWK. They proposed to cultivate relationships with (West) Berlin factories and provide them with necessary raw materials but also to insure that the DWK controlled all their interzonal trade with the west. Berlin was not to be allowed independent economic access to the eastern or the western zones, goals they saw as dependent on their ability to "undermine" the Berlin Magistrat, to "eliminate" it (*schalten ihn aus*).[77] The notes of this meeting make no mention of the Western powers. While this hardly means that the Soviets now saw the British or Americans as a nonfactor in Berlin, it does suggest that the focal point of these particular Soviet and DWK strategies remained the relationship between Berlin (as a whole) and the Soviet zone, a relationship that during the summer of 1948 was proving increasingly difficult to manage.

On July 28, the DWK passed a resolution creating a special trade association for Greater Berlin (*Handelsgesellschaft für Groß-Berlin* or HfGB), with the responsibility to administer the supply of factories in Berlin's western sectors with the necessary raw materials and to manage the sales and distribution of their finished products.[78] Regardless of the level of response elicited from firms in the western sectors, even firms in the Soviet zone did not submit all their Berlin trade to the control of this newly formed body. In late September, the DWK issued a further directive in which all Soviet zone firms were forbidden from signing production and delivery contracts with individual Berlin firms. From that point on, all of its "unplanned trade" with Berlin firms (*außerplanmäßigen Warenverkehr*, i.e., trade not included in official economic plans) was to be carried out through the HfGB.[79] While this directive refers to all Berlin firms and not just those in the west sectors, the Handelsgesellschaft had

77 Unterredung Sokolowsky m. Selbmann [und] Leuschner, July 19, 1948, BA-DDR, DC 15–479, Bl. 23. Handwritten notes of the meeting that were most likely taken by Bruno Leuschner.

78 Sekretariat der DWK, 26th Session, July 28, 1948, BA-DDR, DC 15–342, Bl. 7. For a discussion of the firms who took up the DWK offer, see William Stivers, "The Incomplete Blockade," 586ff.

79 Sekretariat der DWK, 34th Session, September 21, 1948, BA-DDR, DC 15–351, Bl. 8.

220

Black Market, Cold War

been created as a means of expanding DWK influence over *west* sector firms. The DWK's repeated efforts to extend the controls of the HfGB pointed to the ongoing trade between individual Soviet zone and Soviet sector firms with their counterparts in western Berlin that continued to make an end run around DWK controls.

An American report filed with the office of the U.S. Political Advisor for Germany in November 1948 describes an interview with a German businessman whose British sector firm was flourishing in spite of the blockade. Whereas previously his firm had traded primarily with the British zone, it now produced industrial glass products almost exclusively for the Soviet zone. He asserted that the Soviets paid 100 percent in west marks or occasionally even in dollars and cut all red tape to provide the necessary raw materials for products they needed. Especially before controls were tightened on October 18, the border controls could be passed with relative ease, and from that date the Soviets increased their efforts to conclude agreements directly with west sector firms. Interestingly enough, the businessman also reported that his firm (near the Zoo station) received twenty-four hours of electricity a day. The memo refers to newspaper accounts describing the continuous supply of electric current to firms located near S-Bahn lines or rail stations that, even in the west sectors, remained under Soviet control and continued to be supplied with current from the Soviet sector. Of course, this phenomenon was not limited to Soviet-supplied current; persons living near Western military installations also found that they received continuous electric current.[80]

Soviet sector and Soviet zone firms also maintained ongoing links to western Berlin. Often, these contacts were facilitated by branch offices or subsidiary firms with offices on opposite sides of the sector boundaries. Under the guise of transports within the firm, raw materials and finished products could be brought back and forth across the boundary controls with relative ease.[81] Increasingly, Soviet zone officials addressed these trades as a kind of illegal economic assault on the areas under their control. They classified these transactions as acts of economic sabotage, equivalent to those of black marketeers in Berlin and elsewhere in the Soviet zone. By reimagining the blockade as part of an attack on the

[80] Memorandum from Robert M. Berry to James Riddleberger, NA, RG 84, 350/57/18/02, box 216.
[81] On Soviet zone police concern about the possibilities presented by firms with branches in both Berlin and the Soviet zone, see the memo from the MdI Brandenburg, Abt. Polizei (Landeskriminalamt), June 4, 1948, BLHA, Ld. Br. Rep. 203, VP, Nr. 125, Bl. 11. Note that this concern predates the standard starting date of the blockade.

black market, the policies typically associated with the blockade (such as Soviet Order No. 80) become more obviously components of a larger network of developing (economic) control structures being deployed in the Soviet zone and never just a blockade of West Berlin.[82]

Checkpoints, Controls, and Blockade Runners

For the most part, the "Soviet" transport restrictions that comprised the blockade were implemented by German police in the Soviet sector and the surrounding Soviet zone. While the nature of the controls changed over time, the restrictions on access to Berlin did not entail a simple cutting off of traffic to and from the western zones. They were at the same time both less and more than this: Berliners maintained some access to the west (if along indirect routes), and eastern officials undertook additional efforts to control access to the surrounding Soviet zone. These attempts demanded cooperative efforts from diverse sections of the German administration, including the DWK, various branches of the police (rail- and water-police, municipal police, etc.), and local officials in Berlin, Brandenburg, and elsewhere. As this partial listing of responsible bodies suggests, the execution of these controls tended not to be uniform, and conflicts between various departments often hampered control measures.[83] It is more accurate to speak of an ongoing if turbulent flow of goods and supplies into (West) Berlin rather than to portray a tight seal interrupted by an occasional blockade runner. The porous nature of these controls did not reflect a failure to implement a strict blockade but rather resulted largely from the ambiguous ends that these controls sought to serve.

It is important, first of all, to recognize the extent of supply and trade traffic that the Soviets or their German partners officially authorized to pass in and out of the western sectors. In addition to those west sector residents drawing their rations in the east, party and trade union organizations also provided substantial supplies to their supporters living in

---

[82] See the order from the SVA commander in Brandenburg dated October 14, 1948. In this order he notes: "Making use of the fact that the struggle against [illicit transports] is not being carried out with the necessary intensity and that checks on the activities of trading firms and industrial plants by the responsible government organs have dropped off, speculators and criminal elements are buying up foodstuffs and industrial goods in the State of Brandenburg and transporting them illegally (mostly by car) over the borders of Brandenburg." BLHA, Ld. Br. Rep. 203, VP, Nr. 9, Bl. 85.

[83] See Memo from Kreispolizeiamt Teltow (signed Leibholz, Ltr. d. Schupo) to Brandenburg MdI (Abt. Polizei) regarding cooperation between municipal police (Schupo) and rail police, dated August 9, 1948, Ld. Br. Rep. 203, VP, Nr. 31, Bl. 173.

the western sectors. SED members, party officers, and even doctors who belonged to the FDGB requested additional coal supplies from Soviet sector officials. The FDGB made additional foodstuffs and clothing available to some west sector workers. But the propaganda value of such efforts proved tricky. At the November meeting of west sector residents organized by the FDGB, one woman, who clearly supported the SED position, criticized the unions' provision of shoes for women working to build the new airfield in Tegel (French sector). In effect, she criticized union officials for underwriting a building project tied to the airlift, but she also explicitly condemned a decision to supply shoes to women who had decided to work there only because they would be paid in west marks even as "thousands upon thousands of women are walking around Berlin with their feet in shreds and clad only in rags." Although an FDGB official argued that these shoes never came from the FDGB, that didn't matter for this woman. Her readiness to believe what she had heard suggested that, at the very least, she believed the FDGB to be an unprincipled supplier of scarce goods, regardless of what and how much the organization might make available.[84]

Individual Berliners supplementing their food and heating supplies from the Soviet zone played a much larger supply role, both in terms of the volume of material and in terms of political impact. An October article in *Tägliche Rundschau* complained that during the week of September 27 to October 3, 420,000 foragers (*Hamsterers*) had used the outlying S-Bahn lines to reach the surrounding countryside and smuggle an estimated total of 7,000 tons of goods into the west sectors.[85] A similar article in *Neues Deutschland* reported that 30,000 tons of potatoes were smuggled into the west sectors during August and 36,000 tons during September.[86] In remarks to the Central Committee of the Berlin SED, Hermann Matern put the number of scroungers heading out into the Soviet zone from Berlin at 200,000 a day.[87] While these figures must be treated with caution, they

---

[84] See the critical remarks by Frau Granzow in Protokoll d. Aussprache des FDGB Groß-Berlin mit Vetretern d. Westberliner Bevoelkerung, 27.11.1948, LAB, STA Rep. 106, Nr. 234, Bl. 38 and the rejection of her claim on Bl. 61.

[85] "Täglich 61 000 Hamsterer," *Tägliche Rundschau* (Nr. 236 (1041) 4. Jg., October 8, 1948), 1.

[86] "Volkspolizei schafft Ordnung," *Neues Deutschland* (October 20, 1948), in BLHA, Ld. Br. Rep. 203, VP, Nr. 98, Bl. 214. This article seeks to justify intensified control measures implemented by the Brandenburg police. As a comparison, during September, the airlift flew in a total of 38,499 tons of foodstuffs for civilian use. See Deutsches Institut für Wirtschaftsforschung, *Berlins Wirtschaft in der Blockade*, 12.

[87] Protokoll d. Landesvorstandsitzung d. SED, 2.-3.10.1948, LAB, BPA, IV L-2/1/39, Bl. 84.

were not merely for public consumption and at the very least reflected the SED's impressions of the massive problems it faced. Throughout the fall the eastern press increasingly decried this "plundering" of the Soviet zone and more intensive controls were gradually mounted to counter it.

At the same time, these papers used the phenomenon of foragers as one basis from which to assert that there was no blockade. Here, the SED perspective suggested that the ability of West Berliners to find additional food and other supplies in the Soviet zone demonstrated its general economic prosperity and supported the idea that Berliners would be best off linking their fortunes to that of the Soviet zone, an argument that suggested the SED had still not quite escaped its 1946 presumption that increased SED control, and the offer of potential material benefits might still convince Berliners to support the party.[88] This rhetorical ambiguity underscored the extent to which these Soviet and SED headline writers seemed to want it both ways, portraying the SBZ both as a bountiful land of opportunity and as a fragile area of economic development, greatly threatened by marauding forces from the West. In their internal policy discussions, the latter perspective seemed to win out.[89] Yet, as evidenced by ongoing directives from German and Soviet officials, these restrictions again and again proved incapable of controlling economic contacts between the east and west sectors of Berlin or between Berlin and the Soviet zone.

The control measures put in place along the sector and zonal borders were not an entirely empty gesture. On numerous occasions, German policemen or Soviet sentries accompanying them opened fire on persons attempting to pass the control point, killing or wounding them, offering another argument for the relative ordinariness of the August clashes on the Potsdamer Platz that produced such widespread outrage. A municipal police (*Schutzpolizei*) report on police activity in January 1949 described sixteen incidents in which police had fired a total of fifty-nine shots during encounters on the sector border. The report noted that in spite of clearly given stop signals, truck drivers often approached the control points at full speed, which (at least in some cases) led to shots being fired.[90] Yet such

[88] See the caption, "Es gibt keine Bockade," above a photo of a crowd carrying sacks of potatoes after disembarking from a train in Spandau (British sector) in *Neues Deutschland* (October 16, 1948), 4. For a good discussion of the "there is no blockade" rhetoric, see Stivers, "The Incomplete Blockade," 575f.
[89] See the discussion in the SED's Berlin Landesvorstand on 2.-3.10.1948, LAB, BPA, IV L-2/1/39.
[90] Monthly report (January 1949) from the Kdo. Schupo (Pech) to the Police Pres., dated February 3, 1949, LAB, STA Rep. 26, Nr. 215, Bl. 6. On the inherent ambiguity of police

violence or even decisiveness was by no means the norm. An inspection of checkpoints revealed that often sentries asked for nothing more than vehicle papers, making no inquiries about way bills (*Warenbegleitscheine*) or other documentation authorizing the transportation of goods into Berlin. On the "Ring around Berlin," one post had to leave the crossing gate up at night because they had no light to hang on it. In another instance, the crossing gate had been broken off by a truck that forced its way through the checkpoint.[91] Quite often, the sentries were poorly supplied with food, clothing, and heating material and at times had to rely on passing vehicles to provide them with coal or wood to heat their shelters.[92] Controls in train stations encountered logistical difficulties as well. Often the limited number of policemen available made it impossible to carry out thorough checks of train passengers for "smuggled" goods. Jurisdictional conflict between the rail police and Schutzpolizei at times also limited the police's access to train stations to implement their controls.[93] The repeated shortcomings noted in police reports throughout 1948 and into 1949 attested to SED-controlled police efforts to enhance their control of economic life in and around Berlin but also to their recognition of the fact that they continued to fail in that undertaking. The ability and motivation of Soviet zone and Soviet sector police to carry out systematic checks of persons seeking to enter the west sectors with foodstuffs or other materials from the Soviet zone proved marginal at best.

Ordinary Berliners trying to supplement their supplies with additional foodstuffs from the Soviet zone did have to consider the threat of controls when returning from a foraging trip. They developed a wide range of strategies to cope with this danger. Persons traveling by train would pull the emergency brake to force the train to stop before it entered the station, thereby avoiding the checkpoints at the end stop. Others would toss the

orders for vehicles to stop, consider that the first postwar director of the Berlin Philharmonic Orchestra was killed by an American soldier who fired on the passing vehicle when its British driver misunderstood the MP's order to stop. See Andreas-Friedrich, *Battleground Berlin*, 86–91.

[91] Abt. Schutzpolizei: Bericht über die Kontrolle des Ringes um Berlin am 3.11.1948, BA-DDR, DO 1–17/271, Bl. 122.

[92] Bericht der Hauptabteilung über den Ring um Berlin vom 13.12.1948, BLHA, Ld. Br. Rep. 203, VP, Nr. 103, Bl. 2. On efforts to bribe policemen in Berlin, see also the Monthly Report (January 1949) from the Kdo. Schupo (Pech) to the Police Pres., dated February 3, 1949, LAB, STA Rep. 26, Nr. 215, Bl. 6.

[93] See the memo from Kreispolizeiamt Teltow (signed Leibholz, Ltr. d. Schupo) to Brandenburg MdI (Abt. Polizei) regarding cooperation between Schupo and Bapo, dated August 9, 1948, BLHA, Ld. Br. Rep. 203, VP, Nr. 31, Bl. 173.

supplies they had obtained from the train window at some prearranged point.[94] Waiting accomplices could pick them up and make their way into the city on foot. Police reports contain numerous accounts of vehicles with false bottoms or of foodstuffs concealed under other loads, but such methods were less likely to be adopted by individuals merely seeking to supplement their personal supplies. Individuals on foot or on bicycle were often able to avoid checkpoints, passing into the west sectors on unpatrolled side streets or by sneaking through the ruined buildings that lent a porous quality to the Berlin cityscape.[95] A police report from early September describes the crossing point at the Düppel train station, on the boundary between the American sector and the Soviet zone. One German and one Russian sentry manned a crossing gate and allowed pedestrians to pass uncontrolled. Vehicles were stopped, but if their papers were in order, they too were allowed to pass.[96] For those willing to run the risk – often not that great of a risk – there were numerous opportunities to avoid police checks and successfully bring foodstuffs or other materials into the city from the Soviet zone.

In spite of the control measures' material ineffectiveness, they did make a significant impact on life in Berlin or at least on the popular perception of life in Berlin. During the third quarter of 1948 (July 1 to September 29), the Brandenburg Schutzpolizei seized, in connection with the program "Ring around Berlin," a total of 234,622 kilograms of potatoes, 31,273 kilograms of vegetables, and 54,821 kilograms of grain. These amounts did not differ greatly from those of the preceding two quarters, but the methods with which these seizures were implemented resonated powerfully in Berlin.[97] During the period from noon on September 2 to noon September 3, the Brandenburg police commands on the "Ring around Berlin" checked 2,045 vehicles, of which 1,026 were heading into Berlin. These controls netted fairly small amounts of foodstuffs and other materials. For

---

94 Wochenkommunique Nr. 1 des MdI, Abt. Polizei für den Zeitraum 26.2. – 5.3.1949, BLHA, Ld. Br. Rep. 203, Nr. 117, Bl. 319.

95 Hallen and Lindenberger, "Frontstadt mit Lücken," 184ff.

96 Section K (Kriminalpolizei), Daily Report to the Police President, dated September 7, 1948. LAB, STA Rep. 9, Nr. 241, Bl. 418.

97 Daily Report from the Brandenburg Schutzpolizei, dated September 30, 1948, BLHA, Ld. Br. Rep. 203, VP, Nr. 50, Bl. 473. Compare this to 198,381 kg potatoes, 5,122 kg vegetables, and 21,750 kg grain seized during the 1st Quarter and 268,449 kg potatoes, 6,908 kg vegetables, and 21,394 kg grain seized during the 2nd Quarter. BLHA, Ld. Br. Rep. 203, VP, Nr. 50, Bl. 224. The "Ring um Berlin" was a series of thirty-six checkpoints on the roads surrounding Berlin. It was reorganized and expanded at the end of March 1948.

example, the Greater Glienicke Department of the Falkensee Command reported the following seizures during this twenty-four-hour period:

100 kilograms of fruit
148 cigarettes
450 grams of margarine
three tins of cocoa
one tin of milk
one tin of syrup
100 grams of coffee
1990. – DM (East)
5. – DM (West)

All were seized from a single truck, owned by a man living in a town on the outskirts of Berlin.[98] While the report does not indicate whether the truck was heading in or out of the city, the nature of the goods seized pointed to someone heading into the west sectors to sell fruit and trade for west marks. The scope of this single seizure suggests that the driver at least anticipated the possibility that he might successfully negotiate the checkpoint.

Given the widespread evidence of lax controls on other occasions, the lack of any other seizures among the more than 2,000 vehicles checked that day should not be taken as evidence of a complete lack of "illegal" transports. We can only speculate about this particular case: perhaps a higher ranking police officer was momentarily present to prevent any lax control measures, perhaps the driver of this particular truck managed to provoke the guards to action, or perhaps this really was the only vehicle carrying illicit goods into the city. Regardless of the specifics of this case, Berliners' dependence on the agricultural areas just outside of the city remained a very public phenomenon. A notice posted on advertising pillars (*Litfaßsäulen*) throughout the west sectors in the latter part of September called on Berliners to use a Spandau boat company's daily trips to towns in the Havel district to take advantage of the potato and fruit harvests going on at that time.[99] It is clear that many Berliners answered this call, if not on the boats of this or other companies, then by rail, foot, bicycle, or car. The police actions against Berliners seeking to bring

[98] Tagesmeldung vom 2.9.1948 – 12.00 Uhr- bis 3.9.1948- 12.00 Uhr- "Ring um Berlin"-, BLHA, Ld Br. Rep. 203, VP, Nr. 50, Bl. 228ff.
[99] Cited in a report to Police President Markgraf, dated September 21, 1948. LAB, STA Rep. 9, Nr. 50, Bl. 197.

fairly small amounts of foodstuffs into the city, regardless of their limited impact, came increasingly to dominate the popular image of the Soviet zone police and the political administration that stood behind it; but they did not end Berliners' pursuit of those supplemental supplies or Soviet zone farmers' and merchants' willingness to participate in this trade.

In a suggestive indicator of the extent to which police officials worried about the popular image as well as the practical efficacy of their control efforts, a September report from the economic section of the east sector police described some of the jokes making the rounds in Berlin cabarets and variety shows. The report noted that those about the police generally elicited a strong positive response. One joke justified the highest ration card for policemen with the comment that "one has to take into account all [of the goods] that they have to cart off." Another described police raids as "collections for suffering policemen."[100] Even when speaking to the aforementioned FDGB-organized gathering of sympathetic West Berliners, one SED economic official felt compelled to counter the negative impressions of such police seizures from individual Berliners:

If the officers of the People's Police (*Volkspolizei*) of the Soviet Zone of Occupation or if policemen of the Soviet Sector stop the smugglers' vehicles or take away someone's backpack, don't let yourself be made to feel sorry by the cry: "Oh, the poor old woman! Why? The police are so mean!" Think about the fact that the transport of these goods does not occur only with trucks or by train. Rather, there are whole columns of smugglers of 120 or more persons, who are sent out with backpacks from a central point. One brings 50 pairs of stockings, another 80 pair of stockings, and they are all turned in to a central point. There, every one of these – what should I call them – commuter black marketeers gets his wage, and the whole story goes on. Think about the fact that in this hard struggle, resentment is not appropriate. It is necessary to act humanely. But it is also necessary to tackle things firmly and to be clear what effects things have.[101]

The need to address these criticisms posed for the SED the crux of its dilemma: at once threatened by this popular perception of its economic control measures as directed primarily against the individual Berliner, party leaders ultimately believed that even more drastic control measures were necessary and that a battle against the black market remained a viable means with which to stage their efforts to control the city.

---

[100] Confidential report from the Gewerbeaußendienst to Präsidial-Dir. Seidel, dated September 21, 1948. LAB, STA Rep. 9, Nr. 50, Bl. 196.

[101] Protokoll der Aussprache des FDGB Groß-Berlin mit Vertretern der Westberliner Bevölkerung, November 27, 1948. LAB, STA Rep. 106, Nr. 234, Bl. 14–15.

An Expanded Assault on the City Administration

As part of the process that Marshall Sokolovskii had mapped out for DWK leaders in July, Soviet Order No. 80 established a semiautonomous eastern subdepartment within the city administration. For the first time since the Kommandatura took up its work in July 1945, the Soviets installed an administrative structure that sought to directly challenge the authority of the central city government. Ostensibly, the subsection of the Food Department set up under the former district mayor, Paul Letsch, was designed to administer the Soviet offer to supply western sector residents from the Soviet sector. Aided by Soviet liaison officers, this subdepartment proceeded to take over the department's offices and largely ignore the directives of the SPD department head, Paul Füllsack. By August 11, the Food Department had set up a western branch in the British sector and after a brief stint in the Neue Stadthaus, the home of the municipal parliament, Füllsack also moved his offices to the west on August 23.[102] Thus by the end of August, the department was essentially split between east and west. The unified city administration, headed by a democratically chosen Magistrat, had begun to disintegrate.

The motivations that underlay Soviet Order No. 80 were complex, a product of political hopes and economic fears. Certainly, the desire to undermine the Berlin Magistrat, as discussed in the July meeting between Marshall Sokolovskii and DWK officials, was one important factor in creating the subdepartment, but Soviet Order No. 80 marked something less than an absolute decision to split the city administration. While the Food Department's split into east and west occurred fairly rapidly, the continued interaction between the opposing forces within the department, especially between Letsch and Füllsack, demonstrates how competing goals continued to function within the department's structures and only gradually gave way to a complete rupture. The combined pressure of Soviet and SED officials ultimately forced Füllsack to abandon the department's central offices and essentially renounce any jurisdiction over food supply in the Soviet sector. But even in the face of that defeat, he held on to the fiction of central administration as long as possible, thereby contributing to the legitimacy of the Magistrat as the executor of the popular will voiced in the election of October 1946. More importantly, he

---

[102] For a timeline of events affecting the Food Department, see LAB, Rep. 280 (LAZ-Sammlung), Sta.-Ort. Nr. 11307.

managed to draw many department workers to his western office, thus providing a bureaucratic base from which to challenge Letsch and his subordinates.

On July 31, Paul Füllsack wrote to the head of the Soviet Command's section for trade and procurement and complained that a Soviet order had been directed not to him, the director of the Main Food Office but to Paul Letsch. He requested that in the future all orders be directed to him, so as to maintain the orderly functioning of the department.[103] One week later, Füllsack refused to sign an order granting Letsch the authority to make all personnel decisions for those employees working in his subdepartment.[104] In an August 14 letter to Acting Mayor Louise Schröder describing the deteriorating situation in his department, Füllsack explained that Soviet Orders No. 80 and No. 660 had essentially undermined his authority and usurped his staff and equipment in the service of the new subdepartment, the *Unterabteilung Ost*. Although the Soviet Command indicated that only those persons who voluntarily wished to work in the Unterabteilung Ost would have to do so, he believed that the eastern section would only be able to continue its work if persons were forced to remain. He further complained that he was almost entirely excluded from the decision-making processes of the subsection east. Security personnel at the main office on Wallstrasse (Soviet sector) refused to allow entrance for staff with IDs issued by Füllsack. He concluded by noting that he would continue to do all he could to maintain his department's ability to function throughout all of Berlin.[105] His tone suggested little optimism for the future.

On September 10 Letsch offered his interpretation of the situation in a letter to Füllsack. He challenged a directive issued by Füllsack that all significant mail be sent first to his office in Charlottenburg (British sector) noting that while he was technically subordinate to Füllsack, he was head of the eastern subdepartment and therefore wholly responsible for the fulfillment of its duties per Soviet Order No. 80. He pointedly emphasized that he would do everything in his power to ensure the smooth functioning of this section: "formalities will not hamper me in this." The letter accused Füllsack of weakening all intersector departments and essentially splitting

[103] Note from Füllsack to Soviet Command, Section for Trade and Procurement, dated July 31, 1948. LAB, Rep. 280 (LAZ-Sammlung), Sta.-Ort. Nr. 11255.
[104] Notice dated August 6, 1948, LAB, Rep. 280 (LAZ-Sammlung), Sta.-Ort. Nr. 11256.
[105] Letter from Paul Füllsack to Louise Schröder, dated August 14, 1948, LAB, Rep. 280 (LAZ-Sammlung), Sta.-Ort. Nr. 11260.

the Food Office. It concluded, "I regret that such acidity has entered into [our] work. I regret it even more so, as I am convinced that this does not make any easier the orderly supply of the Berlin population."[106] Much more than a real concern for the orderly supply of the Berlin population, Letsch was concerned with the continued ability of Füllsack's office to limit the reach of his subdepartment.

In a letter to Major Gubisch at the Soviet Central Command, Letsch complained that those departments not directly subordinate to the structures set up by Soviet Order No. 80 were continuously losing people to Füllsack's offices in the Deutschland Haus. He warned that those joint departments (i.e., those departments utilized both by the western and eastern branches of the Food Office) would soon be unable to function. Furthermore, he noted that since Füllsack had moved his offices to Charlottenburg, they had received no word from him and did not even officially know his telephone number (obviously, a lack of *official* knowledge should not be equated with an actual inability to obtain the phone number in question). According to Letsch, Füllsack's office had ceased to provide anything but negative leadership and had forced his subdepartment to assume all responsibility.

Soviet officials seemed less eager to so radically expand the scope of Letsch's power. In early November a Soviet memo to Letsch criticized the substantial personnel increase in his subdepartment and warned that those responsible for the arbitrary expansion of personnel levels would be held accountable for any resulting financial waste.[107] Soviet skepticism rested perhaps in the fact that only days after Füllsack had abandoned his offices in the Soviet sector, Letsch requested a substantial amount of fabric with which to redecorate those rooms.[108] Regardless of Soviet plans to undermine the Magistrat, Letsch seemed to be running ahead of them in his pursuit of greater independence and power, not just in the Soviet sector but throughout all of Berlin.

The ongoing give and take between Letsch and Füllsack, however, suggests the limits of an internal assault on the administrative structures of

---

[106] Letter from Paul Letsch to Paul Füllsack regarding his directive to the Poststelle, dated September 10, 1948. LAB, STA Rep. 113, Nr. 39. Two weeks later Füllsack responded with a letter that warned Letsch of substantial difficulties in the public administration if he viewed official obligations as nothing but formalities.

[107] Translation of an order from Major Gubisch to Paul Letsch, dated November 2, 1948. LAB, STA Rep. 113, Nr. 38.

[108] Memo dated August 26, LAB, STA Rep. 113, Nr. 37.

the Berlin city government. Not only did Letsch find that very few West Berliners accepted the Soviet supply offer his office was to administer, he also faced a flight of personnel to the developing western branches of the Main Food Office, even down to the level of cleaning ladies.[109] The development of a parallel administrative structure served less to undermine the city government than to detach the Soviet sector Food Offices from the legitimate authority of the elected Magistrat. Isolated from the normal channels of German administrative operation (through Füllsack's office), Letsch was forced to rely almost entirely on the Soviets to support his position, a precedent that would come to define the SED's position more generally throughout the entire existence of the GDR.

The split of the Berlin police into eastern and western branches was at once more abrupt and more closely linked to the relationship between the German authorities and the Kommandatura. Throughout 1948, tension had been growing between the Magistrat and the Soviet-appointed Police President, Paul Markgraf, whose ongoing promotion of SED interests within the police earned him the animosity of the majority parties in the municipal government.[110] On March 3, the Magistrat had directed Deputy Mayor Friedensburg (CDU) to inform the Kommandatura that given Markgraf's refusal to accept the Magistrat's authority, productive cooperation between the two was no longer possible.[111] The Soviet sector police's failure to intervene in the disturbances at the city assembly meeting on June 23 served further to poison the relationship. In July, Markgraf dismissed a large number of police officers in the Soviet sector, most noticeably the Municipal Police Chief, Hans Kanig.[112] Finally, on July 26, the Magistrat voted to suspend Markgraf and designated his deputy, Johannes Stumm, as acting Police President. It recognized Stumm as the sole head of the police administration for all of Greater Berlin.[113] Markgraf ignored the suspension and refused to vacate his offices. The Soviet Commander

---

[109] Notice filed by Spudich, August 16, 1948, LAB, STA Rep. 113, Nr. 37.

[110] A memo dated November 29, 1947 overtly discussed the relative strength of the SED within the police, LAB, STA Rep. 120, Nr. 3249, Bl. 26.

[111] Protokoll über die 80. (Ordentliche) Magistratssitzung am 3. March 1948. LAB, Rep. 280 (LAZ-Sammlung), Sta.-Ort. Nr. 8503/12. Note the change from Friedensburg's earlier defense of Markgraf.

[112] See the comments in the Stenographisches Bericht der 79. Sitzung der StVV, July 29, 1948.

[113] Protokoll über die 113. (Ordentliche) Magistratssitzung, July 28, 1948. LAB, Rep. 280 (LAZ-Sammlung), Sta.-Ort. Nr. 8503/43. The police president could be removed from office only with the approval of the Allied Kommandatura.

ordered the Magistrat to dismiss Stumm, reinstate Markgraf, and begin
an investigation into this scheme to split the police.[114] It refused to do so.
On August 7, Stumm publicly announced the shift of many central police
offices, including the presidial section, to Friesenstrasse in the American
sector.[115] For all practical purposes, there were now two police forces in
the city.

From the outset, there had been some degree of sector division within
the postwar police administration. Police were generally not to cross sector boundaries in their investigations, nor were they to carry weapons in
a sector other than the one in which they served. Police sector assistants
served as direct links between the police and the occupiers, a channel
of authority largely independent of the central police administration and
able to issue directives independent of the central police administration.
Unlike these earlier administrative divisions, the split that occurred at
the beginning of August 1948 ran down the middle of the police force,
largely independent of sector lines. For the first time, municipal employees faced the need to choose between two Berlin administrations. Many
officers, even those living in the Soviet sector, failed to appear for duty at
their Soviet sector stations, assuming new posts under Stumm's administration.[116] For some, this decision cost them their home or apartment,
seized on order of Markgraf's police.[117] On July 31, Markgraf issued an
order blocking wage payments to any personnel who had taken up duty
in the "illegal break-away presidium." By September, the administrative
favor had been returned: Stumm ordered that all members of the central police administration who failed to report to duty in the new police
headquarters by August 30 be summarily dismissed.[118] At this point,
the respective east and west police forces seemed well entrenched and
irreconcilable.

Despite some examples to the contrary, cooperation between the two
police administrations with regard to criminal matters remained generally

[114] Soviet order dated July 27, 1948, LAB, STA Rep. 9, Nr. 2, Bl. 209. See also Letter from
Kotikov to Louise Schröder regarding dismissal of Markgraf, dated July 27, 1948, LAB,
STA Rep. 101, Nr. 19, Bl. 160.

[115] Announcement from the Police President (Stumm) dated August 7, 1948, LAB, Rep.
280 (LAZ-Sammlung), Sta.-Ort. Nr. 3986.

[116] Präsidialabteilung: Correspondence regarding the Division of the Berlin Police, 1945 –
1948, LAB, Rep. 9, Nr. 2, Bl. 136–51.

[117] See the Letter from Stumm to the Magistrat, August 6, 1948. LAB, Rep. 280 (LAZ-
Sammlung), Sta.-Ort. Nr. 11019.

[118] Memo from Dr. Stumm to all police branches, dated September 16, 1948, LAB, Rep.
280 (LAZ-Sammlung), Sta.-Ort. Nr. 11025.

good.[119] They continued to exchange information with each other and cooperate in criminal investigations. On an ideological level, individual members of the police were not nearly as estranged from each other as might be presumed, a reflection of the fact that, like registering for rations, the decision to cast one's lot with one police administration or the other depended on much more than a simple party political litmus test. A "law-and-order" approach to questions of black marketeering remained a common thread running through police forces regardless of sector, and although mentioned in a report to the Soviet sector president Markgraf, it is not hard to believe the assertion that most members of the western municipal police supported their eastern counterparts' use of firearms in their clash with stone throwers on Potsdamer Platz on August 19.[120] In their day-to-day operations, the police recognized the limits of their power and sought to function as well as possible in spite of political and administrative divides.

On a rhetorical and symbolic level, however, police officials refused to acknowledge any limitation in the two forces' powers. Both sides regularly referred to their opposite as "illegal" and accused it of disrupting the work of the police.[121] In spite of the "reality" of a split police administration, both police presidents portrayed themselves as head of the police for all of Greater Berlin. At the highest level, they denied the practical existence of the other administration, save as a foil for symbolic expressions of their own sweeping power and legitimacy.

A small but telling matter was the conflict between the two police presidents over who should receive the free theater and concert tickets allocated to the head of the department. The police presidium Friesenstrasse (west) sent a directive to all city theaters that free tickets were to be made available only to persons from the western presidium. Theaters also received a similar letter from Markgraf's office. Seeking guidance, the Hebbel-Theater (American sector) wrote to the art section of the Magistrat's Education Department, noting that it was bound by the directive of the American military government not to recognize the "Police President

---

[119] See the Soviet sector police's half-year report for the period July 1 to December 31, 1948 (January 11, 1949). The report cites one example of a murderer sought by the Soviet sector police who was advised by the Friesenstrasse presidium to avoid the Soviet sector as he would likely be arrested there. Certainly, this accusation should be taken with a grain of salt (p. 3). See also the report of police authorization for a church group to use a loudspeaker truck in the east and west sectors, SAPMO DY 30/IV 2/5/298.

[120] Report dated August 30, 1948. LAB, STA Rep. 9, Nr. 241, Bl. 408.

[121] See Paul Markgraf's appeal to the Berlin population, LAB, STA Rep. 9, Nr. 2, Bl. 105.

234 Black Market, Cold War

in the East Sector," and it asked for an opinion on how to respond prop-
erly. In his reply, the head of the Art Department advised city councilor
May to propose that theaters in the western sectors make their free tickets
available to Stumm and those in the Soviet sector make theirs available
to Markgraf. He explained this suggestion with the remark that theaters
in the Soviet sector would perhaps encounter difficulties with the Soviet
Kommandatur if they were forced to provide tickets to Dr. Stumm and his
department.[122] This example suggests the extent to which – at least in fall
1948 – the competing police presidents still found it necessary to turn to
the Magistrat and to acknowledge that they remained part of the city as a
whole. But it also showed how their everyday practices – attending a play
or distributing complementary theater tickets – manifested the intensity
of their clash.

The city assembly continued to meet throughout the summer and
although the escalating political tensions increasingly challenged its ability to function, the opposing parties still found occasional opportunities
to cooperate. In early July, the SPD and SED together sponsored a measure
to aid persons made unemployed by factory closures, but this cooperation
was hardly the norm. During the session on July 29, the SED left the hall
before a vote to adopt a resolution condemning the blockade as a "crime
against humanity."[123] This walkout marked the last time that the city
assembly met as a whole to consider parliamentary business, but the ultimate collapse of the united assembly derived from more than mere party
conflict.

On August 27, Otto Suhr briefly opened the eightieth session of the city
assembly only to close it immediately in light of demonstrators in front of
the building and reports of more on the way. Demonstrators in front of and
inside the Stadthaus had already forced a first cancellation of the session
the day before. At that time, demonstrators delivered petitions calling
for "unity of administration, currency and supply, guarantee of work,
an increase in the real wage, guarantee of the supply of food, housing,
heat, and clothing." They protested vehemently against the "bankruptcy
of the Berlin Magistrat." Suhr noted briefly that most of the petitions were
contained on preprinted forms with the same wording.[124] The *Tägliche
Rundschau* reported that the demonstrating crowd numbered 50,000,
but this was obviously an exaggeration. Two days later a (West) Berlin

[122] LAB, STA Rep. 120, Nr. 1503, Bl. 71, 84, and 85.
[123] Stenographisches Bericht der 79. Sitzung der StVV, July 29, 1948, 51.
[124] Stenographisches Bericht der 80. Sitzung der StVV, August 27, 1948.

paper put the crowd at only 1,000 persons, and even Hermann Matern, cochair of the Berlin SED, referred to only a "couple thousand" party members in front of the Stadthaus.[125] Lost in the tumultuous photographs of crowds storming the Stadthaus in June, August, and September is the fact that the building's entrance opened out on a narrow intersection of two back streets; there was no square in which a massive crowd could gather.

At the meeting of the Central Committee of the Berlin SED, assessments of the demonstration were much more guarded. One delegate reported that only 500 representatives from the west sectors participated in the demonstration, although he noted that the banners and flags made it seem like 2,000 to the inexperienced.[126] Another speaker complained that efforts to organize participants in Berlin factories met with only marginal results. When asked to send workers to the demonstrations, the party members he addressed offered to choose ten. Even at the rail repair yards in the Soviet sector, only a small number of workers were willing to participate.[127] Thus, the SED-organized demonstrators should not be seen as representative of Berlin's workers or even as a decisive show of force by those loyal to the SED. But given the unwillingness of Soviet sector police to take any measures to guarantee the security of the assembly, even moderate demonstrations represented a significant threat to the elected assembly's ongoing work.

Hoping to obtain some security guarantee for the city assembly, Otto Suhr wrote to General Kotikov asking that he approve the law, adopted on June 29 by a four-fifths majority of the city assembly (i.e., opposed only by the SED), to set up a boundary precinct around the Stadthaus.[128] Kotikov responded later that day, wondering sarcastically whether Suhr wanted him to ban all demonstrations to protect the city assembly from

[125] "250 000 erhoben ihre Stimme: Für einheitliche Währung, Verwaltung und Versorgung – Massenkundgebungen vor dem Stadthaus: Keine Stadtverordnetensitzung, da die Mehrheit geflüchtet war," *Tägliche Rundschau* (August 27, 1948), 1. Ann and John Tusa put the number at no more than 5,000. Tusa, *The Berlin Airlift*, 222. Matern's remarks from the Protokoll d. Landesvorstandssitzung, 28.-29.8.1948. LAB, BPA, IV L-2/1/38, Bl. 52.

[126] Comments by General Voigt from the Protokoll d. Landesvorstandssitzung, August 28–9, 1948, LAB, BPA, IV L-2/1/38, Bl. 25ff.

[127] Comments of General Fischer from the Protokoll d. Landesvorstandssitzung, August 28–9, 1948, LAB, BPA, IV L-2/1/38, Bl. 44.

[128] During the Weimar Republic, a boundary precinct (*Bannmeile*) demarcated the government district around the Wilhelmstrasse in which all political demonstrations were prohibited. Hsi-Huey Liang, *The Berlin Police Force in the Weimar Republic* (Berkeley: University of California Press, 1970), 11.

the population of Berlin. Suhr's reply the next day addressed Kotikov's comments point by point. He indicated that he wished to carry out the law as passed by the city assembly and noted that he was turning to the Soviet Commander only because the police in the district (Mitte) refused to honor the directives of the city government. Suhr concluded the letter rather pointedly: First, he denounced the Soviets' decided animosity toward the elected city government and their desire to see a radical change in its composition. Second, he suggested that there was, in fact, an opportunity to change the makeup of the city government and that Soviet inaction made that even less likely. Scheduling the fall 1948 elections was on the agenda of the next (and thus also of the postponed) city assembly meeting.[129] The challenge of new elections had troubled the SED since the spring, and the Soviets certainly worried about them at this point as well.[130] In the end, the SED extracted itself from the electoral process. It would not be part of the body that approved the electoral code in the city assembly's next session.

On September 6, Suhr called for the city assembly to make another attempt to meet in its Soviet sector hall. It was not to be. Before the session started, small groups of demonstrators again gathered in front of the main entrance to the Stadthaus. Columns of marchers, who had assembled at various points of the city, soon joined them, carrying banners and flags. An American report indicated that some of the demonstrators arrived in Soviet vehicles.[131] Before the session (scheduled for noon) could begin, these demonstrators broke the glass doors at the main entrance and forced their way into the building.[132] Pitched battles broke out in the hallways and demonstrators, journalists, and policemen all seem to have been drawn into the fray. Two related elements distinguished these clashes from any of the earlier disruptions of city assembly sessions. Volunteer members of the West Berlin police had been recruited by Deputy Mayor Friedensburg to serve as a defense for the assembly against the demonstrators. In this, they proved ineffective. Members of Markgraf's

---

[129] Letter from Otto Suhr to General Kotikov, August 28, 1948. LAB, Rep. 280 (LAZ-Sammlung), Sta.-Ort. Nr. 6614.

[130] See the memo on the needs for a successful election campaign in the fall of 1948, n.d. (it follows the minutes of the June 12, 1948 Sekretariat session); perhaps prepared by General Hensel. In Protokolle der Sekretariat Sitzungen, June 1948, LAB, BPA, IV L-2/3/99, Bl. 11.

[131] Special reports of the Civilian Administration and Political Affairs Branch of OMGBS, September 10, 1948, NA, RG 260, 390/48/10/1, box 62, 6.

[132] Report from the Polizeipräsident in Berlin, Dr. Stumm on the events at the Neues Stadthaus on September 6–8, 1948, LAB, STA Rep. 101, Nr. 170, Bl. 71.

police entered the Stadthaus as well, eventually arresting many of the West sector police volunteers.[133] Some of those West sector policemen managed to take refuge in the offices of the French and British liaisons to the Magistrat, but they were eventually seized from a French bus as they were being transported back to the western sectors.[134]

While this hostage drama dragged on over several days, the city assembly went ahead and met in the British sector (without the SED) where it voted to hold municipal elections in November (they were eventually held December 5) and to implement the Magistrat's "Winter Emergency Program" for 1948–9. It also selected five persons to represent Berlin at the discussions of the Parliamentary Council, which was meeting to formulate a constitution for a new West German state.[135] The Magistrat continued to meet in the Stadthaus until mid-October, but the pretense of a unified city government had now nearly vanished.

Unruly Berliners

Following the SED-led assault on the city assembly, leaders of Berlin's democratic parties organized a mass demonstration to display the popular willingness to face the SED- and Soviet-led assaults on the city. On September 9, after two days of preparation, more than 250,000 Berliners gathered to demonstrate for freedom on the Platz der Republik in front of the ruined Reichstag. In front of a significant portion of Berlin's population, Ernst Reuter issued his famous call for the world to look to Berlin, that the rest of the world not abandon the city. Drawing together the threads from his March and June speeches, Reuter claimed for (West) Berlin a potent symbolic power that might resonate on a global scale. Even in a city where mass demonstrations occurred regularly, this assembly was truly remarkable. Every effort had been made to enable people to attend the rally: newspapers published the best travel routes, bus and tram service was extended, and employers were encouraged to shut down early

---

133 Foreknowledge of the presence of a Western security presence was at least hinted at in an article in the previous day's *Tägliche Rundschau*. "Stadtparlament will Winternotprogramm beraten: Die 'Rollkommandos' der Stadtvewaltung bereits ausgesucht," *Tägliche Rundschau* (September 5, 1948), 1. An official British statement directed muted criticism at Friedensburg, noting that in the face of ongoing violent decisions, he "was tempted, perhaps unwisely, to try to meet force with force." Cited in *The Times* (September 7, 1948), as transcribed in LAB, STA Rep. 101, Nr. 170, Bl. 37.

134 See Tusa, *The Berlin Airlift*, 227ff.

135 Stenographisches Bericht der 81. Sitzung der StVV, September 6, 1948.

to allow their workers to attend.[136] British authorities in the city worried about the presence of a large crowd so near the boundary with the Soviet sector and issued a decree to go into effect the next day that would limit gatherings near the sector border.[137] This concern turned out to be justified. Following the end of the program, clashes broke out near the Brandenburg Gate, shots were fired, and a fifteen-year-old boy was killed.

Near the conclusion of the demonstration, three discussion groups (each approximately 150–200 persons) gathered on Pariser Platz, south of the Reichstag and just across the sector boundary, on the Soviet side of the line. There was no evidence of any east sector police presence. In the course of the heated debates, a man in the crowd was struck down. At this point, the head of the Police Station Mitte, Police Commissar Engelbrecht arrived at the square, got out of his car, and sought to intervene in this incident. The crowd apparently surrounded him and knocked him down. After freeing himself, he drove to obtain police reinforcements. At the conclusion of the large demonstration, many persons headed east through the Brandenburg Gate toward the Unter den Linden or Friedrichstrasse stations, or toward their residences in the east sector. A detachment of east sector police (approximately fifteen men under the direction of Engelbrecht) arrived at the Pariser Platz and sought to block the Brandenburg Gate, but the crowd forced them back. A second police squad (approximately twenty officers) arrived as the first was being forced east down Unter den Linden. They disembarked from their truck with weapons ready and sought to push back the crowd. When they met with resistance, including thrown rocks, they fired into the crowd. Twelve persons were injured, one fatally (the fifteen-year-old member of an SPD youth organization, Wolfgang Scheunemann).[138]

---

[136] See Tusa, *The Berlin Airlift*, 230. A confidential Soviet sector police report provides an interesting detail about the participants in the demonstration. At a streetcar repair workshop in Wedding (French sector) the SPD-led factory council called on all workers to go and take part in the demonstration. Apparently, only the plant's ninety-five SED members remained at work. During a plant meeting the next day, the head of the SED group was roundly denounced as a "mercenary for the Russians" (*Russensöldner*), and the workers overwhelmingly voted that he should be fired, which he was, one day later. LAB, STA Rep. 9, Nr. 50, Bl. 252.

[137] Mentioned in an excerpt from *Tägliche Rundschau* (September 9, 1948) in the Präsidialabt., Pressestelle: Zeitungsausschnitten zu Fragen der Berliner Polizei, August 1948 – September 1948. LAB, STA Rep. 9, Nr. 116, Bl. 99.

[138] Report from the Kommando der Schutzpolizei to the Police President (Stumm) dated September 14, 1948 on the "Zwischenfälle auf dem Pariser Platz nach der Protestkundgebung auf dem Platz der Republik am 9.9.1948." LAB, Rep. 280 (LAZ-Sammlung), Sta.-Ort. Nr. 11041.

During the clashes with police, some youths climbed up on the Brandenburg Gate and tore down the red flag flying there. The crowd in the square tore the flag into pieces and began to burn it. At this point, Soviet soldiers on guard duty at the Soviet monument a short distance from the Brandenburg Gate drove over and sought to intervene. One Soviet soldier fired a machine gun into the air, but the intervention of a British officer prevented any further firing.[139] Thus, even according to Western accounts of the incident, the Soviet role in the shooting seems to have been fairly minimal, and the principal cause of bloodshed seems to have been the misguided crowd control efforts of the Soviet sector police.

Although admittedly inconclusive, the Soviet sector police's preliminary report on the clashes sought to paint a more sinister picture. Police officers described the crowd as moving with military discipline, halting at times to receive shouted commands from persons behind them. These young people allegedly threatened the police, decrying them as "toadies of the Russian," "Markgraf pigs," and "bloodhounds."[140] On the basis of accounts submitted by individual officers, the report argued that it was clear the first shots were fired *at* the (east) police from the ruins of the Hotel Adlon and of the French embassy on Pariser Platz. These shots were ostensibly fired by west sector police in civilian clothing, because, according to the reports, the shots *sounded* like police shots, and one policeman, Heinz Voss, claimed to have seen a man in civilian clothes firing at him from behind a pillar of the former French embassy.[141] In this report, Soviet sector police portrayed themselves as the victims of an organized assault, directed by Western military officials and carried out by resurgent "fascist" forces, a description that clearly paralleled their understanding of the violent reaction to their raid on the black market on August 19.

---

[139] The British point of view is described in the article, "Berlin/Ruhig und Wirksam," *Die Welt* (September 11, 1948) in LAB, STA Rep. 101, Nr. 171, Bl. 13.

[140] Gustav Noske, an SPD politician and the first defense minister in the Weimar Republic, explained his willingness to organize paramilitary forces in Berlin to crush the January 1919 Spartacist uprising: "someone has to be the bloodhound." His decision helped crystallize the split between Communists and Socialists during the 1920s and 30s. Here, the expression is inverted to describe the Communist-controlled Soviet sector police. See Detlev J. K. Peukert, *The Weimar Republic: The Crisis of Classical Modernity*, Richard Deveson, trans. (New York: Hill and Wang, 1993), 32 and Gordon Craig, *Germany 1866–1945*, Oxford History of Modern Europe (New York and Oxford: Oxford University Press, 1980), 406–10.

[141] Preliminary report of the investigation into the events around the Brandenburg Gate in the evening hours of September 9, 1948; submitted by Section K and dated September 13, 1948. LAB, STA Rep. 9, Nr. 2, Bl. 122–3.

The Soviet sector police detained twenty-eight persons in connection with this incident. Of these, seven were turned over to Soviet officials, and on September 14, a Soviet military tribunal announced a sentence of twenty-five years at hard labor for five of these young men.[142] The sentences unleashed a storm of protest. The West sector press noted that only a few months earlier, a Soviet court had handed down the same sentence to those convicted of war crimes in the Sachsenhausen concentration camp.[143] Even in the Soviet zone, many people perceived the sentence as too harsh, although they generally couched their criticisms in calls for justice to be exacted from the Western politicians who provoked the young people with their "fascist" diatribes.[144] On September 17, General Kotikov adopted precisely this stance in asking that the military tribunal reconsider the sentences imposed on the five Berliners. It imposed reduced sentences several days later. At the same time, the tribunal issued a special decision, accusing a number of West Berlin politicians of gross violations of several ACC directives prohibiting "any militarist or fascist activity or propaganda." In conclusion the tribunal announced that it was forwarding the pertinent documentation to the responsible military authorities.[145] Although this decision marked a new high point in the Soviet and SED assault on the legitimacy of the elected government in Berlin, they also moved increasingly to try to formulate an alternative power structure.

On Sunday, September 12, the Association of the Victims of the Nazi Regime (*Vereinigung der Verfolgten des Naziregimes* or VVN) held its annual commemoration for the victims of fascism. Although the organization had initially been formed as a nonpartisan group for those who had suffered Nazi persecution, the SED assumed an increasingly dominant role in its leadership. Soviet sector officials clearly conceived the demonstration

---

[142] Ibid.

[143] Political Report No. 15, Week ending September 18, 1948, NA, RG 260, 390/48/10/1, box 62

[144] See Informationen über Stimmen zu den Urteilen von 25 Jahren Zwangsarbeit für die 5 jugendlichen Berliner, from Information, Potsdam, September 20, 1948. SAPMO, DY 30/IV 2/9.02/44, Bl. 492. Whether the respondents actually *believed* what they said or were simply learning the appropriate ritual formulations that Soviet zone officials desired remains an open question.

[145] "Faschistische Pogromreden der Reuter und Neuman: Urteil gegen die aufgehetzten Rowdys abgeändert – Akten der Gerichtsuntersuchung an Militärbehörden weitergeleitet," *Tägliche Rundschau* (Nr. 224 [1028] 4. Jg., September 24, 1948), 1. See also the copy of the special decision of the Military Tribunal of the SVA, regarding the events of September 9, 1948. LAB, Rep. 280 (LAZ-Sammlung), Sta.-Ort. Nr. 11524.

as a counterweight to the Reichstag demonstration three days earlier.[146] In his notes on discussions with Soviet officials, Wilhelm Pieck referred to plans for slogans for the September 12 demonstration by referencing the earlier demonstration at the Stadthaus as too weak. Instead of emphasizing the negative aspects of the Berlin situation, the lack of heating material (accompanied by pleas for coal from the Ruhr – with the ambiguous notation, "that means lifting of the blockade") and other supplies, Pieck's notes underscore the need to play up the international component of the "antifascist" struggle as well as the possibilities contained in the economic plans laid out for the Soviet zone.[147] West sector participants in the demonstration readily perceived this new, more programmatic line; an informant in Wilmersdorf (American sector) reported a rash of withdrawals from the VVN in that district. Apparently, many members were concerned about the "Communist" line brought out in the speeches of Ottomar Geschke and an unnamed Soviet speaker. They feared that the VVN would slip completely into the train of the SED, a path seen as increasingly separate from that of the municipal administration.[148]

Already by mid-September, the SVAG had decided that there was no longer any future for a unified parliamentary, governmental, or administration system in Berlin. Thus, the leading organs of the Soviet Command in Berlin had worked out a detailed plan for an SED-dominated provisional Magistrat to be set up on a specific "day X." Once the plans had been consolidated, they were approved by the Soviet military governor, Marshall Sokolovskii.[149] The Soviets acted out of fear that municipal elections to be conducted that fall would end any SED claim for political significance within the city. On August 11, members of the Berlin

---

[146] In a September 10, article, the VVN demonstration at the Lustgarten is overtly posited as a counter to the events of the day before, "Massenkundgebung im Lustgarten," *National-Zeitung* (September 10, 1948), in LAB, STA Rep. 9, Nr. 117, Bl. 7. The competition for a higher number of participants is almost comical. On September 11, the *Tägliche Rundschau* denounced western accounts of up to 300,000 participants at the Reichstag demonstration as "Kudamm arithmatic." The first accounts of participation in the VVN demonstration placed it at 400,000, including many from the west sectors. "Großkundgebung gegen Faschismus und Krieg: Aufmarsch der Kräfte des Friedens und der Demokratie – Demonstrationen in allen großen Städten Deutschlands – Das demokratische Europa im Berliner Lustgarten: Millionen bekennen sich zum Kampfe gegen die Kriegsbrandstifter," *Tägliche Rundschau* (September 14, 1948), 1.

[147] Handwritten notes of Wilhelm Pieck, September 6, 1948 [?]. SAPMO, NY 4036/735, Bl. 143–4 (a typed transcript of the notes begins on Bl. 141).

[148] Confidential report from Section K to the police president (Markgraf), dated September 21, 1948. LAB, STA Rep. 9, Nr. 50, Bl. 197.

[149] Creuzberger, *Die sowjetische Besaztungsmacht*, 170.

SED met with Kotikov, the Soviet commander in Berlin. Stadtrat Waldemar Schmidt argued, "If the Situation in Berlin, if the sentiment of the
masses does not change, we will have no chance of success in the elections."[150] This sense of weakness in many ways characterized the SED's
general sense of inferiority or at least its perception of an unlevel playing field in its dealings with the West. Its inability to compete effectively
within existing structures suggested to Soviet and SED leaders the need
to transform them. Thus on November 30, Ottomar Geschke, the SED
deputy head of the city assembly, called that body – or at least its SED
members – into special session. Joined by members of the "democratic
organizations" linked to the SED, they met in the State Opera House in the
Soviet sector. Delegates selected a new, "provisional" Magistrat, headed
by Friedrich Ebert, whose father had been the first president of the Weimar
Republic.

The elections in the western sectors on December 5 finalized the split
of the city administration.[151] Turnout was high: 86.2 percent of those eligible voted.[152] The SPD won a decisive majority, and Ernst Reuter finally
assumed the post of mayor. Initial fears that the SED would try to disrupt the voting proved inconsequential. The SED limited itself to futile
appeals to the West sector population not to participate. In that respect, at
least, the transition occurred smoothly, but the week preceding the Sunday
elections had been momentous for the city of Berlin. It marked the end to
the political and administrative structures founded on quadripartite rule.
But these changes did not draw any line under the battles for survival that
still comprised everyday life in Greater Berlin, and it was in conjunction
with ongoing efforts to master those conditions that these high political
transformations resonated most powerfully.

In an October 13 order tightening controls on the "Ring around
Berlin," the head of Brandenburg's police explained west sector residents'
need to try to obtain supplemental foodstuffs in the Soviet zone as a by-
product of "the divisive measures of the illegal Magistrat of Berlin and the
resulting poor supply of the west sectors with potatoes, fresh vegetables
and other foodstuffs." The order sought to control much more rigorously

---

[150] Ibid., 169.
[151] For a summary of the election and the administrative steps preceding it, see *Berliner
Statistik*, Sonderheft 8/August 1949, published by the Hauptamt für Statistik und
Wahlen: "Die Berliner Wahl am 5. Dezember 1948," in LAB, Rep. 280 (LAZ-Sammlung), Film Nr. 58, Sta.-Ort. Nr. 11897.
[152] Tusa, *The Berlin Airlift*, 294.

the ability of vehicles and persons transporting rationed goods into Berlin, insisting that even vehicles en route to Berlin's Soviet sector not pass through the western half of the city.[153] Less than a week later, a subsequent order attempted to address perceived inadequacies in this initial directive, reiterating in particular the need to prevent any German vehicles from passing through Berlin and insisting that any vehicle heading to Berlin and transporting goods for daily use only enter the city through the Soviet sector. It further directed local police to keep watch over "foraging sources" (*Hamstererquellen*) and to post a guard (one police officer plus one member of the Volkskontrolle) at town entry points.[154]

Berliners rapidly adapted, developing new techniques to circumvent these restrictions. In mid-November, Brandenburg Police reported to Soviet authorities that large numbers of packages had recently been arriving in post offices near the boundary to Berlin's western sectors. Investigations showed that many of the addressees did not exist, and that the packages full of rationed goods were intended for persons living in (West) Berlin. At the Glienicke/Nordbahn post office, officials found more than a thousand packages and seized 800. In order to prevent any repetition, the order directed post offices to reject any packages larger than 5 kilograms and to insist that addressees present identification before receiving packages.[155] But all these expanded control measures still failed to live up to Soviet zone officials' expectations. An investigation of the "Ring around Berlin" from November 30 to December 3 uncovered continued failures.

Trying to explain these shortcomings, the report emphasized that the "foundation of faultless service on the 'Ring around Berlin' lies first and foremost in ideological training." According to this investigation, the personnel manning the checkpoints showed an inadequate understanding of the larger significance of their assignment.[156] The Brandenburg police's ideological investment in their efforts to control physical sites paralleled the SED's effort to make its battle against the black market the core of its challenge to the authority of the municipal government in Berlin. The

---

[153] Befehl Nr. 52 des Chefs der Polizei des Landes Brandenburg (October 13, 1948), BLHA, Rep. 203 VP, Nr. 1, Bl. 137–9.

[154] Befehl Nr. 53 des Chefs der Polizei des Landes Brandenburg (October 19, 1948), BLHA, Rep. 203 VP, Nr. 1, Bl. 140–2.

[155] Memo from Landeskriminalamt Brandenburg to Sowj. Militäradministration, Abt. Innere Verwaltung (November 15, 1948), BLHA, Rep. 203 VP, Nr. 36, Bl. 379–81.

[156] Befehl Nr. 59 des Chefs der Polizei des Landes Brandenburg (December 17, 1948), BLHA, Rep. 203 VP, Nr. 1, Bl. 151–4.

failure of both campaigns ultimately reflected the inadequacy of their efforts to define as criminal or politically suspect precisely those everyday practices that Berliners continued to see as normal elements of surviving the ongoing postwar period. Only when the terrain of that normalized postwar shifted would the foundation be laid for a relatively stable SED regime.

6

June 1949: Ending the Blockade

At midnight on May 20, 1949, the breakaway western trade union (UGO) declared a strike of railroad workers in Berlin. A remarkable percentage of railroaders heeded the call, far more than the approximately 3,000 UGO members in their ranks.[1] Over the course of the next few days, the strike evolved into a pitched battle for physical control of the train stations and rail infrastructure throughout Berlin's western sectors. Railway officials initially managed to keep the commuter railroad (S-Bahn) running in Berlin's western sectors, but by midmorning on May 22, striking workers seized control of most S-Bahn stations in the west sectors and interrupted the passage of trains. SED and FDGB situation reports read increasingly like battle accounts. A report from Pankow (Soviet sector) described the situation just across the sector border at 12:20 P.M. on May 22:

Train traffic from Wilhelmsruh to Waidmannslust has been interrupted. For half an hour, no trains have run. Waidmannslust is no longer in our hands. No reports are coming from Hermsdorf; we must assume that this base has been lost.[2]

Ten minutes later, another report came in:

The electric rail between Waidmannslust and Hermsdorf has been broken. The Ugo is marching on the Wittenau station.[3]

---

[1] Arthur Schlegelmilch cites an OMGBS report that put the number of strikers at 10,900, those in doubt at 3,000, and the number of "strike breakers" at 1,000. In Schlegelmilch, *Hauptstadt im Zonendeutschland*, 247 n. 402.

[2] Dispatch Nr. 27, May 22, 1949, Pankow, Genossin Grete Neumann (12.20 hrs.), LAB, BPA, IV L-2/10/402.

[3] Dispatch Nr. 28, May 22, 1949, Pankow, General Friedrich (12.30 hrs.), ibid.

MAP 4. Berlin Area Rail Network. *Source:* Villanova University Office of Media Technologies.

In the British sector, clashes at the Charlottenburg and Zoological Garden stations reached violent climaxes. The railroad authority (*Reichsbahndirektion* or RBD) used the S-Bahn to ferry reinforcements of railroad police, SED, and FDJ members to hot spots, and they took up positions in the stations and along the tracks. West sector police assumed perimeter positions around the stations but at times proved incapable of holding back the crowds. An SED situation report from the Zoological Garden Station provides a detailed account of the volatile situation:

Zoo Station 11:00 a.m. very good manning of the station by FDJ, party and Railroad police. The Railroad police has occupied all entrances and carefully checks every passenger. At the Hardenber[gplatz] entrance, approximately 3–400 persons who were being held back by an organized chain of the Stumm-Police [west sector police]. These people's mood was somewhat excited, incited by individual UGO-provocoteurs. Joachimsthalerstr. no massed crowds of people, Stumm-Pol. seal off the station entrance in a very disciplined fashion. Stumm-Pol. restrained (*zurückgehalten*). Young people and children burn ND [the SED party organ *Neues Deutschland*] at four points. 50 armed Railroad pol. with protection of the Stumm-Pol. slipped over to the pol. sta. opposite. Rowdies incited by the UGO attempt several times to storm the railway embankment, forced by the Stumm Pol to go back down. Remaining Railroad Police head out toward Savigny-Platz at the head of the FDJ there and the Party-troop Gesundbrunnen; Rowdies urged on by the UGO throw stones, pieces of the railing, and iron rails from the bridge onto the railway embankment. The Railroad police guarding a switch box about 300m away begin to shoot so that the bullets fly just over the bridge. On the bridge, some comrades have spread out and started numerous discussion groups. Discussion leadership excellent. Stumm-Pol intervenes in the face of a hail of stones and brings it to a stop. People relatively quiet, somewhat disturbed by the shooting, Stumm-Pol extremely disciplined in order to prevent any provocation.[4]

In the shooting and violent clashes in the west sectors, a fifteen-year-old boy died, and many people were injured.[5] Even though some degree of violence had always been part of postwar Berlin political struggles, the extent of these clashes proved unsettling to political and military leaders in the west sectors and even to the UGO (Figure 12).

That this SED report spoke approvingly of west sector police under the direction of Johannes Stumm pointed to its discomfort with unregimented popular action. The incongruity within this report between these acts of popular violence and SED efforts to form *discussion groups* points to party members' uneasy presumption that they could control – if not the crowds – at least the meaning attributed to or appropriated by those crowds. More significantly this description elaborates the ebb and flow of violence in between the official authorities of East and West – to some extent regulated by those authorities but certainly not under their control. It describes a kind of "liminal space" that was at once powerful and unsettling.[6] By forging a new sense of popular danger just as the postwar battle for control of the city seemed to be letting up, the railroad workers' strike helped normalize the sustained experience of thinly controlled tension somewhere between war and peace. As much as Great Power negotiations seemed to draw a clear line under the Berlin Blockade crisis, its uneasy resolution on the ground – despite the assertion of international control – marked the crystallization of the Cold War in practice.

By contrast, in most accounts of the blockade, the beginning of the end came in the coded language of international diplomacy when, on January 31, Joseph Stalin provided answers to four questions posed by

---

[4] Meldung Niki Sternberg – Karl Morgenstern (13.45 hrs.), n.d. but probably 22.5.1949, ibid.

[5] Schlegelmilch, *Hauptstadt im Zonendeutschland*, 246 n. 401.

[6] On the threat to social and political order implicit in liminal spaces, see Victor Turner, *Blazing the Trail: Way Marks in the Exploration of Symbols*, Edith Turner, ed. (Tucson and London: University of Arizona Press, 1992), 153.

FIGURE 12. May 21, 1949: A young crowd watches anxiously as a policeman strikes a vigorous blow in a battle for control of an S-Bahn station in the Tempelhof District (American sector). The figures in the foreground stand on the track and make clear that trains are not running, at least for the moment. On this first day of the railroad workers' strike, SED activists and party youth groups marched on the idled tracks from the Soviet sector, heading west in an effort to occupy the stations throughout the city's western sectors. *Source:* Landesarchiv Berlin.

the American journalist, Kingsbury Smith.[7] In response to a query about the conditions under which the Soviets would lift their restrictions on transportation to Berlin, Stalin made no mention of the currency issue, indicating that Soviet restrictions could be removed if parallel Western restrictions were lifted simultaneously. Charles Bohlen, a senior State Department official and Russia expert, noticed the omission and took it to indicate a significant change in Soviet policy on Berlin.[8] He set in motion a diplomatic process that culminated in the Jessup-Malik agreement, announced on May 5, 1949, and the Paris CFM a little more than two weeks later. These lengthy, secret discussions relied heavily on discrete, personal contacts and took place in almost total isolation from the day-to-day events in Berlin. Although generally recognized as the process that brought an end to the blockade, the unique separateness of these diplomatic dealings from the remainder of the crisis has remained generally unexplored.[9]

Charles Bohlen suggests in his memoirs that Soviet willingness to negotiate stemmed from the Western counterblockade, which "was hurting the Communists a great deal."[10] But because the impact of the counterblockade was, for the most part, no more total than the Soviet control restrictions around Berlin, asking whether the Western counterblockade delivered a crushing blow to the Soviet zone economy is the wrong question.[11] For Soviet zone officials, the crisis they faced in early 1949 did not mark the emergence of new economic pressures but rather reflected their continued inability to effectively manage and control the Soviet zone economy.[12] On February 22, the American Political Advisor to Germany, Robert Murphy, wrote to the State Department and noted that "the economy of the western sectors of Berlin is being maintained not by the airlift but also on an extensive scale by various deals on the part of

---

[7] For the text of both the questions and Stalin's responses, see "Text of Stalin's Statement," *New York Times* (January 31, 1949), 4.

[8] See E. Bohlen, *Witness to History*, 383f. This realization is also discussed at some length in Shlaim, *The United States and the Berlin Blockade*, 380ff.

[9] Philip C. Jessup, "The Berlin Blockade and the Use of the United Nations," *Foreign Affairs* 50, no. 1 (October 1971), 163–73 and especially "Park Avenue Diplomacy," 377–400.

[10] Bohlen, *Witness to History*, 283. Public response in Germany and the United States varied from a cautious wait-and-see attitude to enthusiastic praise. See *New York Times* (January 31, 1949) and the *Tägliche Rundschau* (February 1, 1949).

[11] See Koop, *Keim Kampf*, 211–46.

[12] On the continued movement of people from the western zones into the Soviet zone, even after the tightening of the counterblockade, see, e.g., Report from the Krimialpolizei in Halle/Saale, dated March 21, 1949, LHAM, Rep. K14, Nr. 172, Bl. 81–2.

German firms and individuals with sources of supply in the Soviet Zone of Germany."[13] Such ongoing trade presented a real dilemma to Soviet and SED officials who wanted to promote economic development in their zone but also to tighten their control over those efforts. The contentious relationship between the emerging eastern and western administrations of Berlin highlighted the simultaneous successes and failures implicit in that attempt.

One City – Two Administrations

By the end of 1948, the city seemed split in two. There were now two mayors, two police forces, and two bureaucracies to go along with the two currencies circulating throughout the city. Speaking to the special assembly that created the East-Magistrat on November 30, the newly appointed mayor, Fritz Ebert, tried to justify its creation:

The looming danger of the final tearing apart (*Zerreisung*) of Berlin has been repulsed by this wide-ranging measure, and the constitutional unity of the administration reestablished (applause). With this vanguard action, you, ladies and gentlemen, have torn the wheel from the hands of the splitters of Berlin and created the precondition for a politics directed toward the good of the people, [a step] which can fill all Berliners with justified hope.

He argued that this new East-Magistrat reduced the vote in the west sectors five days later to an empty act and claimed that the *Ost-Magistrat* was the real administrator for all Berliners, regardless of the sector in which they lived.[14] His assertion that this SED-directed assembly had taken the necessary measures to guarantee the "constitutional unity" of the city could not conceal the fact that the decision to create a new administration for Berlin's Soviet sector was a desperate defensive measure designed to counter the continuing erosion of SED power within the city, and the insecurities that drove it did not vanish with the creation of the Soviet sector Magistrat.

Just before the December 5, 1948 elections in Berlin's west sectors, the SED issued a thirty-two-page pamphlet entitled, "Berlin – Worth a new war?" With graphic photos of pre- and postwar Berlin, the pamphlet denounced the destruction of the first "airlift" (British and American

[13] Letter from Robert Murphy to Charles E. Saltzman, Asst. Sec. of State, dated February 22, 1949, NA, RG 84 350/57/18/01 box 12, folder: Ambassador Murphy File February 1949.
[14] Stenographisches Bericht der Außerordentlichen Sitzung der StVV, November 30, 1948 in the Admiralspalast zu Berlin, LAB, STA Rep. 100, Nr. 91, Bl. 14.

bombing during World War II) and asserted that what had been accomplished in the city since the end of the war had been achieved by Berliners with little or no assistance from the Western occupiers. Even more pointedly, it linked the ongoing Western airlift to past and future destruction: "Yesterday phosphorus, today raisins, tomorrow atom bombs." Rejecting the "lie" of a Soviet Blockade, the booklet reminded its readers of the suffering produced by a "real" blockade imposed by the British navy during World War I.[15]

American military officials reacted with consternation, seeing the pamphlet as a crass example of devious and underhanded propaganda with which the Soviets and their SED supporters sought to influence events in the city. The U.S. military government in Berlin reported that the pamphlet was being sold for the modest price of 30 pfennig, mostly in the Soviet sector, but also illegally in the western sectors. The report also described "wide free distribution" and cited cases in which it had been wrapped into copies of the American sector newspaper, *Der Tagesspiegel*. For the American report writer, such a strategy seemed to suggest an insidious sneak attack, a propaganda fifth column, literally hidden in the midst of one of the western parties' staunchest public advocates. Ironically, if this assertion were true, it meant that the SED message reached West Berliners only in conjunction with a newspaper that the pamphlet denounced as a major source of warmongering (*Kriegshetze*) and against which it called its readers to defend themselves. For the SED, which for years had bemoaned its inability to escape the powerful voice of Western papers, such a propaganda "success" would have marked an ambiguous achievement at best. This pamphlet full of over-the-top inflammatory rhetoric – together with the American response – mattered very little for everyday life in Berlin. But that is precisely the point. It remained dramatically disconnected from the ongoing material issues that still mattered most for ordinary Berliners.

In a parallel to American fears about Communist propaganda, Soviet sector officials responded quickly to even very small-scale threats to the explanatory monopoly to which they aspired. A police report from

---

[15] NA, RG 59, 250/38/12/4–5, box 6694: Decimal File 1945–49 from 862.00/12–149 to 862.00 Bondholders/12–3149. The word *raisins* refers to the affectionate term, *Rosinenbomber* (Raisin bombers) given by Berliners to the planes of the airlift, especially those that dropped chocolate and other treats for children as they approached the Tempelhof airfield. Memorandum from Gordon E. Textor, Colonel CE, Information Services Division to The Military Governor, dated December 3, 1948, NA RG 84 350/57/18/01, box 7, folder: Dept. Beam.

January 1949 described how banned Western-licensed printed materials were being laid out in hair salons and other stores. Apparently, journal lenders had been placing these articles under authorized journals in the folders they distributed to these businesses. The municipal police command ordered its officers to confiscate such folders immediately and report all cases to the responsible section of the criminal police.[16] In spite of its newfound administrative independence, the Soviet sector found it impossible to escape the continued incursions of west-sector influences, but the extent to which SED leaders found threatening even the reading material in salon waiting rooms testified to the depths of officials' uneasiness.

The separate municipal administrations notwithstanding, Berlin was by no means a divided city, and it was not only journals that managed to cross sector boundaries. Every day, thousands of people traveled between the eastern and western sectors, to work, visit family, or purchase food and other items, and these border-crossers (*Grenzgänger*) remained a vital part of the economic life in both sectors and continued to tie Berlin to the surrounding Soviet zone. A photo in the weekly *Sie* shows a man carrying a forty liter can of "black market fuel" across the border into the American sector. The caption reports that a kilogram of diesel oil was available for one east mark in free-trade Handelsorganisation (HO) Shops and went for 3.50 east marks or 1.20 west marks on the black market.[17] In what seems to be daylight, the man walks past one of the large signs announcing in four languages the boundary of the American sector, suggesting the degree to which even "black" activities took place in plain sight. Even more explicitly "illegal" trade continued in occasionally spectacular fashion. West Berlin Mayor Ernst Reuter received almost daily reports of trucks running Soviet sector police checkpoints on the sector boundary. In a remarkable number of cases, the reports laconically note that shots were fired – occasionally resulting in a death or injury but most often ending in the truck continuing unabated into the western sectors. Whether a reflection of Soviet sector police officers' poor marksmanship or an indication of their ambivalence about the need to halt this regular transportation of goods, these "border violations" underscored

---

[16] Kdo. d. Schupo: Kommando-Anordnung Nr. 1, dated January 12, 1949, LAB, STA Rep. 26, Nr. 143, Bl. 48.

[17] "Treibstoff für Berlin," *Sie* (April 24, 1949), 3. The first HO shop opened its doors in Berlin's Soviet sector in November 1948. Organized under the direction of the DWK, these "free shops" attempted to counteract the black market and provide access to scarce goods by selling them ration free but at significantly higher prices than those charged in regular shops. Landsman, *Dictatorship and Demand*, 55–73.

how daily practices continued to challenge the concreteness of political division.[18]

For all of the political and administrative changes facing Berliners as they entered 1949, day-to-day material considerations continued to dominate their lives, and there was much more to their survival than the dried potatoes and canned meat flown in by the airlift. Generally, accounts of the blockade have emphasized the increasing economic burdens that its restrictions placed on the western sectors: plant shutdowns, layoffs, and growing unemployment.[19] While such occurrences were a fact of life for many Berliners, the overall Berlin economy continued to function remarkably well, far better than Western experts had initially predicted.[20]

The fact that West Berlin firms could still use east marks to cover many expenses, including at least a portion of wages, provided additional incentive for continued pursuit of Soviet sector and Soviet zone business. Even when Western occupation authorities extended their counterblockade to West Berlin in January 1949, such trade continued – including deals made by the West-Magistrat.[21] This trade played a major part in the relative stability of the west sectors' economy. From July 1948 through March 1949, West Berlin industry produced at 65 percent of the June 1948 level. Unemployment remained much lower than initial predictions had guessed, increasing from 4.4 percent in June 1948 to 13.5 percent in March 1949. Industrial employment remained even more stable with an average of 94 percent of the June 1948 workforce retained by Berlin manufacturers between July 1948 and March 1949. Only with the introduction of the west mark as the sole currency in the west sectors did Berlin's east-west trade drop off substantially, declining to almost nothing by the end of the year.[22]

Nearly four years after the end of World War II, scarcity remained the norm for all zones of Germany. The "official" ration continued to be inadequate to meet real nutritional requirements. Although nutritionists' analysis of body weights in the American zone indicated that the situation

[18] LAB, Rep. 2, Acc. 888, Nr. 452: Polizeiliche Tagesmeldungen, January – July 1949.
[19] See Tusa, *The Berlin Airlift*, 263 and 282.
[20] On this phenomenon, see the detailed account in Stivers, "The Incomplete Blockade," 591–3. Airgram from U.S. Political Advisor for Germany, Berlin, to Sec. of State; No. A-984; December 27, 1948, NA, RG 84 350/57/18/02, box 216.
[21] See BK/O (49) 9 dated January 26, 1949, LAB, Rep. 280 (LAZ-Sammlung), Sta.-Ort Nr. 5998. Koop, *Kein Kampf*, 223–5 and Stivers, "The Incomplete Blockade," 587–8.
[22] Stivers, "The Incomplete Blockade," 590–1. On the economic impact of the dual-currency structure, see the memorandum from John B. Holt to Robert Murphy dated February 19, 1949, NA RG 84, 350/57/18/01, box 12.

had improved significantly since mid-1947, average body weights for men and women still remained significantly below the desirable minimum "for maintenance of health."[23] A report prepared for American officials in early 1949 suggested that daily average food consumption in the American sector of Berlin had actually dropped from December 1948 to January 1949, from 1,642 to 1,579 calories – in both instances significantly less than the allocated ration.[24] Expounding on the same theme, a January 14 article in the SPD newspaper *Telegraf* complained about "paper" calories – nourishment allocated according to the ration schedules but never actually made available. Describing conditions in the Soviet zone, the article ironically cited DWK reports that in the coming year, only 25 percent of food rations would be met with alternative products: sugar for oil, dried vegetables for fresh, and so on.[25]

In the east and west, supplemental sources of foodstuffs drove individuals' decisions about time management, work attendance, and organizational membership. Speaking to an FDGB meeting in January, one trade union leader described the general sense of depression that had settled over the workers at his firm. He indicated that many workers planned to drop their FDGB membership if there were no additional distributions of vegetables and textiles.[26] Soviet and SED efforts to promote expanded foodstuff supply (especially in the form of deliveries from the Soviet Union and other Eastern European countries) met with cynical responses. A Brandenburg police report from mid-March described how workers in plants slated for extra support in conjunction with Soviet Order No. 234 continued to wait for the additional rations promised by DWK press reports. The report went on to note that theater newsreel accounts of foodstuff imports were greeted with "general laughter and catcalls."[27] As these accounts

---

[23] Nutrition: Adult Body Weights (undated report, likely early 1949), NA, RG 260, 390/48/12/05, box 186. See similar document in the same file: OMGUS, Civil Administration Division, Public Health Branch Report (January 5, 1949).

[24] "Daily Food Rationed and Consumed (Calories): U.S. Sector of Berlin: December 1948 and January 1949," NA, RG 260, 390/48/12/05, box 186.

[25] "Kalorien in Ost und West." *Telegraf* (February 14, 1949), in LAB, STA Rep. 113, Nr. 110.

[26] Minutes of the Bezirks-Ausschuss Tiergarten on 11.1.1949; report dated January 20, 1949, LAB, FDGB 136.

[27] Wochenkommunique Nr. 2 for the period 4.-10.3.1949 from MdI, Abt. Polizei (Hirsch) to the Interior Minister, dated March 15, 1949, BLHA, Ld. Br. Rep. 203, Nr. 117, Bl. 322ff. Soviet Order No. 234, issued in October 1947, provided supplemental food and supplies to workers in some factories but essentially introduced Soviet-style labor relations to the Soviet zone. Kopstein, *The Politics of Economic Decline in East Germany, 1945–1989,* 23.

suggest, the economic and supply situation facing SED officials in the Soviet zone remained critical. Even if the details of this supply crisis only rarely garnered discussion at the highest levels of SED leadership, the physical and health consequences for Soviet zone residents were manifest in local reports and help to explain these popular reactions to perceived supply failures. Soviet zone officials' focus on Berlin at the expense of the rest of the zone exacerbated these shortages, especially in the public mind.[28]

Western propaganda played up the image of a "starving Soviet Zone,"[29] but Berliners from all sectors continued to make forays into the surrounding areas to supplement their food supplies. In spite of border controls, these persons constantly developed new techniques to transport goods into the city.[30] The minutes of a meeting of (East) Berlin police section chiefs suggest the extent to which control efforts at the sector border were often ignored: "Numerous incidents provide reason to point out that all vehicles that ignore the signal by municipal policemen to stop, should have their license number noted down and reported."[31] A March 3 directive outlining instructions for border controls in Berlin suggests that even at that date much traffic continued to enter the west sectors with no or only superficial checks. It explicitly instructed the policemen:

Absolutely all vehicles are to be checked: in addition to trucks and their trailers and horse-drawn vehicles, also cars and handcarts. The inspection should not be conducted in a superficial fashion. It must, e.g., include the trunks of cars. With trucks, special attention should be paid to the possibility of a false bottom in the loading area and to any other hollow spaces that could be used as hiding places.[32]

If, as this directive seems to imply, police had been ignoring car trunks, it's hard to believe that great effort was even required to circumvent these controls.

Some indication of the range of Berliners obtaining supplies in the Soviet zone is indicated by the fact that during the first three months of 1949, 5 percent of those persons reported seized by police in Saxony-Anhalt (the western-most state in the Soviet zone) for "unauthorized

---

[28] Koop, *Kein Kampf*, 196–200.
[29] See Stivers, "The Incomplete Blockade," 577 and Kopp, *Kein Kampf*, 157–60.
[30] See the weekly communiqués produced by the Brandenburg police, BLHA, Ld. Br. Rep. 203, Nr. 117.
[31] Niederschrift über die Dienststellenleiter-Besprechung am 4.11.1948 (Kdo. d. Schuztpolizei), LAB, STA Rep. 26, Nr. 150, Bl. 5.
[32] Instructions for checkpoints on the sector border from the Kdo. d. schupo, dated March 3, 1949, LAB, STA Rep. 26, Nr. 143, Bl. 63. Underlining in original.

export of foodstuffs and agricultural products from the Province Saxony" came from Berlin.[33] The significant amounts of west marks (including many with the Berlin "B" stamp) seized in Saxony-Anhalt further attested to the extent that western currency played a significant role in the Soviet zone economy, an economy that by its very nature thus eluded SED and DWK control.[34]

A confidential Berlin *Schutzpolizei* memo dated January 12, 1949 further highlighted eastern authorities' limited power. It discussed the need for Berlin police to receive support from "workers among the Berlin population" in their efforts to carry out controls on S- and U-Bahn trains running into the city's western sectors. According to the description that opens the memo, "Organized gangs (mostly young people) disrupt the controls and harass the police officers by spitting at them, holding the doors shut, etc."[35] In an effort to address "the most dangerous spots," the memo called for the formation of groups from "democratic parties" and trade unions in order to place five support persons in every S- and U-Bahn car. "These civilian forces are assigned to travel back and forth between the last station in the sector and the station that comes before it in order to insure that attacks on municipal policemen are met with discussion in order to guarantee their moral support."[36] The decision to confront this dramatic indication of police weakness and popular power with a call for discussion group interventions underscored yet again Soviet sector officials' failure to grasp Berliners' ability and readiness to confront material crisis with personal action that operated beyond the jurisdiction of any one municipal or occupation authority.

In a dangerous demonstration of this sort of initiative, west sector residents raided Soviet zone coal trains as they passed through the western half of the city. These trains generally had to stop for several hours at a switching yard in the American sector, and, as soon as the coast was

---

[33] Monthly reports on Black Market Trade 1947–9, LHAM, Rep. K 8, Nr. 550. The total figures are 641 persons, 30 of whom came from Berlin. I calculated these totals on the basis of individual monthly reports submitted by local police offices. While I believe that these figures provide an insightful glimpse into the makeup of persons engaged in this "illicit" activity, they should not be taken as comprehensive. These figures may conceal some of those persons coming from Berlin as the information also includes persons from unknown locations. Occasionally, the figures included numbers of items seized, not persons, and I did not use that data in my calculation.

[34] See LBdVP Sachsen-Anhalt: Sekretariat, 1946–50, LHAM Rep. K-14, Nr. 18.

[35] Memo from Kommando der Schutzpolizei, Org.-Abt. (signed Pech) dated January 19, 1949, LAB, STA-Berlin, STA Rep. 26, Bl. 49.

[36] Ibid.

clear, small groups, primarily women, dashed between the cars to fill their bags with coal briquettes. A series of photographs captured one case in which an older woman and her grandson worked together to obtain much needed coal, even more so because the airlift never attempted to supply coal for home heating. While the boy climbed up into the load of coal, his grandmother stood on the coupling holding a bag into which the boy tossed down as many briquettes as it could hold. Looking around nervously she moved quickly away while the boy filled his pockets, and the two of them made their way back on the hazardous path between the train cars that might move with little warning.[37] While this risky behavior demonstrated the desperation that many Berliners continued to feel, a Berlin in which *Soviet zone* trains could be accessed in the middle of the *western sectors* also made clear how tenuous these dividing lines remained (Figure 13).

As Berliners continued to move back and forth across the city, SED officials expressed concern that their "success" in setting up the East-Magistrat risked isolating the party from the city's western half. Speaking to the Berlin SED's Executive Committee, Waldemar Schmidt, the head of the Personnel Department in the new Magistrat, hopefully declared the new municipal administration a decisive step en route to SED power in the city as a whole but warned that the battle for Berlin was not over. He called on his fellow party members to combat Western efforts to make the SED a party of the Soviet sector.[38] In fact, SED leaders in the city were growing irritated with the tendency of members to withdraw from party activity in the three western sectors. Many SED members who lived in the western sectors but worked in the Soviet sector limited their party activities to the factory party group, staying away from SED activities in their home area. Even more troubling for the SED leadership were those SED members who moved to the Soviet sector. In order to prevent such acts of "desertion" the Berlin Secretariat resolved that "comrades" be permitted to move from west to east only with approval of the Berlin Executive Committee.[39] With this resolution, SED leaders sought to invest party membership with an ideological significance that it did not hold for

---

[37] "Jagd nach Kohlen," *Sie* (February 27, 1949), 3. On the physical dangers of stealing coal from train cars, see Heinrich Böll, "Lohengrins Tod," in *Wanderer, kommst du nach Spa...: Erzählungen* (Munich: DTV, 1987), 120–9.

[38] Protokoll d. Konferenz d. Landesvorstandes, Tues., December 14, 1948, LAB, BPA IV L-2/1/42, Bl. 2–4.

[39] See the remarks by Hans Jendretzky, Protokoll d. Konferenz d. Landesvorstandes, Tuesday, December 14, 1948, Bl. 20.

FIGURE 13. A young man leaps from a barge with an armful of stolen coal. Whether or not he netted more than the small armful with which he is shown plunging into the water (or even if that armful made it to shore), his brazen daylight theft pointed both to his material desperation and the opportunity to pursue unrationed sources of supply. Coal barges plying Berlin's rivers and canals offered a visible reminder of the goods moving back and forth across the city's occupation sectors but also provided a mobile platform for black market trading in precious coal briquettes. *Source:* Landesarchiv Berlin.

many members and thereby address an ongoing weakness they recognized with the party.

Some preliminary policy initiatives undertaken by the Ebert administration reflected the Berlin SED's optimistic belief that it could still succeed in both halves of the city. By proposing a winter emergency plan to address Berliners' material needs and moving to implement the expropriation plan passed by the city assembly two years previously, the SED pursued popular support across sector lines. Most clearly though, SED efforts to expand the program by which west sector residents could receive food and heating rations from the Soviet sector gave expression to SED leaders' ongoing hopes that their battle for Berlin was not yet finished. A proposed Magistrat resolution submitted to Ebert explained that the number of west sector residents registering for Soviet sector rations was continuously increasing – an assertion that may have been technically correct, but the numbers never reached much more than 5 percent of the west sector population. Building on this optimistic vision, the resolution emphasized the need to ensure the seamless supply of these persons and proposed to set up storage and sales sites in the western sectors.[40]

A memo dated December 23, 1948 noted that attempts had been made to organize food stores in rail installations in the west sectors (especially in existing stores in S-Bahn stations). Because, as part of the German rail system, these sites were technically under Soviet jurisdiction, SED officials thought that such a step would be legal under existing four-power regulations. These efforts broke off when the necessary small-scale retailers could not be found to run these stores. They allegedly feared repressions in their own sectors. The memo went on to suggest that supplying these stores would have proved extraordinarily difficult, as the "Stumm-Police" and the Western Allies could be expected to confiscate the goods en route.[41] Even then, the effort was not yet dead. In a letter to the Soviet command in early January, Berlin SED head Hans Jendretzky outlined a series of similar measures. He called for Soviet officials to meet with him and Bruno Baum (from the SED's economic section) regarding these "important" proposals. There is no evidence of any Soviet support for the idea, and it apparently ended with this attempt.[42]

Even in the Soviet sector, the new structures of SED control proved less than total. Writing to the Soviet Command on February 7, 1949, Karl Maron, the new head of the Soviet Sector Economic Department, responded to a series of questions directed to him about the distribution

---

[40] Proposed Magistrat resolution submitted by St.R. Spangenberg to OB (Ebert) regarding creation of food stores in west sectors, n.d., LAB, STA Rep. 101, Nr. 711, Bl. 37. According to reports from the Food Department in the Soviet sector, 65,534 West Berliners registered for Soviet sector rations in October; 68,302 in November; and 85,188 in December. While this did amount to a substantial increase, it still remained less than 5 percent of the west sector population. LAB, STA Rep. 113, Nr. 224, Bl. 97, 100, 104.

[41] Memo from St. R. Spangenberg to OB Ebert regarding creation of food stores in west sectors, dated December 23, 1948, LAB, STA Rep. 101, Nr. 711, following Bl. 37.

[42] Letter from Jendretzky to the Soviet Central Commander (attn. General Demidov) regarding supply of West Berliners by the east sector, dated January 5, 1949, LAB, BPA, IV L-2/4/172. Of course, during the post-1961 period, the East German regime did set up shops in the portion of the Friedrichstraße Train Station (in East Berlin) accessible to westerners traveling through East Berlin on the S- or U-Bahn. In particular, many West Berliners used the shops as a source for cheap alcohol and cigarettes. Christoph Links, *Berliner Geisterbahnhöfe: The Berlin Ghost Stations: Les gares fantômes* (Berlin: Ch. Links Verlag, 1994), 70.

of confiscated goods. Maron pleaded that he was unable to answer all of the questions fully in such a short time as he had only been director of the Economic Department since November 30, 1948. He claimed that he found the department in a disastrous state, with much of its personnel and many of its files lost to the west. Thus, he asserted that he could not be held responsible for the distribution of any goods confiscated in 1948.[43]

A more general report from January cited similar concerns. In spite of the fact that the new Magistrat had a smaller population to administer, the report explained that it found the drop in personnel difficult to cope with, as many tasks remained independent of population level. Only about 50 percent of the previous personnel remained following the split. Among higher-ranking personnel, the number of those leaving ranged from 60 to 90 percent. Thus the most experienced and technically qualified personnel tended to head to the western administration, but political conviction played a role in only a small number of the decisions to stay or leave. For the most part, more prosaic considerations influenced their decisions: those living in the western sectors left, those living in the eastern sector stayed with the "Magistrat of Greater Berlin," as eastern officials described themselves in an effort to maintain their fictive claim to speak for the entire city. The report explained that many employees who remained with the East-Magistrat stood in opposition to the SED in spite of having signed the mandatory declaration of loyalty to the new administration.[44] This assessment only heightened SED fears about "enemies" within its new administration or even in the SED and underscored its sense of the party's fragile position.[45]

In some arenas, Soviet sector officials perceived an even more overt Western threat. They couched their understanding of this danger in specific terms of an assault on the economic development in the Soviet sector and as directly targeting the Soviet zone's two-year plan. On October 28,

---

[43] Copy of a letter from Stadtrat Maron (Abt. Wirtschaft) to the Head of the Abt. f. Versorgung u. Handel bei der Zentralkommandantur Berlin, Major Gubisch regarding the distribution of confiscated goods, dated February 7, 1949, LAB, STA Rep. 106, Nr. 206.

[44] Copy of a report on the Reorganization der Hauptverwaltung des Magistrats von Gross-Berlin nach der Spaltung am 30.11.1948, LAB, BAP, IV L-2/13/453. It is interesting to note that this report refers to the creation of the eastern Magistrat on November 30 as the "division" (*Spaltung*) [of the city administration]. In most SED correspondence, the undertaking is not characterized as an act of division but as an act designed to save the unity of Berlin.

[45] Catherine Epstein convincingly argues that their experience of denunciation and betrayal during the Nazi era significantly contributed to postwar Communists' readiness to seek out and find "agents" and "enemies" in their midst. See her *The Last Revolutionaries*, 47.

Tägliche Rundschau reported a failed sabotage attempt at the Klingenberg electric power plant in the Soviet sector. Three days earlier, the paper alleged, the pressure in one of the plant's boilers had suddenly shot up, the result of a valve mistakenly being closed. Supposedly, the cover securing the buttons that controlled this valve had been found suspiciously open.[46] More than a propaganda effort to cover up what seems likely to have been an accident, this incident (or more accurately the image constructed around this incident) helped drive the ever-increasing sense of insecurity that surrounded the SED's efforts to establish independent political and economic power bases.

On November 4, the Soviet sector municipal police commander issued a special order directing the municipal police to take over security at critical industrial sites such as the Klingenberg Power Plant and the Danziger Street Gasworks. The directive explained its decision as necessary to prevent "wide scale destruction," prevent worker deaths, and counter sabotage of the two-year plan.[47] This denunciation of a threat to Berlin's electric supply at a time when Soviet sector power plants remained largely disconnected from the western sectors' power grid was, of course, rich with unintentional irony but also reiterated the SED's sense of weakness, even in the midst of the blockade. In early March 1949, a municipal police directive expanded security measures around critical factories. Citing the need to defend against economic crimes, sabotage, and theft, with which "criminal elements" were seeking to derail the "planned expansion of the democratic economy in the Soviet Occupation Zone and in Berlin," the order established an armed factory guard made up of appropriate members of the factory workforce. It called on "democratic organizations" to promote publicly that workers were for the first time being armed to defend their workplaces, an assertion that continued to manifest the SED's contradictory claims to looming threats and triumphant accomplishment that demanded the kind of conceptual gymnastics that longtime Communists had practiced for years.[48]

A letter from the Bezirksamt Wedding (French sector) to the Food Department (East) regarding some personnel files derisively referred to the

---

[46] "Vereitelter Sabotageakt auf Klingenberg," *Tägliche Rundschau* [B] (October 28, 1948), 2.

[47] Sonder-Anordnung der Kdo. d. Schupo vom 4.11.1948, LAB, STA Rep. 26, Nr. 143, Bl. 33.

[48] Kdo. d. Schutzpolizei – Betriebsschutz-Insp.: Confidential Instructions for the introduction of an armed factory guard, dated March 2, 1949, LAB, STA Rep. 26, Nr. 143, Bl. 59.

eastern administration as the "City Soviet."[49] But complaints were not limited to concerns about the moral and ideological complications of a politics tied so closely to the Soviet Union. Among Soviet sector residents and even SED loyalists, the new administration's ongoing material failings garnered vigorous criticism. Writing to SED-controlled Berlin radio in mid-January 1949, a woman in the Soviet sector complained about the lack of vegetables in the stores there:

Since November 1948, we have not received any vegetables. Why, then, does the radio announce them each day, when there aren't any in the shops. I would very much like to know where all the vegetables are. Of course I realize that vegetables cannot be made available like during the summer. But there at least there should be turnips and carrots. True, today I saw canned turnips, but only pickled; one can hardly cook a dish from those (small coal over 2.–DM). How is one supposed to have enough [cellared] potatoes if one has to cook potatoes every day. If one had vegetables, it would be possible to stretch out the potatoes a bit, but grits and farina alone are not enough.

I personally finished off my potatoes in the middle of February. Other families that I know have the same problem.[50]

For this woman, the problem lay not only in the ongoing material but in the disconnection between that material reality and propaganda assertions of plenty that the radio broadcast every day.

West sector leaders faced similar tensions between ideological desires and ongoing material crisis. Under the leadership of the new mayor, Ernst Reuter, the west sector administration worked vigorously to ensure that at least part of Berlin remained firmly imbedded in the West. Its leaders were less confident that this goal remained a priority of the Western occupying powers. Especially with respect to the city's divided currency, Reuter and other German officials in West Berlin feared that an "international" compromise would be reached at Berliners' expense.[51] On October 27, 1948, the Berlin Magistrat supported the west mark as the sole valid currency for the western sectors and directed its financial representatives to base

---

[49] Attached to a memo from the Abt. f. Ernährung to the OB (Ebert) dated January 10, 1949, LAB, STA Rep. 101, Nr. 659.

[50] Letter from a Fr. Friedel Dobroschek dated January 16, 1949 regarding the lack of vegetables in the stores of the Soviet sector, LAB, STA Rep. 113, Nr. 184.

[51] See Brandt and Löwenthal, *Ernst Reuter*, 463. In the late fall, the currency question was put before a special U.N. committee of "experts." However, in the end, the United Nations played almost no role in shaping policy or the eventual settlement in Berlin. See Jessup, "The Berlin Blockade and the Use of the United Nations," 172.

their discussions with the occupiers on this premise.[52] On November 2, the Central Committee of the Emergency Board on the Berlin Economy (*Notgemeinschaft der Berliner Wirtschaft*), a cooperative organization made up of representatives of industry, trade unions, and the Magistrat under the direction of Klingelhöfer, unanimously called for the introduction of the west mark as the sole currency in the western sectors.[53] This was not a demand motivated by economic necessity. In fact, west sector leaders openly acknowledged that such a step would have significant economic costs because the strength of the west mark and its interaction with the east mark did much to sustain the economic life of the western sectors.[54]

Instead, this call for a second currency reform reflected the desire of Reuter and other west sector leaders to pursue concrete steps to symbolically bind western Berlin to the emerging political structures of a new West German state. They feared that any material compromise on the currency question would eventually entail political compromises to the Soviets and the SED in Berlin. Additionally, these west sector leaders hoped to add West Berlin to the Marshall Plan's European Recovery Program, which at that time included only the three western zones of Germany.[55] Such a step would not only provide additional material assistance but would provide a further institutional link to the West.

Information gathered in the western zones bore out west sector leaders' fear that Berlin was not a primary concern for western Germany. A report prepared for the western sector City Assembly in January 1949 characterized western Germans as generally apathetic about the Berlin crisis. On the basis of interviews and discussions held in preparation for an exhibit on Berlin to be shown around western Germany, the report asserted that many people assumed that Berlin was lost anyway and that scarce resources were being wasted on dragging out the inevitable (a sentiment that also found some proponents in the west zone SPD). Some commented that not knowing what tomorrow will bring, it's not worth

---

[52] *Berlin: Behauptung von Freiheit und Selbstverwaltung 1946–1948*, 683. See also the letter from Mayor Ferdinand Friedensburg to American officials on November 9, 1948, NA, RG 84, 350/57/18/01, box 11, Folder Memoranda October-December 1948.

[53] Ibid., 688. See also Brandt and Löwenthal, *Ernst Reuter*, 463.

[54] According to the testimony of the President of the Berliner Industrie- und Handelskammer in 1951, cited in Keiderling, *"Rosinenbomber" über Berlin*, 187.

[55] See the fragmentary memo by Gustav Klingelhöfer [?] regarding the inclusion of Berlin in the European Recovery Program (Marshall Plan), dated 20 January 1949, LAB, Rep. 2, Acc. 888, Nr. 485.

future shipment to Siberia for the sake of Berlin today. The report concluded with a request to keep this information confidential as the firm did not want its business in western Germany hurt by repercussions from this "negative" evaluation.[56] As of November 1948, a special tax had been introduced in the Bizone to help support Berlin. Every article of mail required a special 2 pfennig stamp as an emergency sacrifice for Berlin (*Notopfer Berlin*).[57] The potential animosity that this could produce was not lost on the West-Magistrat. In January, it responded negatively to a proposal to post placards in the Bizone proclaiming that "Berlin is worth a sacrifice."[58] Although the financial assistance was critical, the image of a city dependent on Western handouts – or at least on handouts other than the airlift – did little to promote the value of Berlin in western Germany.

Like its eastern counterpart, the west sector administration spent much of its time struggling to cope with the logistics of the split. Because most municipal buildings were located in the Soviet sector, finding space for the administration presented significant difficulties. Additionally, the large number of city employees who refused to work for the eastern Magistrat provided the western administration with more workers than necessary. In spite of the recommendations of some of his administrative colleagues, Reuter was loath to dismiss persons who had committed to the new administration.[59] While many of these acts of "loyalty" were less politically than pragmatically motivated, the symbolic power of Reuter's decision should not be discounted. Indeed, symbolic rather than material successes lay at the core of the new administration's political efforts. Klingelhöfer and other officials did lobby the Allies in an effort to gain additional material benefits for west sector residents but met with few

---

[56] Report for the Abgeordnetenhaus Berlin [?]: Die westdeutsche Bevölkerung und das Problem Berlin: Stimmungsbericht, dated Hannover, January 27, 1949, LAB, Rep. 280 (LAZ-Sammlung), Sta.-Ort Nr. 2906. More generally on the half-hearted nature of West German support for Berlin, see Koop, *Kein Kampf*.

[57] This measure was designed to provide 25 million west marks a month in supplementary funds for Berlin. In addition, the Joint Economic Area (Bizone) extended an initial credit of 45 million west marks to the city of Berlin in July 1948. The precarious financial state of western Germany made it impossible for them to advance a further (70 million west marks) credit that, in turn, led to the creation of the "Notopfer Berlin." See Keiderling, *"Rosinenbomber" über Berlin*, 280–2.

[58] Minutes of the 142nd Session of the Magistrat on January 12, 1949, LAB, Rep. 280 (LAZ-Sammlung), Nr. 8503/72.

[59] See Brandt and Löwenthal, *Ernst Reuter*, 460–1. They report that Otto Suhr (the speaker of the city assembly and later mayor of West Berlin) was initially opposed to the decision to keep on all employees who demonstrated their loyalty to the western administration but later came to believe it to have been the correct decision.

successes.[60] But, as demonstrated by the decisive outcome in the December elections, the new administrative could at least point to an abundance of popular support even if the material crisis had not abated.

In the Soviet zone and the Soviet sector of Berlin, SED reference to the promises of the two-year plan remained a cornerstone of the party's efforts to explain and justify its administrative measures and pursuit of municipal control in Berlin.[61] But the lure of the west mark and the enticements of the Western (capitalist) economy continued to undermine these efforts. Already in February, the fact that the DWK had proposed a new regulation on "the punishment of black marketeers and speculators" demonstrated the seriousness with which SED authorities considered these independent economic efforts. This measure called for the death penalty or life imprisonment for the most serious cases of persons "who undermine the planned economic order or the supply of the population, who selfishly obtain excessive criminal advantages and exact great harm to the general good."[62] Such draconian control efforts were not without effect – although to some extent it was not the effect desired. In spite of the transportation restrictions around the city's western sectors, some firms still sought to escape Soviet zone authority by moving production there. At times, these efforts entailed the secret nighttime shift of plants or equipment to sites in West Berlin. On March 5, the Ristow Firm allegedly used "armed force" to transport machinery from Teltow into the adjacent American sector.[63] In another instance, reports reached FDGB officials that a firm from Zerbst (Saxony) was unloading machinery at a firm in West Berlin. Here, the machinery was apparently used for repair work contracted to the Saxon firm by a company in the American sector. Although the firm showed no signs of attempting to abandon Zerbst, it was investigated in response to a warning from the west sector SED.[64]

---

[60] Klingelhöfer appealed for greater amounts of fuel oil to be flown in by the airlift. This request was dismissed by an American official. See his letter dated January 10, 1949, LAB, Rep. 2, Acc. 888, Nr. 485.

[61] See the remarks by Hermann Matern before the SED Central Committee, Stenographisches Bericht der 16. (30.) Parteivorstandssitzung der SED, 12.-13.1.1949, SAPMO, DY 30/IV 2/1/59, Bl. 13f.

[62] 4th Draft of a Verordnung über die Bestrafung von Schiebern und Spekulanten, dated February 12, 1949, SAPMO, NY 4062/80, Bl. 79.

[63] Wochenkommunique Nr. 1 for the period February 26 to March 5, 1949 from the MdI, Abt. Polizei (Gartmann, Dep. Head of the Landespolizei) to the Interior Minister, dated March 10, 1949, BLHA, Ld. Br. 203, Nr. 117, Bl. 315.

[64] Copy of a memo to Roman Chwalek (Berlin FDGB) regarding transport of machinery from the Soviet zone to western sectors of Berlin, dated February 23, 1949, SAPMO, DY 34/31/113/2007.

This case provides evidence both for continuing Soviet zone trade with the west sectors and the SED's real fear that the zone's industries threatened to slip away to the west. Beyond overt force, DWK officials could provide only little incentive for independent Soviet zone firms to participate in its evolving control structures.[65]

At the same time, these officials looked beyond zonal borders in an effort to expand economic supply and sales networks. While its propaganda increasingly emphasized growing ties to the other states in the evolving Soviet Empire, the DWK did not wholly abandon the western zones. Early in 1949, DWK head Heinrich Rau wrote to the head of the Bizone Economic Council, Dr. Hermann Pünder, and invited him to attend the spring trade fair in Leipzig. On 17 February Pünder responded and expressed his appreciation for the invitation to the Leipzig Trade Fair, the most significant symbol of German economic strength and economic unity, but declined the invitation in light of the ongoing political differences, especially the differing interpretations of the measures taken by the occupying powers in Berlin. At the bottom of the letter, he added a handwritten note in which he expressed hope for a meeting in the not too distant future.

Rau drafted a response in which he expressed regret for Pünder's unwillingness to come to Leipzig. Nonetheless, he hoped that the meeting Pünder addressed could come to pass and at least gave lip service to the possibility that German authorities in all zones could work together to force occupation officials to devote greater attention to interzonal trade.[66] It is not clear that this letter was ever sent. While essentially a futile, cursory exchange, this correspondence still strikes me as significant. Rau's comments reflected an accurate assessment of the negative economic fallout from a breakdown of intra-German trade, especially for the less heavily industrialized Soviet zone. His hope for a closely administered form of interzonal trade reflected the incompatible SED desires for expanded access and expanded control. That it eventually gained the latter so decisively also sowed the seeds for eventual East German economic decline.

---

[65] The largest and economically most significant firms were, of course, under direct Soviet control (in the form of SAGs) or under the jurisdiction of the DWK. The fear of further "socialization" undoubtedly played a major role in some business owners' efforts to move their firms to the West.

[66] Letter to Heinrich Rau from Dr. Hermann Pünder (Head of the Economic Council of the Vereinigten Wirtschaftsgebiet) regarding an invitation to attend the Leipziger Messe, February 17, 1949 and draft of a letter by Rau in response to the previously mentioned letter from Dr. Hermann Pünder, dated March 8, 1949, SAPMO, NY 4062/80, Bl. 91–2.

The Second Currency Reform

On March 20, the Western Allies issued an order that dramatically altered the economic face of Berlin. The Third Ordinance for Monetary Reform declared the west mark to be the sole legal currency in Berlin's western sectors.[67] This step sealed the city's political division and established a more profound barrier between West Berlin and the Soviet zone than Soviet restrictions had ever done.[68] While the currency directive of March 20 did not make possession of east marks illegal in the western sectors, it did rule that east marks need no longer be accepted at face value for such important transactions as food purchases or rent payment. Firms in the western sectors were now obligated to pay their employees entirely in west marks. The order established a wage clearance office in West Berlin to adjust the wages of those employed in the Soviet sector and drawing their rations in the western sectors or vice versa. This occurred at varying rates depending on the sector in which one worked, lived, and drew one's rations, and established a four-tier system of west mark wage and salary payment. At the top tier were persons employed and drawing rations in the west sectors; they received 100 percent of their wages in west marks. Those employed in the Soviet sector but drawing their rations in the west sector were entitled to have 60 percent of their salary exchanged into west marks at a rate of 1:1. Employees working and drawing their rations in the Soviet sector could exchange 30 percent of their wages into west marks at the rate of 1:1. Persons employed in the western sectors but drawing their rations in the east sector received only 10 percent of their wages in west marks.[69] All other exchanges of currency had to be conducted at private exchange kiosks in the west sectors with rates that during spring 1949 ranged from 4 to 5.6 east marks for each west mark.[70]

Speaking to Berliners over the radio, Ernst Reuter emphasized the political significance of the step: "Now they can not cut us off [....]" The simple fact of the introduction of the Westmark is worth more than a hundred political declarations, 'We'll stay here!' This is a fact – the

---

[67] For the full text of the order, see LAB, Rep 280 (LAZ-Sammlung), Sta.-Ort.-Nr. 1283.

[68] See Michael Wolff, *Die Währungsreform in Berlin 1948/49*. Veröffentlichungen der Historischen Kommssion zu Berlin 77 (Berlin and New York: Walter de Gruyter, 1991), 3.

[69] See the Third Ordnance for Monetary Reform (Supplemental Currency Ordinance), LAB, Rep. 280 (LAZ-Sammlung), Sta.-Ort Nr. 1283. See also Keiderling, *"Rosinenbomber" über Berlin*, 183ff.

[70] "DM-West und DM-Ost im Berliner Wirtschaftsraum," LAB, Rep. 280 (LAZ-Sammlung), Sta.-Ort Nr. 4165.

Berliner desires facts and is completely justified in that."[71] For Reuter, the economic impact of the currency decision was secondary. He had been looking for a decisive act demonstrating western commitment to the city; with the March 20 currency reform, he found it. The western sectors found the basis of their economic relationship to the surrounding Soviet zone dramatically undermined.

The acting Soviet Commander in Berlin, Colonel Jelisarov, responded to the currency decree with some restraint. In a statement to the press, he noted that the decision to halt use of the D-Mark of the *Deutschen Notenbank* (east mark) in the western sectors reflected the Western powers' efforts to further isolate that part of Berlin. According to his statement, the Western action aimed to further split the Berlin economy. "The newspapers of the Berlin west sectors which act on behalf of western officials, did not for nothing refer to the sector demarcation line as a 'border' and persons who cross this line as 'border crossers' (*Grenzgänger*)."[72] SED assessments were a bit more pointed. The Berlin Secretariat met on April 27 and put "The struggle against the currency crime and the tactics of our party" as the first point on the agenda, but neither the SED nor the Soviets took any retaliatory steps in response to the western currency measure.[73]

The currency switch did have real, material consequences for Berliners. For those workers who now received all wages in west marks, the directive proved an undeniable boon. A report to the Economic Department on March 30 described an interesting case of a worker exploiting the regulations for maximum gain. According to the report, a worker living in Neukölln (American sector) worked in the western sectors and drew his rations in his home district. Thus he received his entire wage in west marks. However, in order to obtain wood, coal, and fresh potatoes per Soviet sector registration, his entire family (wife and children) were registered there. The report continued, noting that this was likely

---

[71] Brandt and Löwenthal, *Ernst Reuter*, 501. According to Brandt and Löwenthal, Reuter also greeted the publication of the text of the North Atlantic treaty [two days earlier] as an indication that West Berlin was now firmly entrenched in the ranks of Western Europe.

[72] "Währungsumstellung der Westsektoren bezweckt weitere Spaltung Berlins: Westmächte tragen die volle Verantwortung für die Folgen – Keine sowjetischen Gegenmaßnahmen zum Schaden der Bevölkerung – Erklärung Oberst Jelisarows," *Tägliche Rundschau* (March 22, 1949), 1.

[73] Protokoll Nr. 8 der Sitzung des Sekretariats vom Mittwoch, dem 27.4.1949, IV L-2/3/109, Bl. 8of.

not an isolated case and called for a corresponding change in the currency regulation.[74]

But the four-tier system of wage clearance also created financial difficulties for many persons. Some of these hardships resulted from complex individual cases that were not effectively addressed by the initial regulations. In one instance, an engineer owned a small firm in East Berlin but had always lived and received his rations in the west. In the new currency regulation, however no provision had been made for persons owning businesses in the east to exchange any east marks at the rate of 1:1. He explained that this made it nearly impossible for him to meet the newly required west mark obligations. West sector firms whose primary clientele were found in the Soviet sector also expressed concerns about their ability to make payments in west marks. In response to these complaints, the west sector Economic Department admitted that these and similar cases had not been addressed in the currency reform and suggested that authorities would look for ways to resolve the situation.[75] But administrative loopholes were not the only problems arising from currency reform. The costs for the west sector administration were tremendous. In fiscal year 1949, the wage clearing office ran a deficit of 30 million west marks.[76]

The fact that all west sector obligations now had to be met in west marks while many persons continued to receive a portion of their income in east marks struck many as unfair. These *Grenzgänger* found it nearly impossible to pay their rent and other regular expenses entirely in west marks. An Economic Department memo from March 29 indicated that renters' assemblies had met and called for individuals to pay rents in west marks only to the extent that they were paid in west marks. In language that paralleled renters' strikes during the last years of the Weimar Republic, these renters' assemblies passed resolutions with the slogans: "Pay with the money they give you! The rent like the wages! Taxes and fees like the salary!" The report warned that this development seemed likely to bring a large number of legal claims before the civil courts and wondered whether a change in the rates of wage adjustment was perhaps

---

[74] Abt. f. Wirtschaft: Probleme aus der dritten Verordnung zur Neuordnung des Geldwesens (Röder and Wagner), dated March 30, 1949, LAB, Rep. 10, Acc. 499, Nr. 101.

[75] See the letter from the engineer Richard Itzel to the Magistrat f. Groß-Berlin, Hauptamt f. Wirtschaft, Referat Handel u. Industrie, dated March 23, 1949, and other documents in LAB, Rep. 10, Acc. 499, Nr. 101.

[76] Wolff, *Die Währungsreform*, 272.

advisable.[77] In its explanation of this popular dissatisfaction, the Economic Department memo referred to east sector press reports that had incited people to action, and the SED did seek to transform negative reactions to the currency reform into a broader political force.

Speaking at a rally in the Soviet sector, Berlin SED head Hans Jendretzky denounced the currency reform as "nothing other [...] than a political provocation carried out with criminal swindler-methods. It is designed to tear Berlin totally apart and give new life to world-warmongering by stirring up the Berlin conflict."[78] There is little evidence that such efforts to tie the currency reform to this global framework were successful. An FDGB report on conversations with workers in the French and British sectors found that most workers did not see the currency reform as an impetus to political action. Even after speaking to the factory council (i.e., the most politically active members of the workforce), the writers of the report came away with the sense that workers' primary concern was to figure out how the reform would work out for them. In fact, rather than looking to the party to counter Western policies, some workers implied that the SED should take additional steps to provide material assistance to those workers receiving only partial west mark wages to help them meet their rent and other expenses.[79]

The bitter strike by Berlin's railway workers presented the most explosive public face of this conflict. Evolving in the first part of April, the dispute centered on the wage requirements of railroad employees in the western sectors. As part of the postwar settlement, the rail system in the three western sectors (including all S-Bahn trains, tracks, and stations) remained under the control of the *Deutshe Reichsbahn* in the Soviet zone. Ironically, the *Reichsbahn* headquarters was located in the American sector. Thus, the West-Magistrat argued, as a firm in the western sectors employing workers *in* those sectors, the *Reichsbahn* was obligated to pay its employees entirely in west marks. As a stopgap measure, the West-Magistrat authorized the Wage Clearance Office to exchange two weeks'

[77] Abt. f. Wirtschaft, Zentralbüro: Probleme aus der 3. Verordnung zur Neuordnung des Geldwesens, II. Nachtrag, dated March 29, 1949 in ibid. On renters' strikes during the Depression years of the Weimar Republic, see Swett, *Neighbors and Enemies*, 45–6 and 204–5.
[78] "Berlin gegen den Währungsbetrug: 500000 demonstrieren gegen Kriegshetze und Währungsgeschwindel – Hans Jendretzkys Aufruf zur Selbtshilfe – Es gibt keine 'Grenzgänger' in Berlin!" *Tägliche Rundschau* (March 27, 1949), 1.
[79] Bericht über Währungsdiskussionen in Betrieben der Westsektoren, dated March 21, 1949, LAB, BPA, FDGB 1557.

wages from east marks to west marks for railroad employees living and drawing rations in the west and one weeks' wages for those living in the west but drawing rations in the Soviet sector.[80] More than 15,000 railway employees lived in the three western sectors, and, as the end of the Magistrat's temporary solution approached, they felt under increasing financial pressure.[81] They demanded payment in west marks, and the SPD-dominated UGO took up their cause.[82]

On May 7, the vast majority of west sector railroaders voted in support of three fundamental negotiating demands: payment of wages and salaries in west marks, unlimited right to organize, and reinstatement of fired railroaders. The RBD refused to negotiate with the UGO, recognizing only the FDGB. Negotiations between the RBD and the West-Magistrat continued through May 19 but failed to reach an agreement.[83] The increasing tension presented significant risks to all parties. The UGO faced the first real challenge to its leadership of the workers that it had led to break with the FDGB. The RBD and FDGB confronted an increasingly mobilized and antagonistic labor force that challenged those bodies' ability to shape the nature of railroaders' employment and pay conditions. Perhaps most significantly, the west sectors and the West-Magistrat saw the apparent end of the blockade and the resumption of "normal" overland supply put in doubt by a labor conflict that threatened to disrupt rail transportation again.

Parallel Endings: The S-Bahn Strike and the Paris CFM

Crossing gates went up on the Soviet zone borders at midnight on May 12 as the provisions of the Jessup-Malik agreement went into effect, and the first trucks set out with supplies for Berlin. Soviet zone officials even

---

[80] Magistratsbeschluss Nr. 234, Geldumtausch für Reichsbahn, dated April 13, 1949, LAB, Rep. 10, Acc. 499, Nr. 101.

[81] An SED report put the number of railway workers (*Eisenbahner*) living in the three western sectors at 15,614; there were 20,932 in the Soviet sector. From Berliner Eisenbahner im Kampf um die Einheit: Tatsachen über die Vorgänge bei der Eisenbahn in Berlin und über die schändliche Rolle der UGO, LAB, BPA, IV L-2/10/403, Bl. 8.

[82] The UGO had already made the formal switch from Independent Trade Union *Opposition* to Independent Trade Union *Organization* following their split from the FDGB at the May 1948 Stadtkonferenz des FDGB. See Schlegelmilch, *Hauptstadt im Zonendeutschland*, 241–2.

[83] Of 12,275 votes cast, 11,522 supported the negotiating package, 549 opposed, and 204 votes were invalid. Schlegelmilch, *Hauptstadt im Zonendeutschland*, 243ff.

limited unrelated traffic on the autobahns to and from Berlin.[84] The Soviet Commander of Berlin, Aleksander Kotikov, ordered the Berlin police to halt all searches on public transportation and remove police checkpoints on the sector borders. At the same time, he directed Police President Markgraf to prohibit the use of West- or B-Marks in the Soviet sector "under the strictest adherence to the pertinent regulations."[85] The decision to lift these transportation restrictions did not throw out all existing control structures. On June 30, the Soviet Command in Berlin issued a directive to the police regarding "heightened controls" on the "Ring around Berlin." Although items such as hand luggage were to be allowed through unsearched, Soviet zone authorities still wanted to control traffic and transport in general.[86] A police directive from mid-July elaborated the underlying unease felt by Soviet sector officials and referred plainly to the experiences of the blockade:

> The results of the expanded traffic controls in the past have shown that not only the transport of goods and wares out of the eastern sector and/or eastern zone but also the transport from the western sectors requires heightened attention in order to prevent a disruption of economic life in the eastern zone and the eastern sector.[87]

Although this order bore traces of the increasingly formulaic rhetoric that would prove so familiar during forty years of Cold War, the principles underlying Soviet and SED desire remained. The expansion and consolidation of SED control in the Soviet zone and Soviet sector of Berlin continued unabated, and the lifting of the blockade should not conceal that fact.

The SED leadership publicly greeted the announcement of the Jessup-Malik agreement as a sign of Western submission. It emphasized the

---

[84] Fernsrpuch/Fernschreiben from the LPB Brandenburg, Abt. Schupo. to all Stadt- u. Kreisaemter, and Kommandanturen 'Ring um Berlin' regarding measures for carrying out SMAD Befehl Nr. 56, dated May 11, 1949, BLHA, Ld. Br. Rep. 203, VP, Nr. 30, Bl., 197.

[85] Kotikov to Markgraf, LAB, STA Rep. 26, Nr. 15, Bl. 86. The German translation of the directive is found on the preceding page in the file.

[86] Auszug aus der Instruktion über Ordnung des Durchlassens der Personen und Ladungen durch die Kontrolldurchlassungspunkte auf der äusseren Grenze von Groß-Berlin ab 12. Mai 1949, LAB, STA Rep. 26, Nr. 143, Bl. 94. A west sector report described how Soviet zone police did confiscate foodstuffs and other goods from travellers' luggage in early July. See "Zugkontrollen und Lebensmitteldiebstähle: Russisches Interesse für Fischkonserven – Bewaffnete Posten an den Ausfallstraßen," *Tagesspiegel* (July 6, 1948), in BA-DDR, DM 1/3135.

[87] Abt. S.: Einsatz-Befehl Nr. 13: Aktion gegen unberechtigten Waren- und Geldumlauf im Ostsektor, dated July 14, 1949, LAB, STA Rep. 26, Nr. 143, Bl., 96.

Western agreement to the Soviet demand for a meeting of the CFM and downplayed the lifting of transportation restrictions.[88] Obviously, the party sought to limit the symbolic resonance of the first supply trucks arriving in Berlin's western sectors and the joyous celebrations with which Berliners greeted their arrival. One issue of special concern for SED leaders was the sudden appearance in the west sectors of high-quality consumer goods (shoes, clothing) and foodstuffs (citrus fruits, fish) and the reactions this elicited in comparison to the situation in the Soviet sector. Shortly after the lifting of the blockade, a memo described how three trustworthy "female comrades" had for several weeks been going through stores in the west sectors to check on the type of goods, the price, and the stock levels available. For comparison, they also made the same observations in the Soviet sector. When confronted with these women's negative conclusions, the memo writer noted: "I cannot escape the impression, that conscious sabotage is being practiced here," a comment striking in its ambiguity.[89]

In the *Tägliche Rundschau* on May 12, the article describing the lifting of transportation restrictions first mentioned trucks heading *from* Berlin toward the western zones. The article went on to describe how factory sirens in the Soviet sector would sound that afternoon to greet "the beginning of understanding (*Verständigung*) that is extending beyond sector and zonal borders." Workers and students were then to be released to attend a demonstration at August-Bebel-Platz to mark the occasion.[90] Of course, the SED-led demonstration was justifiably overshadowed by the 300,000 persons who gathered in the American sector in front of Schöneberg's town hall to celebrate the end of the blockade.[91] The world joined that celebration, marking it as the heroic triumph of the West Berlin population. Yet, even the Soviets and the SED subordinated their interpretation of the end of the "transportation restrictions" to a larger project. The article announcing the "celebrations" in the Soviet sector made it only to the middle of the paper's front page; the principal headline completely overshadowed it: "The German National Front Fights for German Unity:

---

[88] See "Außenministerrat in Paris am 23. Mai: Kommuniqué der Regierungen der UdSSR, der USA, Großbritanniens und Frankreichs über Deutschlandfragen," *Tägliche Rundschau* (May 6, 1949), 1. See also the text of the announcement issued by the SED Central Committee, SAPMO DY 30/IV, 2/1/63, Bl. 172.

[89] Gustav Heinricht to Karl Maron, dated May 16, 1949, LAB, STA Rep. 106, Nr. 182, Bl. 13ff.

[90] "Heute 0.01 Uhr öffneten sich die Schranken: Sirenen begrüßen Beginn der Verständigung," *Tägliche Rundschau* (May 12, 1949), 1.

[91] Kdo. d. Schutzpolizei: Ereignismeldungen, dated May 13, 1949, LAB, Rep. 2, Acc. 888, Nr. 452: Polizeiliche Tagesmeldungen, January – July 1949.

Press Conference on the People's Congress Vote in the German People's Council Building."

In early May the "National Front" movement emerged as an important symbolic component of Soviet and SED efforts to construct a "German Democratic Republic" in the Soviet zone.[92] In a sense, it became the ideological means to link the structural foundations of the DWK with the supposedly national, democratic basis of the People's Congress. Returning to the principles of antifascist *Blockpolitik*, the National Front ostensibly downplayed party ideals for the sake of the nation-state. In the interests of economic and political success, SED leaders directed the party to pursue tactical alliances even with "bourgeois" forces. Speaking to a party activists' meeting in Berlin, Walter Ulbricht emphasized that the "consolidation of the democratic order" depended on the concentrated improvement of all sectors of the economy, including the private capital sectors, in an effort to improve the quality of life of persons in the Soviet zone. His speech entitled "Why National Front?" explained this requirement by positing Soviet zone success as the ultimate means to overcome existing national division. "We want to conduct a competition. Those in the West should go ahead and show what they can do. It won't last long; then the entire population will see how we are developing in the eastern sector and what is happening in the West. Then it will become even clearer what kind of a poor fool this Klingelhöfer is and what kind of an American agent this Reuter is."[93] With his attack on these two SPD leaders, Ulbricht implicitly linked this political program to the difficult economic situation in Berlin's western sectors. He also laid claim to a level of popular support that continued to elude the SED.[94]

On May 15 and 16, the Soviet zone held elections for the Third People's Congress. The representatives to this congress were selected on the basis of a unitary ballot requiring a simple "yes" or "no" vote: it allocated 25 percent of the seats to the SED, 15 percent each to the CDU and LDP, 7.5 percent each to the year-old NDPD and DBD, 10 percent for the FDGB, and the remaining 20 percent to various "mass organizations."

[92] On Soviet direction of the National Front strategy, see Naimark, *The Russians in Germany*, 55ff.
[93] Walter Ulbricht, speech May 17, 1949, SAPMO, DY 30/IV 2/1.01/112, Bl. 27, 29.
[94] By contrast, the Berlin SPD leader Kurt Mattick argued that the decision to lift the blockade marked an effort to prevent the formation of a West German state. Notes for a speech to a party functionaries' assembly in. Neukölln, May 4, 1949, AdsD, SPD-LV Berlin, 3/BEAB000092.

The ballot bundled this up or down vote on the Volkskongress with the plebiscitary question, "Do you want German unity and a just peace?" Even with this suggestive formulation and the open manipulation of the results (all abstentions were counted as "yes" votes), only 61.1 percent of the votes tallied were positive. In the Soviet sector of Berlin, only 51.6 percent of votes were counted as "yes."[95] Despite their public proclamations of success, the SED leadership viewed this result as yet another setback.

One report on the election results cited primarily organizational failings and general overconfidence among SED members as the reason for the "relatively poor result in the delegate elections for the IIIrd [Third] People's Congress." It also referred to shortfalls in ration supply and an increase in "enemy" propaganda as causes that must be addressed in future campaigns.[96] Equating these two causes further highlighted the schizophrenic nature of the SED, which, for all its self-criticism, it could never quite recognize. For its entire existence, the party continually failed to decide whether its route to popular success depended on its ability to deliver material or ideological results. Analysis of the vote submitted to Wilhelm Pieck declared the outcome to be proof that the People's Congress enjoyed the support of the majority of Germans and possessed sufficient legitimacy to ask that People's Council deputies be permitted to represent the German people at the CFM, but the report also described efforts by the party's opponents to undermine the vote:

While the progressive democratic forces promoted the "yes" for unity and peace with open and honest propaganda, the splitters of Germany turned to all the methods of lies, slander, demagoguery, and provocation; they worked with threatening rumors and enticing promises in order to keep the people from a "yes." It became apparent that the illegal opponent works hand in hand with the legal [one]; in their recognition of the significance of this vote, they deployed their full forces.[97]

This sense of fear continued to run as an undercurrent in all SED "successes." In spite of increasingly concrete steps toward a state in which they would exercise almost total control, SED leaders kept looking over their shoulders – especially in Berlin. Speaking to the Berlin Central Committee on June 10, Roman Chwalek cautioned against assuming that the division of Berlin meant an end to the high points of conflict. He warned

95 Kleßmann, *Die doppelte Staatsgründung*, 204.
96 Instrukteurbericht, SAPMO, DY 30/IV, 2/5/1194, Bl. 21.
97 Eine Analyse der Wahlen zum 3. Deutschen Volkskongress, dated June 8, 1949, SAPMO, NY 4036/755, Bl. 130.

that a failure to put forth an all-out effort would result in a "more dangerous situation" for the party and the entire Berlin working class, a warning
issued primarily in the face of the violent clashes unleashed by the Berlin
railroad workers strike.[98]

After five days of clashes, officials stabilized the situation in the city.
The Western Allies directed the railroad police to evacuate west sector
stations and handed over security around the stations to the west sector
police forces.[99] Negotiations on a settlement resumed between the Railroad Authority and the West-Magistrat as well as between U.S. Commandant Howley and the Soviet transportation officer. Occasional incidents
of violence nonetheless continued. Most notably, in the night and early
morning of June 8 and 9, approximately 300 persons stormed the RBD
building in the U.S. sector. By 2:00 A.M. American MPs and western sector
police had cleared them out and sealed off the building. In a discussion
with Heinz Bracht, the head of the UGO rail workers' union, City Assembly President Otto Suhr criticized the lack of control over lower echelons
of union members. According to the report of their conversation, "Suhr
informed Bracht of Howley's viewpoint that Scharnowski was under suspicion of having intentionally wanted to create a situation in which the
western powers could have been forced into ugly complications." He
warned that any subsequent "excesses" could force the Magistrat to abandon its role as mediator.[100]

As the strike dragged on into June, it became an increasing dilemma for
Western officials. The Paris CFM began its meetings on May 23 to discuss
the situation in Berlin and in Germany. At the same time, Western officials
faced the unpleasant reality that the renewed transportation difficulties
(at least with respect to rail traffic) caused by the Berlin strike lent at
least some credibility to long-standing SED claims of a western "self-
blockade." For the most part, Western politicians and military officials
pursued a policy of ongoing deescalation, but the strikers continued to
hold out.

---

[98] Protokoll d. Landesvorstandssitzung, June 10, 1949, LAB, BPA, IV L-2/1/45, Bl. 91ff.
[99] See the account in Brandt and Löwenthal, *Ernst Reuter*, 526. The withdrawal of the
    Bahnpolizei is also described in a Report from the Eisenbahnpolizei Abteilung Berlin,
    May 23, 1949, LAB, STA Rep. 26, Nr. 77, Bl. 31.
[100] Unterredung Dr. Suhr – Heinz Bracht [regarding UGO Strike] on Friday [June 10, 1949?]
    LAB, BPA, IV L-2/10/382. Ernst Scharnowski was an SPD member and leader of the
    UGO. Interestingly, at the June meeting of the Berlin's Landesvorstand, Roman Chwalek,
    criticized *Neues Deutschland* reports about the incident for describing the participants
    as "drunken hordes of thugs" and neglecting its "political background." See the account
    in Nachlaß Walter Urlbicht, SAPMO, NY 4182/906, Bl. 12.

Throughout the immediate postwar period, west sector rail stations remained technically under the control of the Soviet Zone Railroad Authority and its railroad police, and West Berlin police officials had to accept these sites, physically located in the midst of their jurisdictions, as extraterritorial exceptions to their authority. Already in January 1948, American officials explained their inability to respond when drunken Soviet soldiers threw a German from a moving S-Bahn in the American sector by describing the S-Bahn as an extraterritorial site under Soviet control.[101] The SED, however, saw these clashes as part of its efforts to "defend" its S-Bahn in the middle of West Berlin, but rhetorically the party leadership at least sought to integrate this effort into broader assessments of the political situation in Berlin and Germany and to rally support to its cause. An FDGB announcement (*Durchsage*) to its district committees denounced the strike as a threat both to the supply of Berlin and as targeted at the developing understanding between the Great Powers as their representatives prepared to meet in Paris.[102]

SED and FDGB leaders sought to deny that the walkout was a strike. To permit the UGO to appropriate this most potent symbol of militant worker protest would, of course, have legitimated its claims to represent working-class interests in the city. Roman Chwalek, the head of Berlin's SED-dominated FDGB, criticized a discussion in the railway workers' union (not the breakaway union, but the official branch under FDGB authority) that used the terms *strike* and *strikers*. He argued "that it is not about a strike at all; at most, it is an action. It could be very dangerous if even we introduce the ideology of a strike. We must characterize the action of the UGO and the western occupation powers as that which it is."[103] Rather than a worker organization, Chwalek thus sought to tar the UGO by association with the occupiers. The SED was fighting a battle over what this event should be called, a first effort to transform the stance from which the party's supporters could approach it. Party leaders sought to utilize the strike as a propaganda windfall and portrayed the "UGO-putsch" as part of a broad Western plan to counter the Third People's Congress and disrupt the CFM's discussions in Paris. In an introduction to the brochure provided by the East-Magistrat for delegates arriving in

---

[101] Weekly Berlin Political Report, No. 12, January 2–8, 1948 [report p. 6], NA, RG 260, 390/48/10/1, box 62, Microfilm Reel no. 28B.4.

[102] Memo in the subsection Mitte; addressed to all Betriebsausschüsse regarding impending S-Bahn strike, dated May 20, 1949, LAB, BPA, FDGB 136.

[103] Bericht über die Besprechung am May 30, 1949 [IG Eisenbahn?], LAB, BPA, FDGB 84, Bl. 150.

Berlin for the People's Congress, Mayor Fritz Ebert decried the west sector politicians willing to deploy "vandalistic acts of destruction [the S-Bahn strike], designed to destroy the relaxation of the international situation brought about by the peace politics of the USSR, because they fear a normalization of life in Berlin."[104]

By conflating these local and international perspectives, the SED sought to trumpet its own importance. For SED leaders, the "S-Bahn provocation" or "UGO-putsch" became a catch phrase that demonstrated the extent to which they, too, were targets of Western "assaults" on "progressive" forces around the world.[105] The fact that SED officials in Berlin exerted so much effort to mobilize party members and the FDJ to occupy train stations and "defend" them against striking workers suggests that they viewed the strike as much more than a labor dispute.[106] Indeed, this act of "defense" was, for the SED, as important as the specific demands of the strikers. Lena Fischer, an SED delegate from the district of Köpenick, spoke to the Berlin Central Committee about the party's action: "The activity of our party to hinder the S-Bahn provocation was very great."[107] The extent to which SED leaders viewed their role in the first five days of the strike as a success comes across even more pointedly in a speech by Hans Jendretzky to the SED Central Committee on May 27:

The actual instigators have recently carried out a whole series of maneuvers in order to win the game, namely to be able to step up in Paris with a trump card that would burden the conference ahead of time with the Berlin question. That this did not succeed is a testimony to the Berlin party organization. Their recent actions answered [these maneuvers] with a counterattack in such a decisive and emphatic fashion that this tidy plan did not [...] have the desired result.[108]

In other words, the SED's engagement in the S-Bahn strike, like the People's Congress, should be viewed as part of its ongoing effort to assume a role as a legitimate actor in and on behalf of Germany. It sought to

---

[104] Brochure (1949) in Nachlaß Wilhelm Pieck, SAPMO, NY 4036/742. The Third People's Congress was held in Berlin from May 29 to June 3, 1949. Its central act was the adoption of a constitution for a "German Democratic Republic."

[105] It is interesting to note the extent to which SED leaders regularly refer to Communist advances in China as forcing the western hand in Europe and Germany. See the remarks of Otto Grotewohl, Stenographisches Bericht der 20. (34.) Parteivorstandssitzung der SED, July 20–1, 1949, SAPMO, DY 30/IV 2/1/67, Bl. 21.

[106] See the numerous reports from district SED groups on their activities during the strike in LAB, BPA IV L-2/10/402.

[107] Protokoll d. Landesvorstandssitzung, June 10, 1949, LAB, BPA, IV L-2/1/45, Bl. 21.

[108] Stenographisches Bericht der 19. (33.) Parteivosrtandssitzung der SED, May 27, 1949, SAPMO, DY 30/IV 2/1/65, Bl. 35.

demonstrate that it truly did have the ability to sway people's opinions and exert a real force on events in Germany as it moved toward the establishment of two separate states.

Two days before the Third People's Congress, Otto Grotewohl spoke to the SED Central Committee. He emphasized that the party had hurriedly called the *Volkskongress* and promoted the National Front so as to keep pace with developments at the Paris CFM. While noting that events to that point suggested a real effort was being made on all sides to come to an agreement, he pointed to two specific issues that still required resolution: the question of international control of the Ruhr and the halting of steps to establish a West German state. Not surprisingly, Grotewohl remarked positively on the plan offered by Soviet Foreign Minister Vyshinskii to form a new German administration by combining the DWK with the bizonal Economic Council. But this strain of optimism should not be taken as an indication of some radical shift in SED intentions.

In a more subtle turn, Grotewohl hinted that the People's Congress should perhaps focus more strongly on its proposed constitution as a counter to American Secretary of State Dean Acheson's proposal to bring the states of the Soviet zone into a German administration under the auspices of the recently adopted West German Basic Law.[109] His explanation that Wilhelm Pieck would give the opening address and chair the People's Congress so that there would be no diversions from its intended course speaks more directly to the party's ongoing effort to retain strict control over political developments in the Soviet zone.[110] As much as the SED could, with Soviet support, maintain a rigid hold on the institutions of power, it continued to falter in its efforts to direct or even establish effective links to popular assessments of the local and international events in which its policies were imbedded.

Even to the SED rank and file, the leadership's grand explanations were not readily decipherable. The same party member who celebrated the party's actions in response to the S-Bahn strike criticized the motivations of many participants: "We must admit it openly here: for a portion

[109] Ibid., Bl. 3ff. The western zones' Parliamentary Council adopted the West German Basic Law (*Grundgesetz*) on May 8, 1949.
[110] Ibid., Bl. 19. Wilhelm Pieck had been at a spa in the USSR when the lifting of the Blockade was announced. His notes on a conversation with Molotov on May 11 reflect the planning for a state to be formed under the auspices of the People's Congress including the specific persons (of various parties) to fill its top offices. In Nachlaß Wilhelm Pieck, SAPMO, NY 4036/695, Bl. 94ff. (a typed transcription of the handwritten notes begins on Bl. 81).

[of them], it came down to playing civil war. They were disappointed when we demanded political work from them. When we wanted to deploy these comrades as discussion groups, a large group disappeared en route."[111] Adolf Deter, a former KPD member who had returned from exile in the United States, echoed the words of his colleague. Even among those who took part in combating the strike in its first days, there was a lack of understanding of why this was necessary.[112] Among Berliners in general, there was little sense of the larger political implications being ascribed the strike by the SED. A report filed with the criminal police (east) on the situation in Spandau (British sector) indicated that most people felt that the strikers' demands to be paid in west marks were justified but condemned any acts of violence or sabotage that may have taken place. They desired that S-Bahn traffic restart and calm return to the west sectors.[113] The desire for a return to (relative) stability could also describe the underlying motivations of the participants at the Paris CFM.

On June 19, 1949, a *New York Times* headline summed up the results of the Paris meeting of French, British, American, and Soviet foreign ministers that had convened to finalize the settlement of the Berlin Blockade crisis: "The Cold War goes on, but in a more subtle way." Following this headline, the article began:

In the first three weeks there was no real discussion. The Western powers and the Soviet Union presented proposals for the unification of Germany that each side knew the other side could not accept without surrendering its basic position and its essential philosophy. The meeting on Monday will be the last of twenty-two sessions, of which no more than six were devoted to serious consideration of concrete issues with a view to agreement. The rest of the time was spent in academic lectures so remote from any point that they did not even generate heat or tension.[114]

Perhaps we can express a slight sense of amusement at this mixing of metaphors – the lack of "heat" in the midst of a *cold* war – but I would like to take this assertion a bit more seriously. If we demarcate the Cold War by a series of crises – the two Berlin crises (the blockade and building of the Berlin Wall), the Cuban Missile Crisis, and the like – then the easing of tension that the *Times* noted makes perfect sense as part of the ebb and flow of Cold War. But I want to suggest that the spaces in between these

---

[111] Protokoll d. Landesvorstandssitzung, June 10, 1949, LAB, BPA, IV L-2/1/45, Bl. 21.
[112] Ibid., Bl. 72ff.
[113] Report filed May 25, 1949, LAB, STA Rep. 26, Nr. 77, Bl. 35.
[114] Anne O'Hare McCormick, "The Cold War Goes on, but in a More Subtle Way," *New York Times* (June 19, 1949), E3.

presumed Cold War mountain tops are what matter more for our efforts to try to grasp *how* the Cold War operated (as opposed to asking why or to what ends or who is to blame).

The two sides at the Paris conference arrived without expectations for any real breakthrough in east-west relations, and the proposals offered up for discussion suggested little room for compromise. On May 24, Soviet Foreign Minister Vyshinskii proposed to reestablish the ACC and the Berlin Kommandatura in their old format; two weeks later he suggested that preparations be started to conclude a peace treaty with Germany and withdraw occupation troops within a year. The Western powers countered with a proposal to incorporate the states of the Soviet zone into the structures of the West German Basic Law.[115] Charles Bohlen described the conference as designed "essentially [...] to liquidate the Berlin blockade, which it did."[116] He was right – at least in terms of the diplomatic boundaries that had been established for the crisis. Beyond that, it validated the two separate processes of German state formation being pursued in the eastern and western halves of Germany and more or less detached these processes from the postwar institutions that had been set up to administer Germany. Paris proved to be the last CFM.

For both sides in Berlin, the outcome of the Paris conference produced less than desired. Hermann Schlimme (Berlin FDGB) noted that Berliners had expected more from the sixth CFM, at least the elimination of the dual currency in the city.[117] His colleague in the FDGB leadership, Adolf Deter, elaborated one lesson to be learned from the outcome: "the German people must even more join together in the National Front and engage itself even more for German unity and for a just peace treaty. For Berlin it means to expand this National Front beyond the sector borders, in order to combat the economic crisis, to secure work and bread for all workers;

---

[115] Schlegelmilch, *Hauptstadt im Zonendeutschland*, 556–7. For the text of the Soviet and western proposals, see *Foreign Relations of the United States 1949*, vol. 2, *Council of Foreign Ministers; Germany and Austria* (Washington, DC: United Staes Government Printing Office, 1974), 1040–3. For an American assessment of the two proposals as presented to a group of German officials in Berlin at the time of the CFM, see the Aufzeichnung über die Besprechung in Königstein im Victory Guest House, 29.5.1949, LAB, Rep. 200, Acc. 2435, Nr. 56. Ambassador Robert Murphy explained that for the Western Allies, the Soviet proposal was nothing but a return to the structures of Potsdam without addressing the "real material conflicts" (economic reparations, exports and imports, SAGs, national economic deficit, democratic government, police state, allied majority decision). In describing the Western proposal, he suggested that they viewed Potsdam as a structure for the initial phases and not a permanent construction.

[116] Bohlen, *Witness to History*, 286.

[117] Statement by Schlimme regarding Paris CFM, n.d., LAB, BPA, FDGB 1557.

the best precondition for this is the reestablishment of Berlin unity."[118]
For the Soviet sector at least, the path seemed relatively clear: increasing
incorporation into the SED-directed political and economic structures
of the evolving East German state, even if Berlin remained technically
independent.[119]

The situation in the west sectors remained somewhat more ambivalent. For Ernst Reuter and other west sector leaders, the resolution of
the blockade crisis produced increased political and economic insecurity.
Faced with increasing unemployment and a major economic downturn
(in large part as a result of the March currency reform), they feared that
the west sectors' political position (not to mention its economic survival)
could be threatened if ties to western Germany and the Western powers weakened.[120] In spite of the western military governors' failure to
approve the portion of the Basic Law that included Berlin, SPD leaders in the west sectors continued to pursue incorporation into the new
West German state. One day after the CFM ended, the SPD delegation
to the (western) city assembly submitted two urgent resolutions to that
body suggesting that the outcome of the Paris conference had produced
a "new situation" and calling for Berlin participation in the first Bundestag elections in August. On June 30, the AK, now consisting of the
three Western powers, prohibited Berlin participation in the Bundestag
elections and asserted that the Paris conference had produced no change
in the relationship of Berlin to the West German state.[121]

Through the last week of June, the S-Bahn strike still dragged on.
Strikers had overwhelmingly rejected a settlement offer that called for the
Railway Authority to pay workers living in the western sectors 60 percent
of their wages in west marks. Over the course of the strike, UGO membership had increased significantly, and the striking railroaders seemed
poised to wait for acceptance of all of their demands.[122] Sustained in part
by CARE packages distributed to striking workers, the strike depended
on the same kinds of multilayered survival strategies that Berliners had
cultivated for the past four years (Figure 14). Finally, the Western occupiers intervened. In a June 25 directive, they ordered the West-Magistrat

---

[118] Statement by Adolf Deter regarding Paris CFM, dated June 21, 1949, ibid.
[119] The SED had already begun to establish institutional links between its party groups
in Berlin and those in surrounding Brandenburg in April 1949. See LAB, BPA, IV L-
2/3/109.
[120] See Brandt and Löwenthal, *Ernst Reuter*, 533ff.
[121] Schlegelmilch, *Hauptstadt im Zonendeutschland*, 568.
[122] Ibid., 246ff. See also Keiderling, *"Rosinenbomber,"* 299–300.

FIGURE 14. Steglitz Station (American sector): Six days into the S-Bahn strike, a UGO official stands on the platform of the idled S-Bahn and distributes the contents of CARE packages to striking railroad workers. CARE packages, like all international aid in the postwar period, remained but one component of Berliners' strategies for material survival – strikers also received unemployment support from the West-Magistrat and payments from UGO strike funds. But as railroaders lined up to receive their share of coffee, milk, chocolate, and other luxury goods from a CARE package – each one was shared among thirty striking workers – they still confronted physically the relative wealth of the American occupier that ultimately rejected the material claims motivating their walkout. *Source:* Landesarchiv Berlin.

to halt all unemployment payments to railroaders who failed to return to work by June 27. As previously offered, the Railroad Authority agreed to pay 60 percent of wages in west marks. The West-Magistrat and the Western Allies proposed to exchange an additional 15 percent of wages at a rate of 1:1 and 40 percent (i.e., the entire remaining wage) for the next three months.

The strike came to a close, although train traffic did not reach normal levels until July 1. To some extent, the strike's end allowed an "honorable defeat" for UGO leaders. The union had established solid credentials as a powerful force in Berlin, but the fact that a strike against the Soviet-sponsored RBD was brought to an end by direct order of the Western Allies produced some tension between the three Western powers and the "most militantly democratic forces" in the ranks of Berlin workers.[123] Already in May, the SPD youth leader, Kurt Mattick, drafted an article in which he described the SED-led effort to crack down on striking railroaders by seizing control of west sector S-Bahn stations as something altogether new in German history: "Only in America were these methods used at the beginning of the century, when large companies employed private police to crush the trade union movement."[124] That Mattick was prepared – even in an historical analogy – to make conceptual linkages between the United States and the SED underscored just how fluid the ideological spaces were in the city. But this political flexibility was contingent upon the ways that life in Berlin still depended on literal border crossing.

In the midst of the S-Bahn strike, *Sie* published a cartoon arguing that, even after the Paris CFM, the Great Powers' acceptance of an ideologically and politically divided Berlin could not impose that explanatory vision on the practice of daily life in the city. Mixing red and black color in a cover illustration of a Berlin street corner on the edge of the American sector, the drawing renders the sector boundary not as a dividing line but as a demarcation of mutual interdependence. The caption reads:

COLORFUL BERLIN: Goods and currencies pass continuously back and forth across the sector border. The East (in the background) buys in the West and the West in the East, as it is most beneficial. Everything eastern is shown in red,

---

[123] Schlegelmilch, *Hauptstadt im Zonendeutschland*, 249–50. Also, Brandt and Löwenthal, *Ernst Reuter*, 527f.

[124] Kurt Mattick, Entwurf für Jugendtelegraf, May 28 (1949), AdsD, SPD-LV Berlin, 3/BEAB000092: SPD-Landesverband Berlin, Büro Stellv. Landesvorssitzender Kurt Mattick, Tageskopien, 1.1.-31.12.1949.

everything western in black, even if it can be bought "white" [legally] or "black" [illegally]. A western woman has an eastern permanent wave, and an eastern woman is carrying a western fish. A "red" man hides his "black" newspaper, and the market woman, in exchange, wraps the "black" fish in a "red" newspaper. For many, the question of "East in exchange for West" has become question of fate (*Schicksalsfrage*). For some especially wily traders, however, in between the Black and Red in the colorful city of Berlin, gold is lying in the street.[125]

This ironic rendering of the German national colors (black, red, and gold) challenges the validity of any one claim to national legitimacy – east or west, thus embedding these ideological claims within the calculus of survival and material self-interest. Such subordination of ideological divides to everyday practice induced a level of uneasiness, even among most Berlin politicians (east and west) who saw such behavior compromising the political and administrative outcome that had been achieved by the end of the blockade.

Three years later West Berlin municipal authorities sought even more explicitly to embed these sorts of consumer choices firmly in an ideologically charged version of divided Berlin. In a poster campaign that aimed to convince West Berliners not to "betray" the West Berlin economy by exchanging their west marks to buy cheaper goods in the eastern half of the city, the authorities derided Mrs. Disgrace and Mr. Shame (*Frau Schimpf* and *Herr Schande*) – labels chosen from thousands of suggestions submitted in a contest to name the male and female silhouettes on the posters – for their moral and political failures. Despite its efforts to plug into popular sentiment, the campaign proved ineffective at convincing West Berliners to change their consumer habits.[126] For all its symbolic resonance and the political power that explicitly backed it up, this campaign against West Berliner consumer choices found little moral traction. The shadowy figures on the poster could not help but remind Berliners of earlier condemnations of black marketeers, and their own recollections of foraging and "small-scale" black market trade meant that they would find it relatively easy to imagine their own faces behind the denunciatory shade.

Entering the summer of 1949, the financial challenges facing the new West Berlin administration grew, and its SPD leadership struggled to find solutions to the macroeconomic dilemmas posed by the emerging political accommodation in Germany. But already in late May, some Berliners

---

[125] *Sie* (June 26, 1949), 1.
[126] Pence, "Herr Schimpf und Frau Schande, 185–202.

began to express dissatisfaction with an administration whose policy solutions started to seem "doctrinaire." Maverick SPD politician Willi Kressmann, who had been chosen as district mayor in Kreuzberg (American sector) in February, earned popular approval and his party's ire by introducing a "gray market" in his district.[127] While technically illegal, this semiofficial rejection of some rationing restrictions proved particularly unsettling to municipal leaders precisely because it tore the veil that concealed everyday practices – such as black marketeering – on which the SPD's assertions of democratic principle and political independence still depended. The SPD's political success in Berlin came not from its material and administrative efforts but in spite of them. By acting "as if" these practices were not part of its success story, the SPD helped frame Berliners' own participation in delineating the city's symbolic divide.[128]

By like manner, the Cold War as a hegemonic system depended on the tension implicit to blurred conditions on the ground in Berlin. Thus, regardless of the material rightness or wrongness of the striking railroaders' cause, the Western powers sought to prevent a local clash over wages and material survival to develop the potential to radically challenge the German status quo that they had accepted at the Paris conference. Essentially, those Great Powers, including the Soviet Union, had by this time accepted parameters that more or less defined the extent of their engagement in Berlin. Even though this framework would never allow them to master the material and local political components of the Berlin situation, they were unwilling to permit their claims of control to suffer overt challenges. In this sense, the more ambitious goals of the Berlin SPD as well as the continued (if misguided) optimism of many SED leaders fell victim to the symbolic constraints of the Great Powers' vision of their role in Berlin. In the end, the Cold War stability of an iconic location such as Berlin depended on the collaboration of east and west – even if it was an unintentional collusion. Resolving the railroad workers' strike helped formulate these stabilizing boundaries, and although they remained tenuous and not always coherent or even readily recognizable, they came to mark the real start of a Cold War that was never just about the production of tension but about limiting it as well.

---

[127] "Die Kreßmanns," *Sie* (May 29, 1949), 1.
[128] Pierre Bourdieu, *Praktische Vernunft: Zur Theorie des Handelns*, Hella Beister, trans. (Frankfurt am Main: Suhrkamp, 1998), 164ff.

Conclusion

"Let Them Come to Berlin"

On June 26, 1963, fourteen years after the blockade ended and two years after the construction of the Berlin Wall, American President John F. Kennedy spoke to a massive crowd gathered in front of West Berlin's Schöneberg town hall. Standing beside General Lucius Clay, the American hero of the airlift, Kennedy gave a speech that has become one of the defining rhetorical moments of the Cold War. He reiterated the United States' commitment to the city but also endeavored to describe its place in a global conflict. He explained to the enthusiastic spectators:

There are many people in the world who really don't understand, or say they don't, what is the great issue between the free world and the Communist world. Let them come to Berlin. There are some who say that communism is the wave of the future. Let them come to Berlin. And there are some who say in Europe and elsewhere we can work with the Communists. Let them come to Berlin. And there are even a few who say that it is true that communism is an evil system, but it permits us to make economic progress. *Lass*[t] *sie nach Berlin kommen.* Let them come to Berlin.[1]

Freedom has many difficulties and democracy is not perfect, but we have never had to put a wall up to keep our people in, to prevent them from leaving us.

---

[1] *Lasst* is the more grammatically correct German word and better reflects the phonetic notation Kennedy made at the top of the note cards he used for the speech: "Lust z nach Bearleen coma." Diethelm Prowe, "The Making of *ein Berliner*: Kennedy, Brandt, and the Origins of Détente Policy in Germany," in *From the Berlin Museum to the Berlin Wall: Essays on the Cultural and Political History of Modern Germany*, David Wetzel, ed. (Westport, CT and London: Praeger, 1996), 173 and 186 n. 2.

He concluded his speech in resounding fashion:

Freedom is indivisible, and when one man is enslaved, all are not free. When all are free, then we can look forward to that day when this city will be joined as one and this country and this great Continent of Europe in a peaceful and hopeful globe. When that day finally comes, as it will, the people of West Berlin can take sober satisfaction in the fact that they were in the front lines for almost two decades.

All free men, wherever they may live, are citizens of Berlin, and, therefore, as a free man, I take pride in the words *"Ich bin ein Berliner."*[2]

And the crowd roared its approval.

These words sought to explain why Berlin mattered for the Cold War, but most clearly they encapsulated one of its central tensions: the slippage between real places (like Berlin) and the symbolic – even iconic – role that they came to assume in a global Cold War pantheon. In his speech, Kennedy suggested that someone who came to Berlin would truly comprehend what the Cold War was all about. He or she would see the Wall and the literal and concrete division of a city and recognize it as a microcosm of a world that was also divided between two camps: democratic and communist, free and enslaved. But in claiming Berlin as the symbolic capital of the Cold War, in exalting Berliners as archetypes for all free men "wherever they may live," Kennedy simultaneously reduced those "Berliners" who also happened to live in the city to merely interchangeable parts of a universal Cold War apparatus.

Although Kennedy's speech celebrated the status of an iconic Berliner, the evolution of its rhetoric invested these actual Berliners on the square in front of the Rathaus with a different kind of power. The president and his speechwriter, Ted Sorensen, had been developing most of the speech's rhetorical flourishes during their travels in West Germany in the days before they arrived in West Berlin, but its "cold war core" – in which he denounced the "evil" of the Soviet system – emerged only as Kennedy delivered the speech, fresh from a visit to the Wall and energized by the massive crowd before him.[3] After his return to the United States, Kennedy reportedly expressed the belief that if he had ordered the crowd to the Berlin Wall to tear it down, they would have marched. This assertion may have represented more than mere idle speculation – on several occasions

---

[2] Remarks in the Rudolph Wilde Platz, President John F. Kennedy, West Berlin, June 26, 1963, *John F. Kennedy Library and Museum* (December 12, 2002); http://www.cs.umb. edu/jfklibrary/j062663.htm (accessed September 9, 2003).

[3] Prowe, "The Making of *ein Berliner*," 172–3. On the origin of the expression "ich bin ein Berliner," see Daum, *Kennedy in Berlin*, 130–8.

in the preceding decade, West Berlin crowds responded to incidents in Berlin or elsewhere in the Soviet Bloc with violent protest – but neither Kennedy's suspicion of the crowd's irrational adventurism nor his belief that marching on the wall remained impossible reduce his resounding appeals to mere rhetorical flourish.[4]

In a second, very different speech that Kennedy gave in Berlin that June day, he appealed to a student audience at the Free University to "reject slogans and 'face the realities as they actually are.'"[5] Responding to fears of global upheaval beginning in Berlin, this speech seemed to offer the status quo in Berlin as a model for expanding east-west contacts and local cooperation and a way to step back from Cold War tensions. But that impression is deceptive. Together the two speeches demonstrate Kennedy's investment in and commitment to Cold War stability of which détente was one part. From an early 1960s perspective of possible détente, the "irrational" threat to the Cold War settlement in Berlin came from the potential for uncontrolled transgressions of the boundaries that had come both to define and constrain the Great Powers' engagement with the local manifestations of Cold War.[6]

The problem with this means of imagining the Cold War rested in its assertion of a conflict rendered in absolute divides. Kennedy's rhetoric depended on the very instability he feared, an instability founded not on absolute divides but on continual interaction. Rather than positing the Cold War as a battle against totalitarianism, we should rather see in

---

[4] Arthur M. Schlesinger Jr., *A Thousand Days: John F. Kennedy in the White House* (Boston: Houghton Mifflin, 1965), 885. Schlesinger reports that Kennedy "always regarded crowds as irrational." The most recent event that presumably encapsulated the experience of the Wall and provoked a passionate response in West Berlin was the case of Peter Fechter, an eighteen-year-old construction worker from East Berlin, who on August 17, 1962 died after being shot during an attempt to escape to West Berlin. As frantic West Berliners watched, he lay on the ground and slowly bled to death before the East German guards collected his body an hour later. The guards' callousness and the American and West Berlin police's refusal to intervene contributed to a wave of protests in the days that followed in which thousands of West Berliners took to the streets throwing stones and firecrackers over the Berlin Wall, at police, and even at the Soviet soldiers being bussed to stand guard duty at the Soviet War Memorial in the British sector. Among the most graphic accounts of this story, see "The Boy Who Died on the Wall," *Life* 53, no. 9 (August 31, 1962), 16–22.

[5] Prowe, "The Making of *ein Berliner*," 174.

[6] Jeremi Suri, *Power and Protest: Global Revolution and the Rise of Détente* (Cambridge, MA and London: Harvard University Press, 2003); Timothy Garton Ash, *In Europe's Name: Germany and the Divided Continent* (New York: Random House, 1993); M. E. Sarotte, *Dealing with the Devil: East Germany, Détente, and Ostpolitik, 1969–1973* (Chapel Hill and London: University of North Carolina Press, 2001).

the waging of Cold War a tendency toward the totalitarian.[7] The Cold War's broad stabilizing features depended on an unintentional collusion between east and west, and its half-century domination of everyday life depended as well on broad participation in its hegemonic systems.

In looking at Berlin between 1946 and 1949, we can recognize an ongoing "crisis of hegemony" engendered in large part by the destructive violence of World War II but also dependent on the prolonged nature of the postwar period. A focus on the contested terrain of Berlin's everyday life helps make visible the production of the "private apparatuses" of hegemony on which the global formulations of Cold War ultimately depended.[8] Thus, we are able to move between global and local, haltingly perhaps, but still able to negotiate the productive tension between symbolic assertions of absolute divide and the practices that make such assertions possible. In his study of evolving French and Spanish nationalism in Pyrenees, Peter Sahlins writes, "the sense of difference is strongest where some historical sense of cooperation and relatedness remains, as in the Catalan borderland of France and Spain";[9] or in divided Berlin.

A 1983 subway map produced by West Berlin's public transportation authority makes visible the Berlin Wall – here, euphemistically described as the "sector border." In this map the border – indicated by diagonal cross-hatching – does not remain impermeable; it is traversed by two West Berlin subway lines, the U6 and U8, which run through East Berlin on their way from the southern to northern portion of the city's western half. More strikingly, a dashed black line marks the course of the once and future subway line running from Wittenbergplatz – the heart of West Berlin – past Potsdamer Platz and Alexanderplatz en route to East Berlin's Pankow district – the monochrome rendering of this line ("out of service") contrasting markedly with the full-color immediacy of the eight lines that comprised West Berlin's underground rail system.[10]

[7] Hannah Arendt, *The Origins of Totalitarianism*, rev. ed. (New York: Harcourt Brace, 1973), esp. 364–88.

[8] Antonio Gramsci, *Selections from the Prison Notebooks*, Quintin Hoare and Geoffrey Nowell Smith, eds. and trans. (New York: International Publishers, 1971), 210.

[9] Peter Sahlins, *Boundaries: The Making of France and Spain in the Pyrenees* (Berkeley: University of California Press, 1989), 271.

[10] West Berlin's subway lines numbered 1–4 and 6–9. Line 5, although included in the map (again in black) was part of the East Berlin system. BVG U-Bahn-Liniennetzkarte (1983), http://www.schmalspurbahn.de/netze/Netz_1983BVG.jpg (accessed August 4, 2003). The East Berlin subway map quite explicitly halted at the sector border. In fact, in the 1984 and 1988 versions of the East Berlin S- and U-Bahn map, West Berlin is compressed to such an extent as practically to disappear. Berliner Reichsbahn, Reichsbahndirektion Berlin, "Linien- und Preisstufenübersicht" (1984), http://www.schmalspurbahn .de/netze/Netz_1984_klein.gif (accessed August 4, 2003).

In the early 1980s, a passenger on (West) Berlin's U6 or U8 subway line could travel underneath the Berlin Wall and, without any sort of visa, pass through an underground world that seemed to offer a front row seat on a material reality that summed up the Cold War. Although pedestrians on the East Berlin streets above felt only a distant rumble of the passing subway beneath their feet, as the cars passed slowly through the dimly lit stations, the passengers on board caught sight of armed guards standing along the platforms and tile walls that had remained largely unchanged at least since the Wall went up in August 1961. Like the platforms erected at various points throughout West Berlin to offer tourists a chance to look over the Wall, a western subway rider traveling past these "ghost stations" could glimpse an exotic, other world (East Berlin), a dangerous and different space, produced presumably by the Cold War divide imposed on the city.[11] Thus a ride on these lines facilitated passages through time as well as space.

If the 1990 Two plus Four Treaty that enabled German reunification marked the final resolution of World War II and a reentry into European history,[12] the Cold War thus comprised an artificially extended passage between the end of war and the conclusion of peace. This tension also manifested itself in the course of this subway journey: passing through but not stopping at the stations whose evolution as part of postwar Berlin remained arrested as well. The opportunity to apprehend this static, physical "reality" on display – the separateness of divided Berlin – was what Kennedy called the world to "come to Berlin" to see;[13] but this call failed

---

[11] In his fictional imagining of late–Cold War Berlin, Peter Schneider offers an ironic version of this gaze from an observation platform back and forth across the Berlin Wall. He describes two tourist groups, one on either side of the Wall, simultaneously adjusting their binoculars as they gaze at a watch tower in the no-man's-land between the walls, while the guards in the tower gaze back at them. Peter Schneider, *Der Mauerspringer: Erzählung* (Darmstadt and Neuwied: Luchterhand, 1984), 24–5. The English-language citation is Schneider, *The Wall Jumper*, 27–8. The vast majority of riders on these heavily traveled lines remained West Berlin residents whose work took them from north and south to the opposite end of West Berlin. For images of the "ghost stations," see Links, *Berliner Geisterbahnhöfe*.

[12] Tony Judt, *Postwar: A History of Europe since 1945* (New York: Penguin, 2005), 3.

[13] As early as 1958, W. Philips Davison suggested in the title of his history of the Berlin Blockade that Berlin offered a case study for a larger set of issues. See Davison, *The Berlin Blockade*. The German translation renders the sense of Berlin as an experimental test case even more explicit: *Die Blockade von Berlin: Modellfall des kalten Krieges* (Frankfurt am Main: Alfred Metzner Verlag, 1959). Of course, the opportunity for westerners to view these aspects of life on the other side of the wall or that the subway system could continue to function across sector boundaries depended on evolving agreements between east and west about managing the day-to-day logistics of life in Berlin. On the nature of these contacts and negotiations between West Berlin and the GDR, see

to grasp the critical point: it was the passing through that really mattered. Only in this fluid, interstitial space can we encounter the workings – as opposed merely to the declamations – of Cold War. And as much as the American President's speech referenced the building of the Wall and the tension-filled years since 1949, his speech's iconic deployment of Berlin as a Cold War symbol depended on a set of meanings and practices cultivated in Berlin during the period this book examines.

Making the Cold War in Berlin

Speaking on the topic "Between war and peace," Kurt Mattick, the secretary for the SPD delegation to the city assembly, addressed an election assembly in Wilmersdorf (British sector) shortly before the west sectors' December 1948 election. He argued that World War II had not really ended, and that Berlin now found itself in a new war, this time a battle for peace. In this struggle, he suggested, Berlin could serve as a model for the Social Democrats' vision for a "new democratic order" and was uniquely positioned to influence the future shape of a unified Germany.[14] Mattick's understanding of 1948 Berlin's location *between war and peace* effectively captured the productive possibility inherent in the city's liminal state, but it also reflected the limits of any effort to realize that potential in policy achievements alone. Berliners' potential to transform their world remained – if along slightly different lines than Kennedy would presume in 1963 – inherently dangerous. It threatened to explode the increasingly comfortable high political accommodations within which the emerging superpowers were gradually crafting their post–World War II settlements.[15]

Gerhard Kunze, *Grenzerfahrungen: Kontakte und Verhandlungen zwischen dem Land Berlin und der DDR1949–1989*, Studien des Forschungsverbundes SED-Staat an der Freien Universität Berlin (Berlin: Akademie Verlag, 1999). More generally on Berliners' movement across Berlin's Cold War political boundaries, see Erika Hoerning, *Zwischen den Fronten: Berliner Grenzgänger und Grenzhändler 1948–1961* (Cologne: Böhlau Verlag, 1992) and Conradt and Heckmann-Janz, *Berlin halb und halb*.

[14] Kurt Mattick, notes for a speech to a voter assembly in Wilmersdorf (November 26, 1948), AdsD, SPD-LV Berlin, 3/BEAB000093: SPD-Landesverband Berlin, Büro Stellv. Landesvorssitzender Kurt Mattick, Tageskopien, 1.1.-31.12.1948. Arno Scholz, the long-time SPD activist and founder of the SPD paper in Berlin, *Der Telegraf*, used the same title for his 1956 collection of *Telegraf* editorials. *Zwischen Krieg und Frieden; Beiträge zum politischen Geschehen der Gegenwart* (Berlin-Grunewald: Arani Verlag, [1956]).

[15] Marc Trachtenberg, *A Constructed Peace* (Princeton: Princeton University Press, 1999) and Granieri, *The Ambivalent Alliance*, 151–2.

This study has argued that the belief that one could "come to Berlin" and catch an up-close glimpse of a global conflict dramatically misconstrues the convoluted means with which its participants constituted the Cold War. Berlin's symbolic resonance for the Cold War depended both on its spatial and political dividedness and on the ways that practices *on the ground* sustained and undermined the global assertions of that divide. It was not the construction of a local, concrete version of the Iron Curtain, but the forty-plus-year practice of boundary crossing – and the rituals that accompanied these quotidian acts – that most powerfully elaborated the symbolic contours of Cold War Berlin. Or perhaps boundary crossing is not quite right. That suggests a state of arrival that fails to connote the liminality of a process that remained one of becoming, the sense of continually standing on the threshold. Addressing a very different topic, Victor Turner wrote: "A limen is a threshold, but at least in the case of protracted initiation rites or major seasonal festivals it is a very long threshold, a corridor almost, or a tunnel which may become a pilgrim's road [. . . .] Let us refer to the state and process of midtransition as 'liminality' [. . . .] Those undergoing it [. . .] are betwixt and between established states of politico-jural structure. They evade ordinary cognitive classification, too, for they are not this or that, here or there, one thing or the other."[16]

Like Berlin and Berliners, the Cold War existed "betwixt and between," at once an interruption of "normal" historical time but also imbedded in its particular sites and intertwined with the actors who sought to master and/or transform that history. Much like the rites of passage that Victor Turner elaborated on in which the participants were part but not part of their communities (after all, only by means of the rite does the initiate fully enter adult society), the tension-filled terrain of postwar Berlin also constituted an alternative form of social organization – "antistructure" – that contained, at least potentially, a threat to the symbolic structures that would sustain the emerging Cold War.[17] The Cold War has undoubtedly been defined by its rituals, but primarily in the sense of distinct, extraordinary *events* that demarcated an authoritative discourse of a new kind of power. But ritual can also refer to the repeated and ordinary, the quotidian and decidedly "nonevent," to something very much part of the everyday.[18]

---

[16] Turner, *Blazing the Trail*, 49.

[17] Ibid., 133. Paul Steege, "Finding the there, there."

[18] Harootunian, *History's Disquiet*, 56 and 151. See also William Sewell, cited in Ronald Grigor Suny, "Back and Beyond: Reversing the Cultural Turn?" *AHR* 107, no. 5 (December 2002), 1498; Eley, "Labor History, Social History," 297–343, esp. pp. 300 and 313.

Looking back at his diaries from the 1970s, the British historian Timothy Garton Ash ironically quotes a journalist friend's remark about "living in the heat of the Cold War." But he notes that, in spite of living in Berlin during the "last great confrontation of the Cold War," big historical events were almost entirely absent from his entries.[19] Rather than taking this "gap" in his personal record as evidence of a young scholar whose enthusiasm for Berlin's night life and late night intellectual exchange overshadowed his attention to "serious" international affairs, we should see a profound insight into how the Cold War actually worked in this absence of *great events* from his Cold War account. The Cold War depended on the productive tension between the "hegemonic discourses" that presumably marked its boundaries and complex everyday events that simultaneously undergirded and undermined those discourses.

Paying close attention to "how power works" offers us the chance to address a question that scholars have generally not bothered to ask: where did the Cold War take place?[20] In its focus on the continuities and ruptures that made up everyday experiences in Berlin after World War II (digging through the rubble, riding the U-Bahn, walking through the black market – all as part of Berliners' ongoing efforts to cope with the world of scarcity in which they found themselves), this book offers one possibility. In the tension-filled spaces in which ordinary Berliners lived out their lives, we discover that these Berliners were personally complicit in producing the hegemonic structures of the Cold War.[21] But we also discover that making sense of the emerging culture of the Cold War depends on finding a way to locate it in the often ephemeral passages of everyday life.[22]

This book started with a vision of the Berlin Blockade that explained it in absolute terms: total blockade and total airlift. In the subsequent chapters, it sought to relocate the postwar struggle for Berlin, shifting our

---

[19] Timothy Garton Ash, *The File: A Personal History* (New York: Vintage Books, 1997), 27.

[20] Connelly, *A Diplomatic Revolution*, xi.

[21] In a somewhat different context, see Ash, *The File*, 45.

[22] Cf. Guy Oakes, *The Imaginary War: Civil Defense and American Cold War Culture* (New York and Oxford: Oxford University Press, 1994). Ironically, one of the reviewers of Oakes's book commends it for its insight into the "politics of everyday life" of the Cold War. While the book is an outstanding critique of the political production and manipulation of culture, it is precisely in the sense in which culture remains an object of policy that the book does *not* interject broader everyday agency into the mix. See JoAnne Brown, "Guy Oakes, The Imaginary War: Civil Defense and American Cold War Culture," review of *The Imaginary War: Civil Defense and American Cold War Culture*, by Guy Oakes. *The Journal of American History* 83, no. 4 (March 1997), 1481.

focus instead to the back alleys of the *Zusammenbruchgesellschaft*, the devastated society where Berliners made their postwar world. These were fluid spaces with fluid populations, but they were spaces that nobody in Berlin could avoid. The encounters in these spaces – between privileged and impoverished Berliners, occupying forces, refugees, and professional black marketeers – were necessarily uneven, but they also produced opportunities for these diverse actors to craft or reshape the worlds in which they moved. In the world of the black market, disparities of possession and power were readily apparent but also eminently negotiable. This is where the Cold War was forged.

On August 27, 1948, just a week after the violent clash between Soviet sector police and demonstrators at the Potsdamer Platz black market, American soldiers and a Soviet officer engaged in a high-speed chase and shootout in the same streets on the edge of the American sector – the major arteries running through the American sector offered Soviet forces their most direct route from the Soviet zone into their sector of Berlin. According to the American report, U.S. MPs sought to stop a Soviet amphibious jeep for speeding. When the vehicle refused to stop, the MPs pursued the vehicle. Shots were fired by both sides, and the jeep sideswiped an MP on a motorcycle. The report went on to explain the Soviet officer's desire to escape the MPs by referencing "erroneous false propaganda" according to which American forces sought to detain "for intelligence purposes" any Soviet soldier they found in their sector. In rejecting this assertion, the report notes that had the Soviet officer stopped, he would have gotten off with a warning "for speeding and breaking the rules in the American Sector" but that no "incident" would have resulted.[23] This event did not quite rise to the level of significance to merit inclusion in West Berlin's official chronology of 1946–8; even three years into the postwar occupation, this sort of "wild west" moment was hardly unheard of. In fact, for ordinary Berliners living in a world with 150 daily break-ins into the city's grocery stores, where occupation forces provided a vital cog in the operation of the city's black market, and where "bandits in Russian uniform" made regular appearances in the city's police reports, a few more shots fired literally over their heads were unlikely to make much impact.

The American report's claim for this event's significance depended on an interpretation extracted from the particular details of its Berlin context.

---

[23] Report of August 29, 1948 submitted by David J. Krichevsky to OMGUS Public Safety Branch, NA, RG 260, 390/48/27/3, box 902.

What mattered for its status as an "incident" was a *Soviet* decision driven by "erroneous false propaganda." It claimed a larger ideological significance for an action that is more appropriately discussed in terms of the cityscape, traffic patterns, and German civilians who encountered these speeding vehicles. Two months into what generally figures as the first great battle of the Cold War (the Berlin Blockade), the Soviets and Americans in Berlin were exchanging shots over a speeding ticket.

Ultimately, the end of the blockade crisis in 1949 marked the real beginning of the Cold War. With their assertion to have settled the crisis, the Great Powers claimed for themselves the power to define the nature of *their* conflicts. By collaborating to settle the S-Bahn strike, and supported by the Western powers' acceptance of West Berlin as the limit of their symbolic challenge to what would become East Germany, these World War II allies sought to eliminate the potential for Berliners to publicly challenge their claim to that definitional authority. Although the Wall would help crystallize Berlin's symbolic value in the Cold War as a series of *events* – extraordinary departures from the everyday that seemed to impose a foreign Cold War world upon the city – it could not conceal the fact that these grand gestures depended on the multifaceted, daily practice of the Cold War taking place in Berlin. It is in these practices and the locations in which they occurred that the events of 1946 to 1949 hold so much explanatory power.

Faced with an ongoing struggle to master a situation in a Berlin that remained incomprehensible for them, the Great Powers nonetheless believed in the validity of their ritual commitments to the city. But this international conflict to which they pledged mutual allegiance ultimately was defined by its disconnect from the complicated and difficult conditions on the ground. Ironically, this lack of understanding and the relative freedom it offered local individuals to act on their own behalf exerted pressure on this symbolic Cold War framework – even as they sought to exploit it – and tightened its explanatory hold on a battleground for which its actual descriptive power was really quite minimal.[24]

On the night of November 9, 1989, the Cold War ended, as it had begun, in Berlin. Although the fall of the Berlin Wall did not mark the total dissolution of the Soviet Empire or even the end of the GDR, it did mark the end of a particularly potent public assertion of the Cold War's universal explanatory power. That this power was illusory now seems clear, and,

---

[24] I develop this point in greater detail in my essay, "Finding the There, There: Local Space, Global Ritual, and Early Cold War Berlin."

with the fall of the Wall, Berlin broke free from its artificial place in the Cold War pantheon. While the events of East-Central Europe in 1989 have convinced scholars and pundits to grant to "ordinary people" in the streets of Prague, Berlin, and Budapest the power to *end* the Cold War,[25] they are much more hesitant to grant these same "ordinary people" the power to have made it. By focusing on everyday life in Berlin, this study has strived to elaborate the means by which Berliners on both sides of the city's emerging divide played vital roles in shaping the Cold War. As such, it offers a challenge to all "ordinary people" to consider their complicity in the making of their worlds, but also their potential to transform them.

[25] John Lewis Gaddis, *The Cold War: A New History* (New York: Penguin, 2005), 259.

Bibliography

Archival Sources

Archiv des Polizeipräsidiums, Berlin
Files are uncataloged.

Brandenburgisches Landeshauptarchiv, Potsdam
Ld. Br. Rep. 202B: HA Innerdeutscher Handel, Außenhandel, Materialversorgung
Ld. Br. Rep. 202C: HA Wirtschaftsplanung
Ld. Br. Rep. 203: Ministerium des Innern
Ld. Br. Rep. 203, VP: MdI: Landesbehörde der Volkspolizei Brandenburg
Ld. Br. Rep. 204A: Ministerium der Finanzen
Ld. Br. Rep. 206: Wirtschaftsministerium
Ld. Br. Rep. 209: Ministerium für Handel und Versorgung
Ld. Br. Rep. 332: SED Landesvorstand Brandenburg

Bundesarchiv, Abteilung DDR, Berlin-Lichterfelde
DC 15/: Deutsche Wirtschaftskommission (DWK)
DM 1/: Ministerium für Verkehrswesen
DO 1–17/: Deutsche Verwaltung des Innern (DVdI)
X1/: SMAD-Befehle

Bundesarchiv, Stiftung Archiv der Parteien und Massenorganisationen der DDR, Berlin-Lichterfelde
DY 30/IV 1/1/: Parteitage der SED
DY 30/IV 2/1/: SED ZK: Tagungen des Parteivorstandes
DY 30/IV 2/1.01/: SED ZK: Konferenzen und Beratungen des Parteivorstandes der SED
DY 30/IV 2/2/: Politbüro Beschlüsse
DY 30/IV 2/2.025/: ZK der SED: Sekretariat Otto Meier
DY 30/IV 2/2.1/: SED Zentralsekretariat – Beschlüsse, 1946–49
DY 30/IV 2/5/: SED ZK – Parteiorgane
DY 30/IV 2/6.02/: SED Zentralkomitee, Abteilung Wirtschaftspolitik

DY 30/IV 2/9.02/: Abteilung Agitation des ZK der SED
DY 30/IV 2/9.06/: Abteilung Kultur des ZK der SED
DY 30/IV 2/12/: SED ZK – Sicherheitsfragen
DY 30/J IV 2/3/: Beschlüsse – Kleine Sekretariat
DY 30/J IV 2/201–201: SED ZK – Büro Ulbricht
DY 32/: Zentrales Bestand der Gesellschaft für deutsch-sowjetische Freundschaft
DY 34/: FDGB Bundesvorstand
DY 55/V 278/: Generalsekretariat Vereinigung der Verfolgten des Naziregimes
  (VVN)
NY 4036: Nachlaß Wilhelm Pieck (1876–1960)
NY 4062: Nachlaß Heinrich Rau
NY 4073: Nachlaß Karl Litke
NY 4076: Nachlaß Hermann Matern
NY 4090: Nachlaß Otto Grotewohl
NY 4182: Nachlaß Walter Ulbricht (1893–1973)
NY 4406: Nachlaß Adolf Deter (1900–69)
NY 4416: Nachlaß Hermann Schlimme (1882–1955)

Landesarchiv Berlin

My research in the Landesarchiv paralleled the consolidation of separate East and West Berlin archives into a single institution and the subsequent move of the archive's holdings to its new location in Berlin-Wittenau. This move also entailed the reorganization and renumbering of the files. Documents from the postwar period are now organized in two broad categories:

Tektonikgruppe B includes material from West Berlin offices and institutions, offices responsible for federal funds, leading communal associations, and the women's archival collections.

Tektonikgruppe C includes material from East Berlin offices and institutions, parties and mass organizations, people's factories (VEBs), and industrial combines.

The listing in the following text lists archive record groups as previously divided between the East Berlin (Breite Str.) and West Berlin (Kalckreuthstr.) branches of the Landesarchiv. Record group titles remain generally accurate, but the numbering system has now changed to reflect the archive's new organizational structure.

Landesarchiv Berlin (Breite Str.)
STA Rep. 9: Der Polizeipräsident in Berlin
STA Rep. 26: Präsidium der Volkspolizei Berlin
STA Rep. 100: Stadtverordnetenversammlung und Magistrat von Groß-Berlin/
  Magistrat
STA Rep. 101: Magistrat von Groß-Berlin/Oberbürgermeister
STA Rep. 106: Magistrat von Groß-Berlin, Abteilung Wirtschaft
STA Rep. 113: Magistrat von Groß-Berlin, Abteilung Handel und Versorgung
STA Rep. 114: Magistrat von Groß-Berlin, Abt. für Verkehr und Versorgungsbe-
  triebe
STA Rep. 120: Magistrat von Groß-Berlin, Abteilung Volksbildung
STA Rep. 370–06: Sammlung Fotodokumentation
STA Rep. 411: VEB Transformatorenwerk Karl Liebknecht (TRO)

STA Rep. 420–015: *VEB Berlin Chemie (Schering), BGL*
STA Rep. 432: Bergmann Borsig
STA Rep. 752: VEB Energiekombinat Berlin (BEWAG)
STA Rep. 775: VEB Berliner Verkehrsbetriebe (BVG)

Landesarchiv Berlin (Kalkreuthstr.)
BPA FDGB/: FDGB Bezirksvorstand Berlin – Archiv
BPA IV L-2/: SED Landesleitung Groß-Berlin
BPA IV 4/6: SED Kreisleitung Prenzlauer Berg
BPA IV 4/27: SED Kreisleitung Spandau
BPA IV 4/31: SED Kreisleitung Wedding
Rep. 2: Der Regierende Bürgermeister von Berlin/Senatskanzlei
Rep. 10: Senatsverwaltung für Wirtschaft
Rep. 10B: Ernährung
Rep. 200, Acc. 1704: Nachlaß Otto Suhr
Rep. 200, Acc. 2435: Nachlaß Gustav Klingelhöfer (1888–1961)
Rep. 280: Landesarchiv Zeitgeschichtliche (LAZ-) Sammlung

Landeshauptarchiv Sachsen-Anhalt, Magdeburg
Rep. K3: Ministerium des Innern
Rep. K8: Ministerium für Handel und Versorgung
Rep. K14: Ministerium des Innern – Landesbehörde der Volkspolizei Sachsen-Anhalt

National Archives of the United States, College Park, MD
RG 59: Department of State
RG 84: Foreign Service Posts
RG 260: Records of the United States Occupation Headquarters World War II
CIA Records Search Tool (CREST)

Newspapers and Periodicals
Berliner Statistik
Daily Telegraph
Einheit
Der Kurier
Life
Neues Deutschland
New York Times
Sie
Der Sozialdemokrat
Der Tagesspiegel
Tägliche Rundschau
Der Telegraf
Tribüne

Printed Sources

Albrecht, Willy, ed. *Die SPD unter Kurt Schumacher und Erich Ollenhauer 1946 bis 1965: Sitzungsprotokolle der Spitzengremien*, vol. 1, *1946 bis 1948*. Bonn: Verlag J. H. W. Dietz Nachf., 1999.

Befehle des Obersten Chefs der Sowjetischen Militäverwaltung in Deutschland. Berlin: SWA-Verlag, 1946.

Bonwetsch, Bernd, Gennadii Bordiugov, and Norman Naimark, eds. *SVAG: Upravlenie propagandy (informacii) i S. I. Tiul'panov 1945–1949: Sbornik dokumentov.* Seriia 'Perviia Publikacii.' Moscow: Rossiia molodaia, 1994.

Brandt, Willy. *Berliner Ausgabe,* vol. 3, *Berlin bleibt frei: Politik in und für Berlin 1947–1966.* Siegfried Heimann, ed. Bonn: Verlag J. H. W. Dietz Nachf., 2004.

Deutscher, Isaac. *Reportagen aus Nachkriegsdeutschland.* Hamburg: Junius Verlag, 1980.

Deutsches Institut für Wirtschaftsforschung, ed. *Berlins Wirtschaft in der Blokkade.* Berlin and Munich: Duncker und Humblot, 1949.

Dokumente zur Geschichte der SED, vol. 2, *1945–1971.* 2nd ed. Berlin (East): Dietz, 1981.

Forschungsinstitut der Deutschen Gesellschaft für Auswärtige Politik e.V., Bonn in Zusammenhang mit dem Senat von Berlin. *Dokumente zur Berlin-Frage 1944–1966.* 3rd ed. Munich: R. Oldenbourg Verlag, 1967.

German Democratic Republic, Ministerium für auswärtige Angelegenheiten. *Um ein antifaschistisch-demokratisches Deutschland: Dokumente aus den Jahren 1945–1949.* Berlin: Staatsverlag der DDR, 1968.

Germany (West). Bundesministerium für Gesamtdeutsche Fragen. *SBZ.* Bonn, 1945/54–1959/60 (Annual).

Gröschner, Annett, ed. *"Ich schlug meiner Mutter die brennenden Funken ab": Berliner Schulaufsätze aus dem Jahr 1946.* Reinbek bei Hamburg: Rowohlt Taschenbuch Verlag, 2001.

Hauptamt für Statistik, Berlin-Wilmersdorf, ed. *Berlin in Zahlen 1947.* Berlin: Berliner Kulturbuch-Verlag, 1949.

————, ed. *Berlin in Zahlen 1950.* Berlin: Kulturbuch-Verlag, 1950.

Heidelmeyer, Wolfgang and Guenter Hindrichs, eds. *Documents on Berlin 1945–1963.* Munich: R. Oldenbourg Verlag, 1963.

Institut für Theorie des Staates und des Rechts der Akademie der Wissenschaften der DDR. *Geschichte des Staates und des Rechts der DDR: Dokumente 1945–1949.* Berlin (East): Staatsverlag der DDR, 1984.

Kindleberger, Charles P. *The German Economy, 1945–1947: Charles P. Kindleberger's Letters from the Field.* Westport, CT and London: Meckler, 1989.

Kleßmann, Christoph and Georg Wagner, eds. *Das gespaltene Land: Leben in Deutschland 1945–1990: Texte und Dokumente zur Sozialgeschichte.* Munich: Beck, 1993.

Kromer, Karl. *Schwarzmarkt, Tausch- und Schleichhandel: in Frage und Antwort mit 500 praktischen Beispielen.* Recht für jeden 1. Schloß Bleckede an der Elbe: Otto Meißners Verlag, 1947.

Kynin, G. P. and J. Laufer, eds. *SSSR i germanskii vopros 1941–1949: Dokumenty iz Arkhiva vneshnei politiki rossiiskoi federatsii,* vol. 2, *SSSR i germanskii vopros: 9 maia 1945 g.-3.oktiabria 1946 g.* Moscow: Mezhdunarodnye otnosheniia, 2000.

Michaelis, Herbert and Ernst Schraepler, eds. *Die staatliche Neuordnung Deutschlands: Die Berliner Blockade – Die Errichtung der Bundesrepublik – Das grundgesetz der Bundesrepublik Deutschland – Die Gründung der*

Deutschen Demokratischen Republik. Ursachen und Folgen Vom deutschen Zusammenbruch 1918 und 1945 bis zur staatlichen Neuordnung Deutschlands in der Gegenwart: Eine Urkunden-und dokumentensammlung zur Zeitgeschichte 26. Berlin: Dokumenten-Verlag Dr. Herbert Wendler and Co., n.d.

Die Militär- und Sicherheitspolitik der SED 1945 bis 1988: Dokumente und Materialien. Berlin: Militärverlag der DDR, [1989].

Ministerstvo Inostannykh Del SSSR, *Sovietskii Soiuz i Berlinskii Vopros (Dokumenty).* Moscow: Gospolitizdat, 1948.

Nationale Front des Demokratischen Deutschlands. *Programmatische Dokumente der Nationalen Front des Demokratischen Deutschland.* Berlin: Dietz, 1967.

Protokoll der Verhandlungen des zweiten Parteitages der SED: 20. bis 24. September 1947, in der Deutschen Staatsoper zu Berlin. Berlin: Dietz, 1947.

Reuter, Ernst. *Schriften, Reden,* vol. 3, *Artikel, Briefe, Reden 1964 bis 1949.* Hans J. Reichhard, ed. Berlin: Propyläen Verlag, 1974.

Ruhm von Oppen, Beate, ed. *Documents on Germany under Occupation 1945–1954.* London: Oxford University Press, 1955.

Selbmann, Fritz. *Für eine gesamtdeutsche Wirtschaftspolitik: Rede gehalten in Frankfurt (Main) am 9. Juni 1949.* Berlin: Deutscher Zentralverlag, 1949.

Senat von Berlin, ed. *Berlin: Quellen und Dokumente 1945–1951.* 2 Halbbände. Schriftenreihe zur Berliner Zeitgeschichte, vol. 4. Berlin: Heinz Spitzing Verlag, 1964.

Smith, Jean Edward, ed. *The Papers of General Lucius D. Clay: Germany 1945–1949.* 2 vols. Bloomington and London: Indiana University Press, 1974.

Stenographische Berichte der Stadtverordnetenversammlung von Berlin. I. Wahlperiode. 3 vols. Berlin, 1946–8.

Suckut, Siegfried, ed. *Blockpolitik in der SBZ/DDR 1945–1949: Die Sitzungsprotokolle des zentralen Einheitsfront-Ausschusses: Quellenedition.* Mannheimer Untersuchungen zu Politik und Geschichte der DDR 3. Cologne: Verlag Wissenschaft und Politik, 1986.

Ulbricht, Walter. *Brennende Fragen des Neuaufbaus Deutschlands.* Berlin, 1947.

_____. *Die gegenwärtigen Aufgaben unserer demokratischen Verwaltung.* Berlin, 1948.

United States, Department of State, ed. *The Berlin Crisis – A Report on the Moscow Discussions.* Department of State Publication No. 3298, European and British Commonwealth Series No. 1. Washington, DC: U.S. Government Printing Office, 1948.

_____, ed. *Germany 1947–1949 – The Story in Documents.* Department of State Publication No. 3556, European and Commonwealth Series No. 9. Washington, DC: U.S. Government Printing Office, 1950.

_____, ed. *The Conferences of Malta and Yalta – 1945.* Department of State Publication No. 6199. Washington, DC: U.S. Government Printing Office, 1955.

_____. Historical Office. *Documents on Germany 1944–1959: Background Documents on Germany, 1944–1959, and a Chronology of Political Developments Affecting Berlin, 1945–1956.* Washington, DC: U.S. Government Printing Office, 1959.

————, ed. *The Conference of Berlin – 1945*. Department of State Publication No. 7163. Washington, DC: U.S. Government Printing Office, 1960.

————, ed. *Foreign Relations of the United States 1947*, vol. 2, *Council of Foreign Ministers: Germany and Austria*. Washington, DC: U.S. Government Printing Office, 1972.

————, ed. *Foreign Relations of the United States 1948*, vol. 2, *Council of Foreign Ministers: Germany and Austria*. Washington, DC: U.S. Government Printing Office, 1973.

Weber, Hermann, ed. *DDR, Dokumente zur Geschichte der Deutschen Demokratischen Republik, 1945–1985*. Munich: Deutscher Taschenbuch Verlag, 1986.

Wulf, Werner, ed. with the assistance of Harald Edel. *Trümmer, Tränen, Zuversicht: Alltag in Hessen 1945–1949*. Frankfurt am Main: Insel Verlag, 1986.

Zakharov, V. V., ed. *Deiatel'nost' Sovietskikh voennykh Kommendatur po likvidacii pocledstvii voiny i organizacii mirnoi zhizni v Sovietskoi zone okkupacii Germaniii 1945–1949: Sbornik dokumentov*. Moscow: Rosspen, 2005.

Memoirs and Diaries

Andreas-Friedrich, Ruth. *Battleground Berlin: Diaries 1945–1948*. Anna Boerresen, trans. New York: Paragon House Publishers, 1990.

Anonymous. *A Woman in Berlin: Eight Weeks in the Conquered City*. Philip Boehm, trans. New York: Metropolitan Books, 2005.

Bohlen, Charles E. *Witness to History 1929–1969*. New York: W. W. Norton and Company, 1973.

Bourke-White, Margaret. *"Dear Fatherland, Rest Quietly": A Report on the Collapse of Hilter's "Thousand Years."* New York: Simon and Schuster, 1946.

Boveri, Margret. *Tage des Überlebens: Berlin 1945*. Rev. ed. Munich: R. Piper, 1985.

Brandt, Willy. *My Road to Berlin*. New York: Doubleday and Co., Inc., 1960.

Chuikov, Vasili I. *The Fall of Berlin*. Ruth Kisch, trans. New York: Holt, Rinehart and Winston, 1968.

Clay, Lucius D. *Decision in Germany*. New York: Doubleday and Co., 1950.

Deutschkron, Inge. *Ich trug den gelben Stern*. Munich: Deutscher Taschenbuch Verlag, 1985.

Enzensberger, Hans Magnus, ed. *Europa in Ruinen: Augenzeugenberichte aus den Jahren 1944–1948*. Frankfurt am Main: Eichborn Verlag, 1990.

Friedensburg, Ferdinand. *Es ging um Deutschlands Einheit: Rückschau eines Berliners auf die Jahre nach 1945*. Berlin: Haude and Spenersche Verlagsbuchhandlung, 1971.

Gelfand, Wladimir. *Deutschland-Tagebuch 1945–1946: Aufzeichnungen eines Rotarmisten*. Elke Scherstjanoi, ed., Anja Lutter and Hartmut Schröde, trans. Berlin: Aufbau-Verlag, 2005.

Gniffke, Erich. *Jahre mit Ulbricht*. 1966. Reprint. Cologne: Verlag Politik und Wissenschaft, 1990.

Güstrow, Dietrich. *In jenen Jahren: Aufzeichnungen eines "befreiten" Deutschen.* Berlin: Severin und Siedler, 1983.

Haffner, Sebastian. *Defying Hitler: A Memoir.* Oliver Pretzel, trans. New York: Picador, 2003.

Howley, Frank. *Berlin Command.* New York: G. P. Putnam's Sons, 1950.

Kennan, George F. *Memoirs 1925–1950.* Boston and Toronto: Little, Brown and Co., 1967.

Klimov, Gregory. *The Terror Machine: The Inside Story of the Soviet Administration in Germany.* H. C. Stevens, trans. London: Faber and Faber, 1953.

Leonhard, Wolfgang. *Die Revolution entläßt ihre Kinder.* Cologne and Berlin: Kiepenhauer and Witsch, 1955.

_____. *Child of the Revolution.* Chicago: H. Regnery Co., 1958.

McBride, Gisela R. *Memoirs of a 1000-Year-Old Woman: Berlin 1925–1945.* Bloomington, IN: 1stBooks, 2000.

Murphy, Robert. *Diplomat among Warriors.* Garden City, NY: Doubleday and Co., 1964.

Schmidt, Erich. *Meine Jugend in Groß-Berlin: Triumph und Elend der Arbeiterbewegung 1918–1933.* Bremen: Donat Verlag, 1988.

Selbmann, Fritz. *Acht Jahre und ein Tag: Bilder aus den Gründerjahren der DDR.* Berlin: Verlag Neues Leben, 1999.

Shirer, William L. *End of a Berlin Diary.* New York: Alfred A. Knopf, 1947.

Speer, Albert. *Inside the Third Reich.* Richard and Clara Winston, trans. New York: Collier Books, 1981.

Speier, Hans. *From the Ashes of Disgrace: A Journal from Germany 1945–1955.* Amherst: The University of Massachusetts Press, 1981.

Stolten, Inge. *Das alltägliche Exil: Leben Zwischen Hakenkreuz und Währungsreform.* Bonn: Verlag J. H. W. Dietz Nachf., 1982.

Tjulpanov, Sergei. *Deutschland nach dem Kriege (1945–49): Erinnerungen eines Offiziers.* 2nd ed. Berlin (East): Dietz Verlag, 1987.

Vance, Heidi Scriba with Janet Barton Speer. *Shadows over My Berlin: One Woman's Story of World War II.* Middletown, CT: Southfarm Press, 1996.

Vassiltchikov, Marie. *Berlin Diaries, 1940–1945.* New York: Vintage Books, 1988.

Welty, Joel Carl. *The Hunger Year: In the French Zone of Divided Germany, 1946–1947.* Beloit, WI: Beloit College Archivist, 1993.

Secondary Sources

Books

Adomeit, Hannes. *Soviet Risk-Taking and Crisis Behavior: A Theoretical and Empirical Analysis.* London and Boston: Allen and Unwin, 1982.

_____. *Imperial Overstretch: Germany in Soviet Policy from Stalin to Gorbachev.* Internationale Politik und Sicherheit 48. Baden-Baden: Nomos Verlagsgesellschaft, 1998.

Allen, Keith Richard. "Eating Out in the Age of Industry: Public Policy Toward Food in Berlin, 1870–1950." PhD diss., Carnegie Mellon University, 1997.

Altmann, Normen. *Konrad Adenauer im Kalten Krieg: Wahrnehmungen und Politik 1945–1956.* Mannheimer historische Forschungen, 3. Mannheim: Palatium-Verlag im J-und-J-Verlag, 1993.

Anderle, Alfred, ed. *Zwei Jahrzehnte deutsch-sowjetische Beziehungen, 1945–1965: Beiträge von einem Kollektiv beim Institut für Geschichte der Völker der UdSSR an der Martin-Luther-Universität Halle.* Berlin (East): Staatsverlag der DDR, 1965.

Anderson, Benedict. *Imagined Communities: Reflections on the Origins and Spread of Nationalism.* Rev. ed. London and New York: Verso, 1991.

Auer, Peter. *Ihr Völker der Welt: Ernst Reuter und die Blockade von Berlin.* Berlin: Jaron Verlag, 1998.

Azeryahu, Maoz. *Vom Wilhelmsplatz zu Thälmannplatz: Politische Symbole im öffentlichen Leben der DDR.* Schriftenreihe des Instituts für deutsche Geschichte der Universität Tel Aviv, 13. Kerstin Amruni and Alma Mandelbaum, trans. Gerlingen: Bleicher Verlag, 1991.

Badstübner, Rolf, and Heinz Hetzer, eds. *Die DDR in der Übergangsperiode: Studien zur Vorgeschichte und Geschichte der DDR 1945 bis 1961.* Berlin: Akademie-Verlag, 1982.

Balfour, Michael. *Vier-Mächte Kontrolle in Deutschland 1945–46.* Düsseldorf, 1955.

Barclay, David E. *Schaut auf diese Stadt: der unbekannte Ernst Reuter.* Berlin: Siedler Verlag, 2000.

Barclay, David E. and Eric D. Weitz, eds. *Between Reform and Revolution: German Socialism and Communism from 1840 to 1990.* New York and Oxford: Berghahn Books, 1998.

Bark, Dennis L. *Die Berlin-Frage 1949–1955: Verhandlungsgrundlagen und Eindämmungspolitik.* Veröffentlichungen der Historischen Kommission zu Berlin 36. Berlin and New York: Walter de Gruyter, 1972.

Bark, Dennis L. and David R. Gress. *A History of West Germany,* vol. 1, *From Shadow to Substance 1945–1963.* Oxford and Cambridge, MA: Basil Blackwell, 1989.

Beevor, Antony. *The Fall of Berlin 1945.* New York: Viking, 2002.

Bender, Peter. *Unsere Erbschaft: was war die DDR, was bleibt von ihr?* Hamburg: Luchterhand, 1993.

Bentley, Amy. *Eating for Victory: Food Rationing and the Politics of Domesticity.* Urbana and Chicago: University of Illinois Press, 1998.

Berlin kommt wieder: ein Buch vom wirtschaftlichen und kulturellen Aufbau der Hauptstadt Deutschlands. Berlin: Arani Verlag, 1950.

Berlin (West Berlin) Landesarchiv. *Berlin: Behauptung von Freiheit und Selbstverwaltung 1946–1948.* Schriftenreihe zur Berliner Zeitgeschichte, vol. 2. Berlin: Heinz Spitzing Verlag, 1959.

———. *Berlin: Kampf um Freiheit und Selbstverwaltung 1945–1946.* 2nd ed. Schriftenreihe zur Berliner Zeitgeschichte, vol. 1. Berlin: Heinz Spitzing Verlag, 1961.

———. *Berlin: Ringen um Einheit und Wiederaufbau 1948–1951.* Schriftenreihe zur Berliner Zeitgeschichte, vol. 3. Berlin: Heinz Spitzing Verlag, 1962.

Bessel, Richard and Dirk Schuman, eds. *Life after Death: Approaches to a Cultural and Social History of Europe during the 1940s and 1950s.* Publications of the German Historical Institute. Cambridge and New York: Cambridge University Press, 2003.

Bezirksamt Tempelhof, ed. *Landing on Tempelhof: 75 Jahre Zentralflughafen: 50 Jahre Luftbrücke.* Austellungskatalog. Berlin: Westkreuz Druckerei, 1998.

Bluhm, Lothar. *Das Tagebuch zum Dritten Reich: Zeugnisse der Inneren Emigration von Jochen Klepper bis Ernst Jünger.* Studien zur Literatur der Moderne 20. Bonn: Bouvier Verlag, 1991.

Boelcke, Willi A. *Der Schwarzmarkt 1945–1948: vom Überleben nach dem Kriege.* Braunschweig: Westermann, 1986.

Böll, Heinrich. *Wanderer, kommst du nach Spa...: Erzählungen.* Frankfurt am Main: DTV, 1987.

Bohleber, Wolfgang. *Mit Marshallplan und Bundeshilfe: Wohnungsbaupolitik in Berlin 1945–1963.* Berlin: Duncker und Humblot, 1990.

Bondarev, Iurii. *Das Ufer.* Düsseldorf: Claasen, 1978.

Botting, Douglas. *From the Ruins of the Reich: Germany 1945–1949.* New York: Crown Publishers, 1985.

Bourdieu, Pierre. *Die verborgenen Mechanismen der Macht.* Margarete Steinrück, ed., Jürgen Bolder, et al., trans. Schriften zu Politik und Kultur 1. Hamburg: VSA-Verlag, 1992.

_____. *Praktische Vernunft: zur Theorie des Handelns.* Hella Beiste, trans. Frankfurt am Main: Suhrkamp, 1998.

Bouvier, Beatrix. *Ausgeschaltet! Sozialdemokraten in der Sowjetischen Besatzungszone und in der DDR.* Politik- und Gesellschaftsgeschichte 45. Bonn: Dietz, 1996.

Bradley, Mark. *Imagining Vietnam and America: The Making of Postcolonial Vietnam, 1919–1950.* Chapel Hill and London: University of North Carolina Press, 2000.

Brandt, Willy and Richard Löwenthal. *Ernst Reuter: Ein Leben für die Freiheit.* Munich: Kindler Verlag, 1957.

Braun, Hans-Joachim. *The German Economy in the Twentieth Century.* London and New York: Routledge, 1990.

Brecht, Bertolt. *Die Dreigroschenoper* in Siegfried Unseld, ed., *Bertolt Brechts Dreigroschenbuch: Texte, Materialien, Dokumente.* Frankfurt am Main: Suhrkamp Verlag, 1960.

_____. "The Modern Theater Is the Epic Theater." In *Brecht on Theater: The Development of an Aesthetic.* John Willett, trans. and ed. New York: Hill and Wang, 1964.

_____. *The Threepenny Opera.* Ralph Manheim and John Willet, trans. New York: Vintage Books, 1977.

Breloer, Heinrich, ed. *Mein Tagebuch: Geschichten vom Überleben 1939–1947.* Cologne: Verlagsgesellschaft Schulfernsehen, 1984.

Brewer, John and John Styles, eds. *An Ungovernable People: The English and Their Law in the Seventeenth and Eighteenth Centuries.* New Brunswick: Rutgers University Press, 1980.

Broosch, Karten. *Die Währungsreform 1948 in der sowjetischen Besatzungszone Deutschlands: Eine Untersuchung zur Rolle des Geldes beim Übergang zur sozialistischen Planwirtschaft in der SBZ/DDR.* Herdecke: GCA-Verlag, 1998.

Broszat, Martin and Hermann Weber, eds. *SBZ-Handbuch: Staatliche Verwaltungen, Parteien gesellschaftliche Organisationen und ihre Führungskräfte in der Sowjetischen Besatzungszone Deutschlands 1945–1949.* Munich: R. Oldenbourg, 1990.

Broszat, Martin, Klaus-Dietmar Kenke, and Hans Woller, eds. *Von Stalinsgrad bis Währungsreform: zur Sozialgeschichte des Umbruchs in Deutschland.* Quellen und Darstellungen zur Zeitgeschichte 26. Munich: R. Oldenbourg Verlag, 1988.

Brunner, Detlev. *Sozialdemokraten im FDGB: von der Gewerkschaft zur Massenorganisation, 1945 bis in die frühen 1950er Jahre.* Essen: Klartext Verlag, 2000.

Buffet, Cyril. *Mourir pour Berlin: La France et l'Allemagne, 1945–1949.* Paris: A. Colin, 1991.

Certeau, Michel de. *The Practice of Everyday Life.* Steven Rendell, trans. Berkeley: University of California Press, 1984.

Charles, Max. *Berlin Blockade.* London: Alan Wingate, 1959.

Collier, Richard. *Bridge across the Sky: The Berlin Blockade and Airlift 1948–1949.* New York: McGraw-Hill 1978.

Connelly, Matthew. *A Diplomatic Revolution: Algeria's Fight for Independence and the Origins of the Post-Cold War Era.* Oxford and New York: Oxford University Press, 2002.

Conradt, Sylvia and Kirsten Heckmann-Janz. *Berlin halb und halb: von Frontstädtern, Grenzgängern und Mauerspechten: Berichte und Bilder.* Frankfurt am Main: Luchterhand, 1990.

Corni, Gustavo and Horst Gies. *Brot, Butter, Kanonen: Die Ernährungswirtschaft in Deutschland unter der Diktatur Hitlers.* Berlin: Akademie Verlag, 1997.

Creuzberger, Stefan. *Die sowjetische Besatzungsmacht und das politische System der SBZ.* Schriften des Hannah-Arendt-Instituts für Totalitarismusforschung 3. Weimar, Cologne, and Vienna: Böhlau Verlag, 1996.

Crew, David F. *Germans on Welfare: From Weimar to Hitler.* Oxford and New York: Oxford University Press, 1998.

———, ed. *Consuming Germany in the Cold War.* Oxford and New York: Berg, 2003.

Crockatt, Richard. *The Fifty Years War: The United States and the Soviet Union in World Politics, 1941–1991.* London: Routledge, 1995.

Cumings, Bruce. *The Origins of the Korean War,* vol. 2, *The Roaring of the Cataract 1947–1950.* Princeton: Princeton University Press, 1990.

Dalby, Simon. *Creating the Second Cold War: The Discourse of Politics.* Geography and International Relations Series. London: Pinter et al., 1990.

Daniels, Robert V., ed. *A Documentary History of Communism,* vol. 2, *Communism and the World.* Rev. ed. Hanover and London: University Press of New England, 1984.

Daum, Andreas W. *Kennedy in Berlin: Politik, Kultur und Emotionen im Kalten Krieg.* Paderborn: Ferdinand Schöningh, 2003.

Davis, Belinda J. *Home Fires Burning: Food, Politics, and Everyday Life in World War I Berlin.* Chapel Hill and London: University of North Carolina Press, 2000.

Davis, Lynn E. *The Cold War Begins: Soviet-American Conflict over Eastern Europe.* Princeton: Princeton University Press, 1974.

Davison, W. Phillips. *The Berlin Blockade: A Study in Cold War Politics.* Princeton: Princeton University Press, 1958.

Deutscher Militärverlag. *Für den zuverlässigen Schutz der Deutschen Demokratischen Republik: Beiträge zur Entwicklung der Nationalen Volksarmee und des Systems der sozialistischen Landesverteidigung.* Berlin: Deutscher Militärverlag, 1969.

Diefendorf, Jeffrey M., Axel Frohn, and Hermann-Josef Rupieper, eds. *American Policy and the Reconstruction of West Germany, 1945–1955.* Publications of the German Historical Institute. Cambridge: Cambridge University Press, 1993.

Dinter, Andreas. "Die Seuchen im Berlin der Nachkriegszeit 1945–1949." PhD diss., Freie Universität Berlin, 1992.

——. *Berlin in Trümmern: Ernährungslagge und medizinische Versorgung der Bevölkerung Berlins nach dem II. Weltkrieg.* Geschichte(n) der Medizin. Berlin: Verlag Frank Wünsche, 1999.

Doernberg, Stefan. *Die Geburt eines neuen Deutschlands 1945–1949: Die antifaschistisch-demokratisher Umwälzung und die Entstehung der DDR.* Berlin (East), 1959.

Eisenberg, Carolyn Woods. *Drawing the Line: The American Decision to Divide Germany, 1944–1949.* Cambridge and New York: Cambridge University Press, 1996.

End, Heinrich. *Zweimal deutsche Außenpolitik: internationale Dimensionen des innerdeutschen Konflikts 1949–1972.* Cologne: Verlag Wissenschaft und Politik, 1973.

Engert, Jürgen, ed. *Die wirren Jahre: Deutschland 1945–1948.* Berlin: Argon Verlag, 1996.

Eppelmann, Rainer, Bernd Faulenbach, and Ulrich Mählert, eds. *Bilanz und Perspektiven der DDR-Forschung.* Paderborn: Ferdinand Schöningh, 2003.

Epstein, Catherine. *The Last Revolutionaries: German Communists and Their Century.* Cambridge, MA and London: Harvard University Press, 2003.

Falk, Barbara. *Sowjetische Städte in der Hungersnot 1932/33: Staatliche Ernährungspolitik und städtisches Alltagsleben.* Cologne: Böhlau Verlag, 2005.

Fichtner, Volkmar. *Die anthropogen bedingte Umwandlung des Reliefs durch Trümmeraugschüttungen in Berlin (West) seit 1945.* Abhandlungen des Geographischen Instituts Anthropogeographie 21. Berlin: Selbstverlag des Geographischen Instituts der Freien Universität Berlin, 1977.

Fijalkowski, J., et al. *Berlin – Hauptstadtanspruch und Westintegration.* Cologne: Opladen, 1967.

Fischer, Alexander. *Sowjetische Deutschlandpolitik im Zweiten Weltkrieg, 1941–1945.* Stuttgart: Deutsche Verlags-Anstalt, 1975.

——, ed. *Studien zur Geschichte der SBZ/DDR.* Berlin: Duncker und Humblot, 1993.

Fischer, Wolfram and Johannes Bähr, eds. *Wirtschaft im geteilten Berlin 1945–1990: Forschungsansätze und Zeitzeugen.* Einzelveröffentlichungen der Historischen Kommission zu Berlin 76. Munich: K. G. Saar Verlag, 1994.

Förster, Uwe, Stephanie v. Hochberg, Ulrich Kbisch, and Dietrich Kuhlgatz, eds. *Auftrag Luftbrücke: Der Himmel über Berlin 1948–1949.* Berlin: Nicolai Verlag, 1998.

Foschepoth, Josef C., ed. *Kalter Krieg und Deutsche Frage: Deutschlnd im Widerstreit der Mächte 1945–1952.* Göttingen and Zurich: Vandenhoeck and Ruprecht, 1985.

Fricke, Karl Wilhelm. *Politik und Justiz in der DDR: Zur Geschichte der politischen Verfolgung 1945–1968.* Cologne: Verlag Wissenschaft und Politik, 1979.

Fritzsche, Peter. *Rehearsals for Fascism: Populism and Political Mobilization in Weimar Germany.* New York: Oxford University Press, 1990.

Führe, Dorothea. *Die französische Besatzungspolitik in Berlin von 1945–1949: Déprussianisation und Décentralisation.* Berlin: Weissensee Verlag, 2001.

Gablentz, O. M. *The Berlin Question and Its Relations to World Politics, 1944–1963.* Munich: Oldenbourg Verlag, 1964.

Gaddis, John Lewis. *The United States and the Origins of the Cold War, 1941–1947.* New York and London: Columbia University Press, 1972.

———. *The Long Peace: Inquiries into the History of the Cold War.* New York and Oxford: Oxford University Press, 1987.

———. *We Now Know: Rethinking Cold War History.* Oxford: Clarendon Press, 1997.

———. *The Cold War: A New History.* New York: Penguin, 2005.

Garton Ash, Timothy. *In Europe's Name: Germany and the Divided Continent.* New York: Random House, 1993.

———. *The File: A Personal History.* New York: Vintage Books, 1997.

Gerhardt, Gunther. *Das Krisenmanagement der Vereinigten Staaten waehrend der Berliner Blockade (1948/1949): Intentionen, Strategien und Wirkungen.* Historische Forschungen, 25. Berlin: Duncker and Humblot, 1984.

Geyer, Michael and Konrad Jarausch. *Shattered Past: Reconstructing German Histories.* Princeton: Princeton University Press, 2003.

Giangreco, D. M. and Robert E. Griffin. *Airbridge to Berlin: The Berlin Crisis of 1948, Its Origins and Aftermath.* Novato, CA: Presidio Press, 1988.

Gienow-Hecht, Jessica C. E. *Transmission Impossible: American Journalism as Cultural Diplomacy in Postwar Germany 1945–1955.* Eisenhower Center Studies on War and Peace. Baton Rouge: Louisiana State University Press, 1999.

Gill, Ulrich. *Der Freie Deutsche Gewerkschaftsbund (FDGB): Theorie – Geschichte – Organisation – Funktionen – Kritik.* Opladen: Leske und Budrich, 1989.

Gimbel, John. *The American Occupation of Germany: Politics and the Military, 1945–1949.* Stanford: Stanford University Press, 1968.

Glaser, Hermann. *The Rubble Years: The Cultural Roots of Postwar Germany 1945–1948.* Franz Feige and Patricia Gleason, trans. New York: Paragon House Publishers, 1986.

Gleason, Abbott. *Totalitarianism: The Inner History of the Cold War.* New York: Oxford University Press, 1995.

Goedde, Petra. *GIs and Germans: Culture, Gender, and Foreign Relations, 1945–1949.* New Haven and London: Yale University Press, 2003.

Goldgeier, James Marc. "Soviet Leaders and International Crises: The Influence of Domestic Political Experiences on Foreign Policy Strategies (Stalin, Khrushchev, Brezhnev, Berlin Blockade, Cuban Missilie Crisis)." PhD diss., University of California, Berkeley, 1990.

Gottlieb, Manuel. *The German Peace Settlement and the Berlin Crisis.* New York: Paine-Whitman, 1960.

Graebner, Norman A. *The Cold War: Ideological Conflict as Power Struggle?* Boston: Heath, 1963.

Granieri, Ronald J. *The Ambivalent Alliance: Konrad Adenauer, the CDU/CSU, and the West, 1949–1966.* Monographs in German History 9. New York and Oxford: Berghahn Books, 2003.

Granlund, Christopher. "Regimes of Truth: The Reconstruction of the Press in the Soviet and United States Sectors of Post-War Berlin, 1945–1947." PhD diss., University of Wales College of Cardiff, 1988.

Gravelmann, Birgit and Annette Weickert. *Weibliche Selbständigkeit als Phänomen der Nachkriegszeit? Vier Berliner Frauen berichten über ihren Alltag.* Veröffentlichungen von hervorragenden Diplomarbeiten. Berlin: Fachhochschule für Sozialarbeit und Sozialpädagogik, 1991.

Gray, William Glenn. *Germany's Cold War: The Global Campaign to Isolate East Germany, 1949–1969.* Chapel Hill and London: University of North Carolina Press, 2003.

Gries, Rainer. *Die Rationengesellschaft: Versorgungskampf und Vergleichsmentalität: Leipzig, München und Köln nach dem Kriege.* Münster: Verlag westfälisches Dampfboot, 1991.

Hahn, Hans Joachim. *The 1848 Revolutions in German-Speaking Europe.* Harlow and London: Longman, 2001.

Halle, Louis J. *The Cold War as History.* Rev. ed. New York: Harper Perennial, 1991.

Harootunian, Harry. *History's Disquiet: Modernity, Cultural Practice, and the Question of Everyday Life.* New York: Columbia University Press, 2000.

Harrison, Hope. *Driving the Soviets up the Wall: Soviet-East German Relations, 1953–1961.* Princeton and Oxford: Princeton University Press, 2003.

Hartl, Hans. *Fünfzig Jahre Sowjetische Deutschlandpolitik.* Boppard am Rhein: Boldt, 1967.

Hauch, Ulrich. *Die Politik von KPD und SED gegenüber der westdeutschen Sozialdemokratie 1945–1948.* Frankfurt am Main, Bonn, and Las Vegas: Lang, 1978.

Haydock, Michael. *City under Siege: The Berlin Blockade and Airlift, 1948–1949.* Washington, DC: Brassey's, 1999.

Hellwig, Reinhard, ed. *Dokumente deutscher Kriegsschäden: Evakuierte, Kriegssachgeschädigte, Währungsgeschädigte: die geschichtliche und rechtliche Entwicklung,* vol. IV/2, *Berlin-Kriegs- und Nachkriegsschicksal der Reichshauptstadt.* Bonn: Bundesminister für Vertriebene, Flüchtlinge und Kriegsgeschädigte, 1967.

Herzfeld, Hans. *Berlin in der Weltpolitik 1945–1970*. Veröffentlichungen der Historischen Kommission zu Berlin 38. Berlin and New York: Walter de Gruyter, 1973.

Hildebrandt, Reinhard. *Kampf um Weltmacht: Berlin als Brennpunkt des Ost-West-Konflikts*. Opladen: Westdeutscher Verlag, 1987.

Hinds, Lynn Boyd. *The Cold War as Rhetoric: The Beginnings 1945–1950*. New York: Praeger, 1991.

Hixson, Walter. *Parting the Curtain: Propaganda, Culture, and the Cold War, 1945–1961*. New York: St. Martin's Press, 1997.

Hoerning, Erika M. *Zwischen den Fronten: Berliner Grenzgänger und Grenzhändler 1948–1961*. Cologne: Böhlau, 1992.

Hoffmann, Dierk and Hermann Wentker, eds. *Das letzte Jahr der SBZ: Politische Weichenstellungen und Kontinuitäten im Prozeß der DDR*. Veröffentlichungen zur SBZ-/DDR-Forschung im Institut für Zeitgeschichte. Munich: R. Oldenbourg Verlag, 2000.

Höhn, Maria. *GIs and Fräuleins: The German-American Encounter in 1950s West Germany*. Chapel Hill and London: University of North Carolina Press, 2002.

Hunter, Allen, ed. *Rethinking the Cold War*. Philadelphia: Temple University Press, 1998.

Hurwitz, Harold. *Die politische Kultur der Bevölkerung und der Neubeginn konservativer Politik*, vol. 1 of *Demokratie und Antikommunismus in Berlin nach 1945*. Cologne: Verlag Wissenschaft und Politik, 1983.

———. *Autoritäre Tradierung und Demokratiepotential in der sozialdemokratischen Arbeiterbewegung*, vol. 2 of *Demokratie und Antikommunismus in Berlin nach 1945*. Cologne: Verlag Wissenschaft und Politik, 1984a.

———. *Die Eintracht der Siegermächte und die Orientierungsnot der Deutschen 1945–1946*, vol. 3 of *Demokratie und Antikommunismus in Berlin nach 1945*. Cologne: Verlag Wissenschaft und Politik, 1984b.

———. *Der Kampf um Selbsbehauptung, Einheit und Freiheit*, pt. 1, *Führungsanspruch und Isolation der Sozialdemokraten*, vol. 4 of *Demokratie und Antikommunismus in Berlin nach 1945*. Cologne: Verlag Wissenschaft und Politik, 1990a.

———. *Der Kampf um Selbsbehauptung, Einheit und Freiheit*, pt. 2, *Zwischen Selbsttäuschung und Zivilcourage: Der Fusionskampf*, vol. 4 of *Demokratie und Antikommunismus in Berlin nach 1945*. Cologne: Verlag Wissenschaft und Politik, 1990b.

———. *Die Stalinisierung der SED: Zum Verlust von Freiräumen und sozialdemokratischer Identität in den Vorständen, 1946–1949*, Schriften des Zentralinstituts für sozialwissenschaftliche Forschung der Freien Universität Berlin, Band 79. Opladen: Westdeutscher Verlag, 1997.

———. *Die Stunde Null der deutschen Presse: Die amerikanische Pressepolitik in Deutschland 1945–1959*. Cologne: Verlag Wissenschaft und Politik, 1972.

Huschke, Wolfgang J. "Die Luftbrücke nach Berlin 1948/49: Ihre technischen Voraussetzungen und deren erfolgeiche Umsetzung." PhD diss., Technische Universität Berlin, 1998.

_____. *The Candy Bombers: The Berlin Airlift 1948/49: A History of the People and Planes.* Berlin: Metropol Verlag, 1999.

Inglis, Fred. *The Cruel Peace: Everyday Life in the Cold War.* New York: Basic Books, 1991.

Intriligator, Michael D. and Hans-Adolf Jacobson, eds. *East-West Conflict: Elite Perceptions and Political Options.* Studies in International and Strategic Affairs Series. Boulder, CO: Westview, 1988.

Jackson, Robert. *The Berlin Airlift.* Willingborough, England: Stephens, 1988.

Jaeger, Manfred. *Kultur und Politik in der DDR: ein historischer Abriss.* Cologne: Edition Deutschland Archiv, 1982.

Jarausch, Konrad H., ed. *Dictatorship as Experience: Towards a Social-Cultural History of the GDR.* New York and Oxford: Berghahn Books, 1999.

Johnson, Robert H. *Improbable Dangers: U.S. Conceptions of Threat in the Cold War and After.* New York: St. Martin's Press, 1994.

Judt, Tony. *Postwar: A History of Europe since 1945.* New York: Penguin, 2005.

Jungermann, Peter. *Die Wehrideologie der SED und das Leitbild der nationalen Volksarmee vom sozialistischen deutschen Soldaten.* Stuttgart: Seewald, 1973.

Kaeble, Hartmut, Jürgen Kocka, and Hartmut Zwahr, eds. *Sozialgeschichte der DDR.* Stuttgart: Klett-Cotta, 1994.

Kaldor, Mary. *The Imaginary War: Understanding the East-West Conflict.* Oxford and Cambridge, MA: Blackwell, 1990.

Kaminsky, Annette. *Wohlstand, Schönheit, Glück: kleine Konsumgeschichte der DDR.* Munich: Verlag C. H. Beck, 2001.

Kanon, Joseph. *The Good German: A Novel.* New York: Henry Holt and Co., 2001.

Karlsch, Rainer and Jochen Laufer, eds. *Sowjetische Demontagen in Deutschland 1944–1949: Hintergründe, Ziele und Wirkungen.* Zeitgeschichtliche Forschungen 17. Berlin: Duncker and Humblot, 2002.

Keiderling, Gerhard. *Die Berliner Krise 1948/49: Zur imperialistischen Strategie des kalten Krieges gegen den Sozialismus und der Spaltung Deutschlands.* Berlin: Akademie Verlag, 1982.

_____. *"Gruppe Ulbricht" in Berlin April bis Juni 1945: von der Vorbereitungen in Sommer 1944 bis zur Widergründung der KPD in Juni 1945: eine Dokumentation.* Berlin: Verlag Arno Spitz, 1993.

_____. *Wir sind die Staatspartei: die KPD-Bezirksorganisation Groß-Berlin April 1945–April 1946.* Berlin: Verlag Arno Spitz, 1997.

_____. *"Rosinenbomber" über Berlin: Währungsreform, Blockade, Luftbrücke, Teilung.* Berlin: Dietz Verlag, 1998.

Kennedy-Pipe, Caroline. *Stalin's Cold War: Soviet Strategies in Europe, 1943 to 1956.* Manchester and New York: Manchester University Press, 1995.

Kleßmann, Christoph. *Die doppelte Staatsgründung: Deutsche Geschichte 1945–1955.* 5th ed. Bonn: Bundeszentrale für politische Bildung, 1991.

_____, ed. *The Divided Past: Rewriting Post-War German History.* Oxford and New York: Berg, 2001.

Kofsky, Frank. *Harry S. Truman and the War Scare of 1948: A Successful Campaign to Deceive the Nation.* New York: St. Martin's Press, 1993.

Kölm, Lothar. "Die Befehle des Obersten Chefs der SMAD 1945–1949: Eine ana-
lytische Untersuchung." PhD diss., Berlin, n.d.

Königseder, Angelika. *Flucht nach Berlin: Jüdische Displaced Persons 1945–1948.*
Berlin: Metropol Verlag, 1998.

Koop, Volker. *Kein Kampf um Berlin? Deutsche Politik zur Zeit der Berlin-
Blockade 1948/1949.* Bonn: Bouvier Verlag, 1998a.

————. *Tagebuch der Berliner Blockade: von Schwarzmarkt und Rollkommandos, Bergbau und Bienenzucht.* Bonn: Bouvier Verlag, 1998b.

Kopstein, Jeffrey. *The Politics of Economic Decline in East Germany, 1945–1989.*
Chapel Hill and London: University of North Carolina Press, 1997.

Kornai, János. *The Socialist System: The Political Economy of Communism.*
Princeton: Princeton University Press, 1992.

Krisch, Henry. *German Politics under Soviet Occupation.* New York and London:
Columbia University Press, 1974.

————. *The German Democratic Republic: The Search for Identity.* Boulder, CO:
Westview Press, 1985.

Krönig, Peter. *Schaut auf diese Stadt: Berlin und die Luftbrücke.* Berlin: Bebra
Verlag, 1999.

Kruse, Peter, ed. *Bomben, Trümmer, Lucky Strikes: Die Stunde Null in bisher
unbekannten Manuskripten.* Berlin: W. J. S. Verlag, 2004.

Kuby, Erich. *Die Russen in Berlin, 1945.* Munich: Scherz, 1965.

Kunze, Gerhard. *Grenzerfahrungen: Kontakte und Verhandlungen zwischen dem
Land Berlin und der DDR 1949–1989.* Studien des Forschungsverbundes SED-
Staat an der Freien Universität Berlin. Berlin: Akademie Verlag, 1999.

Kurz, Thomas. *"Blutmai": Sozialdemokraten und Kommunisten im Brennpunkt
der Berliner Ereignis von 1929.* Berlin and Bonn: Verlag J. H. W. Dietz Nachf.,
1988.

Kuznick, Peter J. and James Giblert. *Rethinking Cold War Culture.* Washington,
DC and London: Smithsonian Institution Press, 2001.

Landsman, Mark. *Dictatorship and Demand: The Politics of Consumerism in
East Germany.* Cambridge and London: Harvard University Press, 2005.

Lange, Gunter. *Otto Suhr: im Schatten von Ernst Reuter und Willy Brandt: eine
Biographie.* Berlin: Dietz, 1994.

Langguth, Gerd, ed. *Berlin: Vom Brennpunkt der Teilung zur Brücke der Einheit.*
Cologne: Verlag Wissenschaft ud Politik, 1990.

Large, David Clay. *Berlin.* New York: Basic Books, 2000.

Larres, Klaus. *Politik der Illusionen: Churchill, Eisenhower und die deutsche Frage
1945–1955.* Veröffentlichungen des Deutschen Historischen Instituts London,
35. Goettingen: Vandehoeck und Ruprecht, 1995.

LeCarré, John. *The Spy Who Came in from the Cold.* New York: Scribner, 2001.

Leffler, Melvyn P. *A Preponderance of Power: National Security, the Truman Administration, and the Cold War.* Stanford: Stanford University Press,
1992.

————. *The Specter of Communism: The United States and the Origins of the
Cold War, 1917–1953.* New York: Hill and Wang, 1994a.

————, ed. *Origins of the Cold War: An International History.* London: Routledge, 1994b.

Liebovich, Louis. *The Press and the Origins of the Cold War, 1944–1947*. New York: Praeger, 1988.

Links, Christopher. *Berliner Geisterbahnhöfe: The Berlin Ghost Stations: Les gares fantômes*. Berlin: Ch. Links Verlag, 1994.

Lippmann, Walter. *The Cold War: A Study in U.S. Foreign Policy*. London and New York: Harper and Brothers Publishers, 1947.

Loftus, Robert Anthony. "The American Response to the Berlin Blockade." PhD diss., Columbia University, 1979.

Loth, Wilfried. *The Division of the World 1941–1955*. New York: St. Martin's Press, 1988.

_____. *Stalins ungeliebtes Kind: Warum Moskau die DDR nicht wollte*. Berlin: Rowohlt, 1994.

Löwenthal, Fritz. *News from the Soviet Zone*. London: Gollancz, 1950.

Lüdtke, Alf, ed. *The History of Everday Life: Reconstructing Histarial Experiences and Ways of Life*. William Templer, trans. Princeton Studies in Culture/Power/History. Princeton: Princeton University Press, 1989.

MacCauley, Martin. *The German Democratic Republic since 1945*. New York: St. Martin's Press, 1983.

_____. *The Origins of the Cold War*. 2nd ed. London and New York: Longman, 1995.

Mai, Gunther. *Der Alliierte Kontrollrat in Deutschland 1945–1948: Alliierte Einheit – deutsche Teilung?* Quellen und Darstellugnen zur Zeitgeschichte 37. Munich: R. Oldenbourg Verlag, 1995.

Maier, Charles S., ed. *The Origins of the Cold War and Contemporary Europe*. New York: New Viewpoints, 1978.

_____, ed. *The Cold War in Europe: Era of a Divided Continent*. New York: Markus Wiener Publishing, 1991.

Major, Patrick and Jonathan Osmond, eds. *The Workers and Peasants' State: Communism and Society in East Germany under Ulbricht 1945–71*. Manchester and New York: Manchester University Press, 2002.

Malycha, Andreas. *Die SED: Geschichte ihrer Stalinisierung 1946–1953*. Paderborn: Schöningh, 2000.

Malzahn, Manfred. *Germany, 1945–1949: A Sourcebook*. London and New York: Routledge, 1991.

Mastny, Vojtech. *The Cold War and Soviet Insecurity: The Stalin Years*. New York and Oxford: Oxford University Press, 1996.

McInnis, Edgar, Richard Hiscocks, and Robert Spencer. *The Shaping of Postwar Germany*. London: Dent, 1960.

Medhurst, Martin J., et al. *Cold War Rhetoric: Strategy, Metaphor, and Ideology*. Contributions to the Study of Mass Media and Communications, 19. New York: Greenwood Press, 1990.

Mehringer, Hartmut, ed. *Von der SBZ zur DDR: Studien zum Herrschaftssystem in der Sowjetischen Besatzungszone und in der Deutschen Demokratischen Republik*. Munich: R. Oldenbourg, 1998.

Merz, Kai-Uwe. *Kalter Krieg als antikommunistischer Widerstand: die Kampfgruppe gegen Unmenschlichkeit, 1948–1959*. Studien zur Zeitgeschichte 34. Munich: R. Oldenbourg, 1987.

Meuschel, Sigrid. *Legitimation und Parteiherrschaft: zum Paradox von Stabilität und Revolution in der DDR, 1945–1989.* Frankfurt am Main: Suhrkamp, 1992.

Meyer, Sibylle and Eva Schulze. *Von Liebe sprach damals keiner: Familienalltag in der Nachkriegszeit.* Munich: Verlag C. H. Beck, 1985.

Miller, Roger G. *To Save a City: The Berlin Airlift 1948–1949.* Air Force History and Museums Program. Washington, DC: U.S. Government Printing Office, 1998.

Morris, Eric. *Blockade: Berlin and the Cold War.* New York: Stein and Day, 1973.

Mosse, George L. *The Nationalization of the Masses: Political Symbolism and Mass Movements in Germany from the Napoleonic Wars through the Third Reich.* New York: Howard Fertig, 1975.

Naimark, Norman. *The Russians in Germany: A History of the Soviet Zone of Occupation, 1945–1949.* Cambridge: Harvard University Press, 1995.

Nelson, Walter Henry. *The Berliners, Their Saga and Their City.* New York: D. McKay, 1969.

Nettl, J. P. *The Eastern Zone and Soviet Policy in Germany.* London and New York: Oxford University Press, 1951.

Neugebauer, Gero. *Partei und Staatsapparat in der DDR: Aspekte der Instrumentalisierung des Staatsapparats durch die SED.* Opladen: Westdeutscher Verlag, 1978.

Nicolai, Britta. *Die Lebensmittelversorgung in Flensburg 1914–1918: zur Mangelwirtschaft während des ersten Weltkrieges.* Schriften der Gesellschaft für Flensburger Stadtgeschichte 39. Husum: Druck- und Verlagsgesellschaft, 1988.

Nieckisch, Wieland Werner. "Politik der Staerke: die Geschichte einer deutschlandpolitischen Ersatzkonstruktion." PhD diss., Freie Universität, Berlin, 1995.

Niedbalski, Bernd. "Die Deutsche Wirtschaftskommission (DWK) in der sowjetischen Besatzungszone Deutschlands und ihre Bedeutung für die Herausbildung neuer zentraler Strukturen beim Aufbau von Wirtschaft und Staat." PhD diss., Freie Universität Berlin, 1990.

Nieden, Susanne zur. *Alltag im Ausnahmezustand: Frauentagebücher im zerstörten Deutschland 1943 bis 1945.* Berlin: Orlanda Frauenverlag, 1993.

Niethammer, Lutz, ed. *"Hinterher merkt man, daß es richtig war, daß es schiefgegangen ist": Nachkriegs-Erfahrungen im Ruhrgebiet,* vol. 2, *Lebensgeschichte und Sozialkultur im Ruhrgebiet 1930 bis 1960.* Bonn and Berlin: J. H. W. Dietz Nachf., 1983.

Nolte, Ernst. *Die Weltkonflikt und Deutschland: Die Bundesrepublik und die DDR im Brennpunkt des kalten Krieges 1949–1961.* Munich: R. Piper, 1981.

———. *Deutschland und der kalte Krieg.* 2nd ed. Stuttgart: Klett-Cotta, 1985.

Oakes, Guy. *The Imaginary War: Civil Defense and American Cold War Culture.* New York and Oxford: Oxford University Press, 1994.

Paeffgen, Hans-Ludwig. "The Berlin Blockade and Airlift: A Study of American Diplomacy." PhD diss., University of Michigan, 1979.

Parrish, Thomas. *Berlin in the Balance 1945–1949: The Blockade, the Airlift, the First Major Battle of the Cold War.* Reading, MA: Addison-Wesley, 1998.

Paterson, Thomas G. *On Every Front: The Making and Unmaking of the Cold War.* Rev. ed. New York and London: W. W. Norton and Co., 1992.

Patton, David F. *Cold War Politics in Postwar Germany*. New York: St. Martin's Press, 1999.

Pennacchio, Charles F. "The United States and Berlin, 1945–49." PhD diss., University of Colorado, 1996.

Peterson, Edward N. *Russian Commands and German Resistance: The Soviet Occupation 1945–1949*. Studies in Modern European History, 29. New York: Peter Lang, 1999.

Phillips, Ann L. *Soviet Policy Toward East Germany Reconsidered: The Postwar Decade*. Contributions in Political Science 142. New York, Westport, CT, and London: Greenwood Press, 1986.

Poiger, Uta. *Jazz, Rock, and Rebels: Cold War Politics and American Culture in a Divided Germany*. Berkeley: University of California Press, 2000.

Pollman, Bernhard. *Daten zur Geschichte der Deutschen Demokratischen Republik*. Düsseldorf: Econ Taschenbuch Verlag, 1984.

Prell, Uwe and Lothar Wilker, eds. *Berlin-Blockade und Luftbrücke: Analyse und Dokumentation*. Berlin: Verlag Arno Spitz, 1987.

Raack, R.C. *Stalin's Drive to the West 1938–1945: The Origins of the Cold War*. Stanford: Stanford University Press, 1995.

Ratchford, B. U. and Wm. D. Ross. *Berlin Reparations Assignment: Round One of the German Peace Settlement*. Chapel Hill: The University of North Carolina Press, 1947.

Raven, Margot Theis. *Mercedes and the Chocolate Pilot: The True Story of the Berlin Airlift and the Candy that Dropped from the Sky*. Chelsea, MI: Sleeping Bear Press, 2002.

Redding, Kimberly A. *Growing Up in Hitler's Shadow: Remembering Youth in Postwar Berlin*. Westport, CT: Praeger, 2004.

Reed, Laura W. "The Roads Not Taken: The United States Security Debate Over Germany, 1944–1949." PhD diss., Massachusetts Institute of Technology, 1995.

Reichhardt, Hans. J. *Raus aus den Trümmern: Vom Beginn des Weidersaufbaus in Berlin 1945*. Ausstellungskataloge des Landesarchivs Berlin 7. Berlin: Transit Verlag, 1987.

Reynolds, David, ed. *The Origins of the Cold War in Europe: International Perspectives*. New Haven and London: Yale University Press, 1994.

Ribbe, Wolfgang, ed. *Geschichte Berlins*, vol. 2, *Von der Märzrevolution bis zur Gegenwart*. 2nd ed. Munich: Verlag C. H. Beck, 1988.

Richie, Alexandra. *Faust's Metropolis: A History of Berlin*. New York: Carroll and Graf Publishers, 1998.

Ritter, Gerhard, ed. *Angst als Mittel der Politik in der Ost-West-Auseinandersetzung*. Schriftenreihe der Gesellschaft für Deutschlandforschung, 17. Berlin: Duncker und Humblot, 1986.

Robson, Charles B., ed. *Berlin: Pivot of German Destiny*. Chapel Hill: University of North Carolina Press, 1960.

Roth, Margit. *Westliches Konzessionsverhalten in der Ost-West-Auseinandersetzung: Berlin-Frage, Deutschland-Frage, europäische Sicherheit*. Frankfurt am Main and New York: P. Lang, 1993.

Ross, Corey. *The East German Dictatorship: Problems and Perspectives in the Interpretation of the GDR*. London: Arnold, 2002.

Sandford, Gregory W. *From Hitler to Ulbricht: The Communist Recon-struction of East Germany 1945–46.* Princeton: Princeton University Press, 1983.

Sarotte, M. E. *Dealing with the Devil: East Germany, Détente, and Ostpolitik, 1969–1973.* Chapel Hill and London: University of North Carolina Press, 2001.

Saull, Richard. *Rethinking Theory and History in the Cold War: The State, Military Power, and Social Revolution.* Portland, OR and London: Frank Cass, 2001.

Scherstjanoi, Elke, ed. *Provisorium für längstens ein Jahr: Protokoll des Kolloquiums die Gründung der DDR.* 1993.

Schissler, Hanna, ed. *The Miracle Years: A Cultural History of West Germany, 1949–1968.* Princeton and Oxford: Princeton University Press, 2001.

Schivelbusch, Wolfgang. *In a Cold Crater: Cultural and Intellectual Life in Berlin, 1945–1948.* Kelly Barry, trans. Berkeley: University of California Press, 1998.

Schlegelmilch, Arthur. *Haupstadt im Zonendeutschland: Die Entstehung der Berliner Nachkriegsdemokratie 1945–1949.* Schriften der Historischen Kommission zu Berlin 4. Berlin: Haude and Spener, 1993.

Schlesinger, Arthur M., Jr. *A Thousand Days: John F. Kennedy in the White House.* Boston: Houghton Mifflin, 1965.

Schneider, Peter. *The Wall Jumper: A Berlin Story.* Leigh Hafrey, trans. Chicago: The University of Chicago Press, 1998.

Schulz, Klaus-Peter. *Auftakt zum Kalten Krieg: Der Freiheitskampf der SPD in Berlin 1945/46.* Berlin: Colloquium Verlag, 1965.

Sebald, W. G. *Luftkrieg und Literatur.* Munich and Vienna: Carl Hanser Verlag, 1999.

Shlaim, Avi. *The United States and the Berlin Blockade, 1948–1949: A Study in Crisis Decision-Making.* Berkeley: University of California Press, 1983.

Slussar, Robert, ed. *Soviet Economic Policy in Postwar Germany.* New York: Research Program in the USSR, 1953.

Smith, Arthur L., Jr. *Kidnap City: Cold War Berlin.* Contributions to the Study of World History 100. Westport, CT and London: Greenwood Press, 2002.

Smith, Jean Edward. *The Defense of Berlin.* Baltimore: The Johns Hopkins University Press, 1963.

Smyser, William R. *From Yalta to Berlin: The Cold War Struggle over Germany.* New York: St. Martin's Press, 1999.

Staritz, Dietrich. *Die Gründung der DDR: Von der sowjetischen Besatzungsherrschaft zum sozialistischen Staat.* Munich: Deutscher Taschenbuch Verlag, 1984.

Staritz, Dietrich and Hermann Weber, eds. *Einheitsfront, Einheitspartei: Kommunisten und Sozialdemokraten in Ost- und Westeuropa, 1944–1948.* Cologne: Verlag Wissenschaft und Politik, 1989.

Stein, Mary Beth. "Berlin/Berlin: The Wall in the Expressive Culture of a Divided City." PhD diss., Indiana University, 1993.

Steininger, Rolf. *Deutsche Geschichte, 1945–1961.* Frankfurt am Main: Fischer Taschenbuch Verlag, 1983.

Stüber, Gabriele. *Der Kampf gegen den Hunger 1945–1950: die Ernährungslage in der britischen zone Deutschlands, insbesondere in Schleswig-Holstein und Hamburg.* Neumünster: Karl-Wachholtz Verlag, 1984.

Teuschner, Gertraud et al., eds. *Fünfzig Jahre Triumph des Marxismus-Leninismus.* Berlin: Dietz Verlag, 1967.

Thomas, Hugh. *Armed Truce: The Beginnings of the Cold War, 1945–46.* London: Hamilton, 1986.

Thompson, E. P. *Customs in Common: Studies in Traditional Popular Culture.* New York: The New Press, 1993.

Thurnwald, Hilde. *Gegenwartsprobleme Berliner Familien: Eine soziologische Untersuchung von 498 Berliner Familien.* Berlin: Weidmannsche Verlagsbuchhandlung, 1948.

Till, Karen E. *The New Berlin: Memory, Politics, Place.* Minneapolis and London: University of Minnesota Press, 2005.

Trachtenberg, Marc. *A Constructed Peace: The Making of the European Settlement 1945–1963.* Princeton: Princeton University Press, 1999.

Trittel, Günter J. *Hunger und Politik: Die Ernährungskrise in der Bizone (1945–1949).* Historische Studien 3. Frankfurt am Main and New York: Campus Verlag, 1990.

Turner, Henry Ashby, Jr. *The Two Germanies since 1945.* New Haven and London: Yale University Press, 1987.

Turner, Victor. *The Forest of Symbols: Aspects of Ndembu Ritual.* Ithaca and New York: Cornell University Press, 1967.

———. *Dramas, Fields, and Metaphors: Symbolic Action in Human Society.* Ithaca and London: Cornell University Press, 1974.

———. *Blazing the Trail: Way Marks in the Exploration of Symbols.* Edith Turner, ed. Tucson and London: University of Arizona Press, 1992.

Tusa, Ann and John Tusa. *The Berlin Airlift.* New York: Athenaeum, 1988.

Van Hook, James C. *Rebuilding Germany: The Creation of the Social Market Economy 1945–1957.* Cambridge and New York: Cambridge University Press, 2004.

Verheyen, Dirk. *The German Question: A Cultural, Historical, and Geopolitical Exploration.* Boulder, CO: Westview Press, 1991.

Vernohr, Wolfgang. *Die roten Preussen: vom wundersamen aufstieg der DDR in Deutschland.* Erlangen: Straube, 1989.

Vogt, Timothy R. *Denazification in Soviet-Occupied Germany: Brandenburg, 1945–1948.* Cambridge and London: Harvard University Press, 2000.

Wagnleitner, Reinhold. *The Coca-Colonization of the Cold War: The Cultural Mission of the United States in Austria after the Second World War.* Diana M. Wolf, trans. Chapel Hill and London: University of North Carolina Press, 1994.

Weber, Hermann. *Von der SBZ zur "DDR." 1945–1968.* 2nd ed. Hannover: Verlag für Literatur und Zeitgeschehen, 1968.

———. *Geschichte der DDR.* 3rd ed. Munich: R. Oldenbourg Verlag, 1989.

———. *Aufbau und Fall einer Diktatur: kritische Beiträge zur Geschichte der DDR.* Cologne: Bund-Verlag, 1991a.

———. *DDR: Grundriß der Geschichte 1945–1990.* Hannover: Fackelträger, 1991b.

Weber, Wolfgang. *DDR-40 Jahre Stalinismus: ein Beitrag zur Geschichte der DDR.* Essen: Arbeiterpresse Verlag, 1993.

Wehling, Hans-Georg, ed. *Politische Kultur in der DDR.* Stuttgart, Berlin, and Cologne: Verlag W. Kohlhammer, 1989.

Wehner, Gerd. *Die Westalliierten und das Grundgesetz, 1948–1949: Die Londoner Sechsmächtekonferenz.* Freiburg im Breisgau: Rombach Verlag, 1994.

Weisz, Stephan, ed. *OMGUS-Handbuch: Die amerikaniscche Militärregierung in Deutschland 1945–1949.* Quellen und Darstellungen zur Zeitgeschichte, 35. Munich: Oldenbourg Verlag, 1994.

Weitz, Eric D. *Creating German Communism, 1890–1990: From Popular Protests to Socialist State.* Princeton: Princeton University Press, 1997.

Westad, Odd Arne, ed. *Reviewing the Cold War: Approaches, Interpretations, Theory.* Portland, OR and London: Frank Cass, 2000.

Whitfield, Stephen J. *The Culture of the Cold War.* Baltimore and London: The Johns Hopkins University Press, 1991.

Wildt, Michael. *Der Traum vom Sattwerden: Hunger und Protest, Schwarzmarkt und Selbsthilfe.* Hamburg: VSA-Velag, 1986.

_____. *Am Beginn der "Konsumgesellschaft": Mangelerfahrung, Lebeshaltung, Wohlstandshoffnung in Westdeutschland in der fünfziger Jahren.* Forum Zeitgeschichte 3. Hamburg: Ergebnisse Verlag, 1994.

Windsor, Philip. *City on Leave: A History of Berlin 1945–62.* London: Chatto and Windus, 1963.

Winkler, Heinrich August. *Der Weg in die Katastrophe: Arbeiter und Arbeiterbewegung in der Weimarer Republik 1930 bis 1933.* Berlin and Bonn: Verlag J. H. W. Dietz Nachf., 1987.

Wolfe, Nancy Travis. *Policing a Socialist Society: The German Democratic Republic.* Contributions in Criminology and Penology 34. New York, Westport, CT, and London: Greenwood Press, 1992.

Wolff, Michael W. *Die Währungsreform in Berlin 1948/49.* Veröffentlichungen der Historischen Kommssion zu Berlin 77. Berlin and New York: Walter de Gruyter, 1991.

Woods, Randall Benett and Howard Jones. *Dawning of the Cold War: The United States' Quest for Order.* Athens: University of Georgia Press, 1991.

Wrede-Bouvier, Beatrix and Horst-Peter Schulz, eds. '. . . *die SPD aber aufgehört hat zu existieren' Sozialdemokraten unter sowjetischer Besatzung.* Bonn: Dietz, 1991.

Zieger, Gottfried. *Die Haltung von SED und DDR zur Einheit Deutschlands 1949–1987.* Cologne: Verlag Wissenschaft und Politik, 1988.

Zubok, Vladislav and Constantine Pleshakov. *Inside the Kremlin's Cold War: From Stalin to Khruschchev.* Cambridge and London: Harvard University Press, 1996.

Zweiniger-Bargielowska, Ina. *Austerity in Britain: Rationing, Controls, and Consumption, 1939–1955.* Oxford and New York: Oxford University Press, 2000.

Articles

Akhalkatsi, Dimitrii S. "Berlinskii krisis 1948 g. v sovetsko-amerikanskikh otnosheniiakh," *SShA: Ekonomika, Politika, Ideologiia* 8 (1991): 39–48.

Alrich, Amy. "Black Market? Black Butchering? Other Prohibited Activities? How German Expellees Coped with the Economic Crisis in Their Postwar Communities." Paper presented at the annual meeting of the American Historical Association, Washington DC, January 11, 2004.

Ambrose, Stephen and Douglas Brinkley. "'Like Music to our Ears': How the Happy Drone of American Planes in the Berlin Airlift Signaled the Shape of the Cold War," *Newsweek* (May 25, 1998): 42.

Badstübner, Rolf. "Zum Problem der historischen Alternativen im ersten Nachkriegjahrzehnt: Neue Quellen zur Deutschlandpolitik von KPdSU und SED," *Beiträge zur Geschichte der Arbeiterbewegung* 33, no. 5 (1991a): 579–92.

———. "'Beratungen' bei J. W. Stalin. Neue Dokumente," *Utopie Kreativ* 7 (March 1991b): 99–116.

Badstübner-Peters, Evemarie. "Kulturdebatten im Vorfeld des Zweijahrplans 1948," *Zeitschrift für Geschichtwissenschaft* 30, no. 4 (1982): 304–21.

Balz, Dan. "Clinton, in Berlin, Joins Kohl to Hail: '48 Airlift," *International Herald Tribune* (May 15, 1998).

Baring, Arnulf. "Die Rolle Berlins seit dem zweiten Weltkrieg," *Jahrbuch für Geschichte Mittel- und Ostdeutschlands* 34 (1985): 21–9.

Bedurftig, Friedmann. "A People without a State: Post VE-Day Germany," *History Today* 45, no. 5 (May 1995).

"Beginn der Feiern zum Luftbrückenjubiläum: 12. Mai 1949: Ende der Blockade," *Der Tagesspiegel* (May 12, 1998): 15.

Brown, JoAnne. "Guy Oakes, the Imaginary War: Civil Defense and American Cold War Culture," review of *The Imaginary War: Civil Defense and American Cold War Culture,* by Guy Oakes. *The Journal of American History* 83, no. 4 (March 1997): 1481.

Castillo, Greg. "Domesticating the Cold War: Household Consumption as Propaganda in Marshall Plan Germany," *Journal of Contemporary History* 40, no. 2 (2005): 261–88.

Confino, Alon and Rudy Koshar. "Regimes of Consumer Culture: New Narratives in Twentieth-Century German History," *German History* 19, no. 2(2001): 154–6.

Cooper, Susan. "Snoek Piquante," in *Age of Austerity*. Michael Sissons and Philip French, eds. London: Hodder and Stoughton, 1963.

Crown, Melvin. "Soviet Uses of the Doctrine of the 'Parliamentary Road' to Socialism: East Germany 1945–1946," *American Slavic and East European Review* 17, no. 3 (October 1958): 302–15.

Crown, Melvin and Carl J. Friedrich. "The East German Regime and Soviet Policy in Germany," *The Journal of Politics* 20, no. 1 (February 1958): 44–63.

Cumings, Bruce. "'Revising Postrevisionism,' or, the Poverty of Theory in Diplomatic History," *Diplomatic History* 17, no. 4 (Fall 1993): 539–69.

Daum, Andreas. "Historicizing the German Question: Toward an International History of the Cold War," *Diplomatic History* 29, no. 5 (November 2005): 869–74.

Delage, Christian. "Berlin, Guerre des Images d'une Memoire Partagee (1945– 1989)," *Vingtième Siècle* 34 (1992): 85–105.

Divine, Robert A. "The Cold War and the Election of 1948," *The Journal of American History* 59, no. 1 (June 1972): 90–110.

Eley, Geoff. "Labor History, Social History, 'Alltagsgeschichte': Experience, Culture, and the Politics of Everday – A New Direction for German Social History?" *The Journal of Modern History* 61, no. 2 (June 1989): 297– 343.

Enssle, Manfred J. "The Harsh Discipline of Food Scarcity in Postwarr Stuttgart, 1945–1948," *German Studies Review* 10, no. 3 (October 1987): 1–19.

———. "Five Theses on German Everyday Life after World War I," *Central European History* 26, no. 1 (1993): 1–19.

Eppler, Erhard. "In der Hand der Sieger: Aus dem Krieg heimgekehrt," *Der Spiegel* (May 17, 1999): 100–7.

Erker, Paul. "Revolution des Dorfes? Ländliche Bevölkerung zwischen Flüchtlingszustrom und Landwirtschaftlichen Strukturwandel," in *Von Stalingrad zur Währungsreform: Zur Sozialgeschichge des Umbruchs in Deutschland*. Martin Broszat, Klaus-Dietmar Kenke, and Hans Woller, eds. Quellen und Darstellungen zur Zeitgeschichte 26. Munich: R. Oldenbourg Verlag, 1988.

Faisst, Michael, Harald Hurwitz, and Klaus Sühl. "Die Berliner Sozialdemokratie und die Personalpolitik der Besatzungsmächte 1945/1946," *Internationale Wissenschaftliche Korrespondenz zur Geschichte der deutschen Arbeiterbewegung* 16, no. 3 (September 1980): 313–46.

Filitov, A. M. and Norman M. Naimark. "Germanskii vopros: ot raskola k ob"edineniiu. Novoe prochtenie," *Slavic Review* 54, no. 2 (1995).

Friedman, Thomas L. "Let Them Come to Berlin," *New York Times* (November 3, 2002); wysiwyg://11/http://www.nytimes.com/2002/...RIE.html? pagewanted=print & position+bottom (accessed November 2, 2002).

Fritsch-Bournazel, Renata. "Mourir Pour Berlin? Die Wandlungen der französischen Ost- und Deutschlandpolitik während der Blockade 1948/49," *Vierteljahreshefte für Zeitgeschichte* 35, no. 2 (April 1987): 171–92.

Fulbrook, Mary. "A German Dictatorship: Power Structures and Political Culture in the GDR," *German Life and Letters* 45, no. 4 (1992): 376– 92.

Gallagher, Tom. "Berlin Airlift Should Be Model for Aid," *The Herald* [Glasgow] (April 6, 1999): 7.

Gimbel, John. "Cold War: German Front," *The Maryland Historian*, II (Spring 1971).

Grau, Roland and Volker Steinke. "Zur Führung der Kampfgruppen der Arbeiterklasse der DDR durch die SED," *Beiträge zur Geschichte der Arbeiterbewegung* 31, no. 5 (1989): 605–18.

Grimson, Andrew. "Berlin Blockade 'Showed Air Power Alone Can Win the Day,'" *Daily Telegraph* [London] (May 13, 1999): 24.

Grossmann, Atina. "Home and Displacement in a City of Bordercrossers: Jews in Berlin 1945–1948," in *Unlikely History: The Changing German-Jewish Symbiosis, 1945–2000*. Leslie Morris and Jack Zipes, eds. New York: Palgrave, 2002, 63–99.

_____. "Trauma, Memory, and Motherhood: Germans and Jewish Displaced Persons in Post-Nazi Germany, 1945–1949," in *Life after Death: Approaches to a Cultural and Social History of Europe During the 1940s and 1950s*. Publications of the German Historical Institute. Richard Bessel and Dirk Schuman, eds. Cambridge and New York: Cambridge University Press, 2003, 93–127.

Gruschmann, Lothar. "Korruption im Dritten Reich: Zur 'Lebensmittelversorgung' der NS-Führerschaft," *Vierteljahrshefte für Zeitgeschichte* 42, no. 4 (October 1994): 571–93.

Hallen, Andreas and Thomas Lindenberger. "Frontstadt mit Lücken: Ein Versuch über die Halbwahrheiten von Blockade und Luftbrücke," in *Der Wedding – hart an der Grenze: Weiterleben in Berlin nach dem Krieg*. Berliner Geschichtswerkstatt, ed. Berlin: Nishen Verlag, 1987, 182–200.

Harrington, Daniel F. "The Berlin Blockade Revisited," *The International History Review* 6 (February 1984): 88–112.

_____. "United States, United Nations and the Berlin Blockade," *The Historian: A Journal of History* 52, no. 2 (February 1990): 262–85.

Heineman, Elizabeth. "The Hour of the Woman: Memories of Germany's 'Crisis Years' and West German National Identity," *The American Historical Review* 101, no. 2 (1996): 354–95.

Heitzer, Heinz. "Zur weiteren Ausarbeitung der Strategie und Politik der SED 1948–49: Diskussionen über den Charakter der gesellschaftlichen Verhältnisse in der sowjetischen Besatzungzone und über den Weg zum Sozialismus," *Zeitschrift für Geschichtswissenschaft* 36, no. 3 (1988): 195–218.

Heitzer, Heinz and Gerhard Keiderling. "Zum Wechselverhältnis von kollektiver und nationaler Sicherheit in Europa nach 1945," *Zeitschrift für Geschichtswissenschaft* 33, no. 6 (1985): 507–27.

Henrieder, Wolfram F. "Germany and the Balance of Power," *Polity* 6, no. 1 (1983): 119–36.

Herbert, Maj. Gen. E. O. "The Cold War in Berlin." *Journal of the United Service Institutions* 574 (May 1949).

Herf, Jeffrey. "German Communism, the Discourse of 'Antifascist Resistance,' and the Jewish Catastrophe," in *Resistance against the Third Reich 1933–1990*. Michael Geyer and John W. Boyer, eds. Chicago and London: University of Chicago Press, 1994.

Heuser, Beatrice. "Keystone in the Division of Europe: Germany in the Cold War," *Contemporary European History* 1, no. 3 (1992): 323–33.

Hilton, Laura J. "The Black Market in Germany: Interaction among Jewish DPs, Germans, and Americans." Paper presented at the annual meeting of the American Historical Association, Washington, DC, January 11, 2004.

Jäger, Jens. "Fotografie – Erinnerung – Identität: die Trümmeraufnahmen aus deutschen Städten 1945," in *Kriegsende 1945 in Deutschland*, Beiträge zur

Militärgeschichte 55. Jörg Hillmann and John Zimmermann, eds. Munich: R. Oldenbourg Verlag, 2002.

James, Harold. "The Prehistory of the Federal Republic," *Journal of Modern History* 63 (March 1991): 99–115.

Jarausch, Konrad H. "The Failure of East German Antifascism: Some Ironies of History as Politics," *German Studies Review* 14, no. 1 (1991): 85–102.

————. "1945 and the Continuities of German History: Reflections on Memory, Historiography, and Politics," in *Stunde Null: The End and the Beginning Fifty Years Ago*. Occasional paper no. 20. Washington, DC: German Historical Institute, 1997, 9–24.

Jenkins, Philip. "Policing the Cold War: The Emergence of New Police Structures in Europe, 1946–1953," *Historical Journal* 31, no. 1 (1988): 141–57.

Jessup, Philip C. "Berlin-Blockade and the Use of the United Nations," *Foreign Affairs* 4 (1971): 163–74.

————. "Park Avenue Diplomacy – Ending the Berlin Blockade," *Political Science Quarterly* 4 (1972): 377–400.

Jordan, Gunter. "DEFA's Der Augenzeuge: The Newsreel in East Germany, 1946–1949," *Historical Journal of Film, Radio, and Television* 13, no. 1 (1993): 63–8.

Keating, F. A. "Das Verhalten der roten Armee im Sieg und während der Besatzungszeit," in *Die Rote Armee*. B. Lidell-Hart, et al., eds. Bonn: WEU/Offene Worte, 1956.

Keiderling, Gerhard. "Die Entwicklung Berlins zur Hauptstadt der Deutschen Demokratischen Republik: Die entscheidungsvollen Jahre 1945–1949," *Zeitschrift für Geschichtswissenschaft* 35, no. 6 (1987): 526–30.

————. "Die sowjetische Besatzungsmacht im Meinungsbild der Berliner im Jahre 1948," in *Die "Russen" in Berlin 1945–1949: Zwischen Befreiung und Kaltem Krieg: Erlebtes und Erforschtes – Zeitzeugen und Wissenschaftler im Dialog über Sieg und Niederlage, Befreiung und Neubeginn, Freiheit und zwang, Feinde und Freunde im Nachkriegs-Berlin*. Symposium am 6. Mai 1995 anläßlich des 50. Jahrestages des Sieges der Alliierten über das faschistische Deutschland und der Befreiung Berlins von nationalsozialistischer Herrschaft durch die Rote Armee. N.p., n.d.

Koop, Volker. "Die perfekte Blockade? Über Mythos und Legendenbildung," in *Auftrag Luftbrücke: Der Himmel über Berlin 1948–1949*. Uwe Förster, Stephanie v. Hochberg, Ulrich Kbisch, and Dietrich Kuhlgatz, eds. Berlin: Nicolai Verlag, 1998, 361–9.

Krisch, Henry. "Changing Political Culture and Political Stability in the German Democratic Republic," *Studies in Comparative Commuism* 19, no. 1 (1986): 41–53.

Laufer, Jochen. "Auf dem Wege zur staatlichen Verselbständigung der SBZ: Neue Quellen zur Münchener Konferenz der Ministerpräsidenten 1947." Jürgen Kocka, ed. *Historische DDR-Forschung: Aufsätze und Studien*, Zeithistorische Studien 1. Berlin, 1993.

Leffler, Melvyn P. "The Cold War: What Do 'We Now Know'?" *American Historical Review* 104, no. 2 (April 1999): 500–24.

Lewis, Anthony. "Ends and Means," *New York Times* (April 10, 1999): A27.

Lindenberger, Thomas. "Everyday History: New Approaches to the History of Post-War Germanies," in *The Divided Past: Rewriting Post-War German History*. Christoph Kleßman, ed. Oxford and New York: Berg, 2001.

Lüdtke, Alf. "Organizational order or *Eigensinn*? Workers' Privacy and Workers' Politics in Imperial Germany" in *Rites of Power: Symbolism, Ritual, and Politics since the Middle Ages*. Sean Wilentz, ed. Philadelphia: University of Pennsylvania Press, 1985.

———. "Hunger in der Großen Depression: Hungererfahrungen und Hungerpolitik am Ende der weimarer Republik," *Archiv für Sozialgeschichte* 27, 1987.

Mautner, Karl. "The View from Germany," in *Witnesses to the Origins of the Cold War*. Thomas T. Hammond, ed. Seattle: University of Washington Press, 1982.

May, Ernest R. "America's Berlin: Heart of the Cold War," *Foreign Affairs* 77, no. 4 (1998): 148–60.

Merker, Wolfgang. "Die provisorische Regierung der Deutschen Demokratischen Republik und der Aufbau der sozialistischen Staatsmacht 1949/50," *Archivmitteilungen* 34, no. 5 (1984): 147–51.

Mitchell, Timothy. "The Limits of the State: Beyond Statist Approaches and Their Critics," *American Political Science Review* 85, no. 1 (March 1991): 77–96.

Mitdank, Joachim. "Blockade gegen Blockade: Die Berliner Krise 1948/49," *Beiträge zur Geshcichte der Arbeiterbewegung* 36, no.3 (September 1994): 41–58.

Moran, Joe. "November in Berlin: The End of the Everyday," *History Workshop Journal* 57 (2004): 216–34.

Mosley, Philip E. "The Occupation of Germany," *Foreign Affairs* 28, no. 4 (July 1950).

Mückerberger, Christiane. "The Cold War in East German Feature Film," *Historical Journal of Film, Radio and Television* 18, no. 1 (1993): 49–57.

Murphy, David E. "Spies in Berlin: A Hidden Key to the Cold War," *Foreign Affairs* 77, no. 4 (1998): 171–8.

Mutz, Reinhard. "Die zerbrochene Hauptstadt: Berlin als politisches Symbol des Ost-West-Konfliktes," in *Berlin als Faktor nationaler und internationaler Politik*. Wissenschaft und Stadt: Publikationen der Freien Universität Berlin aus Anlaß der 750-Jahr-Feier Berlins, 7. Hannelore Horn, ed. (Berlin: Colloquium Verlag, 1988), 45–65.

Naimark, Norman M. "The Soviets and the Christian Democrats: The Challenge of a 'Bourgeois' Party in Eastern Germany, 1945–1949," *East European Politics and Societies* 9, no. 3 (Fall 1995a): 369–92.

———. "Die Sowjetische Militäradministration in Deutschland und die Frage des Stalinismus: Veränderte Sichtweisen auf der Grundlage neuer Quellen aus russischen Archiven," *Zeitschrift für Geschichtswissenschaft* 43, no. 4 (1995b): 293–307.

———. "To Know Everything, and to Report Everything Worth Knowing: Building the East German Police State, 1945–49." Working paper no. 10, Cold War International History Project, n.d.

Nakath, Detlef and Siegfried Prokop. "Der imperialistische Wirtschaftskrieg gegen die DDR 1947 bis Ende der sechziger Jahre," *Zeitschrift für Geschichtswissenschaft* 29, no. 4 (1981): 326–38.

Narinsky, Mikhail. "Soviet Policy and the Berlin Blockade." Paper presented at the Conference on the Soviet Union, Germany, and the Cold War, 1945–1952: New Evidence from Eastern Archives, Essen, Germany, June 1994.

———. "The Soviet Union and the Berlin Crisis, 1948–9," in *The Soviet Union and Europe in the Cold War, 1943–53*. Francesca Gori and Silvio Pons, eds. New York: St. Martin's Press, 1996.

Nelson, Anna Kasten. "Illuminating the Twilight Struggle: New Interpretations of the Cold War," *The Chronicle of Higher Education* (June 25, 1999): B4–B6.

Neumann, Franz. "Soviet Policy in Germany," *Annals of the American Academy of Political and Social Sciences* 263 (May 1949).

Niedbalski, Bernd. "Deutsche Zentralverwaltungen und Deutsche Wirtschaftskommission. Ansätze zur zentralen Wirtschaftsplanung in der SBZ 1945–1948," *Vierteljahrshefte für Zeitgeschichte* 33 (1985).

Parrish, Scott D. and Mikhail M. Narinsky. "New Evidence on the Soviet Rejection of the Marshall Plan, 1947: Two Reports." Working paper no. 9, Cold War International History Project, n.d.

Pechatov, Vladimir. "The Big Three after World War II: New Documents on Soviet Thinking about Post-War Relations with the United States and Great Britain." Working paper no. 13, Cold War International History Project, n.d.

Pegg, C. H. "Die Verhandlungen zwischen Ost und West über die Berliner Blockade von Mai bis September 1948," *Europa Archiv* 5 (January 1957).

Pennacchio, Charles F. "The East German Communists and the Origins of the Berlin Blockade Crisis," *East European Quarterly* 24, no. 3 (September 1995): 293–314.

Pike, David. "Cultural Politics in Soviet-Occupied Germany 1945–46," *Journal of Contemporary History* 24, no. 1 (1989): 91–123.

Poiger, Uta G. "Beyond 'Modernization' and 'Colonization,'" *Diplomatic History* 23, no. 1 (Winter 1999): 45–56.

Prowe, Diethelm. "The Making of *ein Berliner*: Kennedy, Brandt, and the Origins of Détente Policy in Germany," in *From the Berlin Museum to the Berlin Wall: Essays on the Cultural and Political History of Modern Germany*. David Wetzel, ed. (Westport, CT and London: Praeger, 1996), 169–89.

Raack, R. C. "Stalin Plans his Post-War Germany," *Journal of Contemporary History* 28 (1993): 53–73.

Randall, Adrian and Andrew Charlesworth. "The Moral Economy: Riot, Markets and Social Conflict," in *Moral Economy and Popular Protest: Crowds, Conflict and Authority*. Adrian Randall and Andrew Charlesworth, eds. New York: St. Martins Press, 2000.

Reynolds, Terry Anderson. "The Origins of the Cold War in Europe," *The Journal of American History* 82, no. 2 (1995): 822ff.

Richardson, James L. "Cold War Revisionism: A Critique," *World Politics* 24, no. 4 (July 1972).

Roesler, Jörg. "Die Wiederaufbau der Berliner Industrie 1945 bis 1947," *Jahrbuch für Geschichte* 35 (1987): 486–538.

_____. "The Black Market in Post-war Berlin and the Methods Used to Counteract It," *German History* 7, no. 1 (1989): 92–107.

Rosenberg, Emily S. "'Foreign Affairs' after World War II: Connecting Sexual and International Politics," *Diplomatic History* 18, no. 1 (Winter 1994): 59–70.

Ruffner, Kevin Conley. "The Black Market in Postwar Berlin: Colonel Miller and an Army Scandal," *Prologue: Quarterly of the National Archives and Records Administration* 34, no. 3 (Fall 2002a); http://www.archives.gov/publications/prologue/fall_2002_berlin_black_market_1.html (accessed February 25, 2003).

_____. "You Are Never Going to Be Able to Run an Intelligence Unit: SSU Confronts the Black Market in Berlin," *The Journal of Intelligence History* 2, no. 2 (Winter 2002b): 1–20.

Samuel, Walker J. "No More Cold War: American Foreign Policy and the 1948 Soviet Peace Offensive," *Diplomatic History* 5, no. 1 (Winter 1981).

Scherstjanoi, Elke. "Die Gründung der DDR. Methodologische, Forschungs- und Darstellungsprobleme," *Beiträge zur Geschichte der Arbeiterbeweung* 34, no. 1 (1992): 95–9.

Scholze, Thomas. "Zur Ernährungssituation der Berliner nach dem zweiten Weltkrieg: Ein Beitrag zur Erforschung des Großstadtalltags (1945–1952)," *Jahrbuch für Geschichte* 35 (1987): 539–64.

Schütrumpf, Jörn. "Vorsatz," *Utopie Kreativ* 155 (September 2003): 787–8.

Schwartz, Thomas A. "The United States and Germany after 1945: Alliances, Transnational Relations, and the Legacy of the Cold War," *Diplomatic History* 19, no. 4 (1995).

Shlaim, Avi. "Britain, the Berlin Blockade and the Cold War," *International Affairs* (Great Britain) 60, no. 1 (1983–4): 1–14.

Short, K. R. M. "'The March of Time', Time Inc., and the Berlin Blockade, 1948–1949: Selling Americans on the 'New' Democratic Germany," *Historical Journal of Film, Radio, and Television* 13, no. 4 (1993): 451–68.

Spencer, Robert. "Berlin, the Blockade and the Cold War," *International Journal* 29 (1967–8).

Staritz, Dietrich. "Das ganze oder das halbe Deutschland? Zur Deutschlandpolitik der Sowjetunion und der KPD/SED (1945–1955)," in *Die Republik der fünfziger Jahre: Adenauers Deutschlandpolitik auf dem Prüfstand.* Jürgen Weber, ed. Munich, 1989.

_____. "Die SED, Stalin und der 'Aufbau des Sozialismus' in der DDR," *Deutschland Archiv*, no. 2 (1991): 687–700.

Steege, Paul. "50 Jahre Berliner Blockade: Die historische Wahrnehmung des Kalten Krieges," *Deutschland Archiv* Heft 3 (May–June 1999a).

_____. "Totale Blockade, totale Luftbrücke? Die mythische Erfahrung der ersten Berlinkrise, 1948–1949," in *Sterben für Berlin? Die Berliner-Krisen 1948: 1958.* Burghard Ciesla, Michael Lemke, and Thomas Lindenberger, eds. Berlin: Metropol Verlag, 1999b.

_____. "Holding on in Berlin: March 1948 and SED Efforts to Control the Soviet Zone," *Central European History* 38, no. 3 (August 2005).

Steiner, André. "Die Deutsche Wirtschaftskommission – ein ordnungspolitisches Machtinstrument?" in *Das letzte Jahr der SBZ: politische Weichenstellungen und Kontinuitäten im Prozeß der Gründung der DDR*. Veröffentlichungen zur SBZ/DDR-Forschung im Institut für Zeitgeschichte. Dierk Hoffmann and Hermann Wentker, eds. Munich: Oldenbourg, 2000.

Stivers, William. "The Incomplete Blockade: Soviet Zone Supply of West Berlin, 1948–49," *Diplomatic History* 21, no. 4 (Fall 1997): 569–602.

Suckut, Sigfried. "Dokumentation: Zu Krise und Funktionswandel der Block-politik in der sowjetisch besetzten Zone Deutschlands um die Mitte des Jahres 1948," *Vierteljahrshefte für Zeitgeschichte* 31, no. 4 (1983): 674–718.

Suny, Ronald Grigor. "Back and Beyond: Reversing the Cultural Turn?" *American Historical Review* 107, no. 5 (December 2002): 1498.

Tiul'panov, Sergei. "Die Rolle der SMAD bei der Demokratisierung Deutsch-lands," *Zeitschrift für Geschichtswissenschaft* 15, no. 2 (1967).

———. "Die Zusammenarbeit der SMAD und der SED im Kampf für Demokratie und Sozialismus," in *Einheit im Kampfe geboren*. E. Kaeble and S. I. Tjulpanov, eds. Leipzig: Karl-Marx-Universität Leipzig, 1975.

———. "V pervye poslevoennye gody na nemetskoi zemle," *Novaia i Noveshaia Istoriia* 2 (1984): 121–36.

Vosske, Heinz. "Für immer mit dem Werden ud Wachsen der DDR verbunden: Friedrich Ebert," *Beiträge zur Geschichte der Arbeiterbewegung* 24, no. 1 (1982): 104–13.

Walker, Stephen G. "Bargaining over Berlin: a Re-analysis of the First and Second Berlin Crises," *The Journal of Politics* 44, no. 1 (February 1982): 152–64.

Weltner, George H. "Millions of Guilty Men," *Harper's* (January 1947): 81–4.

Windsor, Philip. "Berlin," in *The Cold War: A Reappraisal*. Evan Luard, ed. London: Thames and Hudson, 1964.

Woods, Randall B. "Cold War or Cold Peace," *International History Review* 16, no. 1 (February 1994).

Index